W9-AVG-298

24°

48°

44°

22°

26°

Eperjes
Kassa
Ungvar
Munkacs
Satoraljaujhely
Huszt
Nyiregyhaza
Polgar
Szatmar Nemeti
Maramaros Sziget
Visso
Hajduboszormeny
Nagykaroly
Nagybanya
Borsa
Debreczen
Zilah
Des
Besztercze
szentmiklos
Szamos Ujvar
Nagyvarad
Kolozsvar
Szasz Regen
Gyergyo St. Miklos
Bekes
Torda
Maros Vasarhely
Bekescsaba
Enyed
Schassburg
sarhely
Transylvania
Mediasch
Kezdivasarhely
Arad
Muhlbach
Fogaras
Sepsi St. Gyorgy
Maros
Nagyszeben
Temisoara
Vajda Hunyad
Brasso
Lugos
Versecz
Fehertemplom
nat

R U M A N I A

RBIA

Miles
0   20   40   60   80   100

Pre 1914 international boundary of
Hungarian Crown Lands ▪—▪—▪—▪

Post 1919 boundary of Hungary ▬▬▬

Railways ——————   Roads ••••••••••

JORDAN

MEMOIRS OF MICHAEL KAROLYI

THE AUTHOR

MEMOIRS OF
MICHAEL KAROLYI

Faith Without Illusion

Translated from the Hungarian by
CATHERINE KAROLYI

With an Introduction by
A. J. P. TAYLOR

NEW YORK
E. P. DUTTON & CO., INC.
1957

LIBRARY OF CONGRESS CATALOG CARD NUMBER: 57-5683

CONTENTS

CONTENTS

ILLUSTRATIONS

To the memory of
our son
A D A M

INTRODUCTION

EVERY nation in Europe likes to think that it is especially European. But the Hungarians have been especially symbolic of the destinies of modern man. In 1848 Hungary had the most dramatic and successful of radical revolutions. Kossuth became the popular hero everywhere; and when he came to England he received a welcome such as has been given to no other foreigner before or since. Yet, despite this revolution, Hungary was the only continental country with historic continuity, possessing at once the most traditional aristocracy and the only parliament based on more or less unbroken historic rights. In the halcyon days before 1914, Hungary was generally regarded as the most successful of liberal states; yet at the same time this concealed the worst national oppressions — four Irelands instead of one. The First World War began as an attempt to preserve great historic Hungary; and instead it destroyed her. Again and again Hungary set the patterns for others. The first purely European country to experience Bolshevik dictatorship; the first breeding ground of fascism; the heart of the revisionist attack on the peace settlement of 1919; the most devoted, yet most independent, of Hitler's allies; and now the most subservient of Russia's satellites. Hungarians were to be found everywhere. They provided the brightest elements in Weimar Germany and thereafter inspired the Popular Front against National Socialism. The outstanding economist in Soviet Russia — perhaps the only original mind Soviet economics has produced — is a Hungarian; and Hungarians have also supplied the British Labour Party with its few economic ideas.

Michael Karolyi was the Hungarian who above all others concentrated European experience in himself. His *Memoirs* are a human document, the story of a unique personality, buffeted though never overcome by fate. But they are also a parable: the story of what happened to the Europe of high hopes and high ideals. The liberal faith with which Karolyi started was the common stock of the time. What was unusual in him was that he never lost that faith, indeed adhered to it despite increasing sacrifices and disappointments. The Hungary in which he grew up was an aristocratic community which

7

still regarded itself as a Great Power. Karolyi himself was among the greatest of magnates with a fortune which could challenge that of an English duke. The early chapters of this book rank with the writings of Sir Osbert Sitwell as a picture of how the European aristocracy lived in the days before the Fall. Even if they stood alone, they would make the book an historic document of the first importance. Yet they are only the prelude to pages that are more important still.

All Hungarian leaders of the early twentieth century meant to preserve Hungary as a great state. Tisza and his associates thought to do it by becoming the ally of Germany, even willing to shake off the Habsburgs if necessary. Karolyi took the opposite course. He wanted to abandon the German alliance and to bring Hungary back to the association with the western democracies which Kossuth had aspired to in 1848. Other Hungarians dreamt of the same policy. Karolyi was the only one who was ready to carry it to its logical conclusion. Abandonment of Germany meant abandonment of racial oppression inside Hungary; alliance with the democracies meant that Hungary must become a democracy also. By the time of the First World War Karolyi was the advocate of universal suffrage, of national equality, and of the division of the land among the peasants. He intended to destroy 'historic' Hungary so as to preserve her greatness in a new form. It would be mistaken to claim that he saw beforehand how high the price of this policy would be: but as the price became clearer he continued to be willing to pay it. If Karolyi's lead had been followed before the first war or even during it, Hungary would have had to suffer, but she would have survived — and even the great Magyar aristocracy along with her, though in diminished form. In 1918 it was too late. The unhistoric nations claimed their independence. Hungary failed to break free in time from the Habsburg dynasty; and instead was involved in its ruin.

1918 was Karolyi's historic moment — the five months which will give him a place in every textbook. He brought the Habsburg monarchy to an end; became the first President of independent Hungary; and tried to reform central Europe on Wilsonian principles. He failed; but the fault did not lie in him. It lay with the victorious statesmen of England, France and the United States who refused to see that a truly democratic Hungary could be a dependable ally. Their policy first drove Hungary to Bolshevism and then forced on her a reactionary tyranny that was equally detestable. This is not to say that Karolyi could have preserved great historic Hungary even under more favourable circumstances. Hungary had to dwindle in the age of national states. The only question was whether she would become the friend and partner of those states or, remaining irreconcilable, would keep the door open in central Europe for a new German war. Horthy and the statesmen of Paris decided between them on the second course. Karolyi was almost alone in the inter-war years in continuing to believe in a Danubian federation of democratic communities.

It was Karolyi's strongest and most endearing quality that he always continued to believe in something. Disappointment made him more hopeful for the next round. Wilsonian liberalism had failed him in 1918. He drew from this the moral that he must move further and further to the Left. Though he was less important as an historical personage after 1918 than before, he was perhaps more striking as a symbol. He represented perfectly the inter-war Left—the idealists who repented of their idealism, admired the hard realism of Moscow and yet, when it came to the point, repudiated the cynicism which that realism turned into. Every Socialist who is worth anything has believed at some time or other that the rulers of Moscow were creating Utopia; and has had a rude awakening. Where Karolyi differed from others who made this pilgrimage was in his refusal to round on his former idol and beat it. He had been deluded about Moscow; he had been defrauded and cheated. But that was no reason for turning against the ideal which he had hoped to find in Russia. He remained firm to his last day that the one thing worse than a Communist was an anti-Communist. He did his best to hope for a new sort of Communist after 1945; and even when he was once more disappointed, he refused to condemn the good with the bad.

It would be possible to criticize Karolyi for his unshakable idealism; to say that he had too great faith in human goodness and too little awareness of human evil. Perhaps he was too good for this world, though it would never have occurred to him to say so. The strange thing is that this noble, unselfish man, who made unparalleled sacrifices for his beliefs, has often been attacked as a monster of wickedness. Karolyi alludes here and there to the charges made against him — charges ranging from treason to financial dishonesty. Though among the wealthiest men in Europe, he is supposed to have become a revolutionary in order to shake off his debts; and even after the second war he was accused of remaining friendly with the Communists in order to recover his property. The calm way in which he sacrificed this property and — what was far more bitter to him — went again into exile is the best answer to these accusations. The truth is that Karolyi committed one heinous crime: he was a traitor to his class. From a great Magyar aristocrat he became a democrat and a believer in national equality; and aristocrats everywhere, not only in Hungary but throughout Europe, hated him for it. Even in the Second World War, when Hungary was an enemy state, and democratic Hungarians, one might have thought, our only friends, the British Foreign Office looked with favour on Horthy, Kallay and the rest, while Michael Karolyi was held at arm's length. Karolyi describes his conversation with Ernest Bevin soon after the end of the war. He does not mention, and perhaps did not know, that his letters, asking for a meeting, never reached the Foreign Secretary and that Ellen Wilkinson finally approached Bevin privately at my prompting. Not that the meeting did any good. As Karolyi describes, the members of the Foreign Office soon made it clear that they had no time for him. Maybe they were right. Maybe the statesmen of Paris were right in 1919 when they pushed Hungary into the arms of Bela Kun. Maybe democracy is a hopeless cause anywhere east of the Rhine. But in that case why make such a parade of our principles, why complain against the Communist dictatorships if we hold them to be inevitable? Michael Karolyi stood for all those principles of tolerance and social democracy which are our special boast; and our country repaid him for the most part by failing to treat him with even common courtesy.

Karolyi speculates in one passage of his *Memoirs* what I thought of him. The answer is simple: I loved him. He was not an intellectual, but a man of action. He was impatient, restless in thought and deed. Yet, with it all, he was pure gold all through, the noblest man I have ever known. He was guileless, a man to whom idealism came naturally. He had a great sense of fun. Though he had suffered much and been greatly disappointed, he found it somehow ridiculous that all these things should have happened to him. It made him laugh that he had once been worth £25,000,000 and that now he was carrying his own coal-scuttle up three flights of stairs. He laughed at his disappointments, at himself, at the way life had treated him; he even laughed the last time

I met him at being again an exile after having firmly resolved to leave Hungary no more. There was nothing bitter or harsh in this laughter. It was the deep-seated gaiety of a man who had enjoyed the great game of life from start to finish, taking his winnings when they came (which was rarely) but paying up when he lost with equal cheerfulness. As a politician, Michael Karolyi failed completely: failed to make a democratic Hungary after the first war, failed to moderate the Communists after the second. And yet, when I think of my dear dead friend, success and failure are words that mean nothing. If the pure Socialist State is ever achieved, Michael Karolyi will be numbered among its saints.

A. J. P. TAYLOR

PART ONE

FEUDALISM

MY BACKGROUND

Life can only be understood backwards; but it must be lived forwards.
KIERKEGAARD

IN 1909 I was taking the cure in Karlsbad with my cousin Leopold Berchtold.[1] We used to take our coffee and rolls on the terrace of the Altewiesen with André Tardieu.[2]

One day he asked Berchtold: 'What nationality do you consider yourself — German, Hungarian or Czech, as there is no such thing as Austrian nationality?'

'I am Viennese,' said Berchtold.

'But in case of trouble between the different races of the Monarchy, what side would you choose?'

'The side of the Emperor,' was the reply.

'But supposing the Empire should come to an end?' went on Tardieu.

'I would remain what I am, an aristocrat, *Ce n'est pas beaucoup, mais c'est toujours quelque chose,*' replied Berchtold with his slightly supercilious smile.

Berchtold's attitude was typical of the Austrian aristocrat and also of a certain Hungarian milieu which felt itself to be a race apart. A seven-year-old Esterhazy nephew of mine had asked his governess: '*Sterben Herrschaften auch?*' (Do gentlefolk die too?)

Nothing, not even the fall of the Monarchy, could shake this mystical faith which was bound up with the theory of Divine Right. It had been deeply engrained in me, as well, by my Catholic education. Catholicism is international or rather super-national and the majority of the Hungarian ruling class was Catholic and loyal to Vienna and to the House of Habsburg. In Hungary the Danube could be taken as the line of demarcation between Catholics and Protestants. To the east the population was Protestant; they formed the opposition and followed the romantic traditions of the year 1848. They would refer to Francis Joseph as 'King' in contrast to the Catholic aristocracy who would speak of him as 'Emperor'.

Foth, the country place of my maternal grandfather Edward, where I spent my childhood, lay on the boundary of these two Hungarys and was an incongruous combination of both elements.

The Karolyis had been *frondeurs* but at the same time rigorously Catholic. They lived in a secluded feudal atmosphere, untouched by the democratic evolution and ideas of the West.

At the beginning of the eighteenth century, after Rakoczi's rebellion, the title of count[3] was given to General Baron Alexander Karolyi. The General, after having fought the Habsburgs, concluded with them the Peace of Szatmar in 1711, and as a reward received from the Emperor the greatest part of the Karolyi estate — an act I deeply deplored as a young man.

It was a curious destiny which made the first Karolyi gain his fortune by fighting and then concluding a peace with the House of Habsburg, whilst I myself, who signed a peace with the Western powers in 1918, lost the same property as a result. General Alexander Karolyi gained his wealth through a compromise with Austria; I lost it fighting Austria, and was instrumental in the abdication of the House of Habsburg.

In the female line my family descends directly from the Prince of Transylvania, Gabriel Bethlen — his wife was a Karolyi — a famous character in Hungarian history who battled for Hungary's independence against the Habsburgs on one side and the Turks on the other. My great-grandfather Stephen was a fervent Catholic. His hobby consisted in building churches. The largest one he erected at Foth, in Roman style, its size being out of all proportion to our small and primitive village. Eldest of three brothers, he was heir to the entailed property. When, after the death of his father, the estate was divided between the three brothers, Stephen inherited the lion's share and was given in addition the 'sand-downs' which were considered a liability; but when, later on, Budapest expanded, the suburbs of the capital were built on these same 'sand-downs' and thus Palota, Ujpest, Rakospalota, Tothmegyer and Alag became the most valuable parts of the Karolyi estate. On the model of the Duke of Westminster's, these lots were leased for a period of ninety-nine years. Stephen's wife, Countess Georgina de Dillon, was daughter of 'le Beau Dillon' of whom it was reported in contemporary memoirs that at a feast at Versailles he was permitted to undo the stays of the fainting Marie-Antoinette.

The three traditions of the Karolyis of Foth were: first, their rigid Catholicism; second, their anti-Habsburgism; and, third, their sympathy for the French *ancien régime*, due to their kinship through the Dillons with the French aristocracy, the Polignacs, Maillets and others. Prince Jules Polignac was the well-known reactionary Prime Minister of Charles X. Traditions based mainly on emotions are usually a conglomeration of inconsistencies and contradictory elements. The attitude of the rebel, contempt for the dynasty, and the help the Karolyis gave to Louis Kossuth and the Carbonari, are hardly compatible with clericalism and Bourbonism.

Great-grandfather Stephen not only built churches but also raised at his own cost the Karolyi Regiment of Hussars, in which his sons distinguished themselves and for which he later suffered a long term of imprisonment at Olmütz and Kufstein in Austria. The Karolyis were among the few magnates who stood whole-heartedly on the side of the Revolution of 1848.

After Stephen's death, his sons were merely religious formalists, keeping up Catholic traditions to safeguard feudalism. I remember his son Edward, my grandfather, who inherited Foth, discussing in advance with his confessor, whom he himself had appointed, how much penance he would allow him to inflict. *Bon viveur*, his religious principles did not prevent him from keeping a regular mistress, for whom he built a large country house. Even on his death-bed he had girls brought up from the street to cheer him in his last hours. Then he sent for his priest and confessed.

The most powerful personality in the family was my father's mother, born Countess Caroline Zichy. A friend of Louis Kossuth, she played an important part in the Hungarian resistance after the defeat. She was threatened with flogging by the imperial commandant of Budapest if she did not give up agitating against the authorities. She fled and spent the greater part of her exile until 1882 at Vicenza in northern Italy. She bore in her heart a deep wound which sustained her hatred for the Emperor Francis Joseph throughout her life — her grief for Count Louis Batthyanyi, her brother-in-law, the first constitutional Hungarian Prime Minister, whom the Emperor had put to death. Batthyanyi was arrested in 1849 in our house in the Egyetem utca in Budapest. Conscious of his innocence, he refused to flee when the imperial troops approached the capital. His son Elemer showed me the dagger with which his father had inflicted a deep wound on his neck so as to prevent them from hanging him. He was carried out dying, and shot. This dagger, sent by my grandmother, was smuggled into Batthyanyi's cell in a loaf of bread by her children's tutor, a French abbé. It was a sharp stiletto with a quaint design on its handle of Adam and Eve and the serpent, and the significant motto: *Ora et Semper* engraved on it. In my foolish youth I had this same motto tattooed on my arm in Ceylon, and have regretted it ever since. Is it true that my grandmother Caroline launched that famous malediction against the Habsburgs over Batthyanyi's coffin? After the cruel strokes of fate that visited the Habsburgs, after Mayerling, when Crown Prince Rudolf committed suicide, and after the assassination of Empress Elisabeth, I saw my grandmother silent and unmoved. We often asked her to write her memoirs, to which she would reply that she could not tell the truth and would not write lies. I remember her as slight, rather thin, with a dark complexion and short-sighted though very expressive eyes. Having lived a long time in Paris she kept up to the last a Parisian air, with her velvet ribbon *à la Winterhalter* like those of the Empress Eugénie. She would play us little 'Lilac Time' melodies on the piano. This was as much as she could do, although as a girl in Paris she had been a pupil of Chopin. She treated her grown-up sons like schoolboys. She would rebuke my uncle Stephen for plumping his hat on if the window was open, for he was bald and feared draughts; she scolded us when she detected the smell of tobacco in the room, so we puffed the smoke surreptitiously up the chimney. Other crimes strictly prohibited in her house in Sasvar were wearing the Emperor's uniform and using the German language. When her grandchildren were doing their year's military service, they had to change into mufti when visiting her. She never spoke about Francis Joseph otherwise than as 'the hangman', and called her own family, the Zichys, the 'Guides of the Russians' because, with other Hungarian magnates, they had appealed to Tsar Nicholas I for help, and had actually led Prince Paskievich's troops into the country, through the Carpathian passes.

I remember a story my father told me. In the autumn of 1866, on the eve of a fresh Austro-Italian war, the Hungarians were preparing a general rising. The cellar of Grandfather Edward was filled with arms received from Bismarck which were being surreptitiously distributed to the insurgents through the Revolutionary Committee. My father, then a very young man, was given the task of bringing over from Italy a sum of 100,000 gulden in gold to the Committee in Budapest. He travelled by a circuitous route, reaching the frontier at Oderberg in Silesia where, having been denounced, he was arrested. He had the presence of mind to ask permission to have his lunch before his interrogation. In those 'happy' days gentlemen seem to have been treated with privilege. At an unobserved moment he turned to his unknown neighbour in the restaurant with the courage of despair, begging him to take charge of the money he had on him. Without a word, his neighbour took it over. At the interrogation which followed, the frontier police having found nothing, my father was released. His unknown rescuer turned out to be the Viennese banker, Baron Nathaniel Rothschild, so the money was in safe hands.

When the news of the final defeat of the Emperor at Sadowa reached my grandfather Edward, he returned thanks to the Almighty by having a mass read in the church of his patrimony.

Edward's daughter was my mother, Georgina; thus I am a child of cousins, Karolyis on both sides. Although in the Hungarian aristocracy marriages between cousins, uncles and nieces, etc., were a usual practice, the Karolyis beat the record in the way of intermarriages. The desire to keep intact the heraldic quarterings left a restricted choice. One of the favourite sayings of my sister Batthyanyi was: '*Il n'y a que nous*' (we mostly talked French in the family): the 'others' did not count. They were beings of a different order.

When I was three years old, my mother died of consumption. I cannot call her to mind, but I do remember her hands — which were supposed to be very fine — probably from those of the painting of her by Cabanel, seen during my childhood. According to reports, she seems to have been an unusual woman. She was an ardent reader of classics, and recorded, in the fashion of those days, the books she read and her opinion of them. Her diary also gave evidence of her active mind and romantic disposition. Like the rest of the family, she loathed the Habsburgs and when, as a young girl, she had to drive through Vienna, she would close her eyes so as not to see the abhorred city. She was dragged all over Europe to be cured, but all efforts proved vain.

Some years after her death my father married another of his cousins, Countess Geraldine Palffy, and my sister Elisabeth and I were given to the care of our maternal grandmother, Clarisse, who had much resented my father's second marriage. Consequently we were kept away from his home and spent our childhood on the property of our grandparents in Foth. In spite of my grandmother's loving care and her repeated unfriendly and veiled insinuations against her son-in-law's second wife, my young stepmother's and my half-sisters' and brothers' gay company had a special attraction for me, and I could not fathom why we were kept away from them.

The large cream-coloured manor house of Foth, built in the Napoleonic era, with its Doric columns, its library of 80,000 volumes collected by my great-grandfather Joseph and his son Stephen, its mahogany shelves, its galleries and winding stairs, its stucco-moulded ceilings and open fireplaces, its 300 acres of park and its lake, was a gilded cage that held us in splendid isolation from the outside world.

It was strictly forbidden for us children to pass the boundary of our park, large enough, I must admit, for a boy to roam in. The village was a *terra incognita*, and we were not supposed to meet even the children of the village notables. On special occasions, the village curé was invited to lunch.

Already as a small boy, I was made to realize that I was a privileged being, a special pet of the Almighty, who had made me heir to such great wealth. I was supposed to expect and obtain respect and exercise authority over the less privileged, who had to be directed, governed and assisted by us. Our attitude could best be compared with that of the English in their colonies, with the slight difference that the 'natives' were our own people.

Foth was a favourite riding-ground for the Empress Elisabeth. I remember well her alighting from her horse in front of the house, and carefully supervising the feeding and grooming of the fine animal. She was brought a glass of Tokay and a few dry biscuits, but would not enter the house. We children kissed her hand, but she patted her horse instead of us.

The place was populated with instructors of all races. My first tutor was a French abbé and later on I had a Hungarian priest. It was a strange upbringing, for when I had done something wrong, I had to go to church twice a day as punishment. I wonder if my anti-clericalism of later years did not derive from this peculiar system. To revenge myself I concealed some pages of Zola's *Nana* (a work on the Index) in my prayer book and relished them during the service.

As a small child, I was often taken to Paris. I remember one day being led through the streets by my French abbé. Suddenly we found ourselves in the middle of a big crowd. Women were crying, whilst nuns were being driven out of their convent. All around us the street started the chorus:

> *Le voilà Gambetta,*
> *Cette grande bête-là,*
> *Cette grande bête-là*
> *Le voilà Gambetta.*

It was 1880 and I was five years old.

I was a weakly child and born with a defect of the palate. At the age of fourteen my grandmother had Doctor Billroth of Vienna operate on me. It was the first operation of this kind and was a matter of life and death. My father opposed it to the last minute. I thought this a weakness on his part. Ever since I have felt indebted to my grandmother for her initiative and strength of mind. I was big enough to realize the danger and before the operation I made serious preparations for death. When lying on the operating table I asked for my sister Elisabeth and we prayed fervently together. Being deeply religious, I was not afraid and trusted Providence. During my convalescence, when for weeks I had to lie dumb in bed, it was this feeling of gratitude for being alive that comforted me and strengthened my faith. When I recovered, there followed a strenuous and exhausting series of exercises in speech, most exasperating and nerve-racking, but they increased my will-power. It was a valuable training for the struggle against the setbacks of later years. It was often said that I was given a golden palate. I may have been born with a golden spoon in my mouth — but not a golden palate. I was surprised to find this legend in a recent book by a well-known writer.

I had little in common with my father and felt no affection for him. I fancied, perhaps wrongly, that subconsciously he resented his son's physical defect and preferred my sister to me. He opposed my studies and wished me to become a country squire and manage the estate and the stud. It was probably for this reason that I developed a special antipathy to farming and country life. The only study he approved of was that of the horse; he wished me to be an expert in this domain. The head of the Veterinary College came regularly to lecture me on the anatomy of that noble animal. My interest in horse-breeding rapidly waned in consequence. He also opposed my matriculation, saying: 'Let him learn to hunt.' But again my grandmother arranged for me to be put surreptitiously through the secondary school course, thus getting a chance of higher education.

My father was what one could call the typical *Grand seigneur*. Easy and free in his ways, his proverbial charm acquired him friends wherever he went. He was President of the Hungarian Jockey Club and Knight of the Golden Fleece, the emblem of which was erected on the façade of our house in Budapest, enabling mass to be celebrated anywhere on the premises. But honours did not mean much to him. He used to hang on his dog Fancy, a white fox terrier, a most distinguished decoration received from a foreign power, which gave us children great joy. He was very handsome and much loved by women, for he had a detached and casual way of approach which was very attractive to them. He had also a great sense of fun.

In his youth my father had travelled a great deal and had visited the U.S.A. during the civil war, in the company of the son of the 'greatest Hungarian' as Count Stephen Szechenyi was called. Before they sailed, they had to swear to my grandmother Caroline that they would not change the Hungarian magnate's dress for a civilian's during their whole stay in America. It was a most inconvenient way of travelling, this tight black and braided uniform with high boots, and rather warm during the summer months! I remember how he shocked me by telling me that all the *good* men were on the side of the South, that is, the slave owners, and against the liberation of the slaves. As I had just read *Uncle Tom's Cabin*, I was distressed to hear this opinion.

As I grew up, I became more and more critical of my father's way of life and his lack of interest in public affairs. I thus became estranged from him and most probably judged him unfairly; he wished to shelter me from the callous and cruel world, which he thought I was not fit to face.

How children at times misjudge their parents and how mistaken I was to believe him a weak man, I realized only later. Some worrying physical symptoms, about which the Hungarian doctors would not enlighten him, made him visit a doctor in Paris and request him to reveal to him in all sincerity the truth about his illness and how long he had to live. He was told that he was suffering from cancer of the throat and that a year was the maximum. I remember him sitting in his armchair in front of the open fireplace, silently brooding, for hours, with his forefinger between his teeth, and I never guessed what a tragedy was going on inside him; for no man could have had a happier life and a more difficult one to leave. I was fifteen years old when he died.

I remember once, when I was about fifteen, dining in one of the big restaurants of Budapest with my tutor, a Catholic priest. The inevitable gipsy band was playing its dismal melodies, as is usual in all Hungarian restaurants. Before leaving, I tipped the obsequious leader of the band, giving him the usual two gold pieces expected from the well to do. My tutor reprimanded me most severely, telling me that I should pay at least double the amount given by anyone else, for I must never forget that I was a Count Karolyi. His reproach was so effective that for a very long while I had great difficulty in restraining myself from over-tipping everyone.

When I reached the age of sixteen, a living in my patronage fell vacant. My uncle Tibor, who was my guardian, presented a candidate to the Archbishop of Erlau in my name, as I was a minor. One day, I was surprised by the visit of the Cardinal-Archbishop Samossa, who explained to me his view that, according to canonical law, my guardian was not entitled to make this presentation. The right, he contended, belonged to me alone, since the concept of minority held by civil law was unknown in canonical law.

The explanation was, of course, that my uncle's nominee was unwelcome to the Cardinal. He was a man of parts and energy, and I yielded at once to his invitation to exercise the right of presentation myself. I presented another chaplain and the Cardinal duly installed him in the living. My uncle Tibor was furious.

It was in the vast, two-halled library of Foth that I first came face to face with the great, strange world of knowledge.

My first prey was the novels of Jules Verne. I devoured them one after another, not guessing that within fifty years most of his fantastic imaginations would have become reality. Then Gaboriau's detective stories captured me; but most thrilling of all was Captain Marryat's *Phantom Ship*, with its strange, uncanny atmosphere.

Later, however, I discovered on upper shelves, where the great ones of the eighteenth century stood in serried ranks, something which impressed me, first, by its size and its dignified uniformity; the great *Encyclopaedia*. My instinct led me well. The first article I turned up was on 'Dieu', written by Voltaire. Whether I really wanted to learn about God, or whether the volume opened at that place because previous generations had often opened it there, I do not know. In any case, I thought I understood what I read there, and the brilliance of the exposition carried me away. I was often drawn back to the great *Encyclopaedia*, and many hours were well spent in its company. Of all the books, however, in the Foth library, the one which made the greatest impression on me was Louis Blanc's *History of the French Revolution*. Even today I regard it as an excellent historical work, which perhaps only Kropotkin has surpassed. It was there that I also made my first acquaintance with some of Guizot's historical works and with Fourier's and Proudhon's theories and Utopias.

The years of my adolescence were marked by repeated spells of melancholia and intense preoccupation with religious and ethical problems. My disposition has always made me follow to its very end a conviction or a principle, so I believed that the only logical behaviour for a religious person was to dedicate his life to the service of God, to enable him to obtain salvation. In consequence I seriously contemplated becoming a priest. The secluded background of Foth, so far from the real world, must have left its imprint on me through life. Later, as a young man, I moved in the restricted circles of the international aristocracy and consequently had little contact with life itself. For the aristocrat's true home, in whatever country, is the aristocracy, and he feels bound to it more intimately and closely than to his countrymen of a different class. Aristocracy is fundamentally international, far more so than the so-called 'International Proletariat', who are soil and language bound. I never learnt how to speak to workmen or peasants except from platforms — a limitation I have always regretted.

I once asked Alexander Esterhazy, who later became Queen Zita's court chamberlain, his opinion of one of Gerhardt Hauptmann's recent novels. 'I somehow cannot get interested in the private lives and love entanglements of people whom I never meet,' he answered. 'Haupt-

mann mostly writes about professors, architects, doctors and those kind
of people.' To him 'those kind of people' represented a big grey mass
of unknown quantity whose problems could be of no more interest
than those, say, of Eskimos. In Hungary the caste system did not apply
only to the upper classes — aristocracy, gentry, middle classes, etc. —
but the feudal hierarchy extended to the lowest ranks as well. For
example, it was considered a misalliance for a peasant-proprietor to
marry the daughter of a harvest-worker; for a daughter of a harvest-
worker to marry a land labourer; for a land labourer's daughter to
marry a shepherd; or for a shepherd to marry the daughter of a
swineherd, for the swineherd occupied the lowest step of the
social ladder.

My casual and desultory reading in the Foth library had contributed
meagrely to my University studies. My favourite subject was mathematics. I enjoyed the logic of figures and would sit up late in the night
working out equations and solving problems. It was from this taste
that my passion for chess derived.

Frequent journeys kept interrupting my lessons, which had never
been systematic. This was, however, of no importance, as I was shown
the questions before the examination, and thus my certificates showed
full marks. So, when I entered the Budapest University to read Law, I
was worse prepared than most.

While I was a student, a monthly allowance of two thousand florins
(£200) was allotted to me, equal in amount to the salary of our
Prime Minister in those days. Out of this sum I had merely to defray
the expenses of stabling the horses that came from my stud at Nagyut.
The rest was my pocket-money.

Soon I fell under the spell of Roman law, which I was studying.
The sharpness of its definitions and the rigid exactness of its system
fascinated me — I had always been keen on systems. I also felt personally concerned with it, as it dealt with matters which I should have
to face on coming of age: the laws of property. It was at this time that
Darwin's writings came into my hands, as well as Renan's *Vie de Jésus*.
I remember the excitement and pleasure I got out of Nordau's *Conventional Lies*, which left a lasting imprint on me. Although it was a hard
nut to crack, I set out to study Herbert Spencer's *First Principles*,
enjoying his methodical way of thought. Among the liberal philosophers John Stuart Mill made a deep impression on me, with his

classical essay on Liberty. These works largely contributed to the change in my religious attitude.

To the surprise of everyone, as well as to my own, I failed my examination, as I had to face Mariska, the most notoriously severe examiner of the University. It was an unheard-of event—an eldest son and a Karolyi not to have been accepted — so not only the severe Professor Mariska, but the whole institution of the University rose in my esteem. I set myself with clenched teeth to work and soon passed, with distinction.

The brightest spot in my recollection of those years is the time I spent with my uncle Alexander Karolyi, my grandmother's second husband. He was the founder of the co-operative movement in Hungary and had devoted his whole life to the public weal. He had no surface brilliancy, but was a profound thinker and a hard worker, something very unusual amongst Hungarian aristocrats. He had no time for the constitutional squabbles which infected our political life, and held that if Hungary wanted to become a strong and prosperous country, economic progress was the essential first step, and of more importance than separation from Austria. He was anxious to make the 'historical' classes fitter for leadership for he realized better than anyone their inefficiency and antiquated outlook. Being anti-semitic, he watched uneasily the growing influence of the richer Jews, which he hoped to counteract by better equipping the ruling classes for the economic struggle, and training them for leadership based on religious principles and moral responsibility. A conservative, he was surely the wisest one that the past generation in Hungary possessed. When I came to him to discuss the books I was reading, and the thoughts they awakened in me, he was much distressed. Not so much on account of my straying from the faith of my youth, but because he feared that I was falling under the influence of the Manchester school of *laisser-faire* and free competition. His altruism and genuine religious faith made him oppose the theory of the survival of the fittest and free competition, and he wished to rescue me from the abyss of materialism and hold me to the practice of Christian virtues, including the protection of the weak. As now my religious zeal had passed and I had absorbed with equal fervour the rationalism of the nineteenth century, he searched for an influence to counteract this Manchester liberalism on its own ground. So he brought me Karl Marx's *Das Kapital* in order to show me what a system of free competition leads to. He knew the work

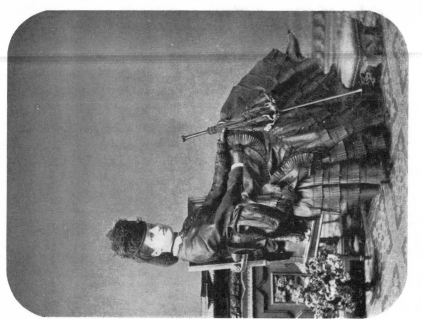

MY MOTHER GEORGINA KAROLYI,
ABOUT 1870

MY GREAT-GRANDFATHER
STEPHEN KAROLYI AT FOTH

MY UNCLE COUNT ALEXANDER IN HIS GIG

MY HOUSE IN THE EGYETEM UTCA IN BUDAPEST

thoroughly and agreed with all that Marx wrote on the anarchy of capitalism, but believed that his own much admired co-operative system would be the solution, for it would exclude the un-Christian and mischievous element of free competition, whilst retaining individual initiative which seemed to him indispensable. Marx might call himself a materialist but my uncle was confident that he would awaken and strengthen idealism in me, for I would find in him a materialist protecting the weak and challenging the right of the stronger to oppress. It is clear to me now that my own approach to life disposed me to agree with him. My uncle's arguments convinced me, and I accepted his criticism of my admired Roman law, whose huge intellectual edifice I now saw was built on egotism. It had stimulated my brain but left my emotions untouched, and I am convinced that in the last resort the emotions rather than the intellect determine a man's acts. I believe that those hours in which I first read Marx decided my whole career, for while it appealed to my reason by its compact, logical system it appealed to my feelings as well. An undisciplined, carefree existence could for a time thrust aside the memory of this great experience, but could not extinguish it.

Later on, the sight of the suffering which followed the First World War, and the muddle and helplessness into which the rulers had steered the people, revived my faith in Marx, and I believed that the only thing worth working for was the deliverance of the oppressed. This conviction ripened into a passion and became the motive force of my life. Had my uncle Alexander lived until the October Revolution, he would have had to admit that I was logically following the path on which I had entered under his guidance twenty years previously. That he would have been the one and only member of his class to stand up for me, I feel certain.

It was not long before my uncle initiated me into his practical activities and I became acquainted with the co-operative movement which he had inaugurated in Hungary. Soon I noticed how little the actual organization corresponded to the theory on which it was based. It was my first glimpse of the blatant difference that so often lies between theory and practice. Co-operation, if true to its doctrine, should have grown from the bottom upwards, and not have been dependent on the arbitrary decision of the central authority. I also deprecated the preponderance of the capitalist element, and considered the Rochdale

system of Robert Owen more equitable. I therefore started to disagree
with my uncle. I studied Charles Gide's writings and the work by
Lavergne, whom I had visited in Paris, *La Co-opération de l'Europe*. In
Lavergne's scheme there would be private competition to start with
but this would wither away when subject to the control of the Co-
operative Society. My first lecture, which was also my first public
appearance, had for its title: 'What, after all, is the difference between
the Co-operator and the Socialist?' and pointed out that both were
fighting against exploitation.

In 1892, at the age of sixteen, I first visited England, in the company
of my uncle Alexander and Albert Apponyi, who was then the leader
of the Independence Party. This visit was made memorable for me by
the luncheon given in our honour at Carlton Terrace by Sir William
Harcourt, at which both Mr. Arthur Balfour and Mr. Joseph Chamberlain were present. The two statesmen, Liberal and Tory, had a lively discussion, chaffing each other in humorous and typically English fashion.
My uncle, who had a sound knowledge of British politics, enjoyed the
subtleties of the argument more than I could. Joe Chamberlain, wearing
his famous eyeglass, sat silent and modest. Uncle Alexander drew my
attention to the fair and equitable tone in which political adversaries in
England discussed their differences, so very unlike the ways of the Continent. After lunch, we were asked to listen to a debate in the House of
Commons. The members in top-hats, their feet high on the back of
the benches, gave the impression of a private club of the privileged, set
against the grand and sombre background of century-old traditions.

What chiefly struck me during my first visit to England was its high
standard of living. One could not help feeling that to have been born
English was a special gift of the gods.

These were the days of security, of the Forsytes, of the man of property, and the rule of the prosperous middle classes, of industrialism
at its height, of elegant turnouts, of hansom cabs, impeccably groomed
horses, shiny paintwork of façades, shop windows filled with all
imaginable luxuries, abundance of woollen materials and leather goods,
and the fastidious elegance of Bond Street. I was struck by the quietness
of the town and the dignity of street manners. England's island quality
could actually be felt; its stability resting on the foundation of accumulated wealth, seemingly secure from any change or upheaval.

2

1900

My salad days when I was green in judgement.
SHAKESPEARE

I SPENT many years in Paris, where my uncle Ladislas Karolyi had acquired a large house on the Quai d'Orsay, which he had taken in exchange for an island near Martinique where there was still slavery: an inheritance from his French ancestors. Thus France became my second home.

In 1900, the year of the Paris Exhibition, the capital was enjoying its golden age; Parisian glamour was at its height. Economically, the Third Republic was making enormous progress, due to the thriftiness of the small man and the influx of foreigners, who, now that travel became easier, poured into Paris. Money was streaming in from all parts of the world. The French capitalist himself did not invest his money in France but lent it at high interest to foreign countries. Among the great attractions of the Paris Exhibition were the carriages of the Trans-Siberian railway. This line, which connected Moscow with Vladivostok, was built with the savings of the French middle classes, amounting to milliards of francs, and lost at the time of the Russian Revolution. Was it not natural, therefore, that the French bourgeoisie fostered a personal grudge against that revolution?

It was the Paris of the Prince of Wales — later Edward VII — the Folies Bergères, the Moulin Rouge, immortalized by Toulouse-Lautrec, of the wild and fabulous Grand Dukes, of le Comte Boni de Castellane, the Chevalier d'Orsay of his time, of Sugar King Lebaudy, nicknamed 'Le petit Sucrier'. In the cabarets they sang about him:

Ah, ah, que t'es rigolo,
Dans ton petit tringolo,
Et tu n'est pas joli garçon,
Mais t'as des yeux de cochon.

Not only the French, but the Hungarians and the Poles, too, had their Chevaliers d'Orsay. Count Roman Potocky, Count Paul Szapary and Count Elemer Batthyanyi were well known on the turf, the Champs Élysées and the Croisette in Cannes.

Elemer Batthyanyi was the best-known Hungarian in the racing world; on one occasion he won the Derby. In his childhood he was supposed to have been the hope of Hungary, as the only son of Louis Batthyanyi; but his ambition did not soar high enough and he turned out to be rather the hope of the turf. One day, when dining with the Prince of Wales, the latter addressed him in German. 'I am sorry, sir,' replied Batthyanyi, who spoke German fluently, 'but even for your sake, I cannot answer you in that language.' He had made a vow, after his father's execution, never to speak the language of the Habsburgs. 'It is for me to apologize,' said the Prince, 'I had forgotten.'

There was another story I remember being told by my uncle Pista, who spent much time in the company of the Prince of Wales. It was after a gay supper in a private room at Larue's. A Polish count asked the Prince for a match to light his cigar. The Prince rang for the maître d'hôtel: *'Monsieur le comte désire sa voiture, faites-la avancer de suite.'* The unfortunate young man was never invited again. On one occasion when the Prince was visiting Hungary, he was the guest of a well-known Jewish banker. A shooting party had been arranged to which the Prince sent out the invitations. Nicolas Palffy, brother of my stepmother Geraldine, received one. He refused the Prince on the grounds that he would not go to the house of a Jew. This illustrates the exclusiveness of the particular milieu in which I was brought up.

One day in 1898, I went to visit the famous clairvoyante, Madame de Thèbes. She lived in a small third-floor room somewhere near the Gare du Nord. I was twenty-two, a young man of the world who little imagined that he would be called upon to play any part in public life. Handicapped by my faulty speech, I simply enjoyed my fortune, gambling, travelling and trying to forget the sentimental troubles in which I was deeply involved. My change of heart came much later in life. Thus, I did not think much of Madame de Thèbes's predictions, regarding them as completely foolish. She told me, holding my hand in hers — she did not know who I was — that I would play a very important part in politics, would have a spectacular career and obtain a high position in public life, but would soon after lose it and my fortune as well. 'Your life will have fantastic ups and downs. You will know what it is to be destitute. Towards the end, for you will live long, your fortunes will rise again. You will marry a girl much younger than yourself, whose most striking feature will be her eyes; they will be unusual eyes, light green in colour.' They are the eyes of my wife, who was hardly born then. The woman I cared for then had blue eyes, so I was not interested.

My French relatives were legitimists, and loyal to the *ancien régime*. To *dorer le blazon*, one of the Polignacs married a Pommery girl, daughter of the champagne manufacturer, a marriage regarded by the Fauberg St. Germain as a misalliance. Later Melchior Polignac, to whose uncle I owed my entry into the Paris Jockey Club, married an American woman belonging to the Morgan family of bankers. Strangely enough, their son, today a brilliant journalist, turned out a militant Socialist, renouncing his wealth and even changing his name.

At that epoch the Jockey Club was so exclusive that even the Austro-Hungarian Ambassador, Count Kevenhuller (nicknamed *l'Ambrassadeur* for his gallant adventures), was not admitted. It was a real power, and the sworn enemy of the Third Republic. I remember the first night of Bernstein's *Après Moi* at the Comédie Française, which ended in a beating-up of Jews by the anti-Dreyfusards and the Camelots du Roi, and the breaking up of the performance; one of the great scandals of the year.

From Paris I returned for short intervals to my vast and empty mansion in the Egyetem utca, with its seventy-two rooms, of which I was the sole inhabitant.

My uncle Laszlo Karolyi used to have shooting parties in his house at Radvany. Although I never liked shooting I was supposed to take part in them. Even when I was a boy, my guardian, Uncle Pista, was keen for me to be a sportsman, but there was nothing I loathed so much as getting up at the crack of dawn and having to watch till a harmless stag or deer came along to be massacred. So I usually got my gamekeeper to spread a rug on the grass in the forest, where I would enjoy a sound sleep. He was delighted to do the same, and naturally never gave me away to my uncle.

At Radvany, at Laszlo Karolyi's place, the guests were supplied not only with stags but also with women. Peasant girls from the village were ordered in for the night by the superintendent. These bachelor parties — as they mostly were — made hilarious by the strong wine of the Matra, would find young girls awaiting them in their beds. One night, in a depressed mood — I usually became depressed when I had to spend days in the company of males only — I found between my sheets a buxom young girl lying in the state in which God had created her. I flew into a rage and most unkindly chased the poor thing out of the room, in spite of her meagre attire. After this my reputation was tarnished, for my uncle, hurt at my 'ingratitude', thought there must be something wrong with me. It was simply that I loved another woman.

My uncle, who now began to realize that I suffered from some sentimental trouble, became suspicious and tried to distract me. Nothing irritated me more than when Uncle Laszlo or Uncle Pista would approach a well-known demi-mondaine, make all financial arrangements with her in advance, and then try to make me believe that she had fallen for me. A famous French beauty, an actress, was supplied to me in this way. She was dark, with jet-black eyes, and although I only liked fair women with light eyes I succumbed to her charms; but the adventure only left me with an acute *malaise* and increased my melancholia.

To beat a servant in those days was quite usual. They would never dare to complain to the authorities. They would resent it if a stick was used on them, but not if their ears were boxed. It was even regarded as a sign of affection. I never indulged in it and remember only once losing my self-control and using a whip on one of my grooms, an action I never regretted. It happened at Parad. I was just going to have a ride when I saw a group of servants, seemingly highly amused, gathered around a tree under which my bulldog Tevrev and some other dogs from the stables were frantically barking. I then saw a red bleeding form crouched on a branch and was told that one of the grooms had 'for fun' skinned a cat and let the dogs loose on it. I had the riding whip in my hand and used it on the culprit with all the vigour of my indignation.

Although an hereditary member of the House of Magnates, I appeared there on rare occasions and it was rather the National Casino's gambling rooms that attracted me. Being a bachelor, this club was my home. To gamble in such restricted company was awkward, as everyone knew the financial situation of his neighbour; when mutually related as well, it was unpleasant to walk off with half of one's brother-in-law's or cousin's wealth in one's pocket. For the gambler money loses its value, and when I thrust the crumpled banknotes on the table, they seemed to be mere dirty pieces of paper. I was a lucky gambler, probably because a rich man can afford losses, for he can wait for his luck to turn. A man with scant means has to stop when he loses or else he runs after his money, which is always fatal. George Pallavicini was one of these and in later years, after I became his brother-in-law, it was most embarrassing when my wife's sister would complain to her the next day that George had lost half his income to me. I had, therefore, for decency's sake, to stay until I returned some of my winnings. The luck I had did not gain me friends, and when I held the bank a dozen times running, the whole table would be holding their thumbs against me, which naturally increased in me the excitement of the game.

My favourite sport was riding and I was also a keen polo player. Polo was a fashionable game in Hungary, brought in by Geza Andrassy, my wife's uncle, who prided himself on his resemblance to Edward VII. I was known not so much for my good as for my dangerously fierce play, so that everyone preferred to be in my team rather than against me. I rode several times in steeplechases, a most enjoyable pastime. In the north of Hungary, on the Andrassy estates, they hunted the fox, with a genuine English pack with an English huntsman and whips. Everyone was immaculately turned out in their Hammond breeches, Lobb boots and pink coats. I remember seeing my future wife, then a girl of twelve, following the hounds with her loose hair floating in the wind whilst she battled with her unruly Irish hunter.

At this time I had grown a long beard which made me appear much older than my years and also gave me the look of a Svengali, with which I hoped to impress my women friends. I never much enjoyed the company of males and although many turned to me when in need of financial help, I had few real men friends. I preferred female society.

It was in those days that Blériot, the French aviator, who some years later crossed the Channel, demonstrated his new plane in Budapest. It was the first time that I had seen actual flying and I could not resist the temptation of trying it out myself. The pilot, who was not Blériot, had strict instructions not to take passengers. But money can do a lot, and he was a Frenchman. I certainly shall never forget the sensation

I had in mid-air; I was seated on a bicycle, clinging desperately to the iron bar in front of me, my legs dangling in space; underneath me I caught glimpses of the roofs of the houses. Luckily I did not suffer from giddiness. I had been in the air once before, but that was a more comfortable journey in a balloon which, changing into a large parachute, descended slowly whilst we were comfortably seated in the gondola.

The interest in the Co-operative movement which Uncle Alexander had aroused in me had not waned and I took the opportunity of combining my lust for travel with acquainting myself with its development in Western Europe. England, as the mother country of the movement, was of special interest to me. One day the Hungarian Agricultural Society asked me to attend a congress of Co-operatives in Cardiff. At the banquet which followed a clergyman said the usual grace, and all present stood up. I was about twenty, going through a materialist phase, and passionately believed myself an unbeliever. I felt that to join the others in prayer and simulate faith would be hypocrisy and moral cowardice, and so with great effort, pale, and holding fast to the arms of my chair, I did not budge. I had not hurt the feelings of the company, as no one seemed to resent my action — thinking, most probably, that this young foreigner did not grasp what was going on; but I had eased my conscience.

My cousin Alexander Palffy was First Secretary to the Embassy in London. Alexander was one of those foreigners who become more English than the English themselves. His greatest ambition was to be taken for a native of the British Isles. On one occasion, his Ambassador, who was the popular Count Mensdorff — related to Edward VII and treated by him as his cousin — put young Palffy in charge of a Hungarian civil servant sent out by the Ministry of Agriculture. Palffy invited him to lunch at St. James's Club. To the consternation of his host, he turned up in a dinner jacket. The miserable Alex tried to convey to him that lunching in that attire was equal to committing murder, and asked him to return for dinner in the evening. This time, the wretched man appeared in tweeds and plus fours. My cousin had not the heart to send him back again, and went through his dinner heroically, although excruciatingly uncomfortable.

My restlessness drove me all round the world. Of my Eastern travels, the one to Ceylon remains unforgettable. I had scarcely arrived at my hotel in Colombo when I was seized with violent fever and dysentery, a malady which in those climates is particularly dangerous. I soon became delirious and, when I regained consciousness, found myself in a rickshaw in a completely apathetic condition. The management of the hotel had removed me, and I was taken to a bungalow in the middle of a forest. It was a small private clinic, where I was well looked after. I spent my convalescence in the hill country at Kandy. For many years afterwards I suffered from malaria contracted there. This fairy island with its luscious foliage, its gorgeous fleshy plants, unsurpassably rich and varied, is nearer to man's idea of Paradise than any place on earth. The scent of cinnamon lingering in the air, and glow-worms as large as oranges illuminating the tropical nights, lend the whole a quality of unreality. I was not interested in colonial politics at the time but I was impressed by British achievements in Ceylon; if we permit roads to be laid out in Paradise, they must be kept like the highroads in Ceylon. If we admit the invasion of the jungle by human habitations, let them be as safe and well organized and hospitable as the English rest-houses, which were open to the foreigner and greatly simplified travel in Ceylon.

During my stay there, I attended a reception at the house of the Governor of Ceylon in honour of the Duke of Connaught and his nineteen-year-old daughter Patricia. The perfection of this occasion remained for ever in my mind.

Lady Patricia, serene and beautiful, like a fairy princess in white silk, stood at the foot of the stairs leading up into the Residency to receive the homage of the native chiefs of Ceylon. They had come on their elephants, with richly embroidered saddles and golden trappings; when arriving in front of Lady Patricia, the huge animals knelt down in salute. The young girl handed each elephant his due reward, and the beast moved slowly away, demonstrating that even a banana can be accepted with dignity. It was as though Asia had paid homage to Europe.

I travelled home on the same ship as the Duke of Connaught and his family, so I had the pleasure of seeing Lady Patricia at close quarters and continued to admire her silently from afar; to my grief, she took no notice of me.

I visited New York for the first time in the year 1905. At that period, it still preserved its colonial character. The Globe, with fifteen storeys, was its highest building, and Fifth Avenue was a strictly residential street. I stayed, as did everyone from Europe, in the Waldorf-Astoria and enjoyed living on the eleventh floor. In those days, I mixed only with New York's so-called 'Four Hundred'. That was before the invasion of titled Europeans, and Americans still kept their illusions with regard to them. We, on the other hand, could not differentiate easily between Americans or understand the finesses of American society. The *Mayflower* tradition, and the difference between a fortune made fifty or a hundred years ago, did not seem important to us. Somehow, every American was regarded more or less as a parvenu.

I remember vividly the big ball at the Vanderbilts' on the occasion of the coming-out of their daughter Gladys, later Countess Szechenyi. It was not the sort of party given by millionaires nowadays. No publicity or ostentation, but a glorious show of flowers and a very timid girl, who whispered rather than talked, as if trying to apologize for being an heiress. I remember, too, the luxurious receptions of the silent Mr. Smith in his house decorated in pure quattrocento style. He possessed one of the world's most famous collections of Dutch and Italian Renaissance masters, but their beauty seemed to have silenced their owner.

One of the society beauties of those days was Mrs. Lydig, who started the fashion of showing her lovely bare back down to the waist. People with lumbago called it the 'Lydig pain'.

When I visited the U.S.A. on another occasion, with Count Antony Sigray who was in search of an heiress, we were invited to a large dinner party at which, to our surprise and embarrassment, we were placed on a couple of throne-like armchairs next to each other. During the courses, a negro pair danced the then fashionable 'cake-walk', while questions were hurled at us as to how it felt to have blue blood. Sigray had a go at two heiresses, daughters of Ogden Mills. After having been rejected by the tall, thin one, he tried her opposite number, the plump, short one, but was equally unsuccessful. Laszlo Szechenyi, also financially broke, had his journey to the States paid for by his moneylender, that being the only hope the latter had of seeing his money back. Szechenyi, however, met his heiress in Karlsbad, not in America.

The independence of American girls was very noticeable by contrast

with those of our society, who were not supposed to go out un-
chaperoned. But here, also, the European guest was likely to commit a
faux pas. He would not distinguish between girls he could invite alone
and those he could not. In Europe in those antediluvian days, a respectable girl would not accept an invitation to a restaurant, while an
invitation to a party had to be given through her parents. In New
York, they would go riding with you in Central Park and even dine
with you, and would be most surprised if you misunderstood them.
Others again, belonging to the so-called *Mayflower* set, were more
strictly brought up. Nevertheless, one could send flowers to any girl or
woman without any deeper meaning being construed; completely
inconceivable in Europe.

At that period Americans had few inherited fortunes and most had
been acquired by labour. They would relate with pride how they had
made their wealth. Eighty-year-old Ogden Mills would tell me how he
drove the post-chaise through the wilds of the Sierra Nevada in 1848,
to the west coast, how he bought out of his earnings a stretch of land
on which later he discovered the yellow metal, and how he had to
defend himself from the attacks of Red Indians. He was a very remarkable old man and had a fascinating way of relating his adventures.

I came to New York as a carefree young man in search of distraction
to make me forget a sentimental attachment, but it was all in vain. The
vivacious American girls could not console me. Like all young people
I imagined the worries of the heart to be eternal. Healthy and wealthy
but not wise, I was not happy; for the gods limit their generosity.
Melancholy, in the then fashionable Byronic mood, I walked beside a
lovely girl by the Gulf of San Francisco; despondent I rode in Central
Park watching the society beauties, wrapped up in furs, driving in
their open carriages; restless I dashed through the American continent in search of the oblivion I could not find.

Although not yet immersed in the social problem, I was deeply
affected by the democratic atmosphere of the New World, so very
different from that of Hungary. Democratic plutocracy in practice
was a new and thrilling experience for me. In one of the hotels they
seated my valet Bakos next to me at meals. The poor soul nearly
passed away in his embarrassment. All my persuasion did not help.
He refused to sit at the same table with his master. This reminds me of
a similar instance of how particular old-fashioned servants are to keep

the distance between themselves and their betters. In the year 1919 when Central Europe was governed by Socialists and Communists, we had engaged an Austrian woman to help with the children. On one occasion when travelling, my wife asked her to sit with us for luncheon in the station restaurant. The same evening she gave notice, giving as her reason that she had thought she was serving genuine aristocrats, who would not demean themselves by eating with their servants.

My uncle Alexander's grave illness put an end for the time to my rovings in foreign lands. In San Francisco, while in bed with pneumonia, I received a cable calling me back to Menton, where he lay desperately ill. Although we had parted on bad terms, for my uncle disapproved of my sentimental attachment and had advised me to become a priest, I remained deeply devoted to him. Against the strict orders of my doctor, I hurried without stopping to his bedside. I had reached Denver when I saw the large headlines of a local newspaper: 'San Francisco utterly destroyed by an earthquake.'

I learned later that the house in which I had lived had collapsed. My uncle's death had saved my life.

3

MY ENTRY INTO POLITICS

I should be a Socialist of the deepest magenta, were I a worker here.
Sir Arthur Nicolson (later Lord Carnock), when British Consul in
Budapest, in a letter to his wife.

WHEN I was twenty-six I made an ill-fated attempt to get into Parliament on the programme of the Party of Independence which at that time supported the Government.[4] The Prime Minister, Szell, had just passed a law against electoral abuses. Few of the members took this law seriously, although the campaign was carried on under the slogan of 'Clean Elections'. My agent in the constituency of Zilah was assailing me with urgent requests for 'constitutional expenses'. I knew what this meant: money for buying votes. Puzzled, I called on the Prime Minister and informed him of the demands of his party machine. 'What should I do?' I asked. 'Pay,' answered the projector of the law against corruption.

Shocked, I did not follow his advice, and I lost the election.

After my uncle's death, I had become a leading member of the Central Co-operative Society, called the 'Hangya' (ant) whose founder he had been. In order to study the movement in all its various aspects, I made several journeys to Belgium, France, England and Italy. I remember meeting for the first time at congresses of the Co-operative Society Sidney Webb and many well-known Socialists of those days, Vandervelde, Leonida Bissolati and others. (The Socialists undoubtedly had the best organized co-operatives.)

In 1909, whilst I was in Paris, the presidency of our most powerful agricultural society, the OMGE (National Hungarian Agricultural Society), which was rightly said to be ruling the country, was offered to me. At the age of thirty-four this was a great honour.

My first aim was to put this exclusive society of landowners onto a much wider basis, for the economic interests and the general outlook of the sixteen hundred members were identical. We soon succeeded in raising the membership of the OMGE to five thousand.

In 1910 I stood a second time for Parliament and was elected. On the question of the franchise I still agreed with Tisza and the entire Magyar ruling class that universal suffrage in Hungary would strengthen the subject races and be detrimental to the supremacy of the Magyars. But I stood for secret ballot, mainly with the idea of purifying the elections from corruption, and was the only one of the OMGE to vote for it. I also founded an agrarian centre, which Members of Parliament from all parties could join if interested in the agrarian and co-operative movement.

Yet, the better acquainted I became with the system of the OMGE the less I liked it. I began to realize that, being based on the unchallenged power and interests of the big estates, its very foundations were wrong, and could be reformed only by changing the system itself. It was therefore on politics that I had to concentrate my activities. My decision to resign the presidency was hastened through happenings in Parliament. Tisza, as President of the Chamber (Speaker), had the Deputies who opposed his armament programme — urged on him by Berlin — led out of Parliament by the police.

After this parliamentary coup, I was pacing up and down in suppressed rage in the rooms of our club, the National Casino, when Tisza entered, and, as if nothing had happened, came up to me with outstretched hand. 'How are you?' I put mine behind my back and walked on. 'Don't you hear?' he asked, turning pale. 'Yes, but after what has happened, I do not care to know you,' I answered. The same day Tisza's seconds called and the next day, at five in the afternoon, the duel took place.

Tisza was a first-rate fencer in spite of his bad sight. We had thirty-four bouts together, lasting over an hour; then he cut my arm, and the seconds stopped the fight. There was no reconciliation. It seems strange today that political controversies should be regulated by duels; another remnant of the feudal past, carried on with gusto in Hungary.

The passivity with which Parliament had yielded to Tisza's violence made me realize that our Constitution was only a sham, and that a Parliament based on corrupt elections, with an open ballot in which only six per cent of the population had a vote, did not represent the country. Now even the Opposition was prevented from doing its duty. The situation became so acute that a Deputy fired his revolver at Tisza in Parliament. I felt that I could no longer serve this pernicious system, nor watch idly from the stagebox of the O M G E presidency, when such vital events were going on. I resigned at the general meeting without prior notice and concentrated entirely on the struggle against the Government, addressing a series of public meetings of protest.

To counteract the dangers of Tisza's uncontrolled power, a democratic Parliament was a *sine qua non*. Until now, the Hungarian Opposition had been concerned solely with gaining independence from Austria, without realizing that this had to be linked with democracy. This had been the programme of the leaders in 1848, and the doctrines of 1848 could still evoke a powerful response in the people. For them the two great ideas of our fight were still a living reality: the political aim of Hungary's independence, and the social aim of raising the standard of living of the agricultural population by freeing them from the yoke of the landlords.

The peasants were Kossuthists, for it was he who had freed their grandfathers from bondage. He had abolished the *corvée*, the tithe and the whipping post. The Kossuth cult was a living protest against the still existing semi-feudal character of Hungary.

The subject races, whom we Magyars used to call 'nationalities' — Rumanians, Slovaks, Croats and Serbs — had never been Kossuthists. The reason for this was that, when the Croats had offered their help to Kossuth, they had been refused. They had more trust in the Habsburgs than in Kossuth, who was a typical representative of the Hungarian gentry. Kossuth's radicalism was a specifically Magyar one. Later, in exile, he realized that his crucial error had been in antagonizing the non-Magyar races. Living outside his country, his vision was clarified by distance, and he drew up the plan for a Danubian Confederation, directed against the Habsburgs. This scheme would have made Hungary the centre of a group of democratic States lying along the Danube, thus giving her the role of pioneer amongst homologous and equal neighbours. His followers did not wish to remember this Kossuth of later years, and it was characteristic that as long as he appealed to national conceit he was considered the greatest Hungarian, but as soon as he launched a scheme of lasting value his popularity diminished. For it implied that Hungary would recognize as equals the alien races within

41

her gates, as she could never succeed without their co-operation. Even today the only solution to the Central European problem is based on this concept of his, and no estimate of Kossuth's statesmanship would be complete which overlooked it.

My aim was to revive Kossuth's plan in a modernized form, and a Slavophile policy was the stepping-stone to this. The events of the past ten years have proved without doubt that Europe's fate would have been very different had a powerful Federal State of 88 millions been able to stand up to Hitler in 1938.[5]

4

THE STRUGGLE

I sit on a man's back, choking him and making him carry me, and yet assure
myself and others that I am very sorry for him and wish to ease his lot by all
possible means — except by getting off his back. LEO TOLSTOY

I ENTERED Parliament in the year 1910 as a member of the
Party of Independence, of which Francis Kossuth was the leader.
It was already divided into two opposing groups. The right wing,
led by Kossuth and Albert Apponyi, were hostile to a democratic
solution of the suffrage question — as it would have included the subject races as well — and in foreign policy they followed the official
Ballhausplatz line. The leader of the left wing was Julius Justh. He
demanded the extension of the suffrage, with more rights for the
minorities, and was for promoting Federation in place of Dualism.
For this purpose he allied himself with the extra-parliamentary group
of the Social Democrats. Anti-German in foreign policy, he aimed at
a break with the Triple Alliance of Germany, Italy and Austria-
Hungary. Friendly to the South Slavs, he adhered to the Fiume
Resolution of 1905,[6] the work of Franjo Supilo, publisher of the
Novi List and leader of Croatia. My place, therefore, could only be on
the side of Justh, in whom I saw the man whose honesty and civic
courage would help my political aims. He had no personal ambition or
vanity, a rare phenomenon in political life. If Hungary had had
several men of his stamp, I believe her fate would have been different.

In striking contrast to Justh's character was that of Francis Kossuth,
the small son of a great man. Brought up in Italy, he had the ostenta-
tious, theatrical manners of his adopted country. Obsessed by the
vanity so often found in children of famous parents, he was so pleased
at receiving from the Emperor whom his father had dethroned the
Grand Cross of the Order of Leopold — a purely Austrian order, by

the way — that he had it added to a portrait of himself, painted before he received the decoration.

The third leader of the Opposition was Albert Apponyi, my uncle.

If a true orator is one who expresses what is in the minds of his audience, there have been few better orators than Albert Apponyi. Instinctively he tried to express nothing else. With miraculous quickness, he found a bond with every kind of audience. With the greatest confidence and optimism — he was a confirmed optimist — he discovered immediately the key that brought him into harmony with the soul of his public. His own talent and the response of his audiences carried him away, especially when speaking *ex tempore*. The orator in him more than once embarrassed the statesman. It happened at times, at the height of a rhetorical flight, that he would express views hardly reconcilable with those which he had up to then represented. His frequent changes from one political party to another were evidently due to this. He was a great and highly cultured European, master of many languages; his French and English were as perfect as his Hungarian and he even spoke Slovak when necessary. He told me that one of his greatest oratorical successes was a speech in Slovak. He had never spoken the language before and his speech, as drafted, was translated for him. He learnt it by heart and delivered it brilliantly, with an almost irreproachable accent. His audience was moved to tears. His comparisons between English and Hungarian parliamentarianism were a scholarly performance, but he would never admit the essential difference — that ours was founded on corrupt elections and administration. For him the fact that the golden Hungarian Charter of 1222 was as ancient as the Great English Charter was all that mattered, for he did not take into consideration that for many centuries we were under absolute government. Debunking our pseudo-parliamentarianism would have put an end to his self-deception and to his smug and sunny outlook. Parliament had to keep up the pretence that the fate of the country was settled by those 413 gentlemen seated under the Gothic arches of the House of Assembly. Not only was it never settled there; it was not even settled in the Prime Minister's office in St. George's Place, but in the Chancellery at the Foreign Office in Vienna, the mansion of Kaunitz and Metternich on the Ballhausplatz, where, on important occasions, the two Premiers and three joint ministers —

of Foreign Affairs, War and Finance — met as a Cabinet of Five. It was this Cabinet that decided on the ultimatum to Serbia. It was inevitable that Parliament came periodically to grief in essaying to keep up this fiction of independence. On such occasions, Tisza, in accordance with his autocratic nature, tried to find a way out by force, as he had done with the Opposition when it obstructed the passing of the Military Laws.

Apponyi, who had been a pupil of the Jesuits in Karlsburg, and was marked by it for life, contributed with his sophistry and rhetoric to the hushing up of the truth. He committed his greatest error when, as Minister of Education, in glaring contrast to the spirit of Deak and Eotvos, he begot the notorious Educational Act, which gave great offence to the non-Magyars, and eventually was the cause of much trouble to us as well. This highly gifted, kind man, with a childlike quality so often found in great men, was completely unfitted for Opposition leader. He was a born pacifist. His moral sense and gentle nature were congenitally opposed to violence. His first laurels were won at the International Pacifist Congresses, and it was he who represented Hungary at the Hague in 1913. A year later, in spite of this, he greeted Hungary's decision to declare war with the memorable outcry: 'at last'. Once again the orator having committed himself for the sake of popularity to an attitude of bellicose ecstasy, the statesman had to follow. He belongs to those who dug the grave of old Hungary.

The divergencies in the foreign policy of the Monarchy gained momentum at the time of the Balkan Wars, forerunners of the great wars to come. The first started in 1912, when the subject nations, Greece, Bulgaria and Serbia, rose against the Turks. The Triple Alliance, to which the Catholic Habsburgs belonged, backed the feudal despotism of Mohammedan Turkey against the Christian peoples of the Balkans. The anti-Slav and anti-democratic line was again what mattered. As is well known, this pro-Turk policy brought the Triple Alliance a formidable defeat.

Turkey collapsed, but the strife continued between Bulgaria and Serbia, when again the Monarchy backed the wrong horse, Bulgaria.

It was only our small group, led by Justh and faced by an overwhelming majority, which opposed the official policy of the Ballhausplatz. Germany's desire to secure a 'place in the sun' and the Berlin-Bagdad plan for the exploitation of the Ottoman Empire, made us realize that war was inevitable if the Monarchy refused to take an independent line; for the more securely our chains were riveted to the German chariot, the more confident Berlin would grow in its aggressive policy.

Placed in the midst of a conflict of rival imperialisms, Hungary's role was of primary importance. We had nothing to gain from the war, and the result, whatever it was, would be disastrous for us. How could we avoid it? Only if the Monarchy could be made to realize that by staying neutral or, if necessary, joining the Entente, it could force the Kaiser and the Junkers to give up their bellicose aims. Federalization was the only way for the Monarchy to carry out an independent policy. If Hungary became democratic and reached an understanding with its minorities, it could exercise a decisive influence on the Ballhausplatz; so the first step towards our ultimate aim was universal suffrage. Tisza's argument that before considering democracy in Hungary ten million non-Magyars had to be Magyarized left little hope that we should ever get it, for the Magyar assimilative capacity has never been great.[7]

The franchise, which was only extended to 6 per cent of the population on the basis of income, was an open one. In a Parliament composed of 414 members the non-Magyar races — Serbs, Slovaks, Rumanians — had an average of eight to ten seats, although 50 per cent of the population was non-Magyar.

Even during the First World War, when Wilson's Fourteen Points were the basis of negotiation, our Members of Parliament considered a two-class franchise, putting the minorities into the second class. Whom the gods wish to destroy, they strike with madness.

In the distribution of land, Hungary was still semi-feudal. In old Hungary the large and medium estates made up 54.4 per cent of the whole territory. Four-fifths of the population had less *per capita* than twenty acres, or no land at all. Three hundred and twenty-four big landowners owned 20 per cent of the arable land with an average of 41,000 acres each. Prince Esterhazy alone owned 570,000 acres. The Roman Catholic Church owned about one million acres. I owned 25,000 acres of forest, about 35,000 acres of meadow and arable land, a coal mine, and the estate of Parad which, on account of its waters, was turned into a spa. Also a glass factory, several houses in Budapest, the mansion in the Egyetem utca, the country estate of Sasvar, and several shooting-boxes. The whole estate was valued at about 25 million pounds.

Justh had now retired from active politics on account of illness. Just at the time when the clouds were gathering for the great tempest, I was elected leader of the United Independence Party, in spite of my youth. This was a blow for my uncle Apponyi, but I never noticed in him any ill-will towards me; his was a generous nature. My leadership was, however, controlled by an executive council composed of the representatives of various shades of opinion in proportion to their numbers in the party, so that Apponyi, who had the majority of followers, remained the outstanding influence.

My elders criticized me, probably with some justice, for my dilettante approach to politics. They suspected that they were for me the pastime of a young man with too much money. Perhaps I conveyed that impression. I remember once being a member of a political delegation which was sent to Vienna to attend a conference. In the express train between Budapest and Vienna we received a message that the conference had been postponed. As I had much more pleasant things to do in Budapest, I waited until the train slowed down a little and then jumped out on to the track, walked to the neighbouring village and hurried home to give a pleasant surprise to a woman friend. My companions, of whom I had not taken leave, looked for me all over the train; but then, as there had been no stop, they imagined that a misfortune had befallen me and pulled the alarm. The track was searched for my body and the papers were filled with the sensational news that Karolyi had leapt from the express when at full speed. I little minded the comments, as long as I could spend my time with the person I cared for.

5

THE QUAI D'ORSAY

IN the autumn of 1913 I felt that the time had come for an attempt to secure a rapprochement between Hungary and those nations with which the Prussian alliance was bound to bring us into conflict sooner or later; also to determine where the Hungarian Independence Party stood, in case of such a conflict. Russia, the leading Slav State, should be approached first. It was by no means easy for an opposition party to approach Tsarist Russia. To get into touch with any of the political parties would have been completely ineffective since, in spite of the Duma, Russia was still under absolute government. The Duma could certainly have done nothing to prevent war. The way to reach the powerful circles of St. Petersburg was through Paris. At the time of the Balkan Wars France had publicly offered moderating counsel to the Russian Government; if the European war did not break out then, it was due in part to the good sense and influence of the French Government. Many features of our struggle for Hungarian independence pointed towards France. Our struggles of the seventeenth and eighteenth centuries coincided with wars waged between Bourbons and Habsburgs for supremacy in Europe.

With this tradition the French orientation of my policy would not have been unpopular in Hungary. To take independent action in foreign policy, proving to Berlin that the Magyar nation did not stand united behind the German Alliance, might have averted war, or, if not, might have preserved Hungary and the Monarchy from it. The way not only to St. Petersburg, but even to our own Slavs, seemed to be through Paris. I made a rash decision; I decided to go to Paris and get into touch with French Government circles. By securing some financial advantage for Hungary, I hoped to effect a change, first in the policy of the party, and then in that of the country as a whole. Albert Apponyi objected to Hungarian affairs being discussed outside the country. This, he thought, would degrade us to the status of a politically outlawed nationality, like the Czechs. He wanted to keep up the pretence of Magyar sovereignty and conceal the fact that the joint Foreign Office in Vienna did not represent Hungary equally with Austria, although no one knew better than he that parity in foreign affairs was a mere fiction and that for forty years Hungarian influence had been scarcely existent. The result of this ambiguous situation was that the Magyars were regarded as pro-German. It was therefore necessary that the Independence Party, which in any case did not stand for the Compromise of 1867, should adopt a new line.

I admitted to Poincaré that, although I was the leader of the party, I had not a majority to back me in the new orientation of foreign policy which I was advocating, but said that if we got encouragement from France or Russia, I should gain a strong following. As I could not approach the Russians direct, I hoped this would be possible through Poincaré's influence. I made it clear to him that if we could secure economic liberation from Austria, and political reconciliation with the Slavs, we should hold the trump cards and could break the front of German-Austrians, Magyars and Rumanians, held by the Triple Alliance. If Hungary broke that chain, war could be avoided.

The President listened attentively to my plan, naturally without committing himself. He showed an intimate knowledge of the subtleties of European politics. When I told him that I was going to discuss my plan with Finance Minister Caillaux, he warned me to be careful; this was because Caillaux was supposed to be pro-German.

The loan I wanted to secure was a hundred million francs for the city of Budapest, to be invested in public improvements. I met Joseph Caillaux several times. He showed the clearest comprehension of my plan; whatever his opponents said, he was not pro-German; but wishing to avoid war he was working for a rapprochement with Germany. He recognized in my politics the counterpart of his own: my mission was to weaken German imperialism, as his was to fight against ultra-chauvinist tendencies in France, and for both of us peace was the aim.

I carried on negotiations with many others besides Poincaré and Caillaux — with Senator Paul Doumer, formerly Governor of Indo-China and virtually the representative of the heavy industries; with André Tardieu, foreign editor of *Le Temps*, and with Georges Clemenceau. Rendered sceptical by his past experience, the latter's main objection to my plan was that it was no longer possible to effect a change of direction, as the Dual Monarchy was already too firmly held in Germany's clutches. But he promised to support us in his paper *L'Homme Libre*. Things were progressing well and I was filled with hope. But we were already in June 1914, and our success was prevented by the war. I was too late.

6

THE END OF SECURITY

Wir gingen almählich der Welt auf die Nerven, und wir selbst haben das bis zum Ende des Weltkrieges gar nicht bemerkt.   CHANCELLOR VON BÜLOW

WHILE waiting for an invitation to St. Petersburg, I decided to tour the United States with a group of M.P.s belonging to the left wing of the Independence Party. Our policy was clear and well defined in all its stages, and no country could offer a better field for spreading our ideas than the democratic States, with their large Hungarian colony. Our party had to move out of its provincialism and inactivity and become a factor to be reckoned with. The vast majority of the half-million Hungarians living in the U.S.A. were people who, either themselves or their fathers, had been driven to emigrate by our intolerable social conditions, and they would certainly not stand for the existing Hungarian social order. Many of them belonged to the subject races, and it was therefore necessary to have on our platform a representative of the Socialists as well, so as not to antagonize them. I invited Sigismund Kunfi, one of the best brains of the Social Democratic party and a fine orator, to accompany us.

At Cherbourg, on the steamer *Vaterland* bound for the U.S.A., a cable was handed to me. It contained the news of the murder of Archduke Franz Ferdinand and his wife at Sarajevo.

We had to make a quick decision whether to get off the ship and hurry home, as the siren for departure had just sounded. No, we would not return now, as everything had been arranged for our reception in New York.

On our arrival there it seemed as if the tragedy of Sarajevo would find a peaceful solution. The exchange of notes and Serbia's apology made it hopeful that war might still be avoided. We therefore started on our propaganda tour, which lasted three weeks. During this time we received no news from home and were left guessing what the future would be.

Arriving in Cleveland in July, we heard of the Austro-Hungarian ultimatum, and realized that we were on the eve of war. The same evening, at a large meeting, I gave vent to my disapproval of the ultimatum and emphasized that the Serb and Hungarian peoples wanted peace, and could live in harmony with each other. The audience and the American press were sympathetic to my declaration. But the tour had to be interrupted and we embarked for Le Havre in the S.S. *Savoie*. Our passage was a slow one, especially through the English Channel. Suddenly over the loudspeaker came the disquieting order: 'All passengers to their cabins.' We knew that war was imminent, but we had not realized that it had actually started. When I reached my cabin a sailor was already busy tarring the portholes. At full speed, in a complete blackout, the *Savoie* was steaming up the Channel.

At 3 a.m. the next morning — August 4th — Captain Tourrette sent me the news that the World War had broken out. Shortly afterwards a squadron of fifteen British warships joined us and, surrounding the *Savoie*, escorted her to Le Havre. We landed in a Europe at war.

On arrival in the harbour, a preliminary sorting out of the passengers took place and we were grouped according to nationality and language. This was my first experience of that system now so natural to Europeans, but which was then in its infancy, of regarding human beings as ciphers. The human rights we were so proud of belonged to the past.

As soon as everyone had been docketed, disembarkation followed. But not for us. We were the enemy and had to await further orders. At last we were informed that we were prisoners of war and asked whether we preferred imprisonment in jail or on board ship. I was granted permission to see the commandant of the town and asked him for leave to live in lodgings, on parole. The commandant was ready to grant this privilege to me but not to my companions. This officer of the French Republic seemed to have more confidence in the word of a count than in that of an ordinary citizen. Naturally I could not accept his offer, whereupon quarters were allotted to us, first in a cargo boat and later in a passenger steamer. But as usual in France the bureaucratic machine did not work efficiently and we soon found out that our imprisonment was contrary to international law, as hostilities had not yet begun between Austria-Hungary and France.

When we realized this, I telegraphed to Poincaré, drawing his attention to this breach and requesting him to intervene and have us released. Consequently on August 6th we were freed and on August 10th we took the train and travelled fifty hours through a France in the throes of mobilization. Callousness towards human suffering was not yet ours and the silent, weeping crowds at the stations, the melancholy waving of handkerchiefs, endless embraces and swooning women, made a deep impression on us. The soldiers I found grave but not enthusiastic; they talked of pushing straight on to Berlin, but their tone betrayed that they had no illusions about a quick, easy victory.

We arrived at Bordeaux on August 12th, just seven minutes after the train in which we could have crossed the Spanish frontier had left. This delay was fateful for us, for in the meantime war had been declared between France and Austria-Hungary. We were again arrested, placed in a closed lorry and transported to the Caserne de Passage which had been turned into a temporary prison camp. There we spent days of deep dejection.

Some weeks later the commandant of Bordeaux informed us that we would be allowed free passage to Spain if we were willing to give our word of honour not to fight against France. I requested the commandant to let me know the exact phrasing of the pledge to be given. In spite of the fact that I had been exempt from military service for reasons of health and that my feelings were anti-war, I wanted to retain full freedom of action for the duration. I wished to leave France without any sort of parole. The text presented to us demanded that we should refrain from any hostile action, either armed or unarmed, against France and her allies.

We refused, with the exception of one of us, who argued that no oath given to the enemy could be binding. This member of our group signed and got away. On reaching home he immediately joined the army. Before the miracle of the Marne, a German victory seemed most probable, and our imprisonment likely to be a short one. Stephen Friedrich, who was one of my companions and who later on, after the Bela Kun interlude, became Prime Minister and conducted the 'White Terror', started a book with the title of *Karolyi, Prisoner in France.*

When taking our daily exercise in the prison courtyard we were watched by a crowd who gazed at us through the iron bars as if we were wild animals in a zoo and shouted insults. I remember a man pointing at me: *'Celui-là a la tête à guillotiner.'*

As the leader of the group and the only one who spoke French like his native tongue, it was my task to confer with the officials. It was an ungrateful one, as my companions resented my behaviour, deeming that an eyeglass dangling on a waistcoat was incompatible with the respect due from a prisoner to his jailers. However, we obtained permission to take private lodgings on parole.

We read with consternation the news of the violation of neutral Belgium and the victorious offensive of the Germans on the Polish plains and in the Balkans.

I spent my time writing to Poincaré and Caillaux. These missives were sent through the housekeeper of the Karolyi palace on the Quai d'Orsay and I also obtained a loan from my relative, Melchior de Polignac.

After the fall of Liège, Louvain and Charleroi, the Germans swept on towards Paris. The news then came that the French Government intended moving to Bordeaux. Soon the Place de la Comédie was crowded with elegant limousines, many familiar faces popped up in the streets and Paris newspapers were printed in Bordeaux. In the press of Central Europe a notice appeared that Michael Karolyi and his companions had been shot in France!

Some time afterwards I got a letter from the Austro-Hungarian Ambassador in Madrid, Prince Charles Fürstenberg, urging me to give my parole not to fight the Allies as it would not in the least reflect upon my honour, since I had passed the age-limit for active service. At home, he argued, this opinion was unanimous. My fiancée's stepfather, Julius Andrassy, wrote to me in the same vein. But in any case this advice arrived too late, for all German and Austrian subjects, even if unfit for active service, had to remain prisoners until the end of hostilities.

One day, without warning and for no apparent reason, our lucky days in lodgings came to an end and we were again taken back to the concentration camp. Soon after our arrival a white-bearded gentleman was brought in. His brilliant conversation made us think that he must be a person of some eminence. Later he introduced himself as Max Nordau, the well-known Zionist author and journalist whose book *Conventional Lies* had had, in my young days, a great influence on me.

The commandant of the camp invited me to have my meals regularly at his home and I gladly accepted, for after the drab prison fare his excellent cuisine was a welcome treat. Max Nordau also was invited and I was asked to choose one of my group to join us. Thus I arranged for my colleagues to take turns. One of them, to gain the goodwill of the commandant and secure for himself a larger portion of the tasty *bœuf Bordelaise*, promised our host that after the war I would present him with a thoroughbred horse from my stud.

The stimulating conversations carried on with Nordau were most pleasant distractions. He shared our opinion that if Germany won it would mean the triumph of reaction. He thought that this war would determine whether the nations would develop on an individualist basis or become 'police states'. He did not foresee social revolution. At that time everyone, including Nordau, believed the war could not last more than six months at the outside.

The days spent in the barracks had many humorous sides. One of our companions was a circus rope-dancer and for our entertainment he spent the evenings practising on the edge of our iron bedsteads, balancing himself with great dexterity over our heads. On September 13th (1914) I received a letter from the foreign affairs editor of *Le Temps*, Eugène Lautier, who had intervened with the Foreign Minister, Delcassé, on my behalf, emphasizing my Francophile sympathies. On September 15th our whole group were set free and obtained passports for Spain. The day before, I received a visit from the American Ambassador in Paris, Mr. Myron T. Herrick, who brought me money from my future father-in-law, Count Andrassy. Thus I left France without having pledged my word.

After obtaining letters of recommendation from the French and Italian Ambassadors in Madrid, we sailed on a Spanish ship bound for Venice and a few days later, at the beginning of October, arrived in Vienna, where I was stormed by journalists, hoping for atrocity stories of French cruelty. When I told them that we had been well treated they were disappointed.

Nobody in Vienna had heard of the battle of the Marne, the importance of which was comparable in history with the battle of the Catalaunian Plains. In fact when I mentioned it they thought I had been taken in by French propaganda.

In Vienna I lunched with Leopold Berchtold, the Foreign Minister, who also pooh-poohed the Marne battle, calling it a strategic retreat on our part. His wife, who was a Karolyi, had told the family how poor Leopold could not sleep on the day when he wrote his ultimatum to the Serbs, as he was so worried that they would accept it. Several times in the night he had got up and altered or added some clause, to reduce this risk.

Now he told me confidentially that within a week the big German offensive would begin again and that in a short time they would be dictating peace terms in Paris. When I suggested that a peace offer based on mutual concessions should be launched, he refused to listen.

I witnessed for the first time how the press, as an instrument of war, disseminated lies, concealing the most important events, and how the public, through the spreading of mass hysteria, was losing the faculty of independent thought and judgment.

PART TWO

THE CHALLENGE

Speaking generally, there is something peculiar in national hatred. We always find it strongest and most vehement on the lower stage of culture. But there is a stage where it totally disappears and where one stands so to say above the nations and feels the good fortune or distress of his neighbour people as if it happened to his own.

GOETHE

. . . I stood
Among them, but not of them; in a shroud
Of thoughts which were not their thoughts. BYRON

MY WIFE,
FROM A PORTRAIT BY QUINCEY ADAM,
1919

THE AUTHOR WITH GYULA JUSTH, 1916

THE AUTHOR ADDRESSING A MEETING
DURING THE OCTOBER REVOLUTION, 1918

A DIFFICULT SITUATION

Everybody saying a thing does not make it right. SHELLEY

ON arriving in Budapest I was bewildered by the ignorance of what was happening in the West. People were convinced that France was on the eve of revolution and would not believe me when I said that there was no such chance.

A hysterical crowd had broken the windows of my house and my friends were concerned for my safety. After six months' absence I felt as though transported into an utterly strange world. No one realized what had happened on the Marne, and that the war situation had completely altered.

My first visit was to Albert Apponyi. I reproached him for having, in my absence, given unconditional support to the war instead of taking advantage of our being indispensable and presenting Hungary's claims for more independence. He replied that he would never adopt such unscrupulous methods, even in politics. Apart from that, he felt sure that the more devotedly the Magyars espoused the Habsburg and Hohenzollern cause, the more certainly could we count, in the event of victory — of which he had not a moment's doubt — on the Emperor's gratitude. I retorted that Francis Joseph's gratitude was the last thing to build on.

Neither then nor later could we agree on the fundamental question of how the nation should meet the new situation and turn it to its advantage. Gone seemed the hope of autonomy, Hungarian co-operation between the different races of the Monarchy, and emancipation from Berlin. Now we were linked to a foreign power and all our resources used for purposes alien to us. We were actually sowing on the battlefields the seeds of future age-long hatreds between ourselves and those others with whom it should have been our mission to live in peace.

I left Apponyi seated at his large desk facing the undulating Buda hills, covered with the tawny leaves of an early autumn. If this was the approach of the great pacifist to what was happening, what would be that of the others, I wondered.

Julius Andrassy junior, who was shortly to become my father-in-law, was the leader of another opposition party — the Party of the Constitution — a Germanophile, and loyal to his father's creation of the Compromise of 1867. He insisted that my policy was bankrupt and advised me, if I had any sense of reality, to retire from active politics. He was pleased that the Opposition had pushed the vacillating Tisza into declaring war, upon which he would otherwise never have ventured.

Tisza's party, on the other hand, boasted of having pressed the Ballhausplatz to take an energetic stand, and claimed that had Tisza not crushed the Opposition, which had obstructed rearmament, we should never have been able to deal with the Serbs and the Russians in a war that had been forced on us.

To speeches of this sort the Independence Party listened with downcast eyes, admitting privately to each other that, after all, Tisza was right. Apponyi's 'at last' was the cry of an uneasy conscience trying to relegate the pacifist past to oblivion. This attitude was very similar to the one adopted by Horthy in 1941.

When the conflict with Serbia started and there were hopes that it would end in a short time, the Hungarian nobles, true to their sporting instincts, volunteered to shoot all Serbs. But when Russia came in and the glorious war turned into a drab duty carried on in cold damp trenches, their enthusiasm dwindled, and wires were pulled to have sons or brothers exempted or placed in safe jobs at Army Headquarters.[1]

The first realization that war was not an operetta and did not consist entirely of beflagged trains, speeches from balconies, women throwing flowers and kisses to uniformed men, came as a shock with the return of the first wounded from the great defeats in Galicia. It had to be counteracted by a most unrealistic campaign carried on by the still unhurt 'Hinterland.' Lies and gullibility became national virtues. The press seemed suddenly to have forgotten that there were discriminating people left in the world. Perhaps they were right, for these were so few and so terrorized by public opinion that they were a negligible quantity. Our National Casino was full of talented strategists. Nicholas Banffy, Foreign Minister in 1921-22, had learnt on reliable authority that the Germans were going to mount guns on rafts, float them across the Channel to the English coast and force England to her knees by bombardment. This mentality spread its suffocating atmosphere over the town like a miasma.

Soon I discovered the painful breach between the victims of the war, the young men in the trenches who had to pay for the errors of their elders, and those who in the safety of their homes and clubs preached war to the finish. Although I was exempt from military service, owing to my precarious health and because I was past the calling-up age, and in any case belonged to the happy few, the owners of entailed property, I found the climate of the 'Hinterland' unbearable. Luckily I had not followed the advice of my friends and given my parole to the French, so I was free to join up. It was a difficult decision to take, for I feared that the act of volunteering would be wrongly interpreted and used for war propaganda. Being against this war and an anti-militarist, had I the right to enlist? After a bitter inner struggle I decided to do so. I felt, now that the war was actually on and the common people were all in the trenches, that it would be senseless for me to keep out of it, especially as I had the right to do so. To remain at home would not have been a demonstration against war; on the other hand, it would be a great advantage for me to use this opportunity of getting to know the people by living with them in the trenches. I also felt that I could not identify myself in the future with a democratic Hungary if I had not shared the hardships of the unprivileged. There was another half-conscious and less estimable consideration as well — the fear of being branded a coward and of taking advantage of my exceptional position to keep safe. I admired the moral courage of the militant anti-militant, of the conscientious objector who suffers imprisonment or is shot for his convictions. As a politician, however, my role was not to sacrifice myself but to save my country from disaster. By giving an individual example of active resistance to war, could I have exercised a stronger influence on events? I do not know. Morally it might have been finer to act on conviction, and braver to appear a coward; but at the time I was not prepared to accept all the consequences involved in anti-militarism. Judging by later events, I believe my choice was the right one.

2

MY MARRIAGE

You were more to me than a wife. In joy and grief, in all you were my companion; companion in fight, in work, in suffering, in hope, companion and true comrade.

SEVERAL years before the war I was the victim of a bad car accident. It was in the days when only the happy few possessed cars in Hungary and the temptation of speeding this new toy at forty to sixty miles an hour was irresistible.

One summer afternoon I landed in a drain which ran right across the main road — a deadly trap. My Mercedes turned a somersault, burying me underneath it. Some kind Swabian peasants, trying to extricate me, dropped the body of the car on my chest, breaking three ribs. I fainted. Regaining consciousness, I found myself in their farmhouse, with my stepmother and sisters kneeling round my bed in prayer.

The papers had announced the news of my death. Catherine Andrassy, a small girl at the time, said to her mother: 'How sad that Karolyi is dead, for he would have been my husband!' We had scarcely met then. Very vaguely I remember in the porch of the Andrassy house in Buda a girl with an auburn mane hanging down her back, and very large green eyes.

I lived, and she became my wife.

The Andrassy and Karolyi families had for many years been antagonistic to each other. The Andrassys had been considered Liberals, as they had supported the separation of Church and State and the institution of civil marriage in opposition to the ultra-clerical aristocracy, to which my family belonged. My wife grew up in an atmosphere permeated with politics and was immersed in them from her earliest childhood. The Andrassys were nationalist, but saturated in German culture, anti-clerical and patrons of the arts, particularly painting. My father-in-law was a collector and connoisseur of the Italian Renaissance and his drawing-room on the Danube embankment was crammed with quattro- and cinquecento paintings, as well as of works of art of all periods — statues, wooden Madonnas, old masters and French impressionists, heavy bronze doors with sculptured figures. The walls were covered with precious oriental carpets, giving the place the look of a museum. The self-portrait of Rembrandt as a young man, a huge Sebastiano del Piombo, a fine Millet, a Corot, a Turner sunset, a Daubigny, a Lawrence and several Canalettos belonged to his collection.

He would sit there in the semi-darkness of his drawing-room, lighted only by the electric bars placed above the pictures, his long thin legs crossed under him in oriental fashion, listening absently to the heated discussions around him, whilst silently contemplating his treasures. Then he would walk around the room, closely examining his favourite objects, stroking them tenderly with his long, delicate fingers. From time to time he would put in a word to correct some inaccurate statement, or smile indulgently at the impassioned utterances of the female members of his family. His opinion on any subject, political, ethical, or artistic, was uncontested. No one ever dreamt of contradicting him — not out of fear, for he was the gentlest of men, but out of admiration and love. He carried on the traditions of Andrassy senior, of the infallible patriarch.

The Andrassy family expected that everyone marrying into it should become an Andrassy and that every female member, although married, should remain an Andrassy.

My wife Katus was the first to break with this tradition. As soon as my activities rose above the usual routine of party politics, acquiring a more human character, she took an enthusiastic interest in them.

It has been said that she has exercised a strong influence over me. This is true in so far as people who live together and love each other are subjected to reciprocal influence. I made her a Socialist, but it was she who drew my attention to the sufferings of the poor during the war and made me feel that the injustices committed against the lower classes were intolerable. She helped me to find myself, to be myself, and made me realize that it was impossible to live two lives, one of atavistic ease and the other of Socialist principles. The circle of the Szent Kiraly utca, where my stepmother Geraldine lived, was a very different one, bound as it was by close ties to the Court of Vienna; it formed a State within the State. They all had their pet archdukes, archduchesses, bishops and, of course, their anti-semitic pet Jews. Prohaszka, the modern bishop, was considered by them a free thinker.

In 'Aunt' Geraldine's blue salon, with its eighteenth-century Louis Seize furniture, they would whisper in French about the world-wide conspiracy of the Israelite Alliance and the Grand Orient Lodge. They were convinced that everything evil, wars and revolutions, emanated from the Jews and the Freemasons, who were the agents of the dark Power, determined to establish its rule. Oddly enough this circle, confessing these strange views, was exceedingly cultured, well-read in *belles lettres*, and especially well-versed in the French memoirs of the pre-revolutionary period. For parliamentary rule and for politics they nourished a deep contempt, mixed with suspicion. They regarded the Chamber of Deputies as an assembly of tradesmen, a low haunt similar to the Stock Exchange, and would whisper: '*Nous sommes tombés si bas*' if one of their protégés stood for Parliament. Their hey-day had been the period of our 'Kultur Kampf', when they had carried on a zealous campaign against religious liberties, and many years later they still harboured a grudge against those who had voted in favour of civil marriage or for the abolition of the laws against the Jews. They hated Count Tisza, the leader of the Conservatives, because he was a Calvinist and his official position was considered an insult to the Roman Church. The war upset their reasoning and puzzled their simplified outlook. They feared victory, for it would increase the prestige of the Protestant Hohenzollerns, and feared defeat as well, as it would beget the revolution of the Jews and rebellion against the dynasty. My stepbrother Joseph was the typical representative of this circle. He and his mother and sisters spent most of their time in Paris and on the Riviera, and belonged in their whole attitude, manners and even looks, more to eighteenth-century France than to Hungary.

These two antagonistic circles were united by our marriage. I myself did not give my allegiance to either of them. Emancipating ourselves from both, my wife and I set off on a new path. They were horrified, but remained attached to me and accepted what they would call my follies. As I was one of their family they refused to imagine that I could seriously believe what I advocated. Katus told them once: 'You care for Michael only as far as you believe him to be a fraud, playing a double game, but when he has proved to you he is honest and acts accordingly, you will turn against him.' This proved later to be only too true.

A strangely prophetic incident happened on our wedding day. After the ceremony in the Matthyias Church in Buda, we drove to my country place, Parad, in the Matra hills. The journey should have taken five hours. We had to cross a mountain range, and had just reached the peak when the car suddenly stopped. We had run out of petrol owing to a hole in the tank. Leaving the chauffeur with the luggage behind, we started off in a downpour of rain right through the forest, with Katus's maid and Tevrev the bulldog following us. At last, completely drenched and exhausted, we arrived in the dark at the cottage of one of my gamekeepers, as the woods we were going through belonged to my estate. We did not disclose our identity to the man, but sitting under the porch inquired to whom the place belonged. 'It belongs to Count Karolyi,' he answered, puffing his cigar, and looking suspiciously at us.

'What sort of man is he?' asked Katus.

'We never see him,' he answered with a grunt, 'but we heard that he is being married in Budapest to a very rich old woman . . .' Katus winced '. . . He rarely comes this way, he prefers foreign countries.'

At last the carriage sent for us arrived and a light dawned on the keeper, who vanished into his kitchen feeling perhaps rather uncomfortable. It was midnight when we drove into the courtyard, where the welcome signs on the gates were blown about by the storm, the lanterns extinguished, the garlands faded, the careful work of our household all ruined. The servants had fallen asleep on their watch and the butler had given up hope of ever seeing us again. This start of our life together was not a good omen. And ever since we have been haunted by a sort of fate preventing us from settling anywhere, chasing us from country to country, without ever acquiring a lasting home.

3

I JOIN THE ARMY

I JOINED the Hungarian cavalry regiment of National Guards, incorporated in the Austro-Hungarian Army. It was supposed to fight only in defence of the country and within its frontiers. The language of command was Magyar. This élite regiment was recruited mainly from the untitled nobility, the aristocracy serving in the joint army.

After completing my military training, I waited in Budapest for my squadron to leave for the front. This lasted for several months. It seemed strange to me that the delay was dragging on so long although I was happy to be able to be with my wife for the birth of our daughter. It was only later that I discovered the actual reason of this welcome delay. An uncle of my wife had pulled strings, and the Minister of War had kept the whole squadron back until the child was born. Indignant, I was prepared to bring the matter up in Parliament, but refrained from doing so as it would have caused a family quarrel and would have appeared most ungrateful towards our uncle, who had acted with the best intentions.

It had also been arranged without my knowledge that I should be attached to Headquarters and become an aide-de-camp to the general in command, Baron Apor.

On my arrival I found an overflow of aides-de-camp: my brother Joseph and my sister's husband were both acting in the same capacity.

It was the period of static trench warfare, and our time was spent in playing bridge and keeping the General jolly. Brother Joseph, who in civil life possessed a wardrobe of 860 suits, brought with him all his 'indispensable' belongings, such as Persian carpets, a dozen special uniforms, hot-water bottles, electric contraptions, and his cook. Each time Headquarters moved, the large private van with my brother's belongings followed. General Apor, who preferred fresh milk to tinned, had a pet cow for his own and his favourites' supply. It was like a family party but defeated the purpose for whichI had joined the army.

One day the Head of the Army Command, General Boroevics, held an inspection of the front and our regiment had orders to take part. Only four aides-de-camp out of eight accompanied the General. This puzzled me at first but before long I discovered the secret. Apor was only entitled to four aides-de-camp; the rest were illegally kept and had to be camouflaged. When I discovered this, I seized the opportunity to volunteer for the front. The Baron, who had pledged my safety to the family, was very disturbed, but grudgingly gave way. The antagonism against me, which became more acute later, started in those days, for they thought it most inconsiderate towards my wife that I should risk my life, arguing that being a pacifist was bad enough, but that I should at least keep myself safe.

Even in the trenches, living in mud and snow, we Members of Parliament were not in as much danger as the others, for each time an offensive started Parliament was convoked and we were automatically given leave.

My general, Count Lubiansky, a Pole, gave permission for my wife to stay with me when our regiment had retired to a village behind the lines, to recuperate. She managed to join me in the capacity of a Red Cross nurse, bringing with her her maid Boske and her dog, an ailing dachshund, her only patient.

This period of the war on the Galician front might have been called *la guerre en dentelles*. My wife rode in the mornings with the regiment at the commander's side and took part in regimental gymkhanas held behind the lines. The Russians, who were at a distance of some two miles, amused themselves by sending over shells in the direction of our playground. This gave more pep to the game and was luckily never fatal. One night I woke to the sound of guitars, flutes and violins outside our window: some officers had had the bright idea of serenading my wife. I now thought it high time for her to go home. My sisters and my brother's wife came to Headquarters as well. They created a sensation when, accompanied by their spick and span husbands with boots, buttons and buckles shining, they would enter the squalid Czernovitz cafés, filled with soldiers. From the dirt and squalor of the trenches the troops would gather here for a day's rest, and gaze in rapture at these heavenly apparitions clothed in the latest Parisian fashion, with Houbigant scent lingering around them.

While serving at the front I witnessed many things which, as I was an M.P., they tried to conceal from me. The officers' mess had excellent food which our quartermaster, 'Uncle Pecsi', could provide only by curtailing the soldiers' rations. Thus 'Uncle Pecsi' was — with the officers — the most popular man in the regiment. My own position was a delicate one, for it was my duty, as an M.P., to disclose this corruption, but it would have compromised the regiment and I would have been considered disloyal to my colleagues.

The actual number of officers in my regiment was ninety, a larger number than necessary, as we had only 500 horse. At the time of our offensive, the ninety dwindled to about ten.

The soldiers, badly fed as they were, and getting far less than their allotted share, had to support the brunt of the attacks. A few rich Jews were allowed to join this élite regiment; but any who succeeded in doing so were made to regret it bitterly. Anti-semitism raged; whatever a Jew did it could never be right. I remember one, a doctor called Gross, who was hated because he dared to be brave. If there was a dangerous job, Gross would be the first to volunteer for it and this enraged his companions. He did so, of course, to prove that not all of his race were cowards, but it worked the other way. 'What an insolent fellow to presume to be as courageous as a Hungarian!'

If a Jew showed fear, however, there was no mercy for him. I remember one in our Hussar regiment who had volunteered for the cavalry so as to gain a social position, but was as terrified of a horse as if it had been a tiger in the jungle. A pathetic sight, grey-faced, he clutched his saddle with trembling hands. He managed to get on the beast's back with the help of a small rope-ladder which he carried surreptitiously with him. When this was discovered, his kind comrades started to whip his horse and make the beast so wild that one day, taking the bit between his teeth, he galloped off through the streets of the town, landing in a café. Another young Jew who dared to join the regiment was continually victimized until he asked for his transfer. One of his martyrdoms was to be obliged to chew up all his favourite gramophone records, which they thrust into his mouth.

On one occasion orders were given for a small Galician village to be evacuated as it was supposed to have an understanding with the enemy. Scapegoats were needed and the Jews of the village had to provide them. They were packed in carts and brought to Headquarters. One of the carts held a load of twelve Jewish girls, but on the way four of them managed to escape. As the sergeant in charge had to deliver twelve, he was quick at finding a solution. He replaced them by four other girls from a neighbouring town, who were promenading happily on a Sunday afternoon. No threats or protests were of any use. The story went round the officers' mess, where the sergeant's resourcefulness was given full credit.

When I returned to Budapest from the Galician front to attend to my duties as a Member of Parliament, I had made up my mind to protest on every possible occasion against total surrender to Germany. I managed to find opportunities for demanding social improvements and national concessions in return for Hungary's sacrifice in men and money. I protested against the intermingling of our troops with the imperial and, later, German forces at the front, as it deprived the Hungarian Government and Parliament of the control of their own armies, preventing any independent step on our part. At the time of the general collapse this blending of the forces proved fatal.

Theodore Batthyanyi, Lovaszy and others began gradually to organize. Gyula Justh, who was already a sick man, gave us his moral support. I was the principal shareholder of the evening newspaper *Magyarorszag* (Hungary), and was anxious to keep an independent organ ready to back our forthcoming struggle. The paper, of course, lost extensively in circulation, but we at least succeeded in owning one journal which held aloof from warmongering and burned no incense at the shrine of the German Alliance. At every considerable victory — and at the start there were a number of victories — Parliament gave a banquet. The Hungarians endeavoured to outdo the Austrians in their zeal for the war, in order to win Berlin's praise, and her recognition that we had done more for final victory than Austria. From the Prime Minister downwards, all the party would rise from their seats and toast the victory.

At these gatherings in which Parliament congratulated itself on the course of the war, I either took no part, or remained in demonstrative silence in my seat.

It was a paradoxical situation that a junior officer with the rank of sub-lieutenant should demonstrate against war, stand up in Parliament and attack his superiors and criticize the Army Command. In my capacity as leader of the Opposition it was my duty to do so.

On one occasion my wife and I visited the Opera in Vienna. After the curtain fell, the portraits of the Kaiser, King Charles and the War Lords were projected and the band played the 'Wacht am Rhein' and the 'Gott erhalte'. The audience rose from their seats. We were in a box next the stage and, when the Kaiser's portrait appeared to the tune of the German National Anthem, we both ostentatiously sat down again. Many heads turned towards us resentfully.

An anecdote told with pride by the Independence Party was that when the Kaiser first launched his 'Big Berthas' — known officially as the 42 gun — he asked Francis Joseph: 'What do you think of my "42"?' To which Francis Joseph replied: 'What do you think of my "48"?' — the Independence Party which had come to heel.

Gradually the public's attitude towards the war was undergoing a change. Those who until now had opposed my opinions started openly airing my arguments; matters at which I had only been able to hint discreetly became the subject of public discussion; a newly coined phrase, 'the penalty of service at the front', adequately expressed the toning down of the bellicose spirit. Everyone who could manage it tried to avoid dying the death of a hero.

Count Stürgkh had still not convoked the Austrian Parliament. Austria was under autocratic government and thus the 'Delegations',[2] the only parliamentary body for foreign affairs, could not meet. Public meetings were prohibited.

In the last months of Francis Joseph's reign the story went around that the only way to shake the old Emperor out of his senile indifference was to tell him about victories won over the Prussians, as he had not forgotten the humiliation of Sadowa and was still under the delusion that he was fighting the Germans.

4

OUR EFFORTS TO KEEP ITALY NEUTRAL

URING the first year of the war the Russians reached the Carpathians and there was danger of their breaking through the front and over-running Hungary. The threat of Italian intervention was gaining momentum. .Rumania, too, had made an agreement with Italy and it would have been fatal if she had come in at that moment.

At the end of January 1915 some members of my group got into touch with a Greek Catholic priest called Török, who was on his way to Rome. We took advantage of this to make him the bearer to responsible quarters in Italy of our attitude towards the war. Through the Italian Consul-General in Budapest I informed Baron Sonnino, whom a couple of years previously I had met in Rome at the house of a relative, Prince Scipio Borghese, of Török's impending arrival. The priest visited Sonnino on March 12th, 1915, and conveyed to him our message that the Hungarian people were not represented by 'official' Hungary, for the Hungarian Government owed its power to a restricted franchise and electoral corruption. A German victory was not in Hungary's interest, as we would then become her vassals and a market for German goods. An independent Hungary was a first-class Italian interest and one of the most important guarantees of a lasting European peace. We appealed to the Italian nation, to their *sacro egoismo*. Hungary was neither Slav nor Teuton. She was not strong enough to harbour territorial ambitions — for instance in the Balkans — but she could oppose a barrier to the territorial ambitions of other States. Török also mentioned the indispensability of a sea coast for Hungary. Sonnino showed interest and informed him of the current Italo-Austrian negotiations. He held out the prospect of Italy's assistance, asked to be acquainted with the extent of our influence at home, promised to procure for us opportunities for negotiating with other great powers, and advised us, first of all, to come to an agreement with

Rumania. He was ready to promote an interview with Bratianu, Rumanian Ambassador in Rome.

Török returned home with these messages and left again for Rome soon after with new instructions from us. On April 22nd Sonnino informed Török that the Triple Alliance would be dissolved at the beginning of May and that by the end of May *se Dio non fa miracolo-fa guerra*. Sonnino put our envoy in contact with the British Ambassador, Sir Rennell Rodd, who also considered that Török should see Bratianu.

We informed Julius Andrassy, whose opinion was that Török should tell Sonnino that a Government representing all parties was in process of formation. The Abbé reached Italy at the moment when, owing to Giolitti's unwillingness to go to war, things had come to a crisis. Sonnino received Török even after the declaration of war, gave him a diplomatic passport, and assured him that, despite the fact that public opinion in Italy was unanimous in demanding the incorporation of territories inhabited by Italians, he would drop the claims to Fiume and to Hungarian coastal territory, and use his whole influence to minimize the demands of Rumania for the possession of Transylvania; provided that on the Hungarian side this new Cabinet was formed, excluding Stephen Tisza who, he said, was regarded abroad as the *spiritus rector* of the war. He promised to remain in communication with the Independence Party even during hostilities. Sonnino emphasized that he considered himself bound by this declaration until the middle of June.

As soon as Török brought us this message, we informed the Hungarian Government, the Austrian Government, the joint Foreign Minister and the King, of our action by way of a memorandum.[3] The reason why I have given so much space to these discussions with Italy is that in 1917-18 the military courts, anxious to find incriminating documents against me, made feverish efforts to obtain details of these negotiations. They were not a little surprised to find that the facts were known, through Julius Andrassy, to the Emperor Francis Joseph, to Burian the Foreign Minister, to Stürgkh the Austrian Prime Minister, and to Tisza, and that we had actually received Burian's special thanks for our efforts.

At my trial in 1922, however, these negotiations were one of the main charges against me.

Although we did not achieve our object of keeping Italy out of the war, we at least kept the way open for mediation with the Entente, which could have been undertaken before feeling ran too high. It is true that the Treaty of London had already been concluded on April 26th, 1915 — although published only on February 28th, 1917, in *Izvestia* — but in that same spring, Ribot and Lloyd George were trying at St. Jean de Maurienne to persuade Sonnino to moderate his claims in the event of the withdrawal of the Monarchy from the German Alliance. The Italians insisted on the Brenner frontier and Trieste. Czernin would have nothing to do with any renunciation of Austrian territory. The loss of Transylvania later to the Rumanians was the consequence. How much more advantageous for Hungary, and even for Austria, to have had a Foreign Minister willing to work for a separate peace, even with territorial sacrifice. A Hungarian statesman, backed by Parliament, could have given him his support.

5

THE END OF AN ERA

THE relationship between Apponyi and myself was heading for a crisis. He gradually fell more and more under Andrassy's influence and looked on Germany's cause as our own. He was even ready to agree to the sending of Hungarian troops to Mesopotamia. In the summer of 1916, while I was in Constantinople on holiday, he accepted the setting up of an Advisory Council for Foreign Affairs, in which, as well as the Government, the Opposition would take part. In this way the Opposition would have assumed responsibility for the conduct of the war without having the power to influence it. I took advantage of this move to make an end of an intolerable situation. With twenty of my followers I broke away from the Party of Independence and formed one of my own, which now at last could follow a clear-cut policy. The time was ripe, I felt, to make a gesture and let the Entente know that in Hungary a party had come into existence which stood for a separate peace treaty and was anti-German. A large section of the press backed us up and, although we were attacked as traitors and madmen, we felt that the man in the street was with us.

I openly challenged the Government to state its war aims and to declare that we would not go on fighting for the Germans and were resolved to regain our independence from Germany. Thus the newly formed Karolyi Party became the party of peace.

What we had desired happened. The Entente papers began to note at last that a party had arisen in Hungary which had broken through the war-time *Union Sacrée*. Inside the country the situation was changing as well. No one any longer trusted our Army Command. The war did not produce a single popular commander. Family allowances were scandalously inadequate, so that the great majority of the families of 'our heroes' were starving in their homes. Erratic payments months in arrears, abuses in connection with contracts for war material, boots with paper soles supplied by army profiteers, aroused bitter indignation all over the country.

In the programme of the International Pacifists I found the perfect expression of my own feelings. Emotionally I was ripe for it, for my loathing of militarism had never been so acute. I got into contact with Kunfi and his group, although this association of mine was strongly disapproved by my own followers. Their pacifism only meant independence from Germany and separate peace. For me it meant much more — a way towards a new international order preventing wars and the creation of a more equitable co-operation between nations.

The situation of the Central Powers was deteriorating. Rumania declared war against us and Brusillov broke through our defences at Luck. A large part of the Monarchy was again in the hands of the enemy, as in 1914-15. Once more we were being saved by the Germans, and their troops occupied Rumania. Falkenhayn had been replaced by Ludendorff and Hindenburg, and the Monarchy was more than ever delivered to the Germans. Its sovereignty was a fiction. The German General Staff was lord in the empire of the dying Francis Joseph.

When the Emperor Charles ascended the throne of his uncle in 1916, everyone was filled with hope. His first act was to have himself crowned King of Hungary in Budapest.

The Hungarian aristocracy was delighted and the excitements and intrigues around the coronation made them forget the worries of war. Titles, orders and honours were distributed. In spite of my revolutionary reputation, my wife was appointed Lady of the Chamber.

But the first disappointment came to them when, as soon as the coronation was over and King Charles had taken off the too-large Crown of St. Stephen — it had sunk over his forehead, the only disturbing note in the ceremony — he hurried back to Vienna. The royal suite prepared for him in the Castle of Buda for the night remained empty.

Yet in the whole of the Monarchy hopes were soaring high. People remembered the gallant way in which the young lieutenant had behaved at the death of his uncle Francis Ferdinand. The murdered archduke had not been given the honours due to his rank at his funeral, for the Emperor could not forget his enmity to his heir, even at the time of his tragic death. Few members of the imperial family were allowed to take part in it. Charles refused to follow this order, attended the funeral and even expressed his disapproval of the way in which it had been conducted. This established his reputation as a man of heart. Also he was known to have been under the influence of Francis Ferdinand and it was inferred that he would favour federalization.

The young Emperor rushed with youthful ardour and good will into his terrible inheritance. He immediately changed his entourage. People were brought to the fore who were known to the public as associated with the Belvedere policy. Tisza and the Hungarian ruling class became nervous. His first act in 1917 was to make a peace offer, jointly with Germany. Had we known that this offer had been made by Germany to counteract President Wilson's efforts at mediation promised to Count Bernsdorff, German Ambassador in Washington, and was therefore unacceptable to America, we should have been less pleased.

My optimism was increased by the appointment of Count Ottocar Czernin to the Ministry of Foreign Affairs, as Czernin's close relations with Francis Ferdinand were well known. Although I did not agree with the ultimate aims of that policy I was ready to co-operate on short-term lines with anyone who would be instrumental in a separate peace. Czernin was not the friend of the Magyar landlords; he disagreed with the oppression of the subject races and recognized, as I did, the danger of a German victory — of which there was, in any case, not much hope left — turning Central Europe into a vast military barracks.

The change in foreign policy was shortly followed by that in home policy. In the Speech from the Throne, the King envisaged the extension of the franchise. On my initiative a franchise bloc was formed between all parties which demanded universal suffrage[4] and a vigorous campaign was started. Andrassy and Apponyi were ready to extend the suffrage, but only to those who spoke, read and wrote Hungarian, and to soldiers who had received the Charles Cross for gallantry in face of the enemy.

The war had not in any way altered the social life of the ruling classes. On the contrary, it was perhaps never so gay and thriftless. During the last years of the conflict the war seemed to have become stabilized and the happy few adopted the attitude of ignoring the beastly thing. Many landowners who were bankrupt at the beginning had restored their finances, owing to the soaring prices of wheat and the products of the land. Also they could pay their debts with the devaluated money. The owners of cattle could sell their stock to the army at the highest prices. Thus it was not only the army manufacturers who were the profiteers of the war, but the landlords as well. In 1917 the wine harvest had been exceptionally good and the proprietors of vineyards had made fortunes. In the Park Club, the meeting place of society, situated in the Varosliget — Garden Suburbs — nothing was changed. After a couple of weeks the old routine of amusements was in full swing and any foreigner stepping into its pleasant and exclusive atmosphere could not have guessed that a bitter and hopeless war was being waged. The Hungarians possess the magic power of changing serious events into an operetta.

As society was exclusive, it was considered cranky to invite to parties writers, artists or prominent journalists, however talented they might be. I remember what havoc it caused when Katus and I went to a reception given in one of the finest houses in old Buda by a titled Jew, a mighty newspaper owner with great wealth and a beautiful wife. The majority of the guests were writers and poets. Some time later we gave a dance in our ballroom and invited, amongst others, some of our new acquaintances and our late host as well. The old house with its chandeliers, its gilded stucco ceilings, its glittering mirrors and shining parquets over which lovely women, in the arms of flashily uniformed men, glided to the tune of 'The Blue Danube', had the atmosphere of pre-war days. In the smoking-room a couple of my wife's uncles were sulking, calling Katus a madcap for having invited such impossible people.

I myself had also greatly profited by this exceptional conjuncture. When I married, my finances had been in a bad way. I was not a good manager of my own affairs. I had spent much on travel, women and gambling. I had also had the unfortunate habit of lending to friends who were in need and few had considered it necessary to settle their debts. I had sold all my non-entailed land. Managers and estate agents profited by my negligence and I was tricked on all sides. Katus had been warned by solicitous relatives what a spendthrift she was going to marry. To economize after our marriage I shut my house in the Egyetem utca and we went around searching for a cheap flat. Katus found the most modest flats far too luxurious, and as the expense of keeping up a large house, even though empty, did not seem to diminish, we gave up our romantic quest and fixed up some rooms in one of the wings of my old house. In a very short time the war proved to be the best of my managers. My income doubled and trebled. Gradually we opened more rooms and, when at home during the sessions of Parliament, we entertained a great deal for political purposes. Our so-called friends, after swallowing with relish the *suprême au volaille* or *homard à l'Américaine* would, as soon as the gate had closed behind them, start biting the hand that had fed them. 'Reds' should not live so well, was the comment. Just as today the ignorant cannot distinguish between Liberals, Democrats, Socialists and Radicals, anyone who was not a reactionary was labelled 'Red'. In England in those days I would have been called a Liberal with Labour sympathies. I still trusted that the ruling classes could be convinced by argument and reasoned with. It was only after bitter experience that I realized the futility of such an effort in Hungary. Katus was passing through the same mental process as I and, being younger, was more intransigent and had qualms of conscience about our way of living. Once when I had bought her a sapphire ring she returned it without my knowledge to the jeweller and exchanged it for a glass imitation one, producing the identical effect. The money returned went to the soldiers' widows. The secret was so well kept that on one occasion she compared her 'sapphire' with those of some women friends, who all agreed that hers was much the better stone. Another time she threw out of the window a huge oil painting, the portrait of one of her ancestors, which I had bought for her out of my winnings at baccarat, a passion of which she fiercely disapproved.

Although I admit that if one is convinced that the social order one lives in is immoral and unjust it is wrong to profit by it, I have always rejected the silly contention so often uttered by the ignorant that a Socialist who is wealthy cannot be sincere and should distribute his fortune to the poor. Socialism is not charity and those who want to bring about a new economic order are not like St. Francis of Assisi, but men living in a capitalist world who should use their money for realizing their aim. But in those days I was not even a Socialist; I had not burnt my boats, for I was not yet ready to break with my background and my friends, to whom I was bound by many sentimental ties.

6

THE NEW ERA

ON January 16th, 1917, I received the first message from the King, brought by Berchtold, who was no longer in office at the time but well known to be the confidant of the young monarch.

In the King's name, Berchtold made two requests: first, that my party should handle the question of a separate peace with discretion, and secondly that we should not attack the German Alliance. I agreed to the first, but declined the second.

Czernin, the Foreign Minister, called on me two months later. I then told him candidly the reasons which led me to pursue an anti-German policy. Czernin's reply was: 'You are right. We are faced by only one danger at the present time, and that is Germany. I shall do all that lies in my power to maintain our freedom of action, a difficult task indeed.' Later I heard that he expressed strong German sympathies in his conversation with Andrassy and Apponyi.

On March 22nd, King Charles summoned me to an audience in Baden, at Army Headquarters. It was the dawn of a new epoch.

The young King was cordial, but with his characteristic hesitancy seemed unable to start the conversation; I had to take the initiative. The King spoke classical Hungarian, using antiquated words. That he had studied the language out of books was noticeable. Nevertheless he spoke it better than many a Hungarian count, and without accent.

In his manner and speech Charles was direct and spontaneous, and he encouraged plain speaking. He was one of those to whom everyone soon laid bare their hearts. That was his special gift. He made one forget that one was in the presence of an emperor.

I was completely outspoken and explained my whole programme: my apprehension of German preponderance, and the necessity of an early and separate peace. In the heat of the discussion, I struck the table with my fist. He took no notice of this breach of etiquette — I dare not think of what Francis Joseph would have done — and agreed heartily with my arguments, repeating: 'You are right, that's just how I feel, that's what I have always said.'

He assured me that as long as he was directing foreign affairs through Czernin there was no chance of the Monarchy being degraded to the position of Germany's vassal. 'I am firmly resolved to bring the war to an end in 1917.' He said these words with impulsive emphasis. At that time he must have already known of Erzberger's memoranda,⁵ and that we had already lost the war.

I asked the monarch whether he approved of the existence of an anti-German party, of which he might make use at the appropriate moment, or would he prefer that it should be dissolved or its policy toned down. He replied that the existence of such a party was very useful, and he saw no reason for me to alter my tactics. This was plain speaking. I then asked him about his message sent to me by Berchtold, warning me to act with discretion in the question of a separate peace and not to attack the German Alliance, this being in contradiction with all he was now saying to me. He replied that he knew nothing of the message. I asked his permission to mention this to Berchtold, but the King, obviously embarrassed, begged me to let the matter rest.

When discussing the problem of the 'minorities' I felt that Charles was strongly under the posthumous influence of his uncle and former political teacher, Francis Ferdinand. He wanted to form a coalition Government and asked my advice. I said that my party could not participate in it, as it would not accept our democratic reforms, but we could be ready to support it so long as it worked for peace.

The King was as incapable of terminating the audience as he had been of starting it. Although anxious to be attentive, he was a bad listener and had difficulty in concentrating. One had the uneasy feeling, even whilst in his presence, that he had forgotten what one had told him at the start.

After an hour, sensing that I had tired him, I asked for permission to leave. With Francis Joseph this would have been unthinkable. I felt happy, confident that I had found an ally in the monarch.

On my return to Vienna my commanding officer, General Apor, called on me and accused me, in the name of the War Minister, of contravening service regulations by joining, as I had done a short while

previously, the Dutch Anti-War Council. The censor had intercepted
my letter to them. I retorted that I wrote the letter in my capacity of
Deputy not of soldier and that only the Chamber of Deputies was competent to decide the matter. Consequently it was brought up in Parliament and came before the Immunity Committee, and I was protected
by the law. The situation was absurd — the Sovereign agreeing to the
necessity of my peace policy while his officials acting in his name were
frustrating my efforts. The King still kept Tisza as his Prime Minister,
the chief supporter of war to the finish, and this made his policy appear
ambiguous.

March 1917: Tsardom overthrown. The peoples of the Monarchy
sensed that they were on the eve of dramatic events.

Along the whole of the Russian front, where the news of this
revolution had spread, our armies were fraternizing with the Russians.
On the Galician front, at Sloteria, where my regiment was stationed,
the soldiers met each other openly during the Easter holidays although
this was strictly prohibited. They were photographed in groups, eating, dancing and embracing one another. No commander dared to
give orders for machine-gunning these happy groups. How could one
expect that, after this, war on the Russian front could be continued with
the same intensity as in the past? Peace was in the air. But the press was
forbidden to breathe a word about fraternization, though it was common knowledge. Diverted from this most vital question, all political
activity concentrated upon home affairs. As it had been the enemy
(President Wilson) who had actually mentioned democratization as a
condition of peace, the peoples of the Monarchy understood that he
who said 'suffrage' meant 'peace'. Therefore the call for universal
suffrage was gaining daily in momentum.

About the time of the Kaiser's famous Easter Manifesto, promising
the long overdue reform of the Prussian three-class franchise, the King
had urged Tisza to submit a draft Bill for the reform of the Hungarian
franchise, in accordance with the first Speech from the Throne. Tisza
sabotaged this reform and it was clear to all that universal suffrage
could never be attained through him.

On May 22nd the King, known for his abrupt decisions, dismissed
Stephen Tisza in a most unorthodox fashion, in the train between
Budapest and Vienna.

The manner in which Charles set about solving the Hungarian crisis after Tisza's fall was characteristic of his inconsistent and impulsive nature. He always agreed with the person with whom he was speaking. On one occasion three Hungarian politicians had audience with the King and each was convinced that the King had appointed him Premier. He also had an unfortunate habit of telling one what he thought of the man who had just left his room. This habit was double-edged: highly flattered, the person to whom Charles had opened his heart would think himself the confidant, but would soon discover what Charles had said about him after he had left. The Hungarians being a talkative race, indiscretions were frequent. To me the King had said of his own Foreign Minister, Burian: 'He is very stupid.' Of Count Hadik when he was on the point of nominating him Prime Minister: 'He tells too many lies, but, if there is no alternative, I will certainly send for him.' About my father-in-law: 'Do not trust him, he is not sincere about the franchise.' The man who had the greatest influence on him was Count Joseph Hunyadi, who would amuse him with inexhaustible gossip and *risqué* stories!

After many futile attempts had been made to form a Government, we had a great surprise. Over the head of Andrassy, the King appointed young Maurice Esterhazy as Hungarian Prime Minister. He invited me to join the Cabinet, but I was so indignant at the mutilation of the Franchise Bill[6] that I refused and put my follower, Batthyanyi, in instead.

7

THE EFFECT OF THE BOLSHEVIK REVOLUTION
ON THE CENTRAL POWERS

They did not understand that politics are a conflict of forces, they supposed that they were a conflict of arguments. A. J. P. TAYLOR

THE news of the Bolshevik Revolution reached me in Switzerland. My first reaction was that of great anxiety. This would naturally stiffen the Prussians' militarist spirit and fill them with new hopes, although the final issue did not even then seem to me doubtful. I remember the desperate letters, filled with apprehension, that I wrote to my wife. On the other hand, if we had been wise, there would have been more hope now for negotiations, for it was to the interest of the Entente to conclude a separate peace with the Monarchy, counterbalancing the setback suffered on the Russian front. Although no one believed that Lenin would last more than a couple of months, it was evident that Russia was out of the war.

On my return to Vienna the Delegations had at last assembled. This was another occasion for banquets and toasts and fine phrases about the *Nibelungen Treue*. I was one of the Hungarian members. 'Make peace', I urged, 'before America gets going.' 'Faint-heartedness', they replied. 'Separate peace with Russia is imminent and our armies in the East will soon be released, so that in spring a decisive victory could be won in the West.'

The gulf between the Government and the country was steadily widening. The parliamentary Opposition was growing more apathetic. I tried to gain support outside of it. Gradually a new movement began, growing day by day in factories, workshops and offices without being organized, without progressing, yet representing the same determination — the destruction of a regime which prevented peace.

At this time Oskar Jaszi was my most valuable collaborator; a professor of Social Science and a sociological and political writer of European reputation, he had courageously opposed the feudal ruling class on the question of the subject races. He was one of the most important Hungarian theoretical politicians and the intellectual leader of the middle-class progressives. The Hungarian middle class was small and negligible and the intellectuals who sprang from it were mostly Jews with whom the Hungarian 'historic class' felt nothing in common; it was a poor testimonial for us that amongst his followers Jaszi could not count a single aristocrat. Over the young intellectuals of the bourgeoisie he exercised an influence similar to that of Masaryk over the young Czechs. It gave me great satisfaction and encouragement that this man, of whom I held so high an opinion, had come independently to the same conclusion as I had on the question of peace; meanwhile I had come over to his views on the minority question. It is a significant and depressing fact that it needed a revolution to enable Jaszi to play any official part in Hungarian politics, and that this exceptional man had to live most of his later life in exile.

An important part in the enlightenment of the workers was played also by Erwin Szabo, one of the founders of the Sociological Society and of the *Twentieth Century* magazine. It was not my good fortune to know him well. In the last year of the war, when I came into touch with his Socialist comrades, his health had broken down under the thankless labour of decades, and it was impossible for this foremost leader of the left-wing Socialists to be any longer as active as his spirit yearned to be. He died in the autumn of 1918. Erwin Szabo's great merits are recognized even in present-day Communist Hungary.

Our great poet Andrew Ady, through the intermediary of his art, served our aims as well. His verses expressed better than any of our speeches the tragic Hungarian fate of being ruled by an obsolete, stubborn and frivolous class, to which he himself belonged, the Hungarian gentry.

But President Wilson had the greatest impact on us. His pacifism and his Fourteen Points determined our internal struggles, just as later his defeat decided the fate of Hungary. In spite of subsequent disillusionment, his influence on the spiritual development of mankind cannot be denied. Between the two wars Wilson's failure made his followers sceptical of the feasibility of his ideas, but today they are still alive, and all efforts to create a united Europe have sprung from Wilsonian principles.

The Entente powers, by inscribing disarmament, international justice and democracy on their banners, made an undeniably skilful move, using these slogans as weapons for the more rapid defeat of the Central Powers. They thus gained the sympathy of the masses and invested the struggle with a new spirit. Pacifism played the part taken by Communism in the Second World War.

Although President Wilson's Fourteen Points and their subsequent completion contained no mention of a league of Socialist States, his pacifism gained innumerable adherents for Socialism, even from the ranks of those who had formerly regarded it as Utopian. In the latter half of the war, owing to the spread of pacifist ideas, Socialism regained its ascendancy. Woodrow Wilson's initiative had the positive result of making people believe that the creation of a social order, excluding war, was within the bounds of possibility and not the Utopian imagination of some cranks. His failure proved that on the present social basis every pacifist effort must fail. People came to realize that responsibility for war did not rest on one nation only, and that capitalism and imperialism were among its causes.

Although I had not yet accepted Marxism, I was beginning to loathe more and more the social order of the old world with its injustice, cruelty, corruption and falsehood; I longed for a more humane one based on the works read in my youth and to which I now reverted, through the impetus of Wilsonian ideas.

The uninitiated imagined that the fall of Bethmann Hollweg in the summer of 1917 meant a change in favour of peace. The contrary happened. Michaelis, his successor, was the representative of the military party in Germany. Shortly after this the Kaiser came to Vienna, and his visit extinguished all our hopes. Moreover, the Emperor Charles's negotiations with the French through Prince Sixtus had been revealed, and greatly damaged the prestige of the Monarchy.

During the summer I received hundreds of letters and telegrams encouraging me to persevere. In the middle of July, on my way from Parad to Budapest, I was surrounded at the station by a crowd of soldiers. They called me the apostle of peace. I felt that I did not deserve this title, for I had done nothing to shorten the senseless misery of these wretched men.

It was now clear to me that we could not count on Czernin. In a letter written to Tisza he had condemned his own policy: 'It certainly is possible to change course and steer in the direction of the Entente, if we believe that the change will succeed. If so, let us have the courage not to stop half way. This coquetting with treachery without committing it is the stupidest of all courses. We lose our footing completely in Berlin, without gaining a hold either in London or Paris.' This was exactly what he had been doing. When I had last seen him I had felt that it was Berlin speaking through Czernin. I told him that I should be compelled to attack him in the future.

Thus my fruitless association with Czernin and the Esterhazy Government had come to an end. I regained my freedom of action. No advance had been made with the reform of the franchise. I took an unorthodox step and broke into a Cabinet meeting in the Prime Minister's office. The Ministers glared furiously at me. I reminded them of the agreement made with the franchise bloc and challenged them to keep to it. It was an ultimatum. I demanded the answer by five o'clock that afternoon. The result was that I secured the secret ballot in one-third of the electoral districts.

I now started a new and independent peace offensive, attacking Czernin's vacillating foreign policy, and publicly demanded a visa for Switzerland. My aim, I admitted, was to get into touch with the Entente.

On October 2nd Czernin, to the general surprise, made a pacifist speech at a dinner given in his honour at Buda by the Hungarian Premier. I had met him previously at our club and he had asked me, in the presence of Andrassy, not to see any Entente politicians if I went to Switzerland. But if I did I should emphasize that he, Czernin, would never betray the Germans or leave them in the lurch. I remarked icily that my policy remained unaltered; that I had every intention of contacting Entente politicians, and that his only way of preventing it would be to refuse me a passport.

The nominal reason for my journey to Switzerland was the Congress of the League for Permanent Peace, held in Berne, to which I had been invited. Although I had no illusions that peace could be brought about by pacifist theorists, this conference afforded me the desired opportunity of meeting neutral and Entente representatives. As I had been cut off from the West for three years, all information, from whatever source, was useful to me. I made the acquaintance in Berne of the great pacifist Alfred H. Fried, Herr Muhlen, Prince Alexander Hohenlohe and, among German politicians, the Socialist Edward Bernstein and the Democrat Walter Schucking. Spies and *agents provocateurs* were on my track, but I disappointed them, for whatever I said corresponded with the views I had repeatedly expressed at home.

I had two important conversations. One with Mr. Wilson, the United States Ambassador, and the other with Haguenin, the Director of French propaganda in Switzerland. I told the Ambassador candidly of our efforts to bring Germany to reason, but if unsuccessful I was confident that there were strong forces inside the Monarchy in favour of a separate peace. I suggested that a neutral power should invite the belligerents to peace negotiations; if Germany accepted, well and good; if not, the Monarchy could declare itself ready to negotiate independently, thus forcing Germany's hand. The Dual Monarchy could in this case give its consent to the restoration of Belgium and to the cession of Alsace-Lorraine. For the sake of an early peace Austria would most probably satisfy the just Italian claims, and cede Galicia to an independent Poland as well. This was the proposal made by King Charles himself in his letter to Prince Sixtus de Bourbon, and by Bülow who, too, was ready to sacrifice the Italian territory belonging to his ally, Austria. The Kaiser was also willing to give Galicia away, as it is easier to be generous with the property of others than with one's own.

Having no right to speak officially, our conversation was simply an exchange of ideas. At the time of my trial for high treason I should have been pleased had the American Government, or Mr. Wilson himself, given an account of this conversation, as the charges against me were chiefly based on these negotiations.

My second and more interesting conversation was with Haguenin. Even after discounting his propagandist statements, I gained an overwhelming impression of the assistance which America was offering her allies on the Western front. The American Army was very much underrated by our leaders, who wished to persuade the people that American assistance was merely a first-rate bluff. I had experienced this same attitude of wishful thinking when I was in Berlin early the same year, at the time when the United States joined in. They were considered as a negligible quantity.

My guiding principle during these discussions and throughout my stay in Switzerland was to convince the Entente politicians that it was in their interest to conclude peace as soon as possible; there was no point in carrying on, if there was a chance of making Germany accept peace.

Even today I am convinced that the psychological moment for negotiations was in 1917, and that Hungary would have fared incomparably better had we come to a compromise with the non-Magyar population. For example, had we acted in unison with the Croats, we could have assured ourselves an outlet to the sea at Fiume. And there would have been no question of the loss of the Banat, the southern Hungarian territory inhabited by Magyars. Serbia in those days had not yet formulated its demands, and the Entente had not committed itself on the subject. Also in the north we should at worst have lost only the counties inhabited by the Slovaks. If the initiative of the negotiations had come from our side, we should have been in a more favourable position, having in those days still something to offer.

Never during my conversations in Switzerland was there any question about Hungary's frontiers. I have described these negotiations in detail as they formed the most serious charges against me at my trial.

The peace negotiations at Brest-Litovsk had started, and the German Foreign Minister, Von Kühlmann, passed through Budapest to attend. I attended a dinner given in his honour, to which only pro-Germans had been asked. They hoped that Kühlmann would convince me that I was backing the wrong horse. After the dinner was over I became involved in a long argument, the Austro-Hungarian Foreign Minister and the others listening indignantly to what I had to say. But not so Kühlmann. The one person who might have had some justification for taking offence at my suggestion that Germany should return Belgium and Alsace-Lorraine for the sake of an early peace, was the only one of the company who displayed sympathy with my plain speaking and did not fly into a rage. Von Kühlmann, a Bavarian Catholic, made a strong impression on me as a man of great intelligence, wide views and calm and clear judgment. I told him the impression which I had formed in Switzerland, and that the chief obstacle to peace was the fact that Germany would not declare her intentions concerning Belgium. Kühlmann, who no doubt knew this as well as I did, without wishing to say so, listened with quiet attention and merely referred to the difficulties involved. The pro-Germans at the dinner were flabbergasted at the objective tone in which Kühlmann discussed this, conveying the impression that he personally would not oppose an agreement on such lines. He distinguished himself at the Brest-Litovsk negotiations through his disagreement with the Supreme Command and its representative, General Hoffmann, who was strongly opposed to his policy.

All along the line reaction lifted its head again, and the Governments of Vienna and Budapest, impressed by the Treaties of Brest-Litovsk and Bucharest — the Bread Peace — and trusting that the danger of democratization had passed, abandoned their reforms. The spurious victories of the Germans provided them with fresh encouragement. Although these victories could only be transitory since the United States had entered the war, they did affect the prospects of democracy at home. Supporters of the franchise were therefore dejected when the military position was favourable and optimistic when the news was bad.

After the session of Parliament I again returned to the front, where fraternization had now seriously started. The spirit of the army was anything but enthusiastic. The positions occupied by my regiment were so close to those of the Russians that we could hear them talking in their trenches. One day in September, when my regiment was stationed behind the lines in Galicia, one of my fellow-officers from the trenches asked to see me privately. He told me that he had received a message from some Russian officers in the opposite trench that they would like to get into touch with 'Karolyi'. They had heard in Russia about my peace campaign and wanted to meet me. The transmission of this message proved, in itself, that already in 1917 the morale of the Austro-Hungarian Monarchy was deeply undermined and that the position on the Galician front, even at the time of the Kerensky Revolution, was hardly tenable. I do not reproach myself for not having followed the call, for Russia would not have been strong enough in those days to be a decisive factor in our struggle for peace. This kept me back from a Hess-like mission.

8

GERMAN SECRET SERVICE IN HUNGARY

IN September 1917, the papers brought the news that the Abbé Török, the young chaplain who had negotiated with Sonnino, had been arrested on some minor charge. During the course of the interrogation the priest mentioned his services to the Karolyi Party, and the Public Prosecutor thought he had made a sensational discovery. Great was his disappointment when, on being called as a witness, I told him that the Foreign Minister had been informed at the time; but this did not end the matter. The Minister of Justice had vowed my destruction and Török had to be induced to give evidence against me, true or false. The priest, although he had nothing to disclose, knowing that he would never be released until he satisfied the authorities, 'confessed' that the documents were deposited in a safe in Zürich. They would be handed either to him, or to me, or to our nominee. Despite the fact that I had no knowledge of compromising documents, I believed Török's confession. His lawyer, who was the agent of the Minister of Justice and an *agent provocateur*, brought me letters and messages regularly from the prisoner. On one occasion he copied a letter of Török's addressed to his friend in Zürich on my notepaper headed with my initials, instructing him to take out the contents of the safe. Unsuspecting, I let him do so.

The next day, this lawyer's clerk rushed to inform me that his chief had been arrested and searched and that the police had found on him the copy of Török's letter. Vazsonyi, the Minister of Justice, had now at last got proof that I was in communication with a prisoner held in jail. He had already informed my father-in-law that he would have me arrested as soon as he had obtained the contents of the safe. It was now a race between me and the Minister of Justice as to who would reach Zürich first. I asked a young relative of mine, who was on her way to Switzerland, to get the mysterious documents. At the frontier, after being searched, she was turned back, although in possession of a special visa given to her by Berchtold. The Government emissary arrived in Zürich, to be told that no such safe existed. The whole story was a pure invention. When I was in office the Public Prosecutor admitted to me that Török had been kept in prison only on account of his mission to Sonnino, as the Minister of Justice wanted to find a pretext to have me arrested.

In January 1918, a letter appeared in the press addressed to me by my cousin, Imre Karolyi, which began with these words: 'Quousque tandem abutere Catiline', and in which he called me 'half a traitor': what half a traitor is supposed to be is not clear to me even today. Imre, son of my uncle Tibor who had been my guardian, had never been a friend of mine. Since my marriage the mutual antipathy of our youth had turned on his side into violent hatred. He had often expressed the hope that his sons would inherit my entailed property, as it was generally supposed that I would not marry on account of my sentimental attachment and that my brother Joseph, although married, would have no issue. With my marriage his hopes had been frustrated and, unable to conceal his feelings, he ostentatiously stayed away from the ceremony. When our son was born, all hope of coming into my property was lost. My political activities gave him an opportunity to satisfy his bitter grudge.

It was about this time that a general strike was proclaimed simultaneously in Vienna and Budapest, the first strike since the outbreak of war. It was a political one, for universal suffrage and peace. It had broken out without the knowledge of the party executive and therefore it was whispered that I had a hand in it. It was meant as a demonstration of strength, but had little effect.

One February morning a private detective named Robinson called on me. He related a fantastic story about having been engaged by a certain German major in Budapest to collect compromising political material against me. He had been informed about some boxes filled with documents which I was supposed to have sent to my country place, Parad. Our housekeeper had sent several baskets of soiled linen to our country laundry and the Major was convinced that important papers were being concealed. Robinson, who had been in his past days a champion wrestler, assured me that he would never have abased himself to spy on a Count Karolyi, but being hard up and not being able to wrestle any more — he was stout and bald — he had to make a living somehow. He begged me with tears in his eyes to supply him with letters, so that at least he could prove that he had been in communication with me. Sympathizing with his plight, I gave him what he wanted. He now called regularly and my secretary made out a series of documents, which Robinson happily carried off with him. We naturally kept duplicates and placed them with my lawyer. The ex-wrestler was doing well, and we also, as we were finding out a great deal about Major Hermann Konsten. He was the head of the German Military Intelligence camouflaged as a commercial representative in Budapest. He was in close business relations with Imre Karolyi and his bank; Imre was the Director of the Hungarian Bank and was also a regular contributor to the leading organ of the Tisza Party on German-Hungarian commercial expansion to the East. The worthy German, becoming confident, hoped to bribe some member of my entourage. He even wanted to get hold of my wife's maid to obtain further information, as the 'documents' did not seem to be interesting enough. Katus was ready to act the part of her own maid and call on Konsten, but I stopped that. I asked a well-known journalist, Paul Keri, to act as my secretary and carry on the game. The Major entertained no suspicion — he had previously worked in Turkey and his faith in corruption was unshakable — and offered my 'secretary' 50,000 gulden for incriminating documents. Keri pretended to hesitate, declaring that if he was found out there would be nothing left for him but suicide. 'You can rely on me,' answered the Major, 'at the worst you will lose your job, but Imre Karolyi will get you a much better paid one in his bank. You need not hesitate, for Michael Karolyi is in any case a lost man. We shall lay the documents you get before his father-in-law, Julius Andrassy, who will then persuade him to retire from political life. If he refuses, we shall be compelled to destroy him. Andrassy will have to help us, for as long as his son-in-law is in politics the Germans will never entrust him with the destiny of the Monarchy.' We thus obtained from the chief German Intelligence Officer of the Eastern Zone precise details of their system of espionage and of the arbitrary interference of the German High Command in the affairs of a Sovereign State and ally. When we had everything well prepared, we spread abroad the news that a sensational disclosure would be made in the House of Deputies. The Major, certain that at last Karolyi was being unmasked, secured a seat in the Gallery.

An independent member of the Opposition opened the debate with the question as to how it was permissible for a military organ of a foreign power to interfere in our national politics and use such disreputable methods against the members of the Chamber? Konsten left the Gallery in haste, leaving his hat behind him.

When I eventually became Prime Minister, all the documents relating to this affair fell into my hands. I learnt that all evidence concerning Török had been supplied to the Major by the Public Prosecutor himself. The Public Prosecutor later admitted to me that he had followed the instructions of his superiors. Accommodating Public Prosecutors were a usual phenomenon during our two revolutions and the counter-revolution, and I fear they still exist. They adapt their views and judgments to the changing regimes.

Intrigues continued secretly against me, and even grew fiercer since I seemed to have won the first round. I remember a typical episode of that period. The Prime Minister, Wekerle, sent for my solicitor in the name of the King and begged him to make me desist from publishing the letters which the King had written to me, and to send him the originals. He had heard from Prince Louis Windischgraetz of my wife's threat that I would produce these letters if the authorities continued to annoy me. I was amazed. I had never received letters from the King and could therefore never have thought of publishing them. My solicitor hurried back to the Premier with the information. 'I have always known the Prince for a liar and a schemer', said the Premier, 'but this is the limit.' 'Excellency,' answered my lawyer, 'the Prince is your pupil.'

The poor King, who must by this time have acquired a complex about letters, did not recollect if he had ever written me any. It was I now who attacked my cousin for slander, but in spite of my solicitor's efforts I failed to get the proceedings concluded. This was the strongest evidence in my favour, for the Public Prosecutor and the military court would have come to his rescue had they had the slightest evidence; all they could do was to sabotage the proceedings. And it was solely on the strength of these absurd fables fabricated by my cousin and the Prussian major that the Law Courts confiscated my fortune in 1923, declaring me a traitor and making me an exile for twenty-seven years.

9

DECAY AND DISSOLUTION

Against stupidity the gods themselves struggle in vain.
SCHILLER

IN the summer of 1918 it was no longer possible to conceal the disaster. The heavy losses on the Piave and the German defeats on the Western front filtered through, making the demand for peace more insistent.

Even at this date, the majority of Parliament stood unanimously against the acceptance of the Fourteen Points, regarding it as open treason. Some members of the National Casino advocated my expulsion from the club. The press, except for organs of the Opposition, attacked me violently.

On September 14th came Count Burian's peace proposals to all belligerent nations. They lacked the one essential thing — acceptance of Wilson's programme. The offer was empty and flaccid, doomed in advance to failure. Three days later, came the crushing reply from the U.S.A.[7]

In spite of the increasing political gulf between me and my father-in-law, our personal relations did not change. My wife was deeply attached to him, and our frequent political arguments, though painful, did not alter my friendship and respect for him. My mother-in-law, too, was violently political; all the women members of the Andrassy 'clan' took an intense interest in politics and, passionately supporting the 'chief', were uncompromising in their approach.

While I was deer-stalking on my father-in-law's estate in Transylvania, the news of the Bulgarian collapse reached us.

We were a family party, with my wife's sisters and their husbands, who were all in politics. At an altitude of over 6000 feet even Hungarian political passions lose their vehemence. Over the entrance of the shack allotted to my wife and me we found the inscription 'Hurrah for the Bolsheviks', put there by my wife's younger sister, Caja. My father-in-law's estate, Dubrin, was not far from Kolozsvar, now Kluj, where we spent the shooting season. Newspapers, much delayed, were brought up by a courier.

Andrassy's constitutional optimism and wishful thinking made him believe that the German retreat was merely strategical and every day he expected to hear that a halt had been called. He said, however, that if I were to be proved right it was the beginning of the end and that if the world were reorganized on Wilsonian principles, which he loathed, he would retire into private life. He would never support a separate peace, or turn against the Germans. 'Better death with honour, than life with dishonour', was his motto. My conception of honour was a different one.

On September 29th the bombshell fell; the Entente had pierced the Bulgarian front. We had seen no papers for days. Andrassy was overwhelmed with anxiety and, visibly shrunken, withdrew from our company. It was a painful situation and I did not derive any satisfaction from being in a position to say: 'I told you so.'

Later that evening my father-in-law admitted that all hope of victory was gone and that we must make peace without losing a moment, but it would no longer be he and his friends who would seek this peace. He himself would retire from politics altogether.

Amid our misfortunes it was a great relief to me to find Andrassy at last ready to give in, for he was the real leader of conservative Hungary and of the Government Party.

Emissaries from the Government rode up the steep, stony roads among the pine forests, begging Andrassy to return immediately. But the shock he had received was so great that he had no wish to leave. His world had crumbled around him. It was not the call of the wild that held him in the mountains — he was a much keener statesman than hunter — but for a lucid moment he realized that politics had ceased to be his hunting-ground.

At daybreak I took a horse to the valley, from where I left in a car for Kolozsvar, leaving my wife with her family, who treated her as if she was personally responsible for the defeat of the Bulgarians; the joyful family party was broken up.

In Kolozsvar I had the most amazing experience of human stubbornness and lack of political insight. Various Transylvanian nobles had gathered at the New York Café to discuss the situation, among them

Count Stephen Bethlen. They were all concerned with how to secure the retention of the Rumanian territory which had been won for Hungary by the Peace of Bucharest in 1917.

In vain did I try to make them understand that the time had passed when we could retain conquered territory and that the problem was now a very different one — how to prevent the Rumanians from taking Transylvania. In vain did I point out that there was only one possible way of preventing this — namely, not only to renounce voluntarily the terms of the Bucharest Peace, but also to make immediate and comprehensive concessions to the Rumanians in Transylvania, to counteract their irredentism. They refused to admit the danger and would not hear of these proposals.

I left for Budapest with Stephen Bethlen. He had an inherited political instinct, qualifying him for traditional home politics, but he had not inherited the invaluable adaptability of the Transylvanian politicians. He was shrewd, but lacking in political vision; in his racial policy he was even narrower and more chauvinist than the others. But he had foresight as far as the danger to his class was concerned; his memorable statement: 'There is but one vital question now, all the rest is secondary and that is, how to save private property', did not sound very patriotic at the time, but was much to the point.[8]

I reached Budapest on the morning of October 1st. In spite of the early hour, a deputation met me at the station. At that time I was far from realizing that we were heading for a revolution and that I should play such a prominent part in it. Thinking back to those days — a month or two before the fall of the Habsburg Monarchy — I feel better able to understand the blindness of Louis XVI when he heard of the storming of the Bastille.

The calendar of revolutions can never be made until afterwards. The day of the Bulgarian collapse was certainly an important date in the process of the fall of the Monarchy. A friend of mine reproached me: How could I hunt at that time? Well, at that time, 'that time' had not yet become 'that time'.

After the Bulgarian collapse, Wekerle summoned the party leaders and informed them of the position. He showed no sign of emotion, but simply stated, with a genial smile and perfect calm, that he had long known that the war was lost and that all that was now happening did not surprise him in the least. The complete collapse of the policy which he had advocated for decades did not appear to disturb him at all. I was dumb with astonishment. 'That means,' I said at last, 'that we ran into the catastrophe with our eyes open?'

This was the second time that a statesman in office — a Minister who knew all that was going on — had told me outright that we had lost the war; first Czernin in the spring of 1917, and now Wekerle.

After his return from Dubrin, Andrassy had completely changed his attitude: he would not hear of Jaszi or his friends taking part in a Government, although Burian had told him that Germany was so broken that it was she who was now pressing for an armistice and an immediate peace on Wilsonian principles. Unless Hungary agreed to this, Germany would leave her in the lurch and accept the Fourteen Points without her. So this was where our stubbornness had led us.

From that day we were no longer called traitors for mentioning peace; but if we mentioned autonomy for the subject races, or raised doubts as to the possibility of maintaining Dualism, we were received with the same uproar. It is true that we had not long to wait for this also to be accepted, but unfortunately it was by then, as usual, too late. Burian's note to President Wilson went off on October 5th and before the answer came King Charles sent Andrassy to Switzerland to begin negotiations with the Entente.

On October 8th the Socialist paper *Nepszava* published a manifesto addressed by the Social Democratic Party to the 'People of Hungary'. Kunfi's brilliant style was recognizable and it thus became evident that the left wing of the party was now taking the upper hand.

I was now ready to try anything to avoid catastrophe. First of all we had to accept the Wilsonian basis, not only because we agreed with Wilson's principles, but for the simple reason that, until we did, there could be no question of America or any other Entente Power being willing to meet us at a conference table. Following Bulgaria's separate peace, the danger was acute that the French army, under General Franchet d'Esperey, supported by Serbian troops and later by the Rumanians, would cross the Danube. Transylvania and southern Hungary would then fall into enemy hands and we should have lost all possibility of treating with our 'minorities'.

We started negotiations with them on the basis of personal union with the Habsburgs. I received valuable assistance from Professor Oskar Jaszi, with whose *Eastern Switzerland* I was in complete accord.

My first meeting was with the leaders of the Slovak National Party, with Matthew Dula, its President and several others, who demanded autonomy for Slovakia; but separation from Hungary was never even mentioned. They showed themselves most tractable and their line of thought largely coincided with ours. When we had closed the discussion, Dula pointed out to me that, although we were in full agreement they could not pledge themselves definitely to a leader of the Opposition, whose word would not be binding upon official Hungary. This was obvious. Even if the Slovaks, after the final victory of the Entente, had broken the pact, Hungary would have been in a stronger position to demand a plebiscite at the time of the treaty.

Negotiations with the Rumanians followed the same lines. Julius Maniu[9] member of the Hungarian Parliament, Alexander Vajda, Ladislaus Goldis and John Erdélyi met in my house. The difficulty was greater than with the Slovaks, for the Rumanians had an army behind them. They demanded far-reaching autonomy for the Rumanian population in Transylvania, with much looser connection with the Motherland than contemplated by us; but even in this maximum demand they explicitly emphasized non-separation from Hungary. The very fact that they treated with me and sought a solution in the form of autonomy gave us hopes that if the King entrusted us in time with the formation of a Cabinet a compromise could be found. Later, Alexander Vajda, who became Rumanian Prime Minister, and Ladislaus Goldis, declared to the Archduke Joseph that the Rumanians desired my appointment, otherwise it would be impossible for them to arrive at any concrete settlement. Erdélyi, later Ambassador in Budapest, expressed a similar opinion.

Dr. Kosta Hadji and Hasha Tomics were in touch with me on behalf of the Serbian Radical Party, giving me definite assurance of their support. I contacted the Croat Deputies as well, Dushan Popovich, Pribicevich and Baron Nickolitch. Tisza had made negotiations rather difficult by his behaviour at Sarajevo, but they knew that Tisza did not represent all the Hungarian people. I had no illusions concerning the possibility of retaining Croatia under the Hungarian Crown, and knew that the Croats would demand complete independence. The South Slav State was a certainty; the only question was the form and degree of unity between Serbia, Croatia, Bosnia, Dalmatia and the Slovene Territory. The only subject for discussion was Fiume.

There, as well, we had the impression that, if a Karolyi Government was now formed, the problem of Fiume, our sole seaport, would be solved in our favour.

I was frequently charged with insisting on my nomination for personal ambition. It is true that I did insist, because I had the strong conviction that only a Karolyi-Jaszi Government could come to an agreement with our neighbours. There was no other Hungarian party whom they would have trusted and who would have been willing to make concessions.

It is of course possible that the non-Magyars, in spite of getting autonomy, would have insisted on separation, but it was clear that we must make this last attempt.

One of the reasons which nourished irredentism was the fact that non-Magyars were excluded from higher posts in the Civil Service. If Hungary had been changed into a federation of autonomous nationalities, these careers would have been thrown open to them and the fangs of irredentism would have been drawn. If a Karolyi Government had been formed in 1917, including the representatives of the non-Magyar population, it would have been perfectly fitted to conclude a separate peace, on Wilson's programme of plebiscite. Even in the case of a German occupation, the plebiscite effected after the victory of the Entente would have been much more favourable to us. The Fourteen Points would have overridden not only the Treaty of London, but also the Treaty of Bucharest. With a plebiscite, Austria would not have lost the portions of south Tyrol inhabited by Germans.

It was obviously disastrous to delay our offer until we were under the guillotine. In October 1918, Andrassy, as Foreign Minister, had to comply with Wilson's demands and give up Slovakia and Croatia. Hungary's complete defeat, the Treaty of Trianon and its logical results — national Bolshevism, the White Terror, the return to power of pro-Germans, the alliance with Hitler — were the consequences of this suicidal policy of stubbornness. A federation of eighty million people would have been able to defend itself against Nazi aggression. The change in the balance of power might have prevented the outbreak of the Second World War.

10

THE END OF DUALISM

ON October 11th the King summoned me to Reichenau. I had been kept away from him for fifteen months. I found him very much altered, showing signs of great mental and bodily fatigue, almost apathetic. When I had last talked to him at Laxenburg he had been filled with youthful energy and optimism. Of all this I now found hardly a trace. I again repeated the old story of the dangers which threatened and which could only be averted by rapid and determined action, if it was not already too late. I told him that our relations with the minorities had reached an acute point and could only be solved by radical measures. I tried to make it clear that at this critical moment it was necessary for us to face the Entente alone, that we must therefore denounce the German Alliance and secure an absolutely free hand for ourselves. New men must come to the helm, for the Entente would enforce harder conditions if the control of our affairs were still retained by those who were responsible for our pro-German policy. America must see that we were not only talking, but acting. I told the King of my experiences in Switzerland, which his advisers had at the time prevented me from reporting to him, and emphasized that it would then have been a particularly favourable moment for negotiation.

The King repeated wearily that I had been right then and was right now. 'But I have always been told,' he added, 'that you have only fifteen people behind you.' He wanted a coalition Government, including the Radicals and myself. I requested the release of all political prisoners, above all Friedrich Adler, in Austria, and the non-Magyar politicians in Hungary.[10]

The audience, which lasted very long, completely exhausted the King. I felt that disappointment in Czernin, the unfortunate Sixtus affair and the attacks against him, had broken his spirit, and that there could be no happy ending for this well-intentioned young monarch.

On October 15th the Committee for Foreign Affairs of the Delegation, held its first sessions in Vienna. These were usually purely formal; the Foreign Minister would deliver his speech and no debate would follow. But I determined to seize this opportunity and, as soon as Burian had made his report I demanded, in defiance of precedent, permission to speak.

Unfriendly, anxious glances were shot at me from all sides but the President let me speak. 'I come to bury Caesar, not to praise him,' I began, and proceeded to say that Burian should have sent out invitations on black-edged cards, with the notice that the joint Ministries were responsible for the death of the Austro-Hungarian Monarchy. I reproached them grimly for their blunders. But, instead of being abused, as I expected, I saw that my words had a shattering effect. The Delegates sat awe-stricken; none of them uttered a word. Silently they left the premises which had for half a century represented the glory of a dynasty.

Two days later, the *coup de grâce* to dying Dualism was given by the Emperor himself. On October 17th a Manifesto was published to his 'Loyal Austrian People' inviting them, in accordance with their right of self-determination, to form National Councils for the purpose of transforming Austria into a Federal State.[11]

The Hungarian Prime Minister threatened Austria with stoppage of food supplies if the Manifesto did not guarantee Hungary's old frontiers. A clause containing this was therefore inserted. The Manifesto filled the ruling circles with horror and caused great excitement in the Chamber of Deputies. For it had freed the minorities in Austria, it had wrecked the foundations of the Dualist system. How many more days of life had the old Hungarian regime left, they wondered.

On October 16th Wekerle announced, at the first sitting of the Chamber, that Hungary now stood on the basis of the Personal Union. 'We must bring to bear the first three paragraphs of the law of the year 1723,' he said, 'that is of the Pragmatic Sanction.' With the dissolution of the realms of the Habsburg dynasty, Hungary, under the terms of the Pragmatic Sanction, automatically regained her independence.

I demanded a complete break with Austria so as to have Hungary independently represented at the Peace Conference. One of my followers, Martin Lovászy, made the challenging statement: 'We are the friends of the Entente.' A terrific uproar followed. Prince Louis

Windischgraetz sprang from his seat and wanted to throw Lovászy out. The sitting had to be suspended. It was a rather unfortunate expression, as we were not friends of the Entente, but friends of democracy and peace. Later, this same Windischgraetz tried to convince the Entente missions that he and his associates had always been their friends in secret, and anti-German. (This undignified comedy was repeated after Hitler's defeat in the Second World War.)

The following day, October 17th, Stephen Tisza rose in the Chamber to answer me. He gave a very different answer from the one expected: 'I will not play with words. I must acknowledge the truth of what Michael Karolyi said in his speech yesterday. We have lost the war.' This fell like a thunderbolt among the stupefied majority. It was clear that, under the pressure of events and the burden of his own terrible responsibility, Tisza had broken down. This was the hardest blow the reactionaries could suffer. Tisza's announcement spread like wildfire throughout the country, in the trenches and behind the lines. Many only now believed the truth, simply because Tisza had spoken.

After the Emperor's Manifesto the process of dissolution had continued at a rapid pace. The German-Austrians were the only nationality which had, in any measure, accepted the terms of the Manifesto and formed their National Council, as proposed by their Deputies in the Austrian Reichsrat. The Czechs and the South Slavs had refused to discuss the matter. Wekerle's mind was not sufficiently elastic to adapt itself to the hurricane rapidity with which the situation was changing. It was necessary to act in the name of Hungary and, as the Parliamentary majority did not represent the people and was incapable of acting itself, my colleagues and I, knowing that the country stood behind us, were forced to take positive action.

On October 22nd I put my Bill for the declaration of the independence of Hungary before the House of Deputies. The Government replied that it could only treat with the nationalities if the idea of an 'Eastern Switzerland' was abandoned, and it rejected a separate peace in emphatic terms. Even discussion of my Bill was outvoted. On this date, October 22nd, a week before the Revolution, the Reaction was firmly united. On one point there was no difference of opinion in the House: the Hungarian troops must be withdrawn from the joint army and recalled to the Hungarian frontiers.

Julius Andrassy, arriving in Budapest from Switzerland this same

day, was horror-stricken at what had happened in the Chamber of
Deputies and in Vienna. In his memoirs he writes about the three
causes of the downfall of the Monarchy: first, the Imperial Manifesto;
second, Tisza's speech; and third, the recall of the Hungarian troops
from the front. He might also have added a fourth: the war and the
whole system responsible for the war, the stubbornness of the Hungarian ruling class.

The cause of the monarch's downfall was not the pacifist agitation,
nor the Karolyi Party, nor the Hungarian Council — formed after the
events mentioned — nor yet the Revolution, which broke out on
October 31st after the collapse of the front, after final defeat and
catastrophe.

Just as the Manifesto, in which the Emperor decreed the federalization of Austria, would in itself have done no harm had it been carried
out, so the recall of the Hungarian troops to the Hungarian frontiers
would not have had such fatal consequences had the Government decided on a separate peace. It was out of the question for Magyar
soldiers to go on fighting when the Croats, Czechs, Slovaks, Rumanians and Poles were withdrawing their soldiers from the army. How
could they go on defending the old Monarchy, which the Imperial
Manifesto had virtually dissolved already, or continue to sacrifice their
lives in a war which the leader of their majority in Parliament, Tisza,
had already declared to be lost? Andrassy's plan to carry on as before —
to keep intact the Monarchy, the joint institutions, the joint Government, the joint army, until after the conclusion of peace — was completely unrealistic. After the collapse of Bulgaria, neither the Entente
nor the nationalities would have agreed to it.

As for the Emperor's action, he failed to consider what to set up in
place of the old system he had destroyed. By a stroke of the pen he
had done away with Dualism, but he still retained his blind Dualist
advisers. At the same time that he dissolved the army into its constituent parts, he failed to bring hostilities to an immediate conclusion
and to ask for an armistice and peace. At the critical moment he, too,
hesitated and left the work half done. This was the immediate cause of
the collapse of the Monarchy and the fall of Charles.

In the Chamber of Deputies a dramatic incident occurred. Whilst I
was listening to the speech of one of my followers, a telegram was
brought to me containing the news that the 79th Croatian Infantry

Regiment had mutinied, disarming the Hungarian Guards and taking prisoner the King's representative. I handed the telegram to the Speaker to read out. The effect was instantaneous. Wekerle sat in his place, completely at a loss, muttering unintelligibly. The sitting had to be suspended and all thronged into the great hall. The leaders of the parties were summoned to the Premier's room, where the Prime Minister informed us that he would announce his resignation. All present agreed on a coalition Government, with seats reserved for us. I declared that we would not enter a Government led by the present majority, but were ready to form a Government on our own programme, and admit representatives of the 'historic classes'.

A gloomy silence prevailed. When the Speaker re-opened the sitting, Wekerle, red in the face, handed in his resignation. When we sat down a journalist shouted from the seats reserved to the press: 'We want the freedom of the press. Down with the censorship.' My party rose and cheered. Tisza sprang up and ran in the direction of the members of the press: 'Throw them out!' he shouted.

This was the last meeting of the House of Deputies except the one declaring its own dissolution and the establishment of the People's Republic on November 16th.

11

THE REVOLUTION

The individual who plays a part in historical events never understands their significance. LEO TOLSTOY

RETURNING home to the Egyetem utca, I found all my followers assembled waiting for me. The leaders of the Social Democrats and the Radicals were there as well. Events in the Chamber proved that the Government had no longer any standing. The longer we delayed in taking matters in hand, the more chaotic the situation would become. National Councils were being formed all over the Monarchy. Although convinced that if we were prevented from forming a Government, a National Council was imperative, we preferred to put off a revolutionary move of this sort until the very last moment. During our meeting I received a message from George Pallavicini that our father-in-law had been appointed Foreign Minister. I immediately informed the gathering, asking them to accept his appointment. But the news provoked the reaction which we had tried to avoid: the decision to set up a National Council without delay. They unanimously insisted that the joint Foreign Ministry should be abolished and a Hungarian Foreign Office set up, as the conclusion of peace must be made by an 'independent Hungary'.

On the following day we were lunching at Andrassy's house on the river bank. I told my father-in-law that I feared his appointment could only prejudice the interests of the dynasty, as well as those of Hungary, and that if he stuck to it our ways must part. He was stern and unconciliatory and I left. My wife stayed on. It was an unfortunate custom of the Andrassy House for the women of the clan — all passionate addicts of politics — to listen in to political discussions. My mother-in-law, her sisters, daughters, cousins, separated only by a curtain from my father-in-law's study, used to be an unadmitted audience and, as they were a talkative family, decisions would soon be known all round the town.

Today, as usual, Katus and her mother sat behind the curtain when Andrassy's followers came to discuss the crisis. Soon Katus heard the Minister of Justice declaring that the only thing to do now was to adopt the Karolyi programme and to carry it out, but without him and his followers. An energetic Government would then be master of the situation. 'I have heard enough,' said Katus to her mother and left the house. On her return home, she told me what had happened. The members of the future National Council were in the middle of their meeting and, when they heard of our opponents' intentions, they decided that the formation of the National Council could no longer be put off.

At noon on October 24th university students, soldiers and officers demonstrated in front of my house. Soon the crowd in the street joined in. John Hock, priest and brilliant orator, addressed them from the windows, referring to the King as the sponsor of peace. To our surprise, cheers for the Republic were the answer. 'The stone has started to roll, where will it stop?' Batthyanyi whispered to me anxiously. The crowd clamoured for a national flag. One was found in the attic. Their intention was to proceed to Godollo, where the King was staying. We dissuaded them from this undertaking. Instead, the procession marched to the Var — the old, high part of Buda — and broke the cordon barring the entrance of the royal palace. The guards put up no resistance. They crowded into the sumptuous halls, nailed the programme of the National Council on the gilt stucco walls, and departed. On their way back they were suddenly surrounded by mounted police, who tried to seize the national flag; several were hurt. In a hysterical state of exultation the crowd flowed back to our house, bringing in their wounded. Katus turned the children's nursery into a hospital, where they were nursed by her and my sister Elisabeth.

The same day a car from the Court arrived, taking me to Godollo. I warned Charles of the danger which, due to his hesitation, threatened the throne, and said that the solution of the crisis would, if necessary, be reached without his consent. In spite of my exasperated tone the monarch showed no irritation. He listened patiently. He said that steps were being taken for an immediate peace and that, all differences having now disappeared, collaboration should be possible between Andrassy and myself. On the question of installing an independent Foreign Office he was adamant.

I drove home with Andrassy, who had also been at Godollo. It was a gloomy ride in the fog and rain of an October day. He was full of bitter reproaches, for the setting up of a National Council was, according to him, a breach of the Hungarian Constitution. The King, he said, could agree to the setting up of National Councils in the Austrian provinces, but not in a sovereign state like Hungary, without the consent of Parliament. In theory he was right, but the Hungarian Parliament was no longer representative of the people, elections being long overdue and the country virtually without a Government.

On October 25th we founded the National Council. We drew up our programme in twelve points and called upon the country to support us. On October 27th the censorship of the press was abolished by the arbitrary action of the journalists, who simply refused to submit their manuscripts to the censor. Consequently, the next morning, the whole country read the proclamation of the National Council.

On the evening of October 26th Andrassy left for Vienna to take up his appointment. I had just received most disquieting news, and sent Katus in great haste to inform Andrassy before he left that the situation was in the highest degree critical. Andrassy took the news calmly, informing Windischgraetz who was accompanying him and who immediately alerted the garrison stationed in Budapest, in case of disturbance.

An open air meeting had been announced for the 27th, in front of the Parliament building. I was to be the main speaker. The same morning the Director of the Hungarian Bank, Simon Krauss, called on me. He had found a way to solve the crisis and the King, he said, had accepted. It was the formation of a left coalition Government, headed by me, with Andrassy staying at his post. The joint Ministry would only function for two months, and would then be automatically replaced by a Hungarian Ministry of Foreign Affairs. It was then generally assumed that the Peace Conference would be called within a very short time. Count Joseph Hunyadi, the court chamberlain, told me that the King had accepted and, if I consented, the crisis would be solved.

Summoned to Godollo, I found the Court in great commotion. The King was receiving swarms of people whom he had never seen before, so as to get acquainted with the desires of his subjects. In the waiting-room, thronged with people, a corner of a long table was laid ready for a single meal. I thought it was prepared for one of the aides-de-camp on duty. No, it had been laid out for Charles IV.

The King received me in the large corner salon of the castle. In the adjoining room were spread out Staff maps, on which he was following the strategic position of our armies. It was already growing dark and the chandeliers were lit. Charles IV, in his field uniform and gaiters, was standing near his writing-table, smoking a cigarette, and seemed to be suffering from great nervous strain. I could not help feeling deep sympathy for him. I told him that I was prepared to settle the crisis on the basis of a compromise of which I had been informed that morning by Simon Krauss and Hunyadi. The King interrupted me, saying that he knew nothing of this plan. 'I agree to the programme,' he said later, 'although I was not acquainted with it before.' But he added pointedly: 'I have always been warned that you want a republic. Is that true?' 'I do not want a republic, I want an independent, democratic Hungary.' The King looked at me searchingly, then said: 'I have decided to appoint you my Prime Minister.' I bowed. He then invited me to take a seat at his side. He offered me a cigarette: 'Tell me your whole programme; take your time. Let us have a good talk and consider what needs to be done in this difficult situation.'

I noticed that the King was tired; his attention began to flag and he did not even ask if his future Ministers were to be Jews or not, a question he rarely failed to put. I read to him, in German, a brief summary of the National Council's programme. He nodded approval: 'Yes, yes, you are right, I agree,' he said several times. When he came to the fourth point of the programme: 'The alliance with Germany is to be denounced', the King interrupted me: 'Andrassy is going to denounce the alliance with Germany; your chief wish will thus be fulfilled.'

We were nearing the end of the programme when the Queen came in. The King presented me. She exchanged a few words in a low voice with her husband and then turned to me. 'His Majesty is so tired,' she said pleadingly, and left us. The King motioned with his hand for me to continue. We sat down again. He accepted all the points. He then asked me to suggest when I would take the oath, as he was travelling to Vienna that same evening, and I should have to get in immediate touch with Lammasch, the Austrian Premier, and with Andrassy, in order to come to an agreement with them over the answer to be sent to President Wilson. I suggested that the oath should be administered in Vienna. The King agreed: 'The essential is for us to accept Wilson's note without reservation.' He knew better than I did that the roof was burning over our heads.

I promised to form the Cabinet as quickly as possible and to come to Vienna. The King then sent for Batthyanyi, Garami, Kunfi and Jaszi, who would be members of my Cabinet. He asked me to have dinner in the castle, so that afterwards we might again discuss the most urgent problems. He dismissed me with the air of a man whose heart has been relieved of a heavy burden.

I had dinner with the ladies of the Court, Count Hadik and several aides-de-camp. The atmosphere was gloomy. No one had received orders. Would the Court leave for Austria? Hadik seemed very nervous and upset. The fact that I was making arrangements and waiting for my audience to be continued did not accord with what he knew — and I did not — that the King had also asked him to form a Government. In Budapest, however, the news had already spread that I was appointed Premier.

At last the embarrassment of waiting together was brought to an end, for the King sent for me. Whilst I was standing for some minutes in the ante-chamber the Queen passed and, recognizing me, came towards me: 'You will be able to help the King and the country, won't you?' — her voice quivered with emotion. 'I shall do everything that lies in my power,' I replied. 'The situation is very grave and the little that we may yet be able to save can only be saved if we act drastically and at once. Even the Queen must be prepared to make great sacrifices, otherwise the throne of Hungary will be lost for the King.' The large, dark, brave eyes of the Queen flashed as she listened; then, deeply moved, she said: 'You will do everything, everything, won't you?' I will not deny that this scene moved me very much.

I then went to the King's study and the discussion continued. The King seemed to be full of good intentions and to have really made up his mind at last. We had not yet come to the end, however, when he was called to the telephone in the adjoining room. It was a good half-hour before he came back, his face flushed and disturbed. Andrassy, it appeared, had given him bad news from Vienna. The King had told him that I was appointed Premier and Andrassy had replied to this that the King might perhaps save the Hungarian throne, but the Austrian would certainly be lost. The King was evidently perplexed. I told him that in Austria, too, Hussarek had been retained too long and Lammasch appointed too late. It was no wonder that there, also, the people had become impatient and distrustful. By tomorrow it might also be too late to calm the Hungarians and there was no Hungarian statesman who could any longer guarantee the course of events in Austria, or even the fate of the Austrian throne. I was a representative of the people and not a courtier and, if I might speak frankly, I should have to say that, in the present hopeless situation, it did not appear probable that the Emperor could retain all his crowns. If he would follow my advice, I could guarantee that the Hungarian throne, at least, could be saved for the present. Assuming that the Austrian throne was for the moment lost, he still had a chance, as King of Hungary, and on the basis of federalization, of regaining it later.

But the King's peace of mind had gone. I heard later that Andrassy, irritated by my appointment, had said to the King: 'If you appoint Karolyi, you might as well send me to a lunatic asylum; I shall be more in my place there.'

'There is nothing else to be done but for you to come to Vienna with us, we shall arrange everything there,' said the King.

The unfortunate Hadik was still waiting. Although the King had virtually appointed him Premier the same afternoon, he had not told him that his services were no longer required and that he had appointed me instead. I followed, taking my place in the suite. I still see the Gargantuan bulk of Hadik standing, sullen and dignified, watching the performance which, naturally, he could not fathom.

During the journey in the special train the King requested me to take immediate steps to ensure that the public meeting, organized by the National Council for the following day, should pass off without incident.

I wrote to Batthyanyi and informed him of my appointment and also of the King's desire. The train was stopped specially to have the letter sent. During the journey I did not speak to the King. In Vienna arrangements had been made for me to stay at Schönbrunn, but I preferred the Bristol Hotel, as I had to carry on the negotiations with Andrassy and Lammasch. I waited for a day, without news from anywhere, and gradually understood that I had been taken to Vienna in order to keep me away from Budapest and the meeting.

At last, after a great deal of trouble, I succeeded in getting Hunyadi on the telephone. I told him that I presumed it was unnecessary for me to wait any longer and that, seeing that the King had no further use for me, I would return to Budapest by the next train. Hunyadi did not detain me. Just before I set off for the station, the news reached me that the Archduke Joseph was travelling by the same train and that I could get all further information from him.

The Archduke invited me into his saloon-carriage; his wife, the Archduchess Augusta, was with him. The first words we exchanged showed that the King had given him no message whatsoever for me. The Archduke referred to the terrible situation at the front and the catastrophe it would involve us in. That was the first I had heard of the disastrous battle of Vittorio Veneto, which had started in the south. The Archduke had come straight from the Tyrol front where, despite the opposition of the Chief of Staff, General Willerding, he had issued a manifesto guaranteeing transport home for the Hungarian soldiers. 'I have told the King that we cannot leave the Hungarian boys at the front, but must make arrangements for their transport home,' the Archduke said. All efforts to persuade the mutinous divisions to obey orders had proved futile. Obviously, King Charles and his advisers had completely lost their heads. Now that I was speaking with the Archduke alone and listening to his plans, I felt instinctively that while the King was rushing headlong to destruction, the Archduke was striving to save what he could for himself.

It was evident that the King had dropped me. I learnt later that, among others, Baron Arz, the Chief of Staff, had described my appointment as disastrous. Someone had hit on the idea of settling the crisis by investing the Archduke with the dignity of Hungarian Palatine (Viceroy).

Towards evening our train came into the West Station at Budapest. The whole town already knew that I had been pushed aside and only taken to Vienna so as to be unable to attend the mass meeting. The news had spread that the King had appointed Archduke Joseph as Dictator, and an enormous crowd filled the station and the large square in front of it. Before the train had drawn into the station, I heard the ominous rumbling of the crowd; some stood closely packed, others sat on the carriage roofs or blocked the gangways, and all shouted passionately against the Archduke: 'Dictator Archduke' — 'We want no Dictator' — 'Down with the Dictator'. It was only by escaping through a back stairway, with the aid of the railway officials, that he was able to avoid being manhandled by the crowd. The ovation I received was fantastic. The cry: 'Since you have not been appointed the King's Premier, we shall make you the People's Premier' was on all lips. The crush in the station prevented me from moving in either direction. My wife, who had come to meet me with Antony Sigray, could not get anywhere near. To avoid recognition, they hired a one-horse cab. Soon it was filled with people standing on the steps and on the driver's seat, yelling: 'The King has misled Karolyi. They played a dirty trick on him. We want Karolyi.' The crowd was completely hysterical. To escape the throng, I climbed over a railing between the station and the square. Seeing a carriage, I jumped into it. In a second the horses were unharnessed and the people seized the shafts. As our progress was slow and I was in a hurry to reach the club, I threw myself into a passing car, begging the driver to get off as fast as possible. The people followed, cheering and yelling. The three small rooms of our political club were filled with people, mostly unknown to me. I scarcely had time to tell my followers of what had happened in Vienna before the crowd, having reached the Gizella Square, now Vorosmarty Square, started to sing the national anthem. The members rushed to the windows and delivered speeches. 'The gentlemen in Vienna no doubt imagine they are playing a game of cards in their club, and do not realize that the stake is a king's crown,' said one of the orators. These words produced an indescribable effect. Loudest in his enthusiasm was Stephen Friedrich, later Prime Minister of the Reaction and White Terror, who called for 'Action, action, action'.

Next morning an official communiqué was issued stating that Andrassy had sent, in the name of the Monarchy, an offer of a separate peace to President Wilson and the Entente. Andrassy's note, in which he accepted the independence of Slovakia, was at the same time an answer in principle to Secretary Lansing's note of October 18th[12] in which Lansing had refused in the strongest terms to consider the peace offer sent by the Austro-Hungarian Foreign Minister on October 4th. Thus it was Andrassy's fate to administer the death-blow to the German Alliance created by his father and to be the first to give up the territorial integrity of Hungary.

The offer of a separate peace by Andrassy demonstrated the hope-lessness of our position. In Austria, where the National groups had already declared their independence and the National Councils had taken over, Andrassy's action aroused passionate indignation. The Czechs declared that Andrassy had no right to speak in their name. The Yugoslavs did the same. These groups had for long been in touch with the Entente and were now endeavouring to legalize their position. They were appointing their own representatives for the Peace Conference. The German-Austrian National Council dispatched a special note to President Wilson, drawn up by the three Presidents of the Council.

Those who wanted to shift all the responsibility for the Treaty of Trianon on to our shoulders invented the fable that if the National Council had not been formed Andrassy could have obtained much more favourable peace conditions, as he had received assurances from Lord Lansdowne and M. Pichon. Those who talked this nonsense had forgotten that Lord Lansdowne was no longer in the Cabinet, that he had been a minister of a sovereign who had died ten years before and that he no longer had any influence. Andrassy's 'reliable' informer was Prince Windischgraetz, who gave him the impression that there was still hope of an acceptable peace. Andrassy was under the delusion that the British Conservatives would prevent the ultimate fall of the Habsburgs.[13]

Czech and Yugoslav statesmen admitted later that there was indeed a time when the Entente was more favourable towards the Monarchy. But at the moment when Andrassy took over they were united in their determination to break up the Dual Monarchy and to give full support to the Czechs and the South Slavs. If the Entente had really sympathized with Andrassy's plan, they would have answered his note. They must have been aware that the Monarchy was heading towards Revolution and they did nothing to prevent it.

12

THE LAST DAYS OF THE HABSBURGS

THE delays and hesitations convinced the people that the King and his advisers opposed the Hungarian National Council. In Austria the National Councils had been recognized; should Hungary alone remain under the dominance of the most retrograde ruling class of Europe? Every evening large crowds demonstrated in front of the Astoria Hotel where we had our headquarters. In the rain and sleet of those autumn days they would stand for hours, even in the night, waiting.

The country was virtually without a Government. The Wekerle Cabinet had resigned, but as there was no other to take its place, it was carrying on without authority. The mechanism of the State had ceased to function. To maintain order and avoid anarchy was a difficult task. Almost every hour, fresh battalions of soldiers who had refused further obedience marched up to the Astoria Hotel to join us. It was from the National Council that orders were expected. All applications came to the Astoria. The soldiers were leaving the barracks, dispersing in all directions; officers came to swear allegiance to the National Council; the workers had armed themselves and the majority of the middle classes had joined us.

Meanwhile, Archduke Joseph was negotiating with the parliamentary parties on behalf of the King. Count Hadik, ruffled and unwilling, was again entrusted with forming the Government. Aware that he could not be successful without the support of the National Council, he was anxious to secure it.

Still hoping to arrive at a peaceful solution and to avoid bloodshed, I started negotiations with the Archduke and Hadik, for the latter was reasonable and shrewd. We were on the point of arriving at a compromise, at the twelfth hour, when an unexpected event destroyed our hopes.

While I was negotiating with the Archduke Joseph in his Palace of

Buda, one of our uncontrollable demagogues — Stephen Friedrich — urged the excited crowd to storm the Archduke's palace in order to force my nomination. Singing the Kossuth Hymn, the procession, led by members of the Parliament, tried to cross the suspension bridge leading to the Var. At the bridge they were held back by a mighty police barrage; but assisted by a detachment of Guards who happened to be passing, they opened a way. From the rear the police fired into the crowd, and the mounted police drove them back at the point of their swords. Dead and wounded littered the pavement. The Revolution had acquired its first victims.

This made negotiations impossible. Indignant, the Council resolved to have no dealings with the authorities. A strike was proclaimed. The next day a representative of the police department called on me, expressing their solidarity with the National Council. One after the other, the postal staff, the railway men, various military bodies, officers, merchants, manufacturers, joined in with us.

Vienna retaliated by appointing the hated General Lukasics to the post of commander of the Budapest town guard. He also was powerless, as the soldiers no longer obeyed his orders. It was rumoured that Lukasics intended to use the Bosnian and foreign troops stationed in Budapest against us.

On the evening of the 28th, the commander of the monitors anchored on the Danube presented us with a telegram received from the naval department at Pola, requesting the National Council to assist them to put down the mutiny which had broken out in the fleet, and which they were unable to suppress. The sailors would only take orders from the Council. This same cry for help was sent to all the National Councils in the Monarchy, to prevent the breaking up of the fleet.

We were ready to send an emissary to negotiate personally with the sailors, should the Prime Minister request us to do so. Wekerle refused. At last, to prevent disaster, we sent two envoys to Pola. They arrived on October 31st and were received with the news that Vice-Admiral Horthy, commander-in-chief of the Austro-Hungarian Navy, had transferred the entire fleet to the Agram National Council — in other words to the South Slavs — by a protocol drawn up on the 31st in which he made mention of 'the people of the FORMERLY EXISTING Austro-Hungarian Monarchy'. It was therefore Horthy, who first declared the non-existence of the Monarchy just as, four years later, by a decree in Parliament, he declared non-existent the rights of the Habsburgs to the throne of Hungary. The handing of the fleet to the South Slavs was the only notable deed of the Admiral who, until then, was only known for his cruel suppression, in the navy, of the use of the Magyar language.

The Croat National Council now proclaimed the independence of Croatia.

After the bloody incident of the suspension bridge and the breaking off of the negotiations with Hadik, I made a last effort to avoid revolution. I sent my wife to Andrassy in Vienna to request him to use his influence with the King, in view of the alarming situation which I was no more able to control. It was my last card. She arrived in Vienna on the 30th and entered the Ballhausplatz at the very moment when the King was asking Andrassy on the telephone whether he should follow Horthy's advice and surrender the imperial navy. Katus heard her stepfather say: 'Hand it over?' and then, in a tone of utter resignation: 'Yes, there is, I suppose, nothing else to do.' Some minutes later, while having breakfast, Andrassy was brought a wire from the Supreme Command on the Italian front, informing him of the final disaster on the Piave and urging an immediate armistice.

Katus made use of all her persuasive capacities and gave her stepfather an accurate account of what was happening in Budapest. Although he took a very serious view of the situation, his contempt for the masses was so deeply ingrained that he could not admit that there were moments in history when their wishes had to be taken into account. The mob was, for this hundred-per-cent aristocrat, a *quantité négligeable*. Public opinion did not exist for him. He deluded himself that everything could be peacefully arranged and the tide of revolution checked if only Hadik would take over and show the necessary energy. On the 29th the people of Vienna had demonstrated against him in front of the Ballhausplatz, and it was said that Prussian officers wanted to kidnap him and carry him off to Berlin. All this did not worry him in the least. He was determined that the armistice should be negotiated by a united Monarchy; and the fact that there was no more Monarchy, and that he himself was representing no one — even the Austrian-Germans had demonstrated against him — made no difference. 'The people have lost their heads completely. That madman Masaryk has even set up a republic,' he said to Katus. 'Michael is capable of the same folly.' Her argument that the only way to avoid a republic would be to give me assistance now, before revolution broke out, fell on deaf ears. His message to me was to appease the 'lunatics and hysterical Jews and to wait for Wilson's answer, after which a Karolyi Government could take over, IN THREE WEEKS' TIME'.

At 5.30 a.m. on the morning of the 30th I was awakened by an unknown officer who declared himself to be the President of the Soldiers' Council, an association recently formed and having nothing to do with the National Council. He informed me that they would seize all the public buildings, occupy the town and demand my appointment. The sailors of the 'men-of-war' were ready to fire on the Archducal palace. I had the greatest difficulty in dissuading him from this project. We were not yet prepared to take over under revolutionary conditions.

Late in the afternoon of the same day we got the news that the garrisons had been seized by the Soldiers' Council. We were appalled. Events were moving independently of us. By the evening the Revolution had gained momentum. One after the other, the garrison posts, the public buildings, the barracks, the General Post Office were occupied without the slightest resistance.

The mutinous soldiers, after occupying the garrison headquarters, brought the commander, General Varkonyi, prisoner to the Astoria. The General stood stiffly saluting before me and with a theatrical gesture unbuckled his sword, with the intention of handing it over to me. I told him there was no such necessity. Suddenly, there came a bang, followed by several others. The General's face lit up and, turning to his aide-de-camp, who had been arrested with him, he said: 'The troops are on their way to set us free. There is no deceiving my practised ear. I can tell machine-gun fire from a long way off.' The bangs proved to be the slamming of doors — the General seemed not to have heard much gun-fire during the five years of war!

If the rumour was correct that the army could not be relied on to shoot at the people, we had won the battle; if not, we were lost and would most probably be courtmartialled next morning. The deserting soldiers had taken the initiative and we were now forced to follow. We had not sufficient armed forces at our disposal to resist Lukasics's regular troops. We could not call on the workers until the following morning as they had by now left their factories and workshops.

Few members of the Council were aware of the critical situation. Most of them had returned home and only a small bunch of us remained, waiting for the incalculable morrow. About 1 a.m. I returned to the Egyetem utca with some sailors to mount guard over my children and my wife, who had just returned from Vienna. A machine gun was placed in one of the windows of the ball-room. I asked the officer in charge if the fleet on the Danube was reliable? The sailor clicked his heels and, saluting martially, said: 'Yes, sir. Sailors are in all circumstances on the side of rebellion.'

Two hours later, a pale and breathless messenger brought the alarming news that the telephone exchange had tapped a conversation between Lukasics and the King, in which the General asked for permission to attack the Astoria with his troops. Immediately I rang up the Archduke, requesting him to prevent Lukasics from carrying out his intention and reminded him that all over the Monarchy the independent National States had been formed without bloodshed. He promised to talk to Lukasics without delay and to let me know the result.

I hurried back to the Astoria with Katus, who refused to stay at home. Approaching the Astoria, we were met with a volley of rifle fire. The nearer we came, the more violent grew the firing and we were convinced that the dreaded attack had started. The darkness and the dense fog made it impossible to see what was actually going on. A mass of people in panic, yelling and cursing, were pushing at the revolving door of the Astoria which, getting jammed, let none in. Eventually we discovered that a battalion of soldiers, ordered to leave for the front, had turned back at the station and marched to the Astoria, shooting off their guns in an ecstasy of joy. Upstairs the remaining members of the Council sat dejected and weary, resolved to hold out to the last. Professor Jaszi, Louis Hatvany and Keri declared the battle lost. It was raining incessantly; the small garrison gradually dwindled, more and more of the men stealing home. We sat silently, waiting for the dawn of October 31st. Suddenly the telephone rang. The Prime Minister was ready to see me. We all breathed again. It was 7 a.m. when Hadik met me in the Prime Minister's office. Clad in pyjamas and slippers, his huge frame seemed to have wilted. He accompanied us just as he was, without a word, to the Archduke's house close by, where Apponyi was waiting immaculately dressed as usual, fresh and rosy.

Hadik began by saying that he wished to tender his resignation. The Archduke accepted it in the name of the King and, turning to me, appointed me Prime Minister, also in the name of the King. There was nothing more said; there were no negotiations, it was complete and unconditional surrender. I assured the Archduke that the Government would be formed without fail during the day. Kunfi vouched that, with the help of the organized workers, order would be maintained. The proceedings — a complete capitulation — had lasted scarcely half an hour.

PART THREE

WHAT PRICE VICTORY?

J'ai vu l'ambition et la fraude prendre le masque de l'adhésion.
GEORGE SAND

THE FIRST WEEK OF THE REVOLUTION

IT was early in the morning of October 31st, when I went down the steps of the Buda Palace Gardens into the city. The rain had stopped, the mist had vanished and the sun was dazzling bright. This walk is among my most vivid memories of those anxious days. Across the shining sea of houses at my feet I caught sight of mine, in the centre of Pest. Today, as in 1848, the heart of the Revolution was beating there. I felt that I belonged intrinsically, that I was one with this so heavily tried city.

Beaming faces greeted me. Lorries, laden with singing, cheering, yelling soldiers and covered with white chrysanthemums, thundered past — rashly driven vehicles are one of the symptoms of revolution. Many lives had been saved from useless sacrifice and young men were no more to be crippled for a lost cause. I felt happy to have contributed to bringing this about. More soldiers were coming towards me; they were emaciated and their uniforms hung loosely about their limbs. They seemed like walking corpses. What would become of them in our defeated country? The only way to save them was to give them land, to satisfy their century-old craving. I felt elated that it was in my power now to give them a country worth having, a country they would feel to be their own.

In the city there was exultant rejoicing at the news of my appointment, for it meant peace. The people were dancing for joy, strangers falling into one another's arms, shedding tears of happiness. White chrysanthemums were distributed and pinned on chests. In their excitement the people had forgotten that they had lost the war. They felt victorious, for they had won the Revolution.

About 9 a.m. I reached the City Hall and resigned the presidency of the National Council. John Hock, the Catholic priest and orator, was elected in my place. Now the pressure of the huge crowd around the City Hall was such as to endanger life, and those who only yesterday condemned now hurried to be the first to congratulate us. The parliamentary parties crowded, unbidden, into the waiting-rooms to swear allegiance.

Our Government was rapidly formed. A Liberal, Socialist and Peasant Coalition, with Batthyanyi and Lovászy representing the Liberals, Garami and Kunfi the Social Democrats, Nagyatadi and Stephen Szabo the peasantry, and Professor Jaszi the Radicals. The latter became Minister for the National Minorities.

At midday I returned home after twenty-four hours on my feet. My wife had been woken in the morning by a cheering crowd gathered in front of our house; when she had stepped on to the balcony she was received with cheers for 'the wife of the President of the Republic'. This was a great surprise to her. No one had, until then, mentioned the republic.

During luncheon, Paul Teleki, later Prime Minister, arrived and congratulated me most cordially. I at once offered him the presidency of the Dependants' Relief Office, which he had held under the preceding Government, and he accepted it very readily.

Count Tisza sent a message that he and his party regarded it as a patriotic duty to rally to the National Council and to support its work. We replied that, owing to the present state of public opinion, it seemed undesirable that he should take over any public office; that the wisest course for him, at the moment, was to retire to the country, and that later it might be possible to consider re-opening negotiations with the politicians of the past and with the classes they represented.[1]

Popular hatred concentrated especially on Tisza, Windischgraetz, General Szurmay and General Lukasics, and, hearing of threats to their persons, I took steps to see that they had police protection. News from Vienna described Andrassy as in danger from the blazing fury which surrounded him, and I took steps for his safety as well.

In the afternoon of the same day I received the news that General Lukasics had been captured by soldiers and brought to the former headquarters of the National Council. When the crowd outside heard this, they demanded wildly that the merciless General who, in the past weeks, had had many deserters executed should be handed over to them. The leaders at the Astoria had kept their heads; they were doing their best to calm the crowd, but could not make themselves heard and sent for me urgently. When I saw the danger of the situation, I went on to the balcony and addressed the population gathered in the square. A roar of enthusiastic applause greeted me and the General was luckily forgotten. While I spoke, I had Lukasics exchange his uniform for civilian clothing; two of my friends took him into the street through a back exit and subsequently to one of their homes, where he lay in hiding for days.

I now went, accompanied by the Members of the Government, to the palace, to take the oath before Archduke Joseph. In the entrance hall we were told that Count Tisza had been murdered in his villa of the Varosliget.[2] This news came five minutes before the swearing-in ceremony and so terrified our future Minister of Justice that, taking to his heels, he vanished and was seen no more. The cowardly murder of Tisza was the first and only stain on the escutcheon of the October Revolution.

I spent the night of October 31st on a camp-bed in one of the offices in the Prime Minister's palace. Hadik, Prime Minister of a day, had fled.

The telephone rang incessantly; from all parts of the country reports came and instructions were demanded. It was clear that the Revolution had not been confined to Budapest alone, but had extended throughout Hungary. The news of the disaster on the Italian front had spread with lightning rapidity. The Emperor's famous proclamation to the army, permitting the soldiers to leave, broke up the unity of the joint army. On the Piave, one regiment after another surrendered. The victory of Vittorio Veneto was an easy one; there were no foes to fight, only voluntary prisoners made. In spite of this the Italians consider it, even today, as one of their major victories.

Peace and the end of a senseless massacre were the aims of our revolution. The end had to come, whatever the cost, and even at the price of violence. Every revolution is an end and a beginning; but in ours, led by men most of whom were not revolutionaries but had been forced into it by circumstances, the end alone was of importance; the beginning of a new era irrelevant. They believed that the conclusion of hostilities would in itself solve all problems. This was a grave error and much trouble was still in store for us.

Aware that the majority of the country had granted its help to us on the basis of our peace programme, and counting on the support of the historical classes of Hungary, we dared not adopt revolutionary tactics.

Our manifesto was strictly constitutional, and had not even the courage to mention what the peasantry was expecting to hear — that the land was to be theirs. It declared instead: 'We have won the battle, we have obtained everything we desired, we have no reason to continue the fight. We are preparing a law on universal suffrage.'

This attitude was typical of a bourgeois uprising which, as soon as power has changed hands, endeavours to stop the revolution before it has even started on its programme, and to restore the 'old-time' order.

The October Revolution was based on the alliance between the Karolyi Party and the Social Democrats. It was a half-hearted alliance, filled with suspicion, for it was only myself and a few of my followers who were seriously concerned to maintain it. As soon as this became clear — as soon as the hopes set on me and my party were dashed — the only possibility for the masses was a Socialist programme, with new values and a new *leit-motif*. Moreover, the organized workers —the Trade Unions — were the only force that could keep order and help to start production. They were disciplined and obeyed their leaders' instructions.

Parallel with war-weariness was anger at those who were responsible for the war, and it was feared that the returning soldiers, 'the great unknown', would take their revenge.

In the first week panic gave rise to rumours that Russian armies were advancing on the city, that the inmates of lunatic asylums had been let loose, that criminals from the prisons were devastating the countryside. None of this was true, but the truth was that the starving and ragged remnants of the defeated armies were streaming home.

Soldiers in the street were tearing the insignia from the uniforms of unresisting officers. We feared that 'Jacqueries' would break out and that we might lose control. We needed a reliable force to run the State machine smoothly. The coal-mines in the north and south were being seized by the enemy. No arrangements had been made for the return of the soldiers, or for demobilization. They would face the winter barefoot and in rags. The factories had to start production of shoes and clothes; coal was the country's most urgent need, and this required the collaboration of the workers.

The Social Democrats held the trumps. The Nationalist Karolyi Party was unwillingly forced to realize that success depended on their support. They could stop the 'Jacqueries', save the landlords, the factory owners, the bank directors. Paradoxically it was the Social Democrats who were the only safeguard of private property.

I have often wondered if it would not have been wiser to refrain from keeping down the passions of discontent during the first weeks and let them loose, as victorious generals allow their armies to run wild for a couple of days. The peasants would then have taken possession of the long-coveted land as they did in 1944, and would thus have been firmly linked to our new order. This would have avoided the regime of Bela Kun as well as the Counter-Revolution. We chose instead the road of legality and order, discarding that of social justice. Five months later the disillusioned masses were driven into the hands of the Communists.

During the first weeks we were besieged by our erstwhile opponents, begging permission to take the oath of fidelity; in the ante-chambers of the National Council in the Town Hall there was a continuous flow of dignitaries, all impatient to swear allegiance, elbowing each other out of the way in their eagerness.

What made the bishops, bank directors, presidents of commercial and agricultural societies, counts and princes, so anxious to render homage to our much-loathed new order? The answer lies in that one word: FEAR. And we, animated by the pacifist spirit which came to us from the army, were filled with forgiveness for our foes of yesterday and of the morrow. We were bitterly to regret this generous attitude.

2

ABSOLUTION BY TELEPHONE

PRESIDENT WILSON had declared that, in order to start negotiations with us, the Entente insisted on democratic regimes inside the Monarchy. Thus the people got the impression that the existence of the Dual Monarchy prevented us from receiving milder treatment at the hands of the Entente. Lansing's note made it clear to the man in the street that the Entente refused to negotiate with the Hohenzollerns and the Habsburgs. This resulted in the proclamation of the German and Austrian republics, and in the formation of the Succession States surrounding us, and made it impossible for us to remain the only State in the Monarchy to postpone its declaration, although none of us had been republicans.

The Government which I headed had sworn allegiance to the King and, in spite of my revolutionary attitude, I would not break my oath. Affected by the feverish atmosphere of the National Councils, the Government decided to ask the King to relieve us from our oaths or to accept our resignation. The National Committees all over the country would then cast their votes as to what form of State they would choose.

The Government having taken this decision, we called on Archduke Joseph. In his palace on the Var nothing was left of Habsburg etiquette. The Archduke actually rushed down the stairs to meet me and took me into his office. His attitude on hearing the Government's decision was a strange one. His first reaction was to ask if all this was not already too late. He knew what at the time I did not — the extent of the imperial armies' defeat at Vittorio Veneto and the result of the plebiscite the King had ordered to be taken amongst the soldiers on the form of State they wanted. The result had been an overwhelming majority in favour of a republic.

The Archduke then said that the resignation of our Government at this time would be a catastrophe. He said that he was willing to advise the King to free us from our oaths. At this moment the telephone bell rang . . . It was the King. Even now I can hear the weak, high-pitched voice of the Archduke: 'Majesty, you have to accept, there is no other way. If your Majesty refuses to free these gentlemen from their oaths, I cannot take any responsibility for the consequence.' After some moments' silence the Archduke, covering the receiver with his hand, turned to me: 'I cannot understand the King,' he said, 'he hesitates, he does not realize the seriousness of the situation and that there is no other way.' He then replaced the receiver and asked whether, if the King consented, the Government would proclaim a republic that same day. I answered that this would depend on the nation's decision at the elections of the National Council. Seemingly perturbed, he answered: 'But won't it be too late then?' The telephone rang again. The Archduke, while listening to the King's words, nodded approvingly and then, turning to us, repeated loudly and clearly the words of the King: 'So your Majesty gives me full power to release Count Karolyi and his Government from the oath they swore to me, as your representative, yesterday.' Then he replaced the receiver. Later he had the absolving document typed and handed over. It was November 1st, 1918. These are the details of this famous telephone conversation with the last of the Habsburg Emperors about which so many lies have been spread.

After my colleagues left I joined the Archduke Joseph in his private sitting-room, where he unburdened his heart to me: 'At last,' he exclaimed, shaking my hand fervently, 'I have succeeded in convincing his Majesty. He will be cross with me, I know, but he has been cross with me for a long time now.'

With the paper in my hand, releasing us from our allegiance to the monarch and signed by the Archduke, we hurried to the National Council where it was unanimously decided that all the National Councils in the provinces must be consulted as to their attitude regarding the future form of the State.

Some days later the Archduke, after taking the oath to the National Council, asked me if it would not be wiser for him to change the name of Habsburg to that of Alcsuti — his property in Hungary was Alcsut. I advised him against it. 'I think,' I said, 'your Highness has a pretty well-sounding name and, if I were you, I would keep it.'

3

THE BELGRADE ARMISTICE

For the sins of your sire, albeit you had no hand in them, you must suffer.

HORACE

FOLLOWING the defeat on the Italian front and the withdrawal of the remaining Hungarian regiments, the Austro-Hungarian chief of staff signed an armistice in Padua on November 3rd with the Italian General Diaz, commander of the Western armies. Owing to the chaotic conditions of those days, Army Headquarters accepted the armistice in our name. We, on principle, opposed the General Staff acting for us, and were all ready and packed to go to Padua ourselves. For technical reasons we could not be there in time, so the signing was done without us. Thus the Armistice of Padua was valid for us as well.

The very day after the armistice had been signed with Diaz in Padua, we received the alarming news that Serbian troops had passed the river Save and that others were following. We had previously received a report that General Franchet d'Esperey, commander of the Eastern armies, demanded the surrender of the Hungarian troops stationed on the borders of the Save and the Danube and the handing over of their entire war material. This made it obvious that the armistice with General Diaz did not include the Eastern Army; and our first concern, therefore, was to get into touch with Franchet d'Esperey, thus ensuring that the forty-seven divisions under his command, which were forcing their way towards Budapest, should be stopped. The General, having defeated Bulgaria, was now planning to attack Berlin through Hungary, instead of going south-east against Constantinople, as originally planned at Versailles. As those armies had at all costs to be prevented from crossing the frontier and penetrating into our country, we decided to send a deputation to General Franchet d'Esperey in Belgrade without delay. Owing to the danger of the situation I headed this deputation myself.[3]

From Szabadka, a town in the south of Hungary, our train moved slowly towards Serbia. Reaching Novisad, we boarded a ship for Belgrade. In my cabin Oskar Jaszi and I prepared the text of the declaration which we were going to present to the commander of the Southern Armies.

We had no illusions; we were the 'citizens of Calais', to be sacrificed for the errors of our predecessors. As we had disapproved of the official policy of the past, the country we represented was confident that we should receive better conditions than the rulers of yesterday. We were less optimistic. Some weeks previously it would have been a different matter, but now it was too late. Hungary was indulging in the wish-dream that, although Germany's ally, she bore no responsibility.

I therefore feared that disillusion would follow; yet I believed that if there was one chance in a hundred of being treated less severely, and of reaching some degree of understanding with our neighbours, it could only be through us. So I felt it a duty to jeopardize my popularity by taking the lead in those desperate days.

It was a sunny November day and we sat, without overcoats, on the deck of the steamer which carried us between the flat banks of the broad Danube towards Belgrade. Dusk was descending over the roofs of the Kalimegdan whilst from the deck we contemplated the outlines of the town which, five years ago, our troops had so mercilessly bombarded. Through our field glasses we saw the ruined streets and the throng of people streaming down to the river. I apprehended that they would receive us with a volley of stones. We hoisted the white flag — a large tablecloth. I saw a crowd standing on the quay and to our surprise we heard shouts of 'Zhivoi'. We were deeply moved by this outburst of generous feeling from a people whom we had treated so badly. This long-suffering city, destroyed by the retiring German armies, deprived of electricity and water and filled with the horrible memories of a cruel occupation, was ready to show its sympathy for us because we brought peace, and because they realized that it was not we who were responsible for the aggression against them.

Ever since then, I have known the Serbs as a generous people, willing at all times to forget the evil done to them. Since that evening at the foot of the Kalimegdan, where I met the Serbs for the first time, my sympathy for them has never waned. In later years, when I lived among them, I came to know them as a peace-loving, humane, brave and proud people, who would rather die than accept slavery. This was proved again in the Second World War and until this very day.

Colonel Milevics informed us that we could choose whether to spend the night on the ship, or in an hotel in town. I decided for the latter.

We approached the Serbs with the knowledge of our guilt towards them, and the declaration we handed over to Franchet d'Esperey bore witness to this. Soon after our arrival at the Hôtel Serbski Kralj, we were informed that the French general would receive our delegation on the following day, November 7th, at 7 p.m. at his private residence.

Through the unlit streets of Belgrade we walked to the General's quarters at 5 Theatre Street, a small building in colonial style, belonging to a Serb professor, which had during the occupation been requisitioned by the Austrian General Staff; later it became the home of the French Ambassador. The small and chilly sitting-room was heated by a log fire and lit by petrol lamps in majolica vases. There we stood and waited for Franchet d'Esperey's arrival. His entrance was that of a victorious general on the stage; I felt that he had rehearsed it beforehand. He wore a light blue uniform and top-boots and had a row of decorations on his chest. He was a bulky, middle-sized man, with broad shoulders, sparkling dark eyes and small turned-up moustache. He came straight up to us with a sprightly, martial walk. Three officers, of whom one was Colonel Azan who later wrote the history of the Armistice, stood at his side. After being presented to the General, I introduced the members of the delegation. At each name he nodded curtly; but when Baron Hatvany's name was mentioned he looked displeased, not even trying to hide his anti-semitism. When the President of the Soldiers' Council was introduced, he exclaimed in horror: '*Vous êtes tombés si bas?*' When I asked if I could read him the text of our manifesto, he took a Napoleonic pose and, leaning with his elbow on the mantelpiece, his hand in the opening of his coat, his legs crossed, he followed each word I read with a vivacious mimicry.

Before starting, I asked the General if it was he or General Diaz who was entitled to sign the Armistice, and received the categoric reply that he had the authority to do so.

Our memorandum pointed out that the past war was the responsibility of the old feudal Monarchy, ally of Prussian militarism, and that Kossuth's Hungary was forced into silence during the conflict. However, we now appeared before him as the representatives of the true will of the Hungarian people. At this, the General interrupted me with a shrill *'Pas Hongrois, Magyar!'* We had, I continued, offered unconditional surrender on November 1st, but the joint army headquarters had cut the telephone lines. As we could not get into direct touch with General Diaz, we had come to him, as representatives of independent Hungary, to open negotiations. We were not responsible for the acts of our past political leaders. We wanted to achieve democracy, give the right to vote to all citizens and the land to those who work it. (*'Que la terre revienne au peuple qui la cultive'*). To our surprise, the General nodded his head in emphatic approval but, when I mentioned Wilson and his democratic pacifist principles, the General waved his hand contemptuously. We requested that, if the country were occupied by foreign troops, they should be French, Italian or American — with the exception of colonial regiments — and not Serbs, Czechs or Rumanians, and asked him to use his influence with the Czechs and Poles not to hinder the delivery of the vitally necessary coal sent to us from Germany; also to re-establish diplomatic relations between us and the Entente and to give our Government his moral support, so as to enable it to cope with its difficult task.

To most of these requests he shook his head negatively. When, owing to the deficient light of the oil lamps, I had some difficulty in reading the text, he reminded us harshly that it was our allies who had destroyed the electricity in the town.

Franchet d'Esperey gave his answer from a short note which he held in his hand. He first asked if the Socialists' representative, Bokanyi, understood French; this, he said was very important, for it was the fate of the poor men whom Bokanyi represented which was at stake, adding ironically that the rich, if they were discontented, could emigrate to Switzerland.

The General now stood straight in front of the fireplace; when he was not looking at his notes, he stared fiercely into our eyes. He emphasized that in the days of Tokoli, Rakoczy and Kossuth, Hungary was respected by the French, for then she was fighting for her independence from Germany. But since 1867 she had become the accomplice of Germany and of her lust for power. 'You marched with them, you will be punished with them. Hungary will pay, it won't harm the rich,' he repeated, 'who can always get off, but the poor ... You suppressed the national minorities and made enemies of them. I hold them in the palm of my hand, the Czechs, Rumanians, Yugoslavs and Slovaks. A word from me and they annihilate you. *Je n'ai qu'un signe à faire, je les lâche et vous êtes détruits.* You offended France and we will not forget how your press insulted us.'

Oskar Jaszi could not refrain from interrupting in his nervous and indignant manner: 'Not all the press, only the chauvinist press.' The General replied impatiently: 'Enough, enough,' but his tone changed after this. His voice dropped, but what he announced was grim: 'You came too late. Your declaration of neutrality might have been of use to you two weeks ago, but not now when I am in Belgrade. My sole reason for having received you is that Count Michael Karolyi is at the head of the delegation. We got to know him during the war as an honest man. In these critical times he is the only one who can help you, *C'est le seul homme qui peut atténuer votre sort. Ralliez-vous autour de lui. Il est votre seul espoir.*'

I felt acutely the drama of the situation. It was too late, I knew it, but had hoped against all reason that I could still save something.

Jaszi and I followed the General into his private study. There he handed us the Armistice terms drawn up in Versailles, the same terms that, four days later, were dictated to the Germans in the forest of Compiègne.

These conditions were grim. The Germans were still carrying on the fight; and it seemed that Franchet d'Esperey intended to march on Berlin, for he demanded the occupation of all strategic points, as well as the seizure of all means of communication.

Clause 17 was of major importance, as it secured Hungarian administration over the whole of Hungary, even the occupied territories, until the peace treaty, with our police forces maintaining order.[4] This emphasized the purely military character of the Armistice. But it was added that in the event of disorder the Entente had the right to take the areas of disturbance under their own administration. This was a double-edged stipulation, for if the Little Entente wished to take over certain parts of Hungary it would only be necessary to encourage the 'national minorities' to create disturbances. We therefore asked to

have this clause altered. We pointed out to the General that disturbances might break out if the Germans and Czechs cut off our coal
supply. The General looked incredulous and asked seriously: 'But
what did you use for heat two hundred years ago?' Jaszi answered that
in those days, there were no trains and no factories in the country, so
that wood was sufficient. 'What industry does Hungary possess?' asked
the General. Jaszi mentioned, among others, the milling industry.
'Why don't you grind your wheat with windmills?' the General
suggested.

The southern demarcation line to which the French troops would
move, was then drawn up.[5]

At last, after much argument, the General assured us that he would
pass on to Paris our request to have the Germans continue to supply
Hungary with coal.

We decided that, before signing the Armistice, we would send a wire
to the High Command in Versailles.[6] When we handed our telegram
to Franchet d'Esperey he would not hear of its transmission, and a
heated argument followed. We told him that if the Entente showed so
little understanding of the new Hungary — their friends who had
demonstrated their loyalty on several occasions during the war — we
were ready to resign. At last the General agreed to send the telegram
and also to have Clause 17 omitted from the text of the Armistice.
The Czech and the Serb press attacked us on the ground that by
barring Clause 17 we got round Franchet d'Esperey and made him
give Hungary the 'right to retain the administration of the whole
country'. The *Narodni Listy* wrote that the Hungarians got the better
of the General, who was not acquainted with the wiles of Hungarian
diplomacy, of which Michael Karolyi was a typical representative.

In London, the great friend of the Slavs Seton-Watson and his
circle felt the same way and I heard later in England that Masaryk and
Benes were indignant with the General as he had, they said, contravened arrangements previously made with them.

On November 8th we returned to Budapest to inform the National
Council of the terms of the Armistice, and to receive their authoriza-
tion to sign. Since the Karolyi Government had come into office, the
representatives of the 'historic' classes had joined the National Council
en bloc and therefore shared responsibility for the Armistice.

The press had published the negotiations in detail. We, who had fought for the liberty of the press, had to be consistent — a fact which we later had bitter reason to regret.

The optimistic public, which had tried to delude itself, now had to face reality. It was a hard test, for those who had yesterday expected wonders from Tisza, and now expected wonders from Karolyi, were bitterly disillusioned. Was this the way the Entente treated their friends? The pro-Germans, hovering in the background, took advantage of the situation, whispering that a treaty similar to Brest-Litovsk would be our lot. If General Franchet d'Esperey was right that the only hope of the country lay with Karolyi, why was he so shamefully handled? Why did the dictators of Versailles not back him up, so as to encourage the nation to rally round him? And if the Wilsonian principles were only catch-words, would not anarchy or Bolshevism be the result? These were the feelings expressed by the free press.

The answer to our telegram to Clemenceau arrived addressed to General Franchet d'Esperey, commander of the Allied South Armies and ran as follows: 'I request you to discuss with Count Karolyi solely military questions, excluding all others. This is my final instruction.' This answer seemed to us satisfactory as it meant that the decisions were not final, being simply military arrangements, and not political. I expounded the situation to the Council with complete frankness, but informing them that refusal would mean the start of fresh hostilities ... the outcome of which was obvious. Also, that the Serbian Army had occupied Ujvidek (Novisad) and was moving towards the centre of Hungary. The Czechs, likewise, were ready to seize the northern districts of the country, to which they considered themselves entitled. It was therefore in our interest to accept the Armistice, for if our neighbours did not keep to it the blame for its infringement would fall on them.

The Council gave its consent, although it felt the terms to be a cruel blow. Yet they were much more favourable than the treaty accepted by Regent Horthy a year later, and this should have silenced our critics once and for all. How well Hungary would have fared if the Treaty of Trianon had accepted our line of demarcation as its frontiers!

Later the Hungarian Counter-Revolution brought against us the dishonest charge that the terms of the Armistice signed with Diaz at Padua had been more favourable, as it guaranteed the frontiers. But if this had been the case, it had already been accepted by us; in fact, it could not and did not influence the final terms of the Peace Treaty.

The truth was that only Franchet d'Esperey had authority to deal with Hungary, although the Monarchy as a whole had signed the Padua Armistice. This was asserted by the representatives of the Entente. Had we not signed, foreign troops would have marched on Budapest. The Belgrade Armistice was a military and not a political one, and the occupied territories should have remained under Hungarian legislation. The legend of the wrong armistice being signed was propaganda invented by our opponents and taken up by Sir William Goode, who had most probably received his information from them. Even the Horthy judges had to drop the charge at the time of my trial, in view of the statements received from the French generals.[7]

4

ABDICATION OF THE LAST HABSBURG

Surtout pas trop de zèle. TALLEYRAND

BEFORE the signature of the Armistice, Baron Julius Wlassics, President of the Upper House, had called on me to inform me of the decision of its members to support the proclamation of a republic, saying that they would themselves request the King to abdicate. As I had asked no one to undertake such a move, it was a most surprising proposal to come from that 'loyal' and feudal institution. They called on me not to defend their sovereign, but to be instrumental in inducing him to give up his throne, abdicate voluntarily, so as to make sure that the danger of a return to the Monarchy would be eliminated.

The reason Wlassics gave for this surprising intervention was that they wished to help me in preserving order and saving the country from chaos. Like the Archduke Joseph, the aristocrats, fearing the wrath of the people, were, with few exceptions, impatient for the Republic to be declared. By assisting it, they hoped to get into its favour. They were eager to convince me that their move was completely voluntary and that my Government should be grateful for their action. In later years these same men declared that they had always remained true to their sovereign and had been forced by terrorism to act as they did.

I made it clear to Wlassics that their action was a purely private move and had nothing to do with us. As to the form of the State, Parliament would decide when it met. Until then, as the King had retired from the direction of affairs in Hungary, his abdication was not urgent and we had many more pressing matters to attend to.

After Wlassics returned from his 'noble' enterprise, he gave me an accurate account of what had happened. At the last moment the Archbishop and Prince Esterhazy had withdrawn from the party. So only

Baron Wlassics, Count Emil Szechenyi and Count Emil Dessewffy
had arrived at Eckartsau, Charles's shooting box in the forest of
Schönbrunn, on November 13th. When the Emperor heard the news
that a group of the Hungarian Upper House had arrived, he hurried in
hopeful expectation to meet them, trusting that they had come to offer
their assistance to their hard-pressed monarch. When Wlassics told
him the purpose of the visit, Charles turned very pale. The nobles
reasoned that if it was in the interests of the country not to oppose the
new order, then the King, too, must not put up resistance, but abdicate.
Charles was difficult to convince. He did his best to persuade the
members of the delegation to change their attitude. He pointed out
that he had never wronged the Hungarians, and had therefore hoped
that he could remain King of Hungary, even if he lost the Austrian
crown. It had no effect on the party; they stuck as one man to their
mission: the King had to abdicate. Charles asked if it would not be
possible to wait until after the Constituent Assembly had been called,
and suggested that perhaps Karolyi would support him. Wlassics
replied that Karolyi, with the best will on earth, could do nothing
against the wishes of the people. 'But the peasants are on my side,'
answered the King. 'Windischgraetz assured me of their loyalty and
surely, if I did not abdicate, Field-Marshal Kovess, at the head of his
troops, could help me to regain my throne?' His 'loyal' subjects assured
their sovereign that these were vain delusions, wishful thinking, that
the future was a different matter, but that his duty today was to
abdicate, if he wanted to save his subjects and not place them in a most
dangerous situation. In order to make him give way, Wlassics mentioned the possibility that a future National Assembly, with a majority
of peasants and Christian Socialists, might bring him back.

The King, broken at last, asked them to give him time to think the
matter over. The gentlemen should stay and wait for his answer.
They waited.

Suddenly there was a commotion in the palace. The King's entourage had discovered the mission of the Hungarian delegation and, as the
King had disappeared by himself, they were seized with panic. He had
been seen leaving the castle with a gun on his shoulder. Could this
weak, unfortunate and abandoned young prince be meaning to end his
life with his own hand? Anxious, they went in search of him. He was
soon found – shooting. This seemed to be the best way for him to

collect his thoughts, to make a decision, to quieten his shattered nerves. On his return he summoned his court chamberlain, Count Joseph Hunyadi. He told him that he was ready to submit to the wishes of the Hungarian Upper House, and asked him to draw up the act of resignation, on the Austrian model, in which he declared his retirement from the present Government of the State and accepted in advance the resolution of the Commons, but without abdication. Then the King, falling into Hunyadi's arms, was seized by a violent fit of sobbing.

The Hungarian Lords now drew up the wording for the abdication, but not on the Austrian model. In their zeal they wanted to go farther than the Austrians had and obtain abdication of his royal rights for good and all. But this the King refused to sign. They had the greatest difficulty in finding paper on which to draft the act; ink, too, was unavailable. At last they found a crumpled sheet on which to copy the King's version of the text. He signed, deeply moved.

On finishing his report Wlassics handed me the sheet with the satisfied air of someone who had done a good job. I now held in my hands this momentous document, the resignation of his throne by the last Habsburg — his abdication, we may call it, for there was little doubt as to what the decision of Parliament would be.[8]

This document, said Wlassics apologetically, might have been better, but *we* have every reason to be satisfied, for the royal signature actually means, he explained, that on this day Charles has ceased to be King of Hungary.

Wlassics's interpretation was upheld by the legal authorities of the Budapest Universities, whose opinion we asked. They declared unanimously that after the ending of the Pragmatic Sanction[9] the decision of the King to retire from public affairs meant, in effect, that the Hungarian nation had the right to choose its own sovereign. It could also re-elect Charles, if it so wished. Later, when the situation had altered, this same Wlassics interpreted the document in the opposite way.

The action of the Hungarian House of Lords was treachery to the aristocratic and dynastic idea, and a flagrant example of the crumbling of moral values, in a period rich in painful revelations of the sort.

Privy Councillors, Chamberlains, Knights of the Order of the Golden Fleece, had received all their honours from the Habsburgs, that most ancient of Christian dynasties. This House which, as

Schwarzenberg had stated, had surprised the world by its ingratitude, was now itself faced with ingratitude. For classes are not grateful; self-interest is their law, and the nobility, reared in the belief that it was their birthright to lead an existence of carefree privilege and to enjoy the best of all worlds, were ready to betray those who proved a hindrance. The King could give them nothing more; he was ballast to be thrown overboard.

Macaulay calls the French aristocracy who fell under the axe of the guillotine the bravest class in history. I refrain from arguing with him, but I know that their opposite numbers, the Hungarian aristocrats, were the most cowardly. A man shows his mettle when exceptional situations arise, not in the ease and comfort of daily life. Even by their own standards, their behaviour during the three Hungarian revolutions was hardly reconcilable with *noblesse oblige*. In April 1918 they were ready, under the lead of Count Schornborn-Bucheim, to force the King's abdication and betray him to the Kaiser; later, in November, to betray him to the Republic; four years after, in 1922, for Horthy's sake, they had him imprisoned and delivered to his former enemies. Sixteen years later, they steered Hungary into Hitler's arms. What has happened since is, in great part, their doing.

Some will retort: 'And you? Aren't you one of them?' Yes, I was. For many years I was their unconscious accomplice. But when I realized that their patriotism was but lip-service, their much-talked-of 'honour' but a code without reality, their loyalty to the sovereign self-interest, their Catholic fervour a means to rule over the uneducated, I left them; I could do no more.

Le vice est de n'en pas sortir, non pas d'y entrer, wrote Montaigne.

5

HUNGARY BECOMES A REPUBLIC

Republics are weak because they appeal to the understanding.

IN spite of our difficulties, during the first weeks we were still confident. We trusted in Wilson's power to put over his ideas and believed that even in the most unfavourable circumstances we should be able to fit into that brotherhood of nations of which he was the most ardent champion. To convince our neighbours that the Hungary of yesterday was definitely dead, we had to complete the break with feudalism.

We intended to convoke the Constituent Assembly for December 25th, to decide on the future form of the State. This body was to be composed of the elected representatives of the various National Councils; but, as so often happens in periods of upheaval, leaders plan and the impatient masses undo the plans. Events forced us to deviate from our original course.

All classes were clamouring for the immediate proclamation of the Republic, as they feared that the delay would be interpreted against us by our neighbours. They would construe our hanging on to the Monarchy as a desire to obstruct their newly acquired independence, and would use it as an excuse to strangle Hungary even more. So it was urgently necessary to prove our *bona fides*.

But there was another reason for declaring the Republic. It was hoped thereby to divert the ultra-left elements from Bolshevism. Hungary was not yet ripe for a Socialist regime and had first to pass through the democratic stage. As we have seen, even the ardent royalists of yesterday were in favour of the Republic, hoping thus to save their property. They seem to have followed Nietzsche's advice that one should push over that which is on the point of falling.

Later, the legend was hatched that the Entente wished the Habsburgs to stay. If so, why did they not inform us of their wish? This would have meant dropping their allies (Czechs, Rumanians, Yugo-slavs) to whom they were committed. That we were right in our judgment was proved by the fact that even after the fall of Bela Kun, Archduke Joseph, who assumed office as regent for the King, was not recognized by the Entente and was forced to resign. When, in April and October 1921, Charles made his surprise visits to Hungary and tried to regain his throne, he was disowned by the Western Powers, made prisoner and deported.

We had but one choice — to declare a provisional republic. At the elections, the people would make their own decision.

The National Council had now taken over the functions of Parliament, which dissolved itself on November 16th. The Upper House closed its session as well and, although not actually dissolved, it was just as dead as the House of Deputies and has never sat since. Only one voice was heard at its last meeting, that of Count Henry Apponyi, who gave a cheer for the People's Republic.

On November 16th, the occasion of my being elected provisional President of the first Hungarian Republic, my valet carefully laid out, in my house in the Egyetem utca, the medieval heavy brocade robes which were the traditional festive attire of the Hungarian nobility. He was grieved when I bade him pack them up in mothballs, for I should never wear them again.

In the Parliament Square, masses had assembled from all parts of the country. The crowd was a huge one, larger than at Louis Kossuth's funeral in 1895, or than at the celebration of Hungary's thousand-year existence in 1896, and certainly much larger than that at the coronation of Charles, in 1916. All Hungary wished to be present in the square.

There could be no doubt of the spontaneity of this demonstration, for one of our defects was our inability to organize the masses. Totalitarian efficiency was as yet unknown.

The provisional Republic was proclaimed in the Kupola Hall (under the Dome), in the Parliament building and I was elected its provisional President. Peasants, workers, soldiers in ragged uniforms and with red insignia, lent the assembly a revolutionary aspect. It was also an unusual sight to see women representatives take their place in the Council. My wife was crouched on the lowest step leading to the Tribune, crushed on all sides by the crowd. Kunfi's speech, with a spark of Danton, vibrated with passion and conviction and moved the audience to tears of enthusiasm. Hock, the Catholic priest, head of the National Council, who was assuming more and more the role of the Abbé Siéyès of the French Revolution, was also an orator on the grand scale. His sharp eyes spied, standing in an archway, a veteran of the '48, a *honved* in shabby brown uniform and blue cap, and he beckoned him to the platform and addressed him in the following words: 'That which you fought for seventy years ago, has now been won . . . Hungary's independence.' It had a dramatic effect.

From the wide stone steps leading to the square, I addressed the crowd. I had the greatest difficulty in making myself understood, as loudspeakers had not yet been invented and my voice did not carry. But in spite of this, I felt the dark, heaving multitude to be one with me, and that, on the brink of despair, all that remained to them was their trust in me. I was hoisted on strong shoulders, a most uncomfortable position, and carried down the steps into the crowd.

Reaction, which eight months later proclaimed Hungary a kingdom without a king, had not yet reared its head. *De facto*, Hungary has remained a republic ever since.[10] It was on this date, October 16th, that Bela Kun arrived from Moscow.

6

THE MISERIES OF OFFICE

The worst thing that can befall a Leader of an extreme Party is to be compelled to take over a Government in an epoch when the movement is not yet ripe for domination and the realization of the measures which this domination would imply . . . What he can do is in contrast to all his previous actions, to all his principles. What he ought to do cannot be achieved. Whoever puts himself in this awkward position, is irrevocably lost. ENGELS

COALITIONS, in most cases, are unsatisfactory. They create an uneasy partnership in which no one is anxious to assume responsibility. Each side has the excuse that it is prevented from executing its programme by the others. A coalition formed for the purpose of intensifying the efforts directed to a common cause, e.g. towards victory in time of war, can be successful; but building up a new regime on a coalition is a game of balance designed to create nothing. Its existence is based on negation.

The Socialists could not carry out their programme because they did not have a majority. We were prevented from accomplishing our land reform because the Socialist Ministers sabotaged it. We could not create the people's army, recruited from the peasantry, for the Socialist Ministers regarded the peasantry as a counter-revolutionary element and threatened to resign if we proceeded with it.

Julius Gombos, later Prime Minister, head of the demobilized officers continually offered to support me, personally, against the Socialists. Had I accepted this, it would have meant casting aside everything we had tried to achieve through our revolution. It would have meant the building up of the new regime on the armed power of the ex-army officers, for momentary gain and to strengthen my personal position. My role then would have been that of Horthy and would have paved the road for Hitler.

The balance of power inside the Cabinet was a strange one. At the start there were only two Socialist Ministers, Sigmund Kunfi, Minister of Education, and Erno Garami, Minister of Industry; but their voices within the Cabinet weighed tenfold, for behind them stood the Trade Unions. It was therefore against them that the enemies of the Republic had to unite. They were an easy target for attack, for it was impossible for them to carry out their own programme. The social laws were not yet working and the Ministry of Welfare was stagnant. There had been no social welfare in Hungary in the past, and even mild reform would have been considered Bolshevik.[11]

The rich peasants had one representative in the person of Istvan Szabo. Although he called himself the Deputy of the landless agricultural workers, their lot was his last concern. A picturesque figure with top-boots and a long moustache, he belonged to the class nowadays known as *kulaks*. We had no little difficulty in handling him. Twice he was on the verge of resignation, first because he didn't get a car as soon as he expected, and the second time because the car was not smart enough!

Day after day, processions representing different strata of the population, some of them armed, marched up the hill to Buda, where the Government offices were situated, clamouring for the immediate realization of their impossible claims. The demobilized soldiers, who considered themselves a privileged caste after having spent five years in the trenches, were the most exacting. Officers of the reserve, lawyers, doctors, undergraduates, industrialists, shopkeepers, aware of the difficulties of the Government, hoped by uniting to obtain whatever they demanded.

Our difficulties were multiplied a thousand times by the ill-will and inefficiency of the different foreign missions in Budapest; the French Mission occupying Hungary was particularly remarkable for its ineptitude.

Although Clause 17,[12] to which we had so energetically objected, had been omitted from the text of the Belgrade Armistice, we received news day by day that foreign regiments had crossed the line of demarcation on the ground that they were 'protecting' the population of the border towns.

Refugees streamed into our dwindling Hungary, but even the most primitive shelter was unavailable in that bitter winter of 1919.

In addition, we were ordered by Colonel Vix to withdraw our troops from the line which, according to the Armistice terms, should have remained under Hungarian administration. At our request that he should inform the competent authorities in Paris of what was happening, Vix replied that, as he did not know the motives underlying our neighbours' action, he would not report to his superiors. This occurred repeatedly during the five months we were in office, with the explanation that the change of frontier was merely a strategic move; but after twenty-four hours these 'strategic' points fell politically, economically and administratively into the hands of the Rumanians and Czechs, so that within a short time three-fifths of the country was in foreign hands.

Although all our requests were turned down by Vix, those of the *ancien régime* were not. These Germanophiles of yesterday, sensing that the Entente was not treating the Government with the consideration that might have been expected, now saw their opportunity. They busied themselves drawing up unfavourable reports on the new Hungary, reports which Colonel Vix, a precursor of Pétainism, was only too pleased to forward to Versailles. Thus a sinister alliance was formed between the French Mission and the pro-Germans of yesterday and tomorrow, resulting in the undoing of Hungary, as we shall see later.[13]

About the beginning of January the situation became so bad that the leading bourgeois Ministers, realizing that the Trade Unions were the only force to be relied on to keep the machinery of State going, and that the Socialists were acquiring more and more control, tendered their resignations. The right-wing Socialist Erno Garami, Minister of Industry, frightened that the Socialists would now have to carry out their programme as they could no longer place the responsibility for not doing so on the bourgeois elements in the Cabinet, strove to induce the executive of the Social Democratic Party to recall him and his colleagues from the Government. There is nothing so worrying for a Social-Democrat Minister as to have the majority.

Without the assistance of the Trade Unions government was impossible; so with the courage of despair I decided to take an unprecedented step; I appeared, without warning, at the committee meeting of the Socialists. I described the crisis and begged them not to forsake the Revolution. Should they withdraw their support, I would resign as well. And if they made it a condition to take over single-handed, I would agree to it.

This intervention on my part, as well as the grim situation I depicted, had the desired effect. I saw tears in the eyes of these tough labour leaders and knew that I had won and that Garami and his faction were defeated. They understood that they could not leave me in the lurch and had to stand by me. After this meeting they became my sole supporters. They demanded one more stronghold in the Cabinet, so I appointed William Böhm Minister of War, instead of Festetich. As they had agreed to the land reform there was no reason for dissension, or so I thought.

Socialists

On February 20th Bela Kun organized an attack against the *Neps-zava*, the Social Democrats' organ, and broke up their premises. A collision with the police followed and several were killed and wounded. At the request of the Social Democrats I had the Communist leader arrested. The next day the free bourgeois press, sensing from where the wind was blowing, published detailed accounts of inhuman and brutal treatment of the Communists, and pathetic portraits of Bela Kun, with bandaged pumpkin face, appeared everywhere. They deliberately made a martyr of him.[14, 15]

7

THE LAND REFORM

THE divergences within our coalition Government on the subject of land reform lasted for months, and we reached agreement only at the beginning of February 1919. These wasted months proved fatal and were the cause of our failure. The increasing animosity of the feudal classes, who felt the sword of Damocles over their heads, could have been neutralized by the support of the peasantry; but the Social Democrats, who had no followers amongst the peasants, were trying to gain time until they could build up their own rural organizations, and therefore sabotaged the reform. In theory they were right, for the peasant in possession is a conservative element, unconcerned with the fate of the rest of the country. Also, the Roman Catholic Church had a strong hold on the peasantry. Yet, in practice, it meant that our adversaries gained time to turn the frustrated peasants against us.[16]

Our moderate reform was finally accepted in February. It left the landowners the right to 500 acres. In certain exceptional cases, and if national interest so demanded, the State could nationalize estates of over 200 acres. These lands, divided into lots of 5 to 20 acres (enough for a family to live on) were then to be allotted to the landless peasants. Large estates of many thousand acres were to be partly turned into co-operatives. The land was valued at the low pre-war rates, and owners were given compensation in the form of heavily taxed State bonds. It amounted, in fact, to a sort of capital levy. The new peasant-proprietors were given a period of several years in which to repay the State for their land.

This reform was similar to those carried out in the neighbouring States. The Hungarian ex-landowners, who opposed it with frenzied bitterness and pursued me with their hatred for decades, are now well aware — as many have admitted to me — that, had it been carried out at that time, it would have meant their salvation.

In the spring the actual division of the land started. As owner of one of the biggest estates, I began with my own property. As expected, this proved to be the last straw as far as my class and relatives were concerned. They had deluded themselves with the hope that all talk of land reform was merely a wily stratagem on my part to make myself popular. Now they realized that they had to act quickly or everything would be lost.

The first public attack against us was made by my brother Joseph Karolyi. In February he summoned the dissolved Assembly of the County and passed a vote of no confidence against my Government, demanding the restoration of the old order. Bishop Prohaszka, who a few weeks before had been our supporter, took part in the meeting against us, thus lining up the Catholics. Encouraged by this attack, the ex-officers of the Austro-Hungarian Army, who had been waiting for the first opportunity to regain their past positions, started to organize illegal military detachments which, needless to say, were dissolved when discovered. They were the forerunners of the M O V E the notorious White Terror detachments of later years. Their leader was Julius Gombos, later Prime Minister.

The rain was falling heavily on that day in March when I distributed my lands. Peasants from all the different parts of my estate stood under their large umbrellas, their deeply furrowed faces lifted up to me in indescribable amazement, wonder and suspicion. They could not believe that their dream was at last to become reality. They had so often been fooled, so often deceived. I felt as if a great weight had fallen from my heart, for I had always felt the guilt of possessing such wealth; in my youth unconsciously, later consciously. I erected a signpost on the soil of Kapolna, which had belonged for so many centuries to my family; it marked the allotment assigned to the agricultural labourer heading the list of claimants. I felt satisfied. The order of things had been restored. It was right. The land now belonged to the peasants of the Matra Valley.

After the distribution of Kapolna, a legend grew around my name, in which I figured as a sort of Tolstoy or Gandhi. I did not deserve this — it being no sacrifice on my part, as I had no developed sense of property. This is more natural to the bourgeoisie, which had accumulated its possessions by its own efforts. But even amongst my own class I was known for feeling no attachment towards my possessions, and therefore my so-called generosity was no merit of mine. It always gave me more pleasure to give than to have.

The Communists and Reactionaries now redoubled their attacks. The livelier the Counter-Revolution became, the more food was furnished for Communist propaganda; the more vigorous the Communist agitation, the more excuse for the Reactionaries to organize. So, complementing and assisting each other, they secretly rejoiced when the danger which they were prophesying increased. Anything was better, they thought, than what existed at the moment. For Reaction, Communism, for Communism, Reaction was the lesser evil. They had only one enemy — Karolyi's 'Third Force'.[17]

We had other dangers to face as well — the perpetual intrigues hatched against us with the Entente Missions stationed in Budapest. No doubt the Hungarian aristocrats were more amusing to meet than Social Democrats. They spoke foreign languages and entertained lavishly, in the company of beautiful women, with music, good wines and tasty food. Our Liberal and Socialist leaders understood only their native tongue and were not brought up in the traditions of international social intercourse. Our young Republic had to carry on an unequal fight, not only against ignorance and stupidity, but against snobbery, which is one of the most powerful allies of Reaction.

The Communist agitation, on the other hand, was winning over the Trade Unions. The Socialist members of the Cabinet felt that they were losing popularity and their hold on the masses. The news was being spread that Trotsky's Red Army was approaching the Galician frontier.

The smallest manifestation on the part of the Entente would have been sufficient to give confidence to those elements which were democratic and pro-Entente. It is superfluous to say that this might have prevented the disaster of later years. The future proved this only too painfully.

The French Government conceived the bright idea of presenting us with their famous ultimatum, thus definitely stabbing Hungarian democracy in the back.

8

THE LEGEND OF MY HANDING OVER THE POWER

THE proclamation by which I was supposed to hand over the power to the Hungarian workers as the result of the Vix ultimatum was a forgery. This proclamation was neither drafted nor signed by me.

The true story is the following: On March 20th Colonel Vix presented an ultimatum ordering us to withdraw our troops from the eastern border and to allow the Rumanians to occupy several thousand square miles of Hungarian territory, including the towns of Szatmarnemeti, Arad and Nagyvarad. This ultimatum had to be accepted within twenty-four hours, evacuation to start within forty-eight hours and to be completed in ten days. Events then gained momentum hourly and a mass meeting was held for the liberation of Bela Kun. A printers' strike was in progress and lack of news increased the panic.

My first question was whether the boundary was just a temporary military one, or whether it was political as well. The answer came that it was a political one and that the Rumanians would take over the administration as soon as our troops left. Nothing could have been a more flagrant violation of the Belgrade Armistice.

It was impossible for my Government to satisfy this demand. The remaining bourgeois members of my Cabinet, representing the nationalist element in the Government, could not accept the responsibility of giving up such extensive territories before the Peace Treaty was signed. Our adversaries whispered that the cause of our harsh treatment at the hands of the Entente was our radicalism. The friendship of Count Istvan Bethlen and Marquis George Pallavicini with the head of the French Mission and their continual visits to the Entente Headquarters made one wonder whether they had not had a direct influence on the drafting of the ultimatum. One fact was known to us — that they had been informed of its contents earlier than we had.

They had been doing their best to convince the Missions of the Entente that Karolyi's regime was a Bolshevik one in disguise and that it would be preferable to have Bela Kun, against whom a holy crusade could be waged; for if Karolyi succeeded in carrying out his land reform and if he won the elections to be held on April 13th, 1919, there would be little chance of getting rid of him.

It was a strange paradox that the Socialists, the Reactionaries and the Entente Missions were equally apprehensive of a democratic land reform. To exasperate the country to such a pitch that it was driven into the arms of Bolshevism was the only way for the old regime to regain power.

Later on, curious scenes were witnessed in one of our main streets, the Vaczi utca. Our nobles were seen falling into each other's arms in joy that the Dictatorship of the Proletariat had been declared. 'Now their end has come,' they whispered.

The next morning, Istvan Bethlen sent a message asking me to accept the ultimatum as there was nothing else to do. Whether this advice was given for the purpose of attacking me later for having surrendered the frontiers of the country, or whether he was scared at the last moment by the Communist danger, I do not know.

We could accept the ultimatum only if we had the agreement of all political parties and I therefore asked Bethlen if he would be ready to head a coalition Government for this purpose, as he was leader of the nationalist element. He refused.

Actually, the new eastern frontiers had been promised to the Rumanians in London in September 1915; but after Wilson had launched the idea of plebiscites, we expected the population to be given a chance to decide for itself to which country it wished to belong. After Wilson's failure, the victorious French generals got the upper hand and it was due to them that the commitments to the Rumanians were satisfied at this most inopportune moment and in this most drastic fashion. Hungary, belonging to the French zone of interest, was the prey of these military men who concocted fantastic plans of revenge against their former allies, the Russians, who had deserted them. For this they needed a bridgehead, for which Hungary was very suitable. They needed a Hungarian Government which would help them to start war against Lenin's Russia. The evidence that the Big Four in Paris were fostering such mad plans, is supplied in the memoirs of the American General Bliss.

No attempt was made to force this policy on Czechoslovakia, where two eminent statesmen, Masaryk and Benes, were in power and where the Czech upper classes had never been as reactionary as ours. The Vix ultimatum was the victory of the Hungarian reaction and our undoing.

On the afternoon of the same day, March 20th, I summoned the Cabinet. The Ministers of the Karolyi Party had tendered their resignation, not having the courage to accept or refuse the ultimatum. I therefore proposed that the Cabinet should resign, after which I would charge the Social Democrats, in conjunction with the Communists, to form a new Government; this proposal was unanimously accepted. We came to this decision because the policy based on a new orientation towards our neighbours and towards the West had failed and the armistice of Belgrade had been violated. Only a homogeneous, strong and united Government, backed by organized labour which the Communists also could support, would have the authority to refuse. Moreover, we had put our hopes in the West and, having been deceived, we had to look for an ally in the East. We were therefore obliged to compromise with the Communists. It was unanimously decided that I should stay at my post.

The next morning, at the meeting of the Social Democratic executive, the leaders, scared by the heated atmosphere of the country and fearing that the Communist revolution would break out and sweep them away, sent a delegation to the Marko utca prison, to open negotiations with Bela Kun.

The prisoner, who still bore on his body the marks of police cudgels, was now the dictator and the Socialist Ministers took his orders. After their return the Executives decided on the fusion of the two Workers' Parties into one under the name of the Hungarian Socialist Party. Bela Kun, as he admitted later, was completely taken aback by this unexpected victory. He had demanded the maximum but had never expected to get it. Power fell into his lap. None of these momentous decisions were known to the non-Socialist members of the Cabinet or to myself.

That same evening, the 21st, I held another Cabinet meeting, during which only administrative problems were discussed. The Socialist Ministers made themselves conspicuous by their silence. Before leaving I called Kunfi aside and told him that, in the event of a new Socialist Government, I would appoint him Premier. He made no comment.[18] Some minutes later these same Ministers appeared before the Workers'

Council and declared, amidst frantic applause, the Dictatorship of the Proletariat.[19] The Public Prosecutor, Vary, the bitterest opponent of Communism, asked for the privilege of personally releasing Bela Kun and to the Communist leader's great surprise he was met at the prison gates by a kowtowing and beaming Prosecutor.

In the royal palace in Buda my secretary, who had just received the alarming news of the latest happenings in the Workers' Assembly, rushed into my study, holding a typewritten sheet which he begged me to sign without delay. It was a proclamation in which I was made to declare that I was resigning and handing over power to the Hungarian working class. It was, my friends believed, the only way to avoid bloodshed. Of course I refused to sign this absurd document, the offspring of hysteria and panic. Some minutes later my secretary returned, pale and distraught. The proclamation, he said, was already in the hands of the *Nepszava*, the Socialist daily.

'Ring them up and tell them to break up the type if necessary,' I declared. Too late — the paper was already on the streets, and posters proclaiming its contents were on the walls of the town. It had been read to the Workers' Assembly and received with frantic enthusiasm. It had been published before being presented to me, and my signature forged. That the signature was not mine was established by Denes Berinkey, the Prime Minister, who swore to this when, later, he was summoned as witness before Horthy's law court; the charge of my handing over the power to the Communists was then dropped.

At my trial the Communist leaders were convicted of seizing power by force, which would not have been the case had they received the power from my hands. But the charge against them was false, too. They did not take it by force, but received it from the hands of the Social Democrats.

I had no means of making a denial. The press was in the hands of the Socialists and no one would have dared to publish it.

I could have rallied my own personal bodyguard; the officers were ready to fight and the regiment of the Seklers who, under General Kratochvil, were protecting our frontiers from the Rumanians, would have been loyal to me. But this would have been tantamount to civil war and, in the event of victory, would have led to the most bloody reaction. It would have been I, instead of Horthy, who would have inaugurated the White Terror.

I did not disclose the truth concerning this forgery during the first years of my emigration for fear of harming those who were already suffering in Horthy's prisons for the errors committed. It seemed to me that it would have been an ignoble gesture had I started to attack my past collaborators for their action. We had only one enemy at that time, the Horthy regime. All else was of no importance.

This is the true story of the Communist *coup d'état* in Hungary in 1919, and my answer to Sir William Goode, who took over the accusation against me from the Horthy propagandists and published it in the *Encyclopaedia Britannica*.

Although I did not hand over power to the Communists, I accept the responsibility for the gradual transfer of power into the hands of the Social Democrats. As I have pointed out, they were the only organization capable of controlling production and preventing chaos. Consequently, the balance turned in their favour day by day. As far as the peasantry was concerned, I was at one with the Socialists in fearing that the creation of a new smallholders' class would put a brake on the progressive, collective, planned economy which was indispensable to a sound agrarian policy. Small units, cultivated by individual peasants, would be unable to produce sufficient for the needs of the country. Also, their political influence would prevent the much-needed rapprochement with our neighbours, on which our future depended. Thus, I was also in favour of Socialist agrarian organizations to support the landless peasantry and build them eventually into large communities on a co-operative basis. I hoped that, in time, the peasants would realize that production would increase and farming become easier if they united their holdings in collective farms, and that it would be to their own interest to make these farms work. Not force, but reason, should lead them to collectivization.

I had appointed William Böhm, an excellent organizer, as Minister of War. The army, our main support in case of crisis, was composed of factory workers, as the agricultural labourers were badly needed on the newly acquired land.

The motive of the Social Democrats' *putsch* against me must have been the fear that they had lost their hold on the workers, for whom Lenin's Soviet Russia, the first Socialist State, was an irresistible attraction. The Socialist leaders had not the courage to take their stand against the *putsch* although the majority did not favour it. They hoped to regain the confidence of the working class by betraying their bourgeois comrades of yesterday. They wanted to prove that the Dictatorship of the Proletariat was entirely their achievement, completed in the face of the Government and even over the head of Karolyi, whom they had confronted with a *fait accompli*.[20]

For the torpedoing of democratic Hungary, and for the Communist *coup d'état*, the Entente was responsible. Nothing remained for me but to retire, with the hope that the new regime, if united and strong, would be better treated by the Entente than we had been.

I was not wrong in this supposition. Under the shock of Bolshevism's first encroachment upon Europe, the Western Powers started those negotiations with Bela Kun which they had refused to take up with me. At last, Versailles took cognizance of Hungary's existence.

General Smuts arrived in Budapest in April.

9

OUR LIFE DURING THE DICTATORSHIP

Hereditary Bondsman! Know ye not
Who would be free themselves must strike the blow.
By their right arms the conquest must be wrought.
Will Gaul or Muscovite redress ye? No!   BYRON

I RETIRED to the Svabhegy, one of the hills overlooking Budapest, and from there we watched the desperate struggle of the country against what it felt to be a grave injustice.

The new Communist Government was headed by Alexander Garbai, a Social Democrat, but its real leader was Bela Kun, Commissar for Foreign Affairs.

The first acts of the Dictatorship were to refuse the French ultimatum, to agree to having elections[21] in the near future, and to build up the Red Army to a size greater than that permitted by the terms of the Armistice which, having been several times violated by our neighbours, was no longer valid.

Within a week the attitude in Paris towards Hungary had changed. The British principle of non-interference in Hungary's internal affairs seemed to have prevailed over the French desire to see her occupied by her neighbours, and the Peace Conference sent General Smuts to negotiate.

So what my Government had not been able to obtain in five months was granted to the Communists after a week, proving that the idea of standing up to the West was not such a bad one. The conditions which General Smuts offered were a marked improvement on those of the Vix ultimatum. The line to which the Hungarian troops had to withdraw was modified to our advantage and formally declared to be a military boundary, without effect on the decisions of the Peace Treaty. The neutral zone between the two lines was to be abolished immediately and a substantial loan granted. The General would advise the Entente to have the representatives of Hungary invited to the Paris Conference, thus enabling them to put forward their point of view. On the other hand, Hungary had to observe the Armistice agreement and discontinue rearming.

These amazingly favourable conditions should have been accepted without delay, but were rejected by Bela Kun, who argued that they would mean a second Treaty of Brest-Litovsk (which at the time he had opposed, even against Lenin) and were unacceptable to a weak Hungary still dominated by the chauvinist element. This nationalist attitude on the part of the Communist leader was paradoxical. Oddly enough, he was a sentimental patriot, who dreaded being thought a less good Hungarian than his countrymen. National Bolshevism, a puzzling contradiction, now appeared in history for the first time. Until then, Communism was supposed to be international.

Kun made a counter-offer to the Smuts proposal, hoping for more concessions. This counter-proposal was, in effect, a refusal, for Smuts had made it clear that his offer had to be accepted as it stood. Kun's colleagues, whom he had the habit of leaving uninformed of the most important events and even of misinforming at times, knew nothing about these negotiations.[22]

Smuts left, and Hungary was now definitely cut off from the West. At the same time the rumour that Trotsky's Red Army was approaching the Galician frontier grew in strength, feeding the illusion that it was only a question of time before the Hungarian Soviets would link up with the Russians and, with them, start the fight against the Versailles Dictatorship.

Frankly, I had never dreamt that such favourable proposals would be offered to Bela Kun. Had they been made to us, they would have prevented Communism. I had wished to deter the country from plunging itself into another hopeless conflict; but that the refusal of the Vix ultimatum did not mean actual war was confirmed by Smuts's visit.

The army had to be built up from nothing. The few battalions permitted by the Armistice were naturally not sufficient for waging war. As active officers could not be relied on, political commissars were attached to them for control.

A week after Smuts's departure, the Rumanians attacked along the whole line and crossed the river Tisza. The Czechs, seizing this opportunity, launched an attack from the north. By the end of April the Rumanian Army was marching on Budapest.

In this dramatic atmosphere of panic on one hand and fanatic exaltation on the other, Budapest celebrated, with grandiose pomp, its Workers' Day, May 1st. All the walls were covered with propaganda posters; mile-long red bunting, spread over the city, looked ominous.

On this memorable day I visited the Hungaria, where the Communist Party had set up its headquarters. In his room, attended by his solicitous wife, Kun lay stretched out on his couch in a state of complete moral collapse. I could not get a reasonable word out of him, so I visited Sigmund Kunfi next door, who told me that Kun had broken down completely and talked of giving up the fight. It was Kunfi who saved the situation, ending a fiery exhortation with the words of the French Jacobins: '*La Patrie est en danger*', which he changed to 'The Revolution is in danger!' He was appealing to the workers' Socialist conscience to fight for the Motherland which was now theirs. Battalions were rapidly formed in the factories from organized workers' units. At the start they had no arms, no supplies, no reserves, nothing but the will to hurl back the invader. It was the same spirit that animated the *Sans-Culottes* to resist the invasion of royalist troops. The French and Serbs had concentrated their forces in the south. Surrounded on all sides, the Communist Army attacked the Czechs in the north and won several victories against overwhelming odds. Even the active officers, who were violent opponents of Socialism, were roused by the general enthusiasm and in their reports praised the astounding courage and self-sacrifice of their men.

In quiet seclusion, and with little hope that all this heroism could have any effect on Hungary's future, we lived with our children, our Alsatian Cora and a cow who provided the milk for the family and grazed placidly on the lawn in front of our sitting-room. I had intended to leave Hungary after my wife's confinement, but as a result of wartime anaesthetics she became ill, and we had to stay until her recovery.

Following information from my cousin Moritz Esterhazy that some members of the National Casino considered it the appropriate moment, now that I had no more power, to make away with me, the Government had put three soldiers on guard in front of our villa. That this 'protection' was at the same time a control and check on me and my visitors, there was little doubt. It did not inconvenience me, as I had no intention of conspiring. Since Tisza's murder had proved that guards were not sufficient protection, we mounted a machine gun on our landing, facing the entrance. We felt it might come in useful in case of undesirable visitors; when the day came when we thought we needed it, we discovered that we had forgotten to load it.

The only friend who remained faithful to me after my loss of office was Esterhazy, who had a most unusual way of paying us visits. He would choose the window instead of the door, for fear of being noticed by our guards and compromising himself in the eyes of the Communists by his association with us. He would praise the land reform of the Dictatorship in comparison with ours, and was full of admiration for the Commissar of Agriculture, Hamburger, of whom he talked as his friend.[23,24]

The first act of the Dictatorship had been to stop the distribution of the land. With the exception of the peasants' dwarf-holdings and the attached buildings, the State seized all land. The Latifundia thus remained intact and were turned over to agricultural labourers, to be worked on co-operative lines. In most places the ex-landowners remained managers of their estates. Bela Kun, who had a soft spot in his heart for the Hungarian nobility, could not bring himself to refuse any of their personal requests. They retained, therefore, the hope that in case of a Rumanian victory the Latifundia would return to their legal owners.

One night while the guards were dozing, a most unlikely visitor, in the person of George Apponyi, the son of Albert Apponyi, sneaked into the villa and whispered that his father was outside, waiting to be let in. Our house was the safest place, for as we had been opponents for years, no one would search for him here. It was unwise for us to shelter him in this small villa, guarded by Reds, for his exceptional height, eagle-like nose and picturesque beard were too well known. He had to be concealed even from the servants. We kept him locked in a room next to my wife who, still keeping to her bed, could share her meals with him, puzzling the cook with her appetite for two.

He would hold long discourses on Communism and his honest and unbiased approach delighted us. His brilliant and youthful mind was not hampered by prejudice. He sensed the ideas of the *Zeitgeist* and was influenced by them.

Some days later his son came to fetch him and with the help of my aide-de-camp he was transferred in the dead of night, wrapped in one of my fur coats, to my sister Pappenheim's country place near Budapest. The police, believing him to be in Austria, gave up the search. During the White Terror, Albert Apponyi was the only man in Hungary who possessed the moral courage to raise his voice against the atrocities committed.[25]

It was about this period that I visited Bela Kun for the last time, with the suggestion that before Hungary suffered complete defeat the Government should be handed over to the Social Democrats, to prevent Rumanian occupation. I also asked him to stop the barbarous measure of taking hostages. Both my requests were refused.

Although on paper the nationalization of the entire land was prescribed, properties up to 100 acres remained in private hands, with the result that more than 48 per cent of the land was not socialized. As the large estates had not been divided and remained under the management of their late owners, the peasants were unaware that anything had been done for them.

Although their wages were raised, prices soared because of the blockade, so there was little difference in their standard of living. Nor was mobilization a popular measure since the peasants, instead of receiving the land and peace they had been promised, got military service and war. The peasant regiments which fought courageously were those situated on the border, whose native villages had been occupied by the enemy. The regiments from the centre of the country were uninterested and completely unreliable; in many cases they joined the Counter-Revolution, proving that the abstract notion of patriotism is alien to the peasant, to whom defence of his country means defence of his own home and family.

Although the churches were not closed and no one was actually persecuted for his religion, anti-religious propaganda, for the purpose of 'enlightening' the rural population, was carried out most tactlessly by Jewish youths from Budapest. This tactlessness was exploited by the Catholic Church and by the Counter-Revolution which, confident in its approaching victory, was now beginning to raise its head. The peasants resorted to their most effective weapon, the concealment of their produce, thus starving the workers in the towns and turning them too against the Dictatorship.

Another mistake was the feverish speed with which all factories and workshops employing more than twenty workmen were nationalized.

Here, too, the lack of experts made it impossible to dispense with the managers of the past, who nearly all remained in their jobs. They were daily harassed and irritated by the control of inefficient bureaucrats, and naturally became embittered enemies, sabotaging as much as they could.

New currency had to be issued, as the printing-press in Vienna refused its supply. The peasants, made suspicious by their landlords, refused to accept the 'white money'. The only success, as far as nationalization was concerned, was in transport. A coal crisis was imminent. Since October 1918 production had fallen to half, and this at a time when enemy troops were closing in on all sides.

The organization of the Communist Army by William Böhm and his Chief of Staff, Stromfeld, an active soldier, Social Democrat and anti-Communist, was an admirable achievement. During the first weeks it scored victory after victory, chased the Czechs out of the occupied territories and pushed the Rumanians over the river Tisza.

Complete economic anarchy was reigning in the capital, for the peasants were starving the workers and they, in their turn, refused to supply reserves for the front. The soldiers' families suffered want, in spite of the promises given to them when they were called up. To allay the discontent of the soldiers, their wives were allowed to visit them at the front. They brought their complaints with them, which did not serve to cheer the men or make them any readier to sacrifice their lives for what was going on at home. The much promised Russian help proved to be a red herring. In vain did Kun produce false telegrams, signed by Clemenceau, stating that the Entente intended to re-install the Hungarian Reactionaries, and others from Tchicherin, saying that the Soviet armies had started their offensive in East Galicia. In vain did he proclaim the approach of the World Revolution. It no longer helped.

The breaking up of the front started with the strike of the railway men in western Hungary, the Hungarian 'Vendée'. The meagre reserves could not reach the front. The strike was naturally camouflaged as one for a rise of wages but, in reality, it was political. Bela Kun who, at the start, showed pluck in handling exaggerated demands,[26] had no longer the courage to do so.

While the real instigators of the country's troubles waited in the ante-chambers of Kun's offices to receive passports to leave the country and enjoyed his protection, retaliation was carried on against small game — discontented peasants and workers.

After the proclamation of the Dictatorship, Szeged, the second largest town in Hungary, had been seized by the French army of Franchet d'Esperey, and turned over to a group of royalist refugees, who formed a Government headed by my cousin Gyula Karolyi. Within a short time they acquired the necessary funds, at high interest, from the sale of the tobacco monopoly, and obtained large credits from financiers who seemed unconcerned by the anti-Jewish agitation of the Szeged Government and the anticipated pogroms.[27]

One day, Mr. H. N. Brailsford, correspondent of the *Manchester Guardian*, came to see me on his way back from Moscow, where he had visited Lenin, Trotsky and other Bolshevik leaders. His understanding and knowledge of the situation made a great impression on me, rousing confidence that there were people in the West, and in England especially, who were not completely ignorant of what was going on in Eastern Europe. In later years our paths often crossed and I was glad to count him amongst my friends.

With the news of the first Rumanian successes, the Counter-Revolution started to rear its head in the villages of western Hungary. At the end of June, when it was clear to everyone that the regime was doomed, ex-officers organized an armed rising and actually counted on the help of the discontented workers to carry it out. Two men-of-war (monitors) started shelling the Margaret Island, in the middle of the town, while the pupils of the Military School, the Ludovica, occupied several buildings. At the sound of the shelling, some citizens, believing that the Rumanians had arrived, rushed into the street, waving flags. This caused the loss of several lives.[28]

Soon the workers got the better of the revolt and even the dissatisfied joined in the defence of the regime. So, for a time, Bela Kun managed to carry on.

PART FOUR

EXILE

I

DEPARTURE

AT midnight on July 4th, 1919, we left Budapest by car for the Austrian border. Katus, a constitutional optimist, said we would be back in three months. I, the pessimist, predicted a year. It proved to be twenty-seven years.

As none of my advice had been followed, it seemed useless for me to await the final catastrophe. With no cash, but a handful of jewels, we started off towards the west. Some of our more valuable belongings were entrusted to the care of my aide-de-camp's father, who for safety's sake buried them in his garden, a fashionable proceeding in those days. The children were taken to the country estate of my sister Elisabeth until they could join us later.

The staff, consisting of my personal valet Bakos, the lady's maid and the cook, stood at the gate to bid us farewell. The women sobbed loudly and I shall always remember the pathetic figure of Bakos, tears running down his cheeks, holding our Alsatian by the lead, as if clinging desperately to his last duty, the care of our dog. His family had served mine for many decades. He had been assigned to me when we were both fifteen years old and had been with me ever since. He had accompanied me on all my journeys to Paris, London and the U.S.A.[1] A year later, when the campaign of calumny started against me, he fell into a deep depression; when his children were persecuted at school because their father had served Karolyi, he could bear it no longer. He put an end to his life by throwing himself from one of the attic windows of my mansion. Over his poor bleeding body Cora stood and moaned, the only living creature who had remained his friend.

Our first shock came at Savanyukut, the Austrian frontier, when, after the car and chauffeurs had left, we missed our suitcase. Having noticed our solicitude for this piece of luggage, the chauffeurs, presuming it to be crammed with jewels, had made off with it. How disappointed they must have been to discover it contained only toilet accessories! But it also contained my wife's diary, which she had been keeping all through the previous eventful year — an irreplaceable loss. We spent the first night in a haystack on the farm of an Austrian peasant. The hay was prickly and dusty and the pigsty was too close. The next morning we had to come to an agreement with our hosts as to how we could be smuggled over the border. The smuggling of refugees brought a regular livelihood to the border population.

The farmer said that there would be no difficulty in disguising my wife as a peasant girl, but I should immediately be detected for what I was.

'What am I?' I asked.

'A Jew, of course,' he answered.

There was an exodus of rich Jews in those days.

The next morning, sitting in a cart filled with potatoes, we were driven over the river Lajta, and from there we set off in pouring rain, with rucksacks on our backs, into Austria. It was not a pleasant excursion; wherever we stopped for food, drink or shelter we were instantly turned out, for anyone on the move was regarded with suspicion. This attitude filled us with apprehension.

Famished and drenched to the skin, we arrived at nightfall in a small Austrian town where we had the usual reception. 'We are full up', we were told, and advised to try our luck in the next town, ten miles farther on. Katus, who had a blistered foot, sat down on the roadside and refused to budge. Her dress was soaked with rain and her face with tears. It was getting dark when at last a cart pulled up. The peasant driver, roused to compassion by her plight, offered us a lift to the next town where, on his recommendation, we were at last given a room. Never did we sleep in a more comfortable bed or eat a more delicious meal, which consisted of eggs fried in margarine of doubtful quality. Having now decided to give up the use of our legs, we took the train to Melk, a town on the Danube, where Oskar Jaszi awaited us with a passport in the name of Koplen and a visa for Czechoslovakia. He was anxious for us to leave Austria immediately as some Hungarian and Austrian noblemen of the Jockey Club had sworn to kill me. I was not much affected by this news as I knew that my countrymen preferred talk to action; but Katus barricaded the door of our hotel room with chairs and tables and sat up all night with a loaded revolver at her side, waiting for the assassins. I have to admit, to my shame, that I slept soundly during her watch.

Sitting in the train bound for Prague, we imagined that the worst was over. But how mistaken we were! At the frontier town at Gmund a passenger recognized me — it seems I never can get off incognito — and reported his momentous discovery to the Austrian frontier officials. The bureaucrats of the old Habsburg regime had no sympathy for Otto Bauer's Socialist Government and were only too pleased to annoy their friends. The Viennese reactionary papers had reported that I had escaped from Hungary with several millions. With this excuse, they searched us from top to toe, then advised the Czech frontier posts that we were travelling under false names. Owing to deficient organization, the Czech authorities had not been informed by Prague of the exact date of our arrival, so after crossing the frontier we were arrested and marched to the Prague train by armed police, between a row of delighted passengers — for people always find special pleasure in the misfortune of others. A short man with a beard, eyes sparkling with gleeful spite, bowed and greeted me as 'Herr Graf'. It gave him particular satisfaction to wreck my incognito. I recognized in him the porter of the Bristol Hotel in Vienna, whom I had regularly overtipped.

In a first-class carriage — a pleasant change from the third-class in which we had started — we spent the time playing cards with our guards. On arrival at Prague we found a huge crowd waiting on the platform, for the evening papers had spread the news that Karolyi had been 'captured' trying to get over the border; but to our great relief the head of the police also was waiting. Greatly embarrassed, he apologized for the *gaffe* of his subordinates. A suite of rooms had been booked at an hotel and the Chief of Police himself brought us excellent wiener-schnitzels from the restaurant opposite, since the service in the hotels was still disorganized.

The next day official apologies poured in from all sides. We were molested by journalists and photographers to such an extent that we were unable to move out of our rooms without having a magnesium light flash at us from somewhere. The following day we were offered rooms in the house of a wealthy widow, Mrs. Lanner, in the Pivovar (beer) district, one of the suburbs of Prague. We hoped that our troubles had come to an end, at least for the time being. But once again we were mistaken. Some days later, entering a local restaurant and being in need of a peg on which to hang my hat, I placed it on a low bust standing in the entrance. The dining-room was empty except for a plump, middle-aged woman and her Pekinese dog, seated near the window. We had only just started our frugal meal when two policemen entered. The plump lady pointed triumphantly at us. We were ordered to accompany them to the police station, as we were under arrest. There I was informed that the lady with the Pekinese had denounced me for having insulted President Wilson by placing my hat on his effigy! After proving my identity we were released. The next day one of the Viennese papers reported that I had met President Masaryk in a restaurant and knocked his hat off, after which I had been arrested. Every day absurd stories were invented about me.

In those days we also learned what it was to be hungry. We had fourteen kronen to spend on food, the equivalent of 8d. a day. As this was not even sufficient for one proper meal, we sucked sweets to still our hunger. Our amiable hostess little suspected that the beer and dry biscuits prepared by her stylish butler as a night-cap, formed almost our only nourishment. And this whilst the Viennese émigré papers were accusing us of wallowing in luxury. But our material situation was the least of our worries; on the contrary it had the charm of novelty and we felt it to be an experience suited to our new way of life.

We spent the exceptionally hot summer of 1919 in Prague. It was a memorable period of my life from many points of view. One was that I had the privilege of coming into close contact with Thomas Masaryk, first President of the Czechoslovak Republic.

I met Masaryk on several occasions in the Hradčin, an architectural gem, built in the Czech version of Maria Theresa baroque, abounding in curves and gilded ornaments. Later, Édouard Benes altered these premises in a modern, Le Corbusier style. Masaryk had the simplicity of the great. His approach was direct and entirely free from the affectations so often found in men who have risen from modest birth to high position. His father had been a coachman, a fact which he and his son Jan often mentioned with pride. An aristocrat of the soul and intellect, his position did not alter him.

This great European did not flatter the primitive instincts of the people for the sake of popularity, as is usual with modern politicians.

When he was an obscure university professor, he had exploded the theory according to which in the thirteenth century the Czech literary language was identical with that of our days. A true Liberal and democrat, he disapproved of the annexation of purely Magyar territories without the consent of the population. He admitted to me that the Csalokoz and Komarom (inhabited entirely by Hungarians) had been thrust upon Czechoslovakia by the Entente without having been asked for. Naturally they were not refused 'and', said he, 'we shall one day have to return these areas to Hungary; but not to a reactionary regime which would wish to restore the Habsburgs'. I did not feel that this was a pretext on his part, as I did when Benes repeated the statement to me.

After our departure from Hungary events moved rapidly. On June 8th a wire from Clemenceau, a genuine one this time, assured the Communist Government that their representatives would be invited to the Paris Peace Conference, and that meanwhile orders had been given to the Rumanian troops to retire to the line of demarcation. He therefore demanded that Hungarians should cease hostilities without delay.

Kun answered that the Communist Army would stop fighting as soon as the Rumanians retired to their demarcation line. Clemenceau replied that the Hungarians must first evacuate Slovakia.

On June 24th Kun gave orders to the troops to halt, and fighting stopped, but the promised evacuation by the Rumanians did not follow.

In those days the British, unlike the French, were anxious to save Hungary from the Rumanian occupation. During the negotiations Colonel Cunningham, head of the British Mission, demanded Bela Kun's resignation and the setting up of a provisional Government with dictatorial powers, to be replaced later by a Government representing all parties. If Kun accepted these conditions, the blockade would be lifted and economic help provided. Böhm, Kun's commander-in-chief, who was carrying on the negotiations in Vienna, went even further than his official mission permitted and declared himself ready to arrest and crush Bela Kun with the aid of his army.[2] Clemenceau mistrusted this Machiavellian offer and thought it wiser to let the Rumanians get on with the job; so when Kun reminded Clemenceau of his promise to get the Rumanians to evacuate, he received the answer that there would be no further negotiations with his Government. Kun now ordered the troops to take the offensive. The general of the staff, Julier, who had worked out the plan for this new offensive, betrayed it to Count Stephen Bethlen in Vienna, and to the Szeged Government, who communicated it to the enemy. The Hungarian Army was thus encircled and partially annihilated in the waters of the Tisza. The final defeat of Hungary was thus promoted by Generals Julier and Craenbrook, and the assumption of power by Horthy, Bethlen and Teleki followed their betrayal. During the last days of the Dictatorship, the émigrés in Vienna did not remain idle. With the help of Ashmead-Bartlett, correspondent of the *Daily Mail*, some Hungarian counts organized an armed hold-up against the Hungarian Legation. They intruded into the offices of the Minister, Elek Bolgar — who in 1949 became Hungarian Minister in London — broke open the safe and seized twenty-five million golden kronen. The spoils were then safely hidden under Ashmead-Bartlett's bed in the Hôtel Sacher. In his memoirs he admitted to having received six millions as reward. The rest of the money was used partly for counter-revolutionary purposes, but the greater part was 'vaporized' on the gambling tables of the Jockey Club.[3]

Soon after this, Kun resigned and, seizing the opportunity offered him by the Austrian Government of Otto Bauer, got into a special train with his family and friends and left for Vienna, where he was put under arrest. Those of his colleagues who had no room on the train were left behind to the mercy of the Rumanian and White Armies.

Though I had from the beginning opposed the ruthless methods of the Dictatorship, as well as the opening of hostilities, I would not join those who after the fall of the Commune spread lies about the terror and cruelty exercised by Bela Kun. The truth is that, compared with the systems which followed and to which Europe became accustomed in later years, the Hungarian Commune was a mild prelude, a sort of operetta in the permanence of which even its leaders did not believe. In feudal Hungary the lower classes harboured no hatred against their rulers as they did in France in 1789 or in Russia in 1917. They could not be convinced that they were the equals of their masters, nor had they any urge for vengeance. The Hungarians are an oriental and a passive race. When they had to arrest a nobleman they did so with a bad conscience, fearing that the wrath of the Almighty would descend upon their disrespectful heads. Often they would ask to be excused. As they had no confidence in the duration of their rule, they treated their landlords with special regard, requesting them not to forget them in their turn when the inevitable change should come: but nothing is less easily forgiven than humiliation at the hands of inferiors; the masters were not charitable and the retribution was terrible.[4]

The Hungarian Dictatorship of the Proletariat was a most unfortunate and inefficient experiment, for which the Entente was largely responsible, carried out by a group of humanitarian idealists, patriotic sentimentalists, Marxist theoreticians and, as in all upheavals, by doubtful characters seeking personal gain and private vengeance. The Communist *avant-garde* in Hungary did not bear comparison with that of Russia — men of the calibre of Lenin, Trotsky, Chicherin, Rakovsky, Bukharin and the others.

The Dictatorship was severest towards the small man — the discontented peasant and unruly workman — who, since it was called the Dictatorship of the Proletariat, innocently imagined that he was the Dictator. The Social Democrats refused to see that, if they accepted Dictatorship, terror would inevitably follow. This remained a controversial point between the parties although the 'terror' was a mild one, tempered by inefficiency and respect for the past. It was a revolt of the slaves, relishing their might, but lacking the courage to carry out their threats. They managed to frighten and humiliate the bourgeoisie, but not to render it innocuous. Böhm states in his memoirs (*In the Fire of Two Revolutions*) that the courts-martial, composed of workers, passed four death sentences in Budapest and twenty-four in the country. But an arbitrary terror detachment was formed during the first weeks by an adventurous character called Cserny, who seized the Batthyanyi mansion in the centre of the town. The awe-inspiring inscription stuck over the entrance — 'Terror Detachment of the Revolutionary Government Council' — made the blood freeze in the veins of the bourgeoisie. But their reign did not last long; threatened by Government troops, they surrendered and were dispatched to the front.

Another much-feared revolutionary organization was that of Samuelly, which was used against armed risings of peasants in western Hungary. Samuelly was one of the most interesting types of that period, the St. Just of the Commune, a fanatic, *un pur*, with great personal courage. Although he was sent to Russia on a mission he returned in the last days to Budapest, knowing that the end was near. He shot himself to avoid falling into the hands of the enemy.

Kun himself, a provincial journalist of humble origin, was deeply flattered when the powerful nobles of yesterday visited him and begged for favours, and found it difficult to refuse them anything. He had the sentimentality of his race and cried easily. When he had to sign a death warrant, even of an ordinary murderer, he would shed tears. He advocated ruthless terror, cruel reprisals, the vengeance of the people, but in reality he was ready to assist anyone who appealed to him personally. Archduke Joseph's son, taken as hostage, was safely guarded in his own mansion, and many other aristocrats were saved by Kun's personal intervention. Other Communists did the same. Proof of this is that only five members of the upper classes, and no leading politicians, lost their lives.[5]

According to the statistics of the White Tribunals in Hungary, the number of the victims of the Red Terror was 234. About 500 were killed in regular battle. The victims of the White Terror, recorded by themselves, numbered 5000.

After Kun's flight, Peidl headed the newly formed Social Democrat Government. The Entente was faced with two Hungarian Governments, one in Szeged, the other in Budapest, each claiming to represent the real Hungary, and refused to recognize either. Colonel Cunningham and General Gorton tried to negotiate a compromise and appealed to the patriots of Szeged to save the country from enemy occupation. After long persuasion, in order to avoid bloodshed, they succeeded in making Stephen Bethlen agree to having the Szeged Government stop one of its members, General Schweitzer, from marching against the capital until a coalition Government representing the whole country could be set up. A couple of days later General Schweitzer and Stephen Friedrich, flanked by two Rumanian brigades, entered the Government buildings and arrested Premier Peidl and his colleagues. Archduke Joseph of Habsburg was proclaimed Governor and appointed Friedrich his Premier. On August 12th Admiral Horthy, having waited for the departure of the looting Rumanian troops, made his entry into the city at the head of his military detachments, riding his famous white horse in Austrian Admiral's uniform. He apostrophized it as the City of Sin and started the punitive White Terror.[6]

Some months later, on November 26th, 1919, Sir George Clark, in the name of the Supreme Council, formally recognized the Horthy regime. It was a recognition on terms. The most striking of the four conditions was that the Hungarian Government 'shall secure to every Hungarian citizen full civil rights, including freedom of the press, freedom of assembly, freedom of speech, and universal suffrage on a secret and democratic basis'. Needless to say, these conditions were never fulfilled. A very powerful weapon used as means to enforce reactionary rule was food relief. The United States food relief under Herbert Hoover and the food relief of Holland were denied to the entire country as long as the Liberals, Social Democrats or Communists were in power. Later under the Horthy Dictatorship, during the period when Sir William Goode was Director of Relief in Europe, food relief was denied to any organization or party which could be accused of left-wing tendencies. The choice for the needy population was submission to the ruling clique or starvation.[7]

It was during that summer that Colonel Josiah Wedgwood visited Hungary with a delegation of M.P.s and gave a detailed report to the House of Commons of the atrocities committed against Socialists and Jews. Sir George Clark also reported the true state of affairs to the Supreme Council, and his reports were in direct contradiction to those of the military missions, especially those of the American, Major-General Bandholtz, who had been completely conquered by the charm of the restorers of the old order and did not bother about the methods they used.

Our first winter was spent in the snows of Moravia, near Reichenau. Favoured until now by the gods, flattered and fawned upon from my earliest years, I now for the first time faced human nature in its nakedness, and got to know people as they actually were when they had nothing to get out of me. It was not an elevating experience. One of the disadvantages of the rich is, that they are mostly surrounded by the worthless. Decent people keep away from them. They have no chance of knowing humanity at its best. And when they are first undeceived, their faith in mankind itself is shattered. It takes some time to discover that there are other sorts of people as well. During the White Terror, the Hungarian papers were publishing day after day the vilest accusations against me and even against my wife. I could not do anything, as no editor would have dared to publish me.

Social Democracy needed me as a scapegoat. As an outsider, I was a convenient cargo to pitch overboard to lighten their vessel, damaged by the loss of prestige suffered in Hungary. For many years, therefore, it was impossible for me to defend myself, or make the truth known. Thus I became Culprit No. 1.

During those grim years of profound disillusionment, 1919 and 1920, I often pondered on the reasons for our failure and the errors committed. My critics have always reproached me with weakness. I admit the charge. I blame myself for the weakness I showed, not towards the Left but towards the ruling classes of Hungary; that, because of my upbringing, I allowed myself to be influenced by chauvinistic prejudices about frontiers and demarcation lines which should have been irrelevant to one whose final aim was a Danubian Confederation. Bela Kun's advent would never have occurred had I ruthlessly crushed reaction. Radical reforms and a strong hand in dealing with the Right would have made Bela Kun's propaganda harmless. Our mistake was too much liberalism and attachment to democratic ideals.

Until then I had believed that a new order based on planned economy could be achieved by democratic methods and that the owners of capital would themselves come to the conclusion that the principle of *laisser-faire* did not pay. I believed that organized production and democracy were not incompatible; but now I realized that democracy, at least for the time being, was an impediment to progress in Eastern Europe. Our ruling classes were too stubborn and too selfish. They could only be tamed by their own methods. I felt that not to recognize the logical deduction of this lesson was pure sentimentality, and might cause more misery. How, I argued, could one stick to the liberal democratic methods of the nineteenth century when those in power had no such scruples in defending their privileges? And were the leaders of Social Democracy, whose political outlook did not extend further than the struggle for wages, fit to be the founders of a new order? My experience in Hungary had proved the contrary.

Corrupted by capitalism, they proved to be venal opportunists, weak when the bourgeoisie was powerful, lacking backbone and authority in time of crisis. I did not reject the theory of evolutionary tactics altogether, but the Second International was, I felt, in those days consolidating capitalism. Therefore, I argued, power had to be seized by revolution and retained by dictatorial measures until a new staff of civil servants could be formed. Democracy was a luxury we could not yet afford. The struggle could not yet be waged without the help of the Communists if we did not want the old feudal system to return, reinforced by up-to-date methods of terror. I had to face these harsh facts; I had no choice.

There are, of course, always emotional reasons for every change of political creed. With me these came from my utter disillusionment with my own class.

Even their patriotism proved a bubble, for it was at their request that the Rumanians occupied Budapest. Not for the purpose of defeating Communism, since Bela Kun cleared out, but simply to overthrow the Social Democrat Government. In later years during the German occupation of France, Belgium, Holland, etc., it became clear that those who had something to lose usually collaborated with the enemy; but in those days it was still a novel experience.

Most of my former friends knew that the charges against me were calumny, invented for political reasons, but on the principle that the end justifies the means they joined the howling wolves. They admitted frankly that political considerations were more important than truth, justice or loyalty. Looking back, we know now that the moral values of the nineteenth century started to disintegrate after the First World War, as well as the standards and principles of political behaviour, and have never recovered since.

The beginning of my exile was the third stage of my political evolution. The first was when I resigned from the presidency of the Landlords' Association because of the nefarious influence of the Latifundia, and when it became clear to me that my colleagues wanted only to defend their own interests. I then realized the necessity of a democratic Hungary.

Through the influence which pacifism exercised on me, the First World War turned me into a Socialist. I had always been attracted by the logical deduction of closed systems, and Marxian dialectic satisfied this urge in me, in the same way as Catholicism did in my youth. The blatant injustices shown up by the war contributed to the moral indignation so necessary to foster a new creed.

Following the Marxist thought to its logical conclusion led me inevitably to Communism, although I was hesitant to adhere to the indiscriminating methods which they used. I never joined the Communist Party, and became more and more a left Socialist, untrammelled by party discipline. Unfortunately, owing to my secluded education, I was incapable of talking to workmen and peasants in their own language and therefore remained remote from that community to which I would have liked to belong. All through my life I missed the comfortable feeling of 'belonging'. Yet it was the only way to keep my independence, the price of which was high — loneliness.

My sister Elisabeth and my stepmother Geraldine, both fervent Catholics, visited us in our exile. They interpreted the teachings of their religion differently from my other relatives. Without their help, especially that of Elisabeth, I believe we would hardly have survived the hardships and material want of the first years.

The letters I sent to Elisabeth by one of my most 'devoted' followers found their way to the desk of the Chief of Police in Budapest. The Chief himself told her this. Unusual times bring to the surface hidden sides of human nature; for me, so long out of touch with the realities of life, these experiences had a shattering effect from which I recovered with difficulty.

In Czechoslovakia we were surrounded by *agents provocateurs* and spies, and only escaped the bullet of a hired assassin through a husband's jealousy; this is the story.

We were spending that summer in Podiebrad, a small watering place near Prague. Czech chauvinism was at its height and we had the greatest difficulty in finding anywhere to live.

One day an agitated young man called on us with a fantastic tale. He belonged to a royalist club — there were such things in the Czechoslovak Republic in those days — and had been approached by Hungarian royalists with the request that he should help over the border a friend with an important mission. Having done so, he invited the Hungarian to his house; after several drinks the stranger confided to his host's wife the purpose of his mission: it was to murder Michael Karolyi. She at once informed her husband and he, although a royalist, felt it his duty to warn me. He would have nothing to do with murder, he said. Our impression was that it was jealousy that prompted his action, for the Hungarian seemed to have taken a fancy to his wife. I sent him to the police, for it was their business to discover whether there was any truth in his story. They hatched a plot. Our Othello was to ring up the Hungarian Don Juan and lure him into a trap, telling him I would be at a certain place at a certain hour. The police listened-in when the appointment was fixed and had no doubt that the story was genuine. Instead of me, two police officers waited for him. He confessed that he had been sent by an officers' organization from Budapest and had been promised fifty thousand pengos if successful. I thought this rather a low price for my life, which was thus saved through a husband's jealousy.

When the news spread that I had escaped an attempt on my life, the Czech workers decided to keep an eye on my safety. A man called Hauser offered me his home. The kindness, understanding and humanity which I experienced in the Hauser family were a real comfort to us. They tried in every way to compensate us for our losses and suffering. My links with the past had now been definitely severed. I had lost those things which are generally supposed to be the most important in life, but I had gained instead something I had not known before. I experienced for the first time that uncalculating generosity of which the mainspring is the heart.

2

MY ARREST IN ITALY

WHEN the Red Army under Tukhachevsky's orders was advancing on Warsaw, Benes asked me whether I would accept a mission to Lenin to deter him from pressing any claims which he might have on Carpatho-Russia, which belonged now to the progressive Czechoslovak State. Feeling, for my part, that these provinces should remain independent so that, in time, they would be able to join the Danubian Confederation, I was prepared to undertake these negotitaions.

Some days later Tukhachevsky was defeated by Pilsudski the Polish general, who had the help of Weygand's advice. The southern Red Army, urged by Stalin and Budyenny, forged ahead towards Lemberg instead of obeying Trotsky's order to hurry to Tukhachevsky's aid. The plan was that Lemberg and Warsaw, for reasons of prestige, should fall simultaneously. Tukhachevsky's defeat ended the Polish offensive and started one of those interminable arguments between Trotskyites and Stalinists.

Peace with Poland followed and Benes had no need to worry any longer about the advance of the Red Army and negotiations with Lenin. He even felt that it might be wise to have me out of the country and therefore suggested with polite diplomacy that I would be happier in a warmer climate, since Czechoslavakia would face a fuel shortage in the coming winter. This was a poor excuse, for the miners of the Kladno district had put in an extra hour of work in order to provide the Karolyi family with free coal.

Accepting the hint, we decided to leave for Italy and started packing our boxes, which by this time were numerous, for my sister was bringing out some of our belongings at great risk to herself. The Czechoslovak Government provided us with a *laisser-passer* and arranged with Rome that we should settle in Italy.

We found rooms in Florence in a *pension de famille*, the other occupants of which were mostly Russian refugees. This did not prevent us from becoming friendly, for we were all companions in poverty; but we little suspected at the time that these friends in 'song and wine' were carrying on a campaign against us which was to have dire consequences. This was revealed to us many years later by Count Sforza, who in those days of 1921 was Minister for Foreign Affairs in the Giolitti Liberal Government.

One day I was invited to tea by the daughter of General Turr, Louis Kossuth's partner, who had emigrated with him after the revolution of 1848 and taken Italian nationality. She, although Italian, seemed to have kept in touch with Hungary and showed sympathy towards me for having achieved what her father had fought for — Hungarian independence. The third person present at the tea party was a young man whom she introduced as her friend. They asked me a great number of questions which I answered candidly, for I had no reason to conceal my political opinions, which were known to everyone.

To my horror, on opening the paper next morning, I saw reported a long interview of mine, which repeated every word I had said and a great many I had not, and interpreted everything in the most fiendish way. Even my appearance was described as satanic. It had been a carefully laid trap into which I had fallen head over heels. Since I was enjoying the hospitality of the Italian Government I would never have dreamed of making a public statement on political matters, and that I appeared to have contravened this custom made an unfavourable impression in Rome. This, of course, was what had been intended. We discovered later that Madame Turr was an agent of the Horthy Government and had been given the job of getting me expelled from Italy. The reason for her special spite against me was that she had come to Budapest as the envoy of D'Annunzio when I was President, and had asked for an audience with me. I refused, since I was advised by the Italian representative not to see her. This was her revenge.

We lived a quiet life, meeting mostly the other inmates of the pension, the Mouraviefs, Narishkins, Olsoufiefs, etc., who in those days were still surrounded with the glamour of imperial Russia and were convinced that their return to St. Petersburg was but a matter of months. I started to write my memoirs with the help of my secretary, Fazekas, a Hungarian refugee who joined me in Florence for the work. We little suspected that Florentine society was watching us with animosity and that our days in the city of the Medicis were numbered.[8]

In the spring of the year we rented the villa Primavera in Fiesole, overlooking the city and surrounded by olive groves. Florence, in those days preceding the march on Rome, was the scene of continual street fights between Fascists and Communists. The Trades Union building in Florence was burnt down by Fascist rowdies under the leadership of the young Marchese Imperiali.[9] Day after day the news of Fascists or Communists being murdered appeared in the papers. The atmosphere was electric. There was shooting in the streets of Florence. We were relieved to have found a remote place in Fiesole, but our happiness did not last long.

We had scarcely been settled a week when, one afternoon while we were basking in the early spring sunshine a small boy appeared behind the stone balustrade of our terrace. He was visibly frightened and pointed towards the gate, making signs that 'they' were looking for us. At the end of the lane leading to our villa we descried a bunch of uniformed men. They did not approach. A quarter of an hour passed. We heard odd noises in the bushes. The uniforms had disappeared. Through the back windows a perplexing sight was visible. Carabinieri, their guns pointed towards the villa, had completely surrounded us. Suddenly an officer accompanied by two men braved the situation and, stepping on to the terrace, told us we were under arrest! Being arrested had by now become the recurring pattern of our lives.

The capture of our villa and its occupants is probably recorded in the annals of Fascist history as one of their victories, like that of the battle of Menton twenty years later![10] Relieved to discover that we had no munitions and did not put up a fight, the carabinieri crept out of their hiding-places. The villa was searched from top to bottom and all contents of cupboards and chests, books, papers and manuscripts, were scattered about. Katus's old Russian maid, whom she had hired in Florence to look after the children and who had been in the service of the Grand-duchess Elisabeth at the time that she was murdered by the Bolsheviks, accepted all that happened with the fatalism of the *mujik*. 'It was just like this in Russia,' she kept muttering between her teeth.

Although they found nothing compromising, my secretary and I were ordered to take seats in the lorry between the armed carabinieri, the women to follow with the children in a car. Accordingly the children were awakened from their afternoon nap and packed up. My wife refused to get in and was allowed to join us in the lorry. Then we were handcuffed. Katus demanded to be handcuffed too, but the officer refused, saying, 'Donnas are not handcuffed'. We drove off with bayonets pointing at our chests — which was unnecessary, I thought, against men who couldn't use their hands. The dutiful barking of the St. Bernard watch-dog accompanied us. I had succeeded in saving him from the murderous intentions of one of the men by assuring him that he was not ours but belonged to the Prince im Thurn und Taxis, which was true.

They drove us through the crowded streets, through the centre of the town, down the via Tornabuoni, in order to show us off as trophies of their victory — all this to the joy of the beaming Fascists. At the police station we were put under lock and key, the children, secretary, Italian nurse and Russian maid in an unfurnished room with stone-tiled floor. Eventually we succeeded in getting rugs for the children to lie on. Whenever they were taken to the lavatory, a soldier with a bayonet accompanied them!

The following morning, when I was at last confronted by the Chief of Police and inquired what were the charges against me, he told me candidly that there were none, but that it was the wish of the Florentine population that we should be expelled. The Italian press was full of fantastic tales about us: I was accused of being the chief organizer of the upheaval in Toscana, the rioting and everything else that happened there was my work; the owner of our villa Primavera was a Socialist, and the brother of the children's nurse was an active member of the Trade Unions. (We had not met either of them, and I had not inquired about the political views of my landlord: landlords as a rule are not Communists.) I had been distributing money from the Bolshevik fund which I was handling; Katus was spying on the Russian refugees and Italian officers. The final proof of my guilt, of which no denial was possible, was the fact that Socialist literature had been found in my library: Marx's *Das Kapital*, Kautsky's and Lenin's works.

My request to wire Giolitti and to have a lawyer was refused. I was asked to which country I preferred to go. My answer was: any, except Austria (since it was accessible to Hungarian Fascists). That same day we were taken to Tarvis on the Austrian frontier. Again handcuffs were fastened on my wrists and I was chained to my secretary. This was hard on poor Fazekas, who was unable to synchronize his steps with mine. The chain was much too heavy for him and he stumbled along after me, begging the guard to unfasten his too tightly screwed handcuffs. Exasperated, I tugged at him. It must have been odd indeed to witness me being pushed up the high steps of the Italian train, unable to use my hands, with Fazekas dangling on the other end of the chain like a fish being dragged from the water.

The journey to the frontier was a strange one. My wife showered abuse in Hungarian on the Italians in general and the carabinieri in particular. Fazekas, who was terrified of angering the officer in charge, translated her in the following manner: 'Madame la Comtesse is saying that she has great sympathy for you and the Italians and that her ardent wish is that you should be her guest in her Salon when she returns to Budapest'; then followed a description of the fabulous wealth of the Karolyis and the Andrassys. Katus, though unable to speak Italian, energetically denied everything Fazekas said. But it was not necessary. Looking at her with sorrowful eyes, the officer repeatedly said: 'Tell her I can well imagine what she is saying. I am sorry, very sorry.' In Venice, in an attempt to appease her, this gallant youth showed her the beauties of San Marco and bought her a bunch of spring flowers! He took touching leave of us at the frontier with many apologies, and expressed the hope that we would meet again in different circumstances.

At Tarvis, on examination of our papers, it was discovered that we had no entry visa for Austria, so we were sent back to Italy. By this time the children were completely exhausted and lay dozing on the trunks. At the Italian frontier the same fuss started all over again. After half a dozen telephone calls we were permitted to re-enter Austria, but would have to endure internment until our fate was decided. Our luggage was taken into custody by the police. Although the greatest part of our papers, documents and books had been seized by the Florentine police, a certain suitcase had escaped their attention. This contained a letter detailing a scheme of General Stromfeld's to overthrow the Horthy regime. Since the names of those involved were mentioned, it would have meant their certain death if discovered. Katus managed to open the suitcase, but a detective who had been secretly watching her noticed her action and confiscated it.

Fazekas, who by now had had enough of being my secretary,

was permitted by the Austrian authorities to proceed to Vienna. So he took the first train and disappeared out of my life.

Being interned in Villach meant that we were relegated to the best hotel of that small town; but as the Hungarian Government was now demanding my extradition on the grounds that I had murdered Tisza and taken four million kronen out of the country, my friends did not think this a safe abode. The workers of Villach feared that we might be kidnapped by Hungarian terrorist detachments and dragged over the frontier, a very common proceeding in those days. They therefore formed a guard of volunteers to stand watch all through the night in front of our hotel. I was, in fact, under the protection of the workers. The sacrifice of their night's rest after a day's work moved me deeply.

I spent the days in my hotel room, writing memoranda to Giolitti and Sforza demanding my rehabilitation and offering to return to Italy and face an investigation in order to justify myself. In pre-Fascist Italy under a liberal Giolitti Cabinet, I believed this was possible. I knew that if I were not cleared of the charge of having fomented the Toscana riots, no country would give me permission to settle. I received no answers to my letters.

Now we discovered also that all our valuables had been stolen by the carabinieri when our trunks had been packed. Our greatest intrinsic loss was Katus's ruby and diamond bracelet and some valuable fur coats, but the confiscation of our library was undoubtedly the hardest blow. When, later, we put in a claim for damages, we received an answer from the Fascist Government that it was an insult to the Italians to impugn the honesty of the carabinieri.

When the Villach comrades got to know about the compromising letter in the hands of the police, they determined to get hold of it. The Chief of Police, an amiable person, one day invited us to tea and there my wife spotted our suitcase on a shelf in the bathroom. The enterprising Villach workers now decided to move quickly and worked out an elaborate plan for taking possession of the suitcase, which luckily was never carried out, for to our relief and surprise the suitcase, still containing the letter, was returned to us the following day. Whether the police had ever read the letter, we never knew.

As so often happens, the papers seized from us by the Italians were of no value to them at all and they let slip the only important one. Still they had my wife's diary, 'translated' by Madame Turr. This journal was later sold to a Hungarian daily whose editor was Imre Karolyi's lawyer, a Mr. Ullein. When it was brought out, the working women in Hungary started a fund collected from their savings in order to engage a lawyer to defend my wife and sue Mr. Ullein, who had seized this opportunity to attack her in Parliament.

The last days in Villach I spent in the home of an engine-driver, called Samek, for the campaign carried on against me in Hungary was considered too dangerous for me to be allowed to continue at the hotel. Samek was a small, dynamic man, the best type of conscientious, level-headed, loyal labour man and I shall always gratefully remember the solicitude which he and his family showed towards me in those days.

Katus, who remained at the hotel with the children, noticed one day that a policeman was discreetly following her. Annoyed at this, she went up to him and asked whether he had orders to watch her. The poor fellow muttered in great embarrassment: 'Yes, but inconspicuously!'

My friends in Vienna, again the loyal Oskar Jaszi and Paul Szende (Minister of Finance during my regime), were active in trying to find a country in which we might settle. They were in touch with the Belgrade Government and at last we received permission to enter Yugoslavia. In 1921 we were supplied with Yugoslav passports, which we held until the end of our exile in 1946.

We bade farewell to Austria and our loyal friends the workers of Villach. Many years later Count Sforza, himself a refugee from Fascism, looked me up in Paris. He told me that in his memoirs, which were about to be published, he had tried to make good the injury done us. He writes that the Hungarian Government had pestered his Government to expel Karolyi and that the Russian émigrés had misled the Italian police by furnishing material which later proved to be pure invention.

3

YUGOSLAVIA

THE following two years we spent in Dalmatia on the shores of the Adriatic. Arriving on this bleak, rocky coast from the mellow Italian scene, we felt for the first time the weight of banishment. The harsh and scorching sun made the shadeless, arid landscape with its cruel cactuses appear to us like Devil's Island.

The Schiller Hotel we settled in was a new, large, barrack-like building standing by itself in a small bay, twenty minutes from the harbour town of Split. This desolate hotel was infested with flies, which settled on our food and drowned in our coffee, harassing our much-tried nerves. The only way to stand the broiling heat was to spend our days in the sea with the children. Not being able to speak the language, we felt completely cut off from the world.

The heat in the narrow streets becomes so unbearable during the summer months, even at night, that the inhabitants carry their bedding to the hillside behind the town to capture some sleep.

Unlike our experience in Czechoslovakia, we did not meet with animosity from the natives. The Dalmatians, accustomed to the wide horizons of sea-faring folk, are free from pettiness. They are kind and generous: a picturesque race, tall and vigorous, with graceful limbs and movements. Living amongst stones, they have developed a talent for sculpture. Many who could not read or write found a satisfying mode of self-expression in hewing and carving their native stone. Remarkable sculpture is found amongst these simple and primitive people: Mestrovics was an unlettered shepherd. Drawn to Vienna at the age of sixteen, he studied at the Academy while working at odd jobs and teaching himself to read. When we met him in Split he was at the height of his fame, having just finished his powerful 'Temple of Kossovo' and his deeply moving bas-relief, 'The Widows'. He was a silent man, with extraordinary hands, a goat beard and the smile of a child.

My gambling passion now changed to chess, a much less dangerous vice. I spent my afternoons in the central café of Split, getting
into touch with local life. The population showed much sympathy
for us, regardless of their old-time antagonism towards Hungarians.
They respected my stand for liberty and justice and were pleased that
I chose to settle amongst them. I had many touching proofs of this.
One day my sandals needed mending and I took them to a cobbler.
When I took out my purse, the man shook his head. From Karolyi he
would accept nothing. He helped the poor when he was rich; now that
he is poor, they would help him, he said. Another time my daughter
contracted typhoid fever, and Dr. Karaman, who attended her all
through her illness, realizing how hard up we were, charged us nothing.

The only social event on the coast was the arrival of the U.S.A. fleet
in the harbour. The flagship of Admiral Nieblack, with destroyers
under Commanders Zogbaum and Robertson, brought something of
the prosperity and luxury of the victorious West to these god-forsaken
shores. The town assumed a festive air. The pretty girls of Split
paraded on the quay in their best clothes to the joy of the intoxicated
U.S. sailors who, since they received higher salaries than Yugoslav
Ministers, could pick and choose. It was the onset of that demoraliza-
tion which increased through the coming years, the prostitution of the
'have not' nations by the 'haves'. It was revolting to see U.S. sailors
throw large pieces of ham and other victuals overboard, as the navy
was forbidden to sell them, and to watch the half-starved natives diving
into the sea to fish them out. . . .

The next year we moved from Split to Dubrovnik, an ancient
fortress town, rising from the sea, which had suffered many alien
dominations. An independent republic, it was in turn a vassal state of
the Byzantines, Venetians and Hungarians. After regaining its independence for a short time, it was once more conquered by Napoleon's
General Marmont, who received the title of Duc de Raguse, and later
by the Habsburgs, until finally it was incorporated into Yugoslavia
in 1919. Called the City of the Seven Banners, since it kept them in
readiness in case of renewed conquest, it is one of the most picturesque
spots of the Dalmatian coast. It has a most ancient, exclusive and degenerate aristocracy which views with contempt the old families of
Venice, whom they consider parvenus, since they themselves trace

their origin back to the sixth century. On one of the many occasions when they were conquered, the nobility unanimously pledged themselves to discontinue propagation. Three broke their vows, and their haughty descendants chose to remain behind their stone walls in their neglected gardens and dilapidated mansions, sulking in their antiquated glory. Life seems to have passed them by.

Dubrovnik was at that time the haven of the remnants of Wrangel's defeated army. After our unfortunate experience in Florence we were again thrown together with those who shared with us the fate of exile. I remember sitting opposite General Wrangel and his staff when we travelled on the Adriatic boat carrying us to Spalato. We viewed each other with aversion, adherents of opposing causes. The members of his army cast on the shores of Dalmatia were a demoralized lot, but they brought with them the careless, happy-go-lucky charm characteristic of the Russian ruling class of pre-Bolshevist days, charm which they lost later in the metropolises of the West. They drank and gambled, took drugs and lived on the earnings of their spouses—the Russian women were more courageous and diligent than their men. They sang, played the guitar, made love to one another's wives and were gay and romantic.

One day an unexpected blessing descended upon the colony. To everyone's surprise the men turned out in fashionable ties, new-made breeches, silk scarves and with smart cigarette cases. Rumour had it that they had got hold of unexpected spoils — a large trunk belonging to one of their 'friends', which had been shipped to the harbour of Durazzo from Constantinople. The unlucky owner had gone to Paris where, they presumed, he would need his belongings less than did his compatriots in the wilds of Dalmatia. They therefore judged it proper to put them up for sale, for the benefit of the needy Russian colony. The town was gayer, with more parties, more champagne and cocaine as the result. One of our friends was old Count Olsofieff who had been Vice-President of the Duma and had been called 'the man of the golden mouth', owing to his oratorical talents. Owner, in the past, of a great fortune, he was completely helpless in his new circumstances. When the biting north wind, the *bora*, blew for its traditional three, six or nine days, he would go to bed, pull the blankets over his head and stay there until the wind subsided, while some kind person would light the fire and bring him meals. Homiakov, who had been President of the Duma, was slightly better off than the rest and was much respected in the colony. Stolypin, son of the well-known Minister who was murdered for trying to create a new class of small landowners (called *kulaks* today) was considered arrogant for, being an admirer of the English, he tried to introduce the hygienic habit of not shaking hands every time one meets. General Lesh, chief of the Russian Third Army, installed a dairy notorious for its doubtful butter. In a ramshackle old house next to our villa in Lapad lived a Georgian prince with his three lovely daughters. Although grown up, they were kept literally sequestered by their tyrannical father, who was even known to use the cane on them if they attempted to acquire independence. This strange man, who had the appearance of a knight of the Middle Ages, had tenderer feelings for his fox-terrier than for his own offspring. When his pet died, he used his scarce money — there never was any for the household and his daughters looked famished — on a luxurious coffin for his 'loved one' and kept it in the living-room on the side table. The putrid odour kept away his daughters' suitors, which was perhaps his aim.

One day a Russian 'friend' offered us a business proposition. Several Russians with means had decided to found a night club, for they considered the Ragusan population was in dire need of a place to spend the night with wine and song. It was supposed to be a gold-mine which would turn them all into millionaires. He had, he said, bought half the shares himself, but, being a friend of ours, would let us have his part as there were no more shares left. We accepted his kind offer gratefully and the major part of our money went into the 'Stella Bar', the name given to this small cabaret in the harbour of Gruz. Now, every night a French *diseuse* sang her meagre repertoire, while the Russians, mostly co-shareholders, not having to pay for their drinks, drank lavishly of champagne. Although the Cossacks performed their dagger dances and a Montmartre atmosphere prevailed, the Ragusan burghers shunned the place, so after some weeks it had to shut, the resources having dried up and of course we never saw our money back. We then discovered that we had been the only shareholders. In any case the Russians had some fun at our expense for a couple of weeks.

The 'friend' who enticed us into this adventure was discovered selling our silver goblets, bracelets and golden cigarette cases after we left, which, he said with tears in his eyes, we had given him 'in remembrance'. He was most charming, cultured and entertaining and I do not doubt that in his peculiar fashion he was sincerely attached to us. He seemed to be haunted by the sight of the mysterious dark island of Lacroma which stretched out in the sea like the back of a seal. It was an unhappy island, bringing bad luck to its owners, who appeared to be predestined to violent deaths. It had belonged to the Archduke Maximilian, shot in Mexico, then to the Empress Elisabeth, stabbed at Geneva, and more recently to the Archduke Franz Ferdinand, killed at Sarajevo. 'I feel the dark forces emanating from that island', he used to say. Twenty-three years later our 'friend' was shot by the Yugoslavs on the island, in the shadow of its old monastery, for having been friendly to the Nazi occupation.

After our experience as bar-owners, we decided to handle our money ourselves. My sister Elisabeth managed to bring out some of my wife's money in a coil of wool which she was knitting during the journey. Katus invested this in a small motor boat, to carry tourists on sightseeing trips along the Adriatic shores and its islands. Clad in oily blue overalls, she tried to gain the confidence of her clients in her capacity of mechanic. One day a Czech family of numerous members hired our boat under the delusion that they had to do with Dalmatian fishermen. Great was their surprise and embarrassment on recognizing us. When we asked where they wanted to be taken, they answered politely 'Wherever the Herrschaften desire to go.' My wife retorted, 'We are not the Herrschaften. You are the Herrschaften,' but to make matters worse the engine broke down and all our efforts to repair it were in vain. In the end we managed to get home with the rudder in front; our passengers seemed deeply relieved when they set foot on land. Soon after this blemish on Katus's reputation as a mechanic a more serious accident occurred, which brought a sad end to our second enterprise as well. We got into one of those storms which arise at a moment's notice on the shores of the Adriatic, and the waves hurled our boat against the rocks beneath the Odak Hotel where we were to pass the evening with friends. To save ourselves we had to get into the water up to our waists, leaving our last investment to go to pieces on the cliffs. We now gave up expecting to make money out of night clubs and motor boats. To earn our living by regular work did not seem possible in those parts which had belonged to the old monarchy and where we were too well known. Not surprisingly there was little trust in the wage-earning or business ability of the Hungarian aristocrat.

I want to mention here a kindness which came to me. It was a loan of 100 dollars, which in those days meant a lot in Yugoslav dinars. It was sent me by an unknown Hungarian living in the States. Help seemed to come mostly from the common people and from strangers.

Some of my followers came to visit us during our stay in Dubrovnik. One of them, Abbé Hock, had been the President of the National Council in October 1918 and was now an exile like myself. One day my wife had prepared a beef ragout which did not meet with his approval, for he was a great gourmet and had been looking forward to consuming that pearl of Adriatic fish, the famous *branzino*. Luckily for him it was a Friday and he had the excuse of having to follow the rule of his church and not eat meat on Fridays. So, accompanied by Katus, he started off in quest of the fish. He visited all the fish restaurants of the port, invariably repeating his story that he could only eat *branzino*, but the fish could not be found. Exhausted and disappointed he sat down to a large steak instead.

After two royalist attempts the situation in Hungary gradually became stabilized, for history does not seem to follow the laws of logic. When a regime is doomed it is sure to last another twenty-five years. So it happened with the Horthy regime. The truth is that it was the Hungarian legitimists who dug the grave of the Habsburg monarchy. Their impatience, shortsightedness and unpopularity were useful weapons in the hands of the adversary. It was in 1922, at the Conference of Genoa, that the Hungarian Foreign Minister, Count Banffy, met for the first time the Governments of the Succession States and was received by Foreign Minister Nincic of Yugoslavia. The émigrés had little chance left. Most of the leaders gravitated towards America and I realized that Yugoslavia had no longer the right atmosphere in which to work successfully. The education of our children, too, made us wish to settle in the West, where I now had more hope of making my ideas known. I received an encouraging message from Caillaux, ex-Prime Minister of France, through a friend of his, Yvette Fouques, with whom during all these years we have remained in close friendship. Caillaux's fate had in some ways been similar to mine, as he was persecuted for his opposition to the war.

My friends, the émigré colony in Vienna, started to break up as well, most of them leaving for the States to prepare the road for me. The Horthy propaganda, as well as my expulsion from Italy, had much harmed my popularity. My first step was to get a transit visa to England in order to get to Canada and wait there for the right moment to start our campaign in the U.S.A., where we might hope to gain the support of the Hungarian colony. The States, I thought, would provide excellent soil for the idea of the Danubian Confederation, as Czechs, Hungarians, Rumanians, Italians and South Slavs, all living together in a larger unit of free states, would be more easily convinced of the necessity of co-operation. English friends had approached Ramsay MacDonald to secure our transit permit. Although I was partly of French origin and had lived much of my life in France and suffered for my friendship for France, I did not attempt to settle there, aware that the French policy, which favoured and backed Horthy, would probably prevent it. I trusted more the liberal traditions and fair play of England, and I proved to be right. Now arose the problem of finding money for the journey. Bozo Banaz, a Yugoslav shipowner, whose boats brought coal from England to Yugoslavia, offered us accommodation on one of them. The only cabin on this cargo boat was that of the captain, who kindly turned it over to us at night; but all day was spent on the sooty deck in the blazing sun, the children and our dog Balalaika being tied with ropes to the mast to prevent them from falling into the sea. We arrived on July 5th, at Barry Dock, Cardiff, where a new phase of our exile began.

The two years I had spent in Yugoslavia were not wasted, for I had come to know that gallant and generous people from close contact. Old Serbia had never experienced feudalism, nor had she a class of nobles sponging on her. I like to believe that the day will come when my country and Yugoslavia will unite in that brotherhood of peoples who live around the Danube and will become strong enough to prevent any imperialist Great Power from inciting them against each other for its own benefit.

4

'GENTLE ENGLAND'

1923

OUR first experience in England was a pleasant surprise. The porters at Cardiff Docks placed our innumerable pieces of hand-luggage, boxes, suitcases, baskets and bags in a third-class compartment of the train to London; but as soon as we stepped in and saw the cushioned seats and the general clean aspect, we started in feverish haste to hurl our belongings out of the window and to carry out the children as well, to the great bewilderment of our fellow passengers; we were convinced that we had got into the first class. After being informed that we were actually in the third, we had to start carrying them back again.

When we arrived from Cardiff at Paddington Station, William Gillies, Secretary of the Labour Party, met us on behalf of Ramsay MacDonald, leader of the party. They had reserved rooms at the Paddington Hotel, little suspecting that the price was much too high for our empty purses. So the next morning we started on our quest for cheaper accommodation in the vicinity.

We at last found rooms in a boarding-house in Stephens Road, a desolate district, where the penetrating smell of cooked cabbage haunted us. Our wild children, accustomed to the free life of the Dalmatian shores where they ran naked without any restraint, were utterly bewildered in their new surroundings. As they spoke only German, we had to silence them in public places, noticing that this language, so shortly after the war, was not favoured. They soon forgot their German, but not having yet learned English they became for a time completely dumb.

My first visit was to Ramsay MacDonald to thank him for his assistance. I met him in the lobby of the House of Commons where he received me in the company of Arthur Henderson, James Middleton,

James Maxton and other of his followers. MacDonald was very friendly. It was thirty years since I had been here with my uncle Alexander and had met Chamberlain, Balfour and Harcourt. The general aspect of Parliament, its top-hatted elegance, had changed, but I felt that these Labour leaders, with their accents and felt hats, were basically as much attached to the Empire as the traditional parties.

Soon after our arrival I fell ill with dysentery — my old illness which I had contracted in India — owing to the heat wave, which was exceptional in London that summer. It was odd that, coming from the hot climate of Dalmatia, I should succumb to heat in London. Katus, who had suffered from continual fevers in Dalmatia, was found to have one of her lungs affected. One day our landlady announced two American gentlemen, Mr. Caldwell and his secretary. I was in bed with fever and my wife had to cope with the task of trying to get rid of them. They persisted, insisting that they had come straight from Prague where they had seen Masaryk and Benes, had heard about me and had worked out a plan for solving the problem of the Succession States which they wanted to put into operation here and now. Accordingly they had to see me. Mr. R. J. Caldwell showered an avalanche of questions on me. As he was deaf, his secretary had to yell my answers into his ear, though they were probably not worth hearing as my fever by now was soaring high. At last, goaded by his secretary, Mr. Caldwell got up and, taking a look at the appalling room filled with luggage and medicine bottles, extracted his cheque book from his pocket, saying sympathetically: 'You do not seem to live under very comfortable circumstances.' He forthwith started to write out a cheque for a thousand dollars with the intention of leaving it on the bed. Exhausted as I was by the nervous strain of this unwelcome visit, this last drop overflowed the cup and I am still ashamed to think how rudely I asked my kind-hearted visitor to leave me in peace and to take his money with him. Seeing the expression on my face, he feared that my discontent was due to the insufficiency of his present and hastily started to make out a second cheque. At last, puzzled, he let himself be jostled out by his embarrassed secretary who, being a European, had grasped my mood. I will come to talk about Mr. Caldwell later, for he became in after years one of our most helpful and reliable friends.

It was most harassing to be laid up, with the prospect of having to leave for Canada in a couple of days. Katus therefore had to call on the authorities to ask for prolongation, and I shall always remember with gratitude those English friends who helped us to overcome this predicament. At last their efforts resulted not only in prolongation but in permission to settle in England. Among those instrumental in getting us the permission were Professor Seton-Watson, Sir Charles Trevelyan and St. Loe Strachey, editor of the *Spectator*. It was in the *Spectator* that my wife made her début as a journalist earning, for the first time, five pounds.

It was a great relief for us to be able to settle in England for, had permission been refused, it would have prejudiced our chances for the future. Being a pessimist, I had had little hope that my request would be granted, knowing the efforts made by my cousin Szapary, Hungarian Minister in London, to have it refused. When at last we got news from Sir John Pedder of the Home Office that I should call on him, I was still somewhat seedy, so I sent my wife instead. I shall never forget how anxiously I waited for her return in the small café opposite the Home Office, the minutes seeming hours. I poured down one cup of bitter coffee after another and watched the clock. Should I win my first victory over the Horthyites or should I be banished from the Old World as well? At last Katus turned up, beaming with the good news. It was a grand day and consequently I got better rapidly.

Although I had known England before, I could not but feel deeply impressed by its objectivity and the fairness which I encountered in all quarters. It was in England that we lost the feeling of being persecuted or ostracized on account of our political views. We became aware of the real meaning of a civilization rooted in liberal traditions, and both felt that at last we had reached a secure haven. I met with no prejudice, no animosity, only goodwill and understanding, and gradually the feeling of loneliness, so acute in the last years, faded away. This was probably due to the fact that I had the good luck to meet the right people, who are, I think, to be found in larger numbers in England than anywhere else.

Although Britain was still on the crest of the wave in those days, I noticed a great change in the exterior of London which we saw from the open bus tops, accompanied by Mr. Gillies: it was no longer the London I remembered. The intensified traffic, cars and buses, which had taken the place of the smart hansoms, the gay coaches, the spick and span turnouts, gave the streets a very different aspect. Devonshire

House was being pulled down. Regent Street had altered its face. But I was also seeing the town from a different angle — from the angle of the man in the street or on the top of a bus, not from that of the wealthy foreigner staying at Claridge's and driving to an exclusive club in Pall Mall for lunch. The greatest difference lay in the appearance of the Londoner himself. Top-hats were much rarer and, although well dressed, men did not seem to give their clothes the same importance as in my youth. On the other hand the quantity and choice of foodstuffs displayed in the shop windows, specially the richness of the fish, so rare in Dalmatia, spread out on ice on the marble slabs of the fishmongers, made our mouths water. The shops with luxury goods not seen by us for nine years were the temptation of Satan himself and made us painfully aware of our lack of cash. It was like stepping into a Garden of Eden, where all the fruits on the trees were prohibited. We took our meals at Lyons' teashops and in the fish and chip saloons for 1s. 6d. When we spent 2s. 6d. we felt we were being too extravagant.

As we were supplied with half a dozen letters of introduction, one of them a most valuable one from the Socialist leader, Bernstein, we were often invited to the houses of our new friends, who scarcely guessed that our finances were in such a dilapidated state.

Mrs. Ruth Cavendish-Bentinck was most hospitable to us, and proved for many years a loyal friend. In her house in Harley Street she would receive in exquisite fashion. Tall and slim, always dressed in black, she had an exotic beauty. An ardent suffragette in past days, she liked to talk about the struggle which she had carried on at the side of the Pankhursts; this was of special interest to Katus. Her outspoken progressive political views, her fierce distaste for snobbery and any sort of prejudice, were most refreshing.

It was Mrs. Bentinck who received for the first time in London the Soviet Ambassador, Christian Rakovsky, and his wife. The invitation card said: Dinner at seven-thirty. At eight o'clock the Ambassador had not yet arrived, but nothing could ruffle the calm of our hostess, who seemed to expect anything from foreigners. 'It is probably the Russian way,' she said philosophically. At eight-thirty a second round of sherry was served. At last, some minutes before nine, Mr. Rakovsky and his wife appeared, casually, without a word of excuse. Miraculously, the dinner was as excellent as usual, and soon the Ambassador's engaging personality, his fascinating talk and his wife's sincere directness made us all forget the incident and we passed a most stimulating evening. We became close friends of the Rakovskys and they often came to our flat, and we went to the Embassy. He was the old type of intellectual Bolshevik with high moral standards and integrity, deeply convinced of the truth of Communism, for which no sacrifice would be too much. He had lived many years in Paris as a gynaecologist, and belonged to the so called 'Westerners', in opposition to the Asiatic group of Stalinists. Highly cultivated, he was well acquainted with Western thought and conditions, subtle and sharp witted, with much humanity, and a sense of humour: in all a delightful companion. His loyalty to his principles and to his friend Trotsky was his undoing; but I do not want to anticipate. In those days he was the Ambassador of another Russia, that of Lenin and Trotsky.

At the Embassy we met Clare Sheridan, who had just returned from Leningrad, where she had made portraits of the leaders. Madame Rakovsky, who was unusually outspoken for the wife of a diplomat, seemed to be rather jealous of this beautiful Englishwoman, and she did not mince her words when giving her reasons for disliking Mrs. Sheridan.

After wandering from one boarding-house to another, where, as undisciplined continentals, we were most unpopular, we found a flat in St. George's Square in Pimlico, opposite an old grey stone church in a patch of garden with chestnut trees. After the conditions in Dubrovnik, my wife thought housekeeping here a pleasure fit for the gods. A gas stove and deliveries to the house were blessings, and it was a divine relief no longer to face the resentful glances of a landlady filled with contempt for 'aliens'.

We were now both searching for jobs, a most difficult, not to say impossible task for foreigners without training in those days of unemployment. Katus answered every advertisement, visited every agency; but her Hungarian nationality, lack of experience and testimonials, rendered her efforts vain. After her success with the *Spectator* our friends encouraged her to take up journalism, but it would not have been sufficient to keep a family of three children. At last she decided to take a course of motoring in Chelsea and become a taxi-driver. Though with little aptitude for mechanics, she seemed to nurse an unhappy passion for them. In addition she had to cope with the cockney accent of the instructor. For me to get employment was an even harder matter. I had no business sense, and my controversial political past limited my scope for journalistic activities. I was neither in my first youth nor in good health. Although my sister Elisabeth had managed to get out of Hungary some pictures which I had purchased at the time as the works of Hogarth and Lawrence, they turned out to be those of their pupils, and the price I received was far less than I expected. In those days I discovered that it is a distressing experience to become a seller instead of a buyer. The charming smile on the rosy face of the sales girl is transformed into a fiendish look when, after you have examined the silver and gilded cigarette cases and heard their price, you suddenly produce your own and shyly ask what she would give you for it.

One day I had the gratification of getting the best of a business deal instead of being done down as usual. It was the first and last time in my life. I had a Burberry, but no money with which to pay the grocer's bill. In spite of the English climate I thought a raincoat less necessary than groceries and walked off to Wilton Road near Victoria Station, where second-hand clothes were bought. I was lucky; they paid me a good price for it, thirty shillings. Encouraged, I returned the next day to sell a superfluous pair of shoes, but as soon as I arrived in front of the shop the owner rushed out in great excitement and let me know that he would never consider buying anything more from me, for the raincoat had its belt missing. After which, every time I passed his shop he would repeat his reproach: 'You, with your raincoat. . . .'

It was about this time that we received a message from Mr. Caldwell, asking to see us. With a feeling of guilt I thought the best way to make amends would be to send my wife to see him. She told him about the job she had undertaken. Mr. Caldwell disapproved. He would get her a situation in the States as a governess, with a high salary. He was on his way home and before leaving he arranged a luncheon party in my honour at Claridge's, his hotel. He asked some people he thought might be useful to us, Mr. J. H. Thomas from the Labour Party, Mr. Dudley Field Malone, a prominent New York solicitor and his wife and a few others.

We went. The toasts delivered were moving tributes to me but, recalling it now, I am afraid my answer did not conform to the traditional etiquette of English banqueting custom. Having at last, after four years' silence, the opportunity of giving vent to my feelings, I felt an irresistible urge to tell these gentlemen that politics in Hungary could not be carried on in kid gloves in the English fashion. I was violent and aggressive and mentioned that terrible phrase 'class war'. It was a reaction to something Mr. Thomas had said about goodwill, understanding and democracy paving the way between parties; my host's dejected air indicated that he felt that his protégé was disgracing him. I never had the qualities of a diplomat, as the reader by now must have recognized, but I admit I overdid it this time. Katus, too, reproached me bitterly. But to our surprise the next day I had a visit from Dudley Field Malone and his wife who were both most enthusiastic, my passion and candour having aroused their sympathy. Those who put up with me that day remained my friends, but the rest I never saw again; that is why, I suppose, I have forgotten their names. Had I been longer in England, in its mellow atmosphere of subdued tones, I should probably not have used the same language, realizing that greater effect can be obtained by understatement.

My trial for high treason had recently opened in Budapest. Dudley Malone, with the charming and disarming spontaneity of the Irish, assured me that he wished to take the matter of my trial in hand. The case was clear as daylight, he said, for under the Trianon Treaty no one could be prosecuted for his friendship to the Entente. He, as an international lawyer, would go to Budapest to assist me.

He was so filled with enthusiasm for the case, and so hopeful, that in spite of the dull sky he brought a ray of sunshine into our flat in St. George's Square. His wife, Doris Stephen, the well-known American suffragette and a very remarkable woman, was more of a realist, and warned us that we should not trust all her husband's promises for he would probably forget all about us in a few days, although, she assured us, he was at the moment completely sincere. All this, mind you, in front of him.

They asked us for the weekend to East Dean, where they had rented a manor house for the summer. Doris met us at the station, accompanied by a short man with light blue, piercing eyes, and a ruddy complexion, whom she introduced simply as H. G. We then recognized him as Wells, whose fame was unsurpassed in Central Europe in those days. I often met Wells in after years, on public platforms, and privately, as we were partners in the same hopeless struggle against dictatorship, aggression and persecution. We had just finished reading his *New Machiavelli*, and to meet him in person, and listen to his brilliant conversation, carried on in that peculiarly high-pitched, feminine voice of his, while we sat on the mossy cliffs overlooking the sea, was most enjoyable. He seemed much attracted to an American girl, a guest of the Malones, and in consequence was in his best form.

Doris was right. Although Malone started with great enthusiasm and actually appeared in Budapest, he was soon daunted by the difficulties and gave up.

One of our first contacts in London was with Herbert Asquith, Lord Oxford, and his wife, Margot. Mr. Baggar, a compatriot of mine, had published a book called *Prominent Europeans*, one chapter of which was devoted to me. Being a friend of Elisabeth Bibesco, he sent a copy to her father. We were asked to 44 Bedford Square for lunch. Lord Oxford was then seventy-six. I got the impression that he had not read Baggar's book and knew little about my history, but the fact that I was a refugee for a liberal cause was sufficient reason for him to show his hospitality. He remembered Katus's parents, whom he had received twenty years previously when he was Prime Minister and my father-in-law was a member of the Hungarian Cabinet. It was at this luncheon that I renewed my acquaintance with Sidney Webb, and met Bertrand Russell for the first time.

Soon afterwards we dined with Sidney and Beatrice Webb in the company of Bertrand Russell and his wife Dora. When the ladies left and we were sipping port, I asked the leading theorist and founder of Fabian thought what would Labour's programme be with regard to India and the Colonies should it win the autumn elections (1923). He surprised me by answering that there could be no question of giving up India, and by being hesitant even about Dominion status. I pointed out that this was in contradiction to Socialist theory. He agreed, but said that one could not settle these matters on logical grounds. For continental Socialists these first contacts with British Socialists are very disconcerting, because few of them realize that the Labour Party is not spellbound by Marxism, and as a matter of fact is not Marxist at all.

During this time Beatrice Webb was explaining to Katus that revolutions did not promote progress, and that the French Revolution with all its bloodshed had not accomplished more than it could have done through evolution. Katus, with the courage of the *ingénue*, held to her own continental opinions. This was the first time we had been in touch with the genuine stuff of old-fashioned Fabianism, and with its two remarkable apostles. It was a surprise to me that in later years they turned into such ardent believers, and supporters of the Soviet Union; considering it as 'Fabianism adapted to Asia'.

Through the Stracheys we met William Rothenstein, the painter, whose greatest attraction for us was that he had been a friend of Oscar Wilde. Wilde had been one of the best known and most admired British writers on the Continent, and we were surprised to discover that in England he was much less appreciated.

Other painters I met were Charles Mason, who made a successful portrait of me, and Derwent Wood, who made a drawing when we attended a party at his house. Colonel Josiah Wedgwood, M.P., later Lord Wedgwood, who had made a report in Parliament on the White Terror, was a most reliable friend. I had a great admiration for this noble fighter for lost causes, whose humanity and kindness for the persecuted manifested itself with unequalled generosity whenever his assistance was needed.

Saturday afternoons we spent mostly with Wickham Steed in Holland Park, where in his large sitting-room furnished in the French style, he received distinguished foreigners for tea. Wickham Steed, who had been correspondent of *The Times* in Vienna for over twenty years, was an expert on the Habsburg Empire and, although Conservative, a violent opponent of Magyar chauvinism and a friend of the Slavs. Over the tea-table the formidable Madame Rose presided, subduing with her imposing personality the motley crowd of Italian anti-Fascist refugees, Rumanians, Czechs and Yugoslavs. They discussed, under her lead, the latest political news, but woe to those who met with her disapproval. Mr. Steed, tall and slim, impeccably turned out, resembled Cardinal Richelieu. He spoke French and Italian without an accent, German and even Hungarian fluently. It was here that I met Don Sturzo, refugee from Mussolini and the head and creator of the Italian Catholic 'Populare' Party. The atmosphere was mostly optimistic, as the opinion prevailed that Fascism was gasping its last breath.

A convenient meeting-place for political men and women of the Left, for painters, writers and actors, was the 1917 Club, founded during the war by Ramsay MacDonald as a pacifist centre; but by the time I was elected an honorary life member, Ramsay MacDonald had become too respectable and rarely visited it. I spent many a stimulating evening listening to the brainy fireworks of Professor Joad, in the company of H. W. Nevinson, Brailsford, Charles Laughton and Elsa Lanchester, who in those days were just beginning to be known. The company compensated one for the uncomfortable furniture; chairs which had but three legs, cups without handles and tasteless, scanty and monotonous food. I remember my bewilderment the first time I lunched there. My neighbour had ordered fish, boiled potatoes and white sauce. After finishing it in the indifferent way in which most English people consume their food, he asked for plums and custard. When he was ready to pay, a flushed and embarrassed waitress informed him that she had mistakenly served custard with the fish and white sauce with the prunes! My neighbour smiled, a kindly English smile, as if such trivialities had no importance whatsoever. 'I never noticed it,' he said. One day I sat next to a tall, bespectacled man, with large loose limbs, whose name I did not know. A conversation ensued on Palestine and as I had been reading the book on the subject by the well-known German writer, Arthur Holitcher, I warmly recommended it to him as being the most brilliant report on Zionism. After having allowed me to praise for some time the qualities of Holitcher's writing, my neighbour introduced himself. 'I am Arthur Holitcher.' After that he cherished a deep affection for me.

The first summer we spent a weekend with the children at Cookham, on the Thames, in the house of Sir George and Lady Young, bathing and punting in the river, a great treat in the hot weather. With my son Adam we swam across the Thames which at that point, although narrow, had a strong current; it was a considerable feat for a boy of five.

One of our first acquaintances in England was Augustus John, to whom we were introduced by the wife of an American captain who had been stationed with his destroyer on the Adriatic coast. John visited us on several occasions in St. George's Square, and we went to some unusual studio parties in Mallord Street which did not correspond to the foreigners' idea of inhibited English entertainment.

On several occasions I visited Bertrand Russell and his vivacious and ambitious second wife, Dora, with both of whom I remained in touch for several years. I often recollect the truth of many of his predictions concerning Soviet Russia. There were few things I enjoyed more than staying with this extraordinary man, whose directness, moral courage, conversational brilliancy, personal charm and spontaneity made him so unusually attractive.

We were asked for weekends to Warwick Castle, offered by the Countess of Warwick to the Labour Party as a holiday resort for Socialists needing rest. Coming from countries where Socialists were outlawed, hounded and imprisoned, we found this a proof of the tolerance so characteristic of England.

The Secretary of the Second International in London in those days was Friedrich Adler, the man who shot the Austrian Prime Minister, Count Stürgkh, in 1916 and who had been sentenced to death but amnestied at the time of the Revolution. He was a surprising choice for London. Since his act, he was a completely changed man. As if drained of all passion, he had become a mild and gentle bureaucrat, loathing direct methods and violence. He was a strange case of split personality. No one could have imagined that this shy, timid little professor with the tawny, unruly mane of thick hair and short-sighted, watery blue eyes, spectacles and awkward movements could ever have dared to shoot at the Austrian Prime Minister in one of the most exclusive hotels in Vienna.

I remember being introduced to Karl Kautsky, the well-known Socialist and Marxist, spiritual leader of the Second International, in the Gower Street club. It was he who published after the war the secret documents of the Berlin Chancery, thus clearly proving German guilt in the war. He seemed prematurely aged for, though only about seventy at that time, he had to be pushed in a bath chair.

It was at the end of the year 1923 that my memoirs were published in Berlin by Karl Novak, who had himself written a book about the collapse of the Monarchy. It was an answer to the false charges made against me at my trial. Banned in Hungary, its clandestine distribution made the book's success. Those who could afford to be objective were startled and began to see things in a different light, but a dictatorship is not much affected by public opinion.

During the summer of 1924 the Horthy Government asked for a loan from the League of Nations. Oskar Jaszi in the States, and I in London, were of the opinion that this occasion should be used to demand the slackening of the dictatorship and that the loan should be granted only if the conditions under which the Horthy regime had been originally set up by the Entente were fulfilled and a guarantee given that it would be used exclusively for productive purposes, not for rearmament against the Allies; that universal suffrage should be re-established and an international commission set up, as had been done in Austria, to see the terms of the agreement carried out.[11] Strangely enough, Benes, although aware of its dangers, did not object to the loan, thus proving our suspicion that he was not really opposed to the Hungarian regime. Realizing Labour's influence in England, Stephen Bethlen sent three Social Democrats whom he had brought to heel, Peidl, Peyer and Garami, to London to gain the support of the Labour Party at the financial committee-meeting of the League in London. Peidl and Peyer had no intention of looking me up, knowing that I would disapprove of their mission; but an impish fate ordained it differently. Taking my place, the only one left, on the top of the Victoria bus to Piccadilly, I found myself seated next to P. and P. whom I had not seen since those memorable days of March 1919. It was an embarrassing moment for them and compromising as well. Who at home, would believe that in the biggest metropolis of the world they had met me by chance? They now felt obliged to look me up next day in St. George's Square and while Peidl was using his gold toothpick — which he had brought with him, having been informed that in England these adjuncts of civilization were unobtainable — they both tried to convince me of the necessity of a loan without conditions. That the toothpick was a gold one was probably to prove to the British working class that in Admiral Horthy's Hungary the workers could afford to clean their teeth with gold!

I asked Ramsay MacDonald for an interview, but could not obtain an answer. Here again chance favoured me. Lunching at the 1917 Club, I found myself facing him. 'I am sorry,' I said, 'for your bad luck!' He had to listen to me, and I tried to make him understand the dangers involved in an unconditional loan, but in vain. Labour's attitude in those days was to help the Central Powers, the 'underdog', the victims of Versailles, Trianon and the Imperialists — a mistake bitterly regretted later. After a robust argument, Ramsay lost his temper, banging on the table with his fist; and I banged the door as we parted, friends no longer. The loan was granted and Hungary, in defiance of the Treaty of Trianon, kept a much larger contingent of armed forces than was stipulated — and this with the knowledge and consent of the Great Powers.

Later I again had reason to disagree with MacDonald — at the time of the public scandal over the forging of French francs. MacDonald was by then under the influence of the smart set and society women of Mayfair and was unrecruitable for Left causes — so our connection ceased.

The behaviour of the Minister in London, Laszlo Szapary, was rather inconsistent with his anxiety to prove that Hungary needed help. His receptions outdid in extravagance those of the other Succession States, which entertained on a much more modest scale. On one of these occasions, a row of sumptuously uniformed guards with plumed shakos and fur-trimmed dolmans were posted on each step of the stairs of the Legation. A Hungarian guest, pleased to see his countrymen, addressed one of them in his native tongue, but to his surprise was answered in the purest cockney: 'It's 'nuff of a bloody nuisance to stand 'ere in this monkey dress wivout 'avin' to understand your bloomin' lingo.'

To the tune of 'Yes, we have no Bananas' Labour won the autumn elections of 1923. The night of the polls we spent as guests of Dr. Marion Phillips in the offices of the Labour Party and saw the excitement and exultation as the results came in. It was the first Labour victory.

My health troubled me quite a lot that winter in London; I was haunted by the fear of spinal trouble. Although this proved wrong, doctor's and chemist's bills drained our last reserves. After having sold a large painting by the Swedish painter, Zorn, we had to turn to my wife's pearls. Through Breitscheid, the German Minister of the Interior in the Weimar Republic and a perpetual candidate for the post of Prime Minister, we met a Berlin *Schieber* — the name given in those days to the Black Marketeers — who was buying jewels from the 'new poor'. Katus had to go to Paris to see him and, after having handed this completely unknown individual her pearl necklace without witness or asking for a receipt, she obtained from him the top price. The next day Breitscheid sent her a message that she should have no dealings with the person he had unwisely recommended, having discovered that he was a notorious crook who had swindled many victims. My wife's naive trust in his honesty, which he probably experienced for the first time, must have disarmed him, for he could have got the necklace without paying a penny for it.

We were still waiting to hear from the American family who would engage Katus as a governess. One day she got a letter from Mr. Caldwell, informing her that he had arranged something more to her liking — a lecture tour through the States. Her article in the *Spectator* had been much appreciated and she was invited to deliver lectures on the same subject, 'Feudalism in Hungary'. The tour would last about six months, all expenses paid. It was not easy for her to leave me and the children but I encouraged her to go, knowing that she would have a success and it would give her satisfaction to add substantial sums to our ebbing income. So she accepted.

At the end of August 1924, on Francis Joseph's birthday, as if he had laid a curse on me, I fell on the pavement at Newbury, while teaching my children to ride a bicycle, and broke my thigh.

One grey October morning Katus left. On crutches and accompanied by a nurse, I saw her off at Southampton. As she was standing on the deck waving me farewell, a man next to her said in German to his companion, pointing at me: 'How ill that wretched man looks, I would not give him another week.'

With this encouragement Katus sailed off to the New World.

I spent the autumn of 1924 in the sombre room to which I had moved in Hampstead, trying to liberate myself from the dangerous narcotic which had been administered to me for soothing pain. The nurse, who had instructions from the doctor to fill my syringe with water, found it more convenient to ensure her night's rest and mine by relieving me with the genuine stuff. Thus my dis-intoxication took a long time.

It was a dismal season with exceptionally dense fogs of the genuine pea-soup variety, and my journeys to the doctor, from Golders Green to Olympia on the opposite side of London, took more than three hours a day.

I shall never forget the torments which I endured under the doctor's treatment. In order to support it I had to visualize the sufferings of those wretched men and women at home who for their political convictions were being tortured in prison cells and concentration camps. I was haunted by the belief, becoming more and more a certainty, that prolonged and intense physical pain can break down even the most gallant resistance and that the moment was bound to come when the victim would consent to whatever was demanded of him. So, lying on the doctor's table, I passed through mental as well as physical anguish.

The saying that 'troubles come not single spies' proved at this time to be true. My trial for high treason unexpectedly came to an end, after having dragged on for three years. I was found guilty. It was a surprise to my lawyers, who had been confident that we should win, public opinion having greatly changed in my favour. The reason for the sudden verdict was that the Government became apprehensive that the League of Nations would try to interfere on the strength of the Trianon Treaty. Soon after the verdict I got a message from a Swiss company that, distrusting the longevity of the Horthy regime, they were ready to exploit my property in Hungary and pay me a yearly income. They had, they said, a way to wangle things with the Hungarian Government. Although the offer was tempting I refused it, as I felt I had no right to dispose of my lands once I had given them away, even if the peasants were no longer in possession of them. My mistake had been not to have invested money outside Hungary as most of my compatriots did: all my wealth was inside the frontiers of Trianon.

My friend Oskar Jaszi visited me in London. The differences between us were beginning to become more evident. We were personally deeply attached to each other, but he was passionately opposed to the Soviet system, while I felt that Social Democracy with its present methods would not bring us nearer to a Socialist State; also that European Socialism needed Soviet Russia's backing, even if we did not agree with the means they employed. Jaszi argued that State Capitalism was just as far or even farther from Socialism than our present system, and that the Soviets were not a help but an obstacle to Socialist progress.

In the States Katus was having a strenuous time battling with her cousin Count Laszlo Szechenyi, Hungarian Minister in Washington, who had started a campaign against her. He had a circular letter sent to all the members of her reception committee, informing them that Katus was 'a bloodthirsty Bolshevik', and referring to our expulsion from Italy. One of them, Mrs. Gerard, the wife of the American Ambassador to Berlin and sister of Countess Antony Sigray,[12] resigned in haste, followed by a bunch of scared ladies. Mr. S. Stanwood Menken, President of the American Defence League, now sent a petition to the State Department requesting that my wife should be prevented from landing and kept on Ellis Island, as a menace to the security of the States. All this had just the opposite effect. The Statue of Liberty which welcomed the pilgrims to the New World started to work. Katus was enthusiastically received. Mrs. Franklin Roosevelt staunchly supported her and she was invited to stay at her house — her husband was being treated at the time in a nursing home. Katus's first public appearance, in the Town Hall, was a great success. She had challenged Mr. Menken to listen to what she had to say and attack her in public if he felt so inclined. The gentleman did not appear.[13]

Shortly before Christmas I got the news that Katus had fallen ill with typhoid fever. I had just received a cheque of a thousand dollars from her for the children's keep. She had sent it off on the day she was taken to hospital and, being destitute, hoped to be admitted to the public ward. This help was a blessing for me, as I could now buy a ticket to join her in New York. Our friends did not agree with her wish to enter the public ward and Mr. Caldwell, with the help of my Hungarian followers, put up the necessary amount for a private room. Mr. Spalding, her doctor, most generously attended her free of charge.

At the news of her illness I hobbled on my crutches to the American consulate and asked for an immediate visa. I received it on condition that I would not deliver any public speeches, give interviews or write articles. Without a moment's hesitation I gave my word. I had only one wish: to cross the Atlantic.

In New York Harbour I was met by Mr. Caldwell with the advice: 'Do not mention the word Socialism. We over here do not believe in it.' I found Katus gravely ill; an urgent operation was necessary. The doctor told me point-blank that there was little chance of her recovery. Dr. Erdmann, one of the best New York surgeons, undertook the operation, also without charge. During her illness the American public manifested much sympathy, which moved me deeply. Some papers even issued a daily bulletin of her condition. The attacks against her and the obvious slander of which she was the victim roused their chivalrous spirit. Since then I have always kept a soft spot in my heart for the American people.

Although I did my best not to attract attention and keep the newspaper men away, it was a difficult task. One day on my way to the hospital I saw a crowd gathered in the street, their heads turned upwards in joyful glee, watching a dishevelled and yelling woman cast out of the window of a skyscraper pairs of pants, shirts, collars, shoes and other useful objects. I was told that she was distributing the wardrobe of her husband in this strange fashion. She was getting what she wanted — publicity — for the reporters were on the spot, camera-men flashing their magnesium lights. To my distress I was recognized and badgered to give my opinion on 'girls' who thrust their husbands' belongings from windows. Bound by my promise not to make public statements I escaped in non-committal silence. My friends, on hearing on what condition my visa was granted, were highly indignant. They felt it a slight on American liberty and suspected it to be due to Szechenyi who, being married to a Vanderbilt, had made use of his social connections. Szechenyi, who in Hungary was nicknamed 'Builty', diminutive for Vanderbilt, was notorious for never having been able to pass an examination — which did not prevent him from becoming a Magyar Ambassador. He certainly failed as an astute diplomat in Washington, having been unmasked by Senator Wheeler for hiring a detective for two thousand dollars to shadow us. Although this sort of thing is done, it is considered reprehensible when found out. 'Builty's' reputation was shaken and he was recalled the year after. My wife seemed to create havoc in the ranks of the Horthy diplomats, for Count Szapary was recalled from London for not having prevented her from getting the visa to go to the States. His defence was that she was more of a danger in London than in New York, a statement with which Szechenyi did not agree.

The liberal and progressive group of Americans proved indefatigable in my defence. Protest meetings were organized requesting the Secretary of State, Judge Hughes, to lift the ban. The press used headlines illustrated with impressive cartoons of the Gagged Man, who had a secret to reveal, but was prevented by the influence exercised on the State Department by the Horthy Government through the Vanderbilts. At meetings I sat in sphinx-like silence, which roused sympathy and assured me success.

This time it was a very different America from what I had known thirty years before: the America of the 'Four Hundred'. On my propaganda tour ten years earlier, shortly before the war, I had contacted only the Hungarian colony; now it was the intellectual, liberal America that received me.

Offers poured in from all sides for lectures, articles and even appearances on the stage, if the ban was lifted. I was asked to hold a public discussion with the Grand Duke Alexander in one of New York's theatres. He would sponsor Tsarism, I Socialism. In the end we were to advertise aspirin. We spent some time in the Connecticut home of the writer Henrik Van Loon, of Dutch origin, whose historical books, among them the *Book of the Bible for Children* with his own witty illustrations, were much in vogue. When his bulky form, in tweeds and knickerbockers, was seated at the head of the oak refectory table, with his jovial physiognomy of a *bon viveur*, his pipe, and his plate overflowing with rich food served by his devoted wife Jimmy, he seemed to have stepped out of a Dutch eighteenth-century canvas. He was a most entertaining conversationalist, always ready to thrust a venomous dart at ignorance and prejudice and to stand up against any sort of injustice.

One day I had a surprising experience. At the house of friends, Roger and Margaret Baldwin — he was President of the American Civil Liberty Union — I had met Mr. Johnson, head of the Union for the Rights of the Coloured People. He himself, white of skin, was a most attractive man and could hardly have been detected as a Negro. He was a talented poet as well and promised to send me an autographed edition of his works. We were staying in a service flat in one of the apartment houses on Lexington Avenue. One afternoon the telephone rang from the hall. The management informed us that a coloured man claiming to be a friend of ours had refused to use the service elevator. I could not at first grasp what was meant and why he was prevented from taking the visitors' elevator. The manager then explained that Negroes were not permitted to use it. I warned him that I would instantly quit the apartment if they stuck to their attitude, as the young man was my friend. Some minutes later, the envoy of Mr. Johnson, whom I had never met before, stepped triumphantly out of the elevator, with a load of books under his arm.

In April we returned to England. That our trip had been so success-ful was in part due to the foolishness of Judge Hughes and Count 'Builty'. When the correspondents of the leading New York papers heard of our departure, they booked seats on the same train to Canada, so as to have an interview with me — the 'forbidden story' — as soon as I crossed the frontier.

I was still asleep when we arrived at the border, and was roused by an eager reporter bending over me with his fountain pen pointed at my head, as menacing as a revolver. Other reporters followed. I pleaded for some more minutes' sleep but there was no mercy. 'The Story' had to be released at midday. So, gathering my wits, I began: 'Now that I am on the free soil of Canada' — Revenge on the State Department was sweet. I ended: 'Best greetings to Count Szechenyi. Tell him that I would be delighted to engage him as my publicity agent on a 10 per cent basis.'

It was not surprising that Szechenyi was called home soon afterwards by his Government, which had discovered meanwhile that it was not sufficient for a Minister to have a Vanderbilt for his wife; he needed brains as well.

For a time it was the standard joke in the States, if someone could not obtain a hearing, to say: Mind you, I am going to Canada.

5

MY TRIAL

MY property was a tempting bait for the Counter-Revolution and they had decided to get hold of it. In a nutshell the story of how they succeeded is as follows:

On January 20th, 1920, during the election campaign, Prince Louis Windischgraetz[14] made a violent attack on me, asserting that I had been in the service of the French since 1916 and had betrayed military secrets to them.

The whole reactionary press responded eagerly to this accusation, as the wounded vanity of chauvinist Hungary acclaimed anyone ready to supply a scapegoat and mitigate the humiliation of a lost war.

On July 6th the Prince delivered his *J'accuse* against me in the National Assembly. He stated that in 1917 great sums of money had been brought from France to Hungary — rather a tricky performance during the war — to be utilized for pacifist and defeatist activities, and were distributed in my presence to the members of the Independence Party. He mentioned the names of two Deputies.[15] He then brought up all the charges which had been collected by Major Konsten, which at the time I had unmasked, and my negotiations with Sonnino and those carried on in Switzerland; he mentioned a memorandum handed by me to Dutasta, Clemenceau's illegitimate son, who was French Minister in Berne in 1917, in which I was supposed to have given up parts of Hungary. He said that Dutasta told him privately that no one in France thought seriously of negotiating with Karolyi, who was their paid agent. He then referred to a sitting of the French Assembly on November 30th, 1917, in which Clemenceau was supposed to have said that his Government 'had seriously considered Karolyi's reports on the military situation of the Central Powers, but as his relations with Soviet Russia were well known we did not think it in keeping with the dignity of the French people to give support to forces which could not be the basis of European consolidation . . .' 'The extreme

Socialists,' went on Windischgraetz, 'Renaudel, Longuet, Moutet, Paul Boncour , had negotiations with Karolyi, who delivered military secrets to them. The French Government admitted that they had sent Karolyi home so that he might carry on an agitation in their interests.'

These facts, he said, were officially communicated to him by the German Legation when he was a member of the Cabinet in 1917 and were founded on investigations by the German General Staff and on the documents of the French Foreign Office, all proving that Karolyi was the bearer of military secrets when in Switzerland.[16]

No proofs of these accusations were produced, but the Prince assured Prime Minister Bethlen that he would supply them in the shortest possible time, so that the necessary action against members of the Independence Party could be launched without delay.

He brought up his charges in such a positive form that the public was completely mystified, and even my closest friends and followers could hardly imagine that the Prince, despite his reputation as an adventurer, would take such a step without some sort of foundation. The Members of Parliament whom he had compromised started a libel action against him.

In the following weeks, the press affirmed that the requisite material had been handed over by the Prince to the authorities.

These preliminaries were necessary to create the atmosphere for the impending trial and to make feasible the confiscation of my estate even before the trial and without proof of my treachery. To render this procedure legal, a special law was passed through Parliament.

I was in Yugoslavia at the time and my answer to the calumnies could not reach the Hungarian public, although published in the press of the Little Entente.

The main reason for this frantic hatred of me was not only political. When my Government had taken over, the Ministry of Food found four million florins missing from a sale of potatoes. The Prince was asked to explain, but he escaped to Switzerland. The papers published the news. Later, at the time of the Counter-Revolution, he candidly admitted having taken this sum to Switzerland 'and having spent it on propaganda'. The Horthy Government did not prosecute him.

The chief envoy of France, M. Foucher, gave an account of Windischgraetz's speech in the Assembly to his Government. At the request of the lawyers representing the Independence Party, Clemenceau sent the following wire to their leader, Count Theodore Batthyanyi: '*Je n'ai prononcé aucune des paroles que m'attribue Prince Windischgraetz.*' The French Minister, Dutasta, wrote to my sister Elisabeth that he had met the Prince once in his life, in the company of the ex-Ambassador Mensdorff-Pouilly, when there was no mention of Karolyi. Then followed the energetic denials of the French Socialists, Renaudel in the *Populaire*,[17] and Léon Blum.[18]

Although the authorities did their best to postpone judgment and gave the Prince five years to collect his material, on January 21st, 1923, my calumniator humbly declared to the court and to the press that he had been misled by 'ill-intentioned informers', withdrew all his charges and apologized to the Party of Independence. He did not apologize to me, as I was an outlaw and could not defend myself. The Prince little minded his disgrace, for he had achieved his aim and enabled the Horthy regime to spread the fable of my treachery and to sequester my estate.

He repeated his accusations in his memoirs, published in Berlin by Ullstein. Now I could get hold of him. I won my libel case against the firm; the memoirs could no longer appear in their original form and the incriminating passages had to be erased.

My estate, which had been valued at 100 million gold florins (£25,000,000) dwindled to one-tenth during the two years of its management by the State. It became the booty of directors, managers and officials.

Being an entailed property (*Fideicommissum*) I was only its beneficiary, not its owner. In order that the State could lay hands on it legally, my son and his heirs had to be deprived of it as well. As the Hungarian laws of 1791 and 1915 did not provide for such a case, a special law had to be fabricated. It was known as Lex-Karolyi and it excluded from the right of possession my five-year-old son, who at the time of the 'treachery' was not yet born. The new law stipulated that 60 per cent of the estate should go to the State, and 40 per cent to another branch of the family, in my case to my brother Joseph and his descendants. Now that the necessary atmosphere was created and the law passed, the trial against me could begin.

It started on June 19th, 1922. My lawyers fought courageously against the inevitable. The charges were the following: my negotiations with Sonnino, and those in Switzerland in 1917; the 'help' I had given to the Entente to defeat us; the signature of the Belgrade Armistice; the formation of the National Council, and preventing the King from exercising his rights. There was no mention of the handing over of power to the Bolsheviks.

The verdict, which found me guilty, was only pronounced three years later, on February 22nd, 1925; as my fortune had already been seized, there was no hurry. Moreover, like Windischgraetz, they had no proofs to justify the verdict. The court refused to give a hearing to any of my witnesses or to accept any evidence on my side. No documents were produced.[19] I was found guilty on the declaration that the charges were public records, and therefore proof was not necessary. The suit would probably have dragged on longer, if the Entente Ambassadors had not reminded the Hungarian Government of the Clause of the Peace Treaty, prohibiting the molestation of anyone for pro-Entente activities during the war. The Horthy Government, fearing interference, thought it wiser to confront the Western Powers with a *fait accompli*.

None of my colleagues, who had shared responsibility with me, had been prosecuted, and some of them even took part in the Horthy Government. Their luck lay in having no fortune to seize.

In 1928 my lawyers, believing that passions had ebbed and that the consolidation of the Horthy regime could afford justice, and also possessing fresh evidence, asked for a re-trial. The evidence was a document signed by the Archduke Joseph in which the laying down of arms had been ordered by him in the name of the Emperor, and had been done by the Karolyi Government, with the Emperor's knowledge, on November 3rd before the Belgrade Armistice.

Masaryk's and Benes's memoirs, which had just been published, gave a detailed account of my efforts to preserve the integrity of Hungary's frontiers, and an unequivocal letter from Clemenceau stated that he and his Government had had no connection whatsoever during the hostilities with me or my party and that he was ready to appear personally before the Budapest courts to give evidence. My wife visited him in his retirement in the rue Franklin, and he had immediately agreed to her request.[20] Paul Painlevé, Head of the Cabinet and Minister of War in 1917, wrote a letter to the same effect. These testimonies were shattering, and the Horthy courts dismissed my request for a new trial, for they realized how compromising for the Government my rehabilitation would be.

In 1946, at the time of the coalition Government of Imre Nagy, Parliament decreed my complete rehabilitation. My property was — on paper — returned to me.

I hesitated to write in detail about my own trial because the world has of late witnessed far greater injustices; but I believe that it is becoming more and more necessary for the student of politics to realize how easily public opinion can be misled and what danger lies in a Government that exercises unlimited power.

6

PARIS IN THE 'TWENTIES

ON our return from the States we moved to France, for life in
England turned out to be too expensive for our meagre means.[21]
In a small house at Bois-Colombes we waited for the autumn,
to return to the States.[22] In sparsely furnished rooms, the children
sleeping on mattresses on the floor, we lived a proletarian existence.
Katus was earning twenty francs a day at the Théâtre St. Martin, where
she acted in the rehearsals of a play on Joan of Arc. She worked also
as a mannequin in one of the dress-making establishments in the Rue
Royale.

On account of her talks in the States a warrant for her arrest was
issued in Hungary. She was charged with being a member of a French
'Anarchist' Society, *La Ligue des Droits de l'Homme*. This league,
the mildest possible of associations, was founded on the humanist
proclamation of the French Revolution, the Rights of Man. Its purpose
was the protection of those persecuted by whatever regime, Fascist or
Communist. Its President, Ferdinand Buisson, and his successor,
Victor Basch, and its Secretary, Henri Guernut, member of the Blum
Government, protested that the seizure of my property by the Hungarian law courts was illegal because the Treaty of Trianon decreed
that no one could be prosecuted for having been friendly to the Entente
during the war.

Our group founded a Hungarian Branch of the League in Paris, of
which I became President, also a daily paper named *The Republic*.

My reception in France contrasted strongly with the kindness I had
received in England and the U.S.A.; few of the French seemed to
understand that the main reason for my exile was my anti-German
stand during the war and that I had worked for closer collaboration
with them. I found very little sympathy. The Frères Tharaud had
just brought out a book, subsidized by the Horthy Government,
entitled *Quand Israel est Roi*, full of calumnies of me and my followers,

all of whom had risked much by being pro-French during the war. As there is no libel law in France, I could not protect myself from these attacks.

The Hungarian colony in Paris was a large one. They all tried to monopolize me, involving me in their petty squabbles. Although Paris was the melting-pot of the uprooted, they could not melt. These intrigues were not exclusive to our colony. They are those of all émigrés in all epochs and to whatever cause they belong. The main reason, I think, is that political outlaws are usually extreme individualists. Freed from old restraints and traditions, they remain subconsciously attached to them and, living in an alien country, they feel a bitter aversion for their hosts, due mostly to envy of their security and success. They often turn into rabid nationalists in spite of their antagonism to their homeland. No one seems to need their exceptional talents, and their hurt vanity and self-centredness grow daily, developing at the same time as a sense of inferiority due to frustration.

The Communist refugees had the best discipline, for their creed made them sacrifice all personal ambition. Giving up their ego completely, they felt themselves to be mere cogs in the wheel, the anonymous soldiers of a cause. This was their main strength and attraction.

Émigrés are usually surrounded by spies or *agents provocateurs*, and are frequently approached with offers of bribes and other shady propositions. Treachery is well paid and one can still get thirty pieces of silver for betraying a friend or even a 'cause'. When émigrés start talking about the necessity for realism in politics, one can be certain that betrayal is in their minds. Most of them lead the life of the Wandering Jew, going from country to country in search of the one where the cost of living is lowest. In the Paris of those days one could live reasonably, and thought was free.

Emotionally the émigrés lived in a state of constant flux from bitter pessimism to brightest optimism. How often would it happen that on the same day a White Russian would gleefully report the imminent collapse of the Bolsheviks and in anti-Fascist circles the news would spread that Italy was rising against the Dictator.

Between the emigration of the 'twenties and that of the 'forties there exists a fundamental difference. The first consisted of Liberals, Democrats and Socialists who were working for a new social order. Those of today are mostly economic refugees, ordinary unpolitical middle-class people. The few political ones form an amorphous mass of all shades and parties, Fascists, Royalists, Social Democrats, Reactionaries, ex-Communists and militant Catholics. Few of them know what they want and they agree only on what they do not want. Purely negative, they exist on hopes of war between the West and the East which might enable them to regain their lost positions. In order to live, all of them are obliged to work for the highest bidder, usually the U.S.A. Thus it is chiefly envy and the need of material reward which are responsible for the antagonism between the different émigré factions.

I was often asked if I felt homesick. I resented this question. For although I felt it less acutely than most of my fellow émigrés, who had lost less than I, and believed myself free from such primitive instincts, it must have been there, concealed in the recesses of the unconscious. My ever-recurring dreams about places and people left behind were proof of this. I was never able to uproot myself completely, for I had been weaned from my surroundings too late. At the age of forty or over, the loss of my male and female friends, however worthless, was bitterly felt. They had belonged to my background, and had the same nursery, the same manners, the same family jokes, had laughed at the same things, had the same quality of humour. However many true and loyal friends I acquired in the West, who ideologically were much closer to me and whom I respected infinitely more, they could never be the same. Also, at times the scent of the elder trees and the acacia blossom which lingered in the air of the dry, hot summer nights, the monotonous croaking of frogs, the melancholy barking of village dogs, the recollection of the juicy flavour of small Hungarian apricots, came vividly back to me, filling me with nostalgia. A longing would assail me to see how much the trees had grown which I had planted on the hillside opposite our country house in Parad, or to stroll carefree up the Kossuth Lajos street watching the pretty women go by, and enter the club, where the waiters would know exactly my tastes and my wishes and be eager to serve me. Yet I refused to admit this weakness even to myself, considering it shallow sentimentality, apt to weaken my struggle and make me give way, as some of my compatriots had done, for the sake of paving the way home. Paris and France had always been my second home, Europe my country, mankind my concern; all the rest I felt was literature and humbug. And last, but not least, I refused to give my enemies the satisfaction of my sorrow. That

I admit this today is a proof that I have now passed beyond all pain and maybe, all joy as well.

But to return to the Paris of those days.

The favourite meeting-place for the European Left was the hospitable house of Madame Aline Ménard Dorian. Widow of a wealthy industrialist, several times a Cabinet Minister, Madame Ménard was a shrewd and witty woman with great personality, whose salon in the Rue de la Faisanderie was in the Dreyfusard tradition, anti-clerical and freemason.

On Sunday afternoons a curious conglomeration of people gathered there. They belonged to the most varied social strata. Wealthy French lawyers, Hungarian workmen, Belgian Cabinet Ministers, Bulgarian peasant leaders, Spanish writers, German Social Democrats, British M.P.s, Italian Professors, Russian Social Revolutionaries and Mensheviks.

Amongst the regular guests I recollect Paul Renaudel, Léon Blum, Edouard Herriot, Paul Clemenceau, the President's brother, Vincent Auriol. Jean Longuet, Marx's grandson, Professor Longevin, the painter Braque, the humanist Unamuno, the writer Ibañez, who hated Alfonso XIII with Spanish passion, the Italian Professor Salvemini, Mussolini's fiercest enemy, and Victor Basch.[23]

The poorer refugees looked forward to these lavish teas, where they could eat their fill and save their evening meal. It was also a good opportunity for meeting distinguished people whom otherwise they would never have known.

I shall always remember my friend Francesco Nitti, ex-Premier of the Italian Cabinet, with his lisping, soft Italian accent and short, corpulent figure, and his very large, very clever and very kind wife, together with their family of five bright children. They took up a great deal of space when arriving together. Nitti, though the most jovial of men, could slay an enemy with one of his dreaded witticisms, brought out in the suavest way. Only the malicious twinkle in his light blue eyes would give him away. The contempt he nursed for Mussolini knew no bounds. From his ever-smiling lips a stream of invective would flow in the sweetest of tones, as if he were confessing his love to a woman. About Count Sforza, whom he loathed, even disputing his right to his title, he used to say that he carried his head as a priest carries the Sacrament, with reverence and veneration.

Nitti was among the last of the liberal politicians, incorruptible and courageous. In his bare rooms near the Luxembourg Garden weird-looking Italians used to visit him secretly, in constant fear of detection by Mussolini's spies, who might land them in jail on their return. No one, therefore, was introduced and names were never mentioned. In this atmosphere of carbonaro conspiracy, the figure of the bourgeois lawyer Nitti seemed somehow incongruous. His children, as is so often the case, were more to the Left than he was. Each time Nitti met my wife he would take her by the hand saying: 'When you return to Hungary, I return to Rome.' This prophecy proved correct as, after the war, Fascism and semi-Fascism having been swept away, we did return to our respective countries. This talented family had a tragic fate. Three of the children died at the beginning of their careers.

Among the habitués of the Rue de la Faisanderie were a young Bulgarian couple, the Trenkas, ardent followers of Stambuliski, the murdered peasant leader: he, a shrewd and promising politician with the Balkan ability for diplomacy, she a dark beauty bursting with vitality and energy. In their Montparnasse home — all political émigrés lived on the left bank — they entertained most generously, evoking the atmosphere of the Balkans with wine, music and song. Their son, a remarkable child of five who we all predicted would one day become Dictator of Bulgaria, attended these parties at whatever time of night. Placed on the table, under the doting eyes of his parents, he would carry on a harangue against Tsankoff's dictatorship. The mother would dance the national folk dances with flashing eyes and quivering bosom, while the guests accompanied her with rhythmical yells of encouragement.

Recollecting those years, I think of a dear friend, Robert Dell, a most enchanting figure of the Paris of the 'twenties. During the World War he had been expelled by Poincaré for an article against the secret treaties. He seemed as proud of this expulsion, although his feeling for the Germans was reversed in later years, as he was of having been sent down from Oxford as a youngster. Although he had lived in France for years, he spoke the language with the most exaggerated English accent, suspected by some to be deliberately put on. A lover of paradox and controversy, with a delightful sense of humour, he was the best of company. During his whole life he was the champion of lost causes, the defender of the under-dog. He had been a fervid supporter of the suffragettes, but dropped them as soon as they had won, insisting later that it had been a youthful error on his part. His motto should have been: *Déplaire est mon plaisir*. I always cherished a soft spot in my heart for this kind of person, found chiefly among the English. A gourmet and connoisseur of wine, he loved the good things of life. He had the embarrassing habit of putting on his spectacles when introduced to a woman, and of discarding them in haste if she failed to please! One of his best friends was the Russian Communist writer and journalist Rappaport, who had been one of Lenin's intimate friends. It was queer to watch these two figures, in appearance so opposite to each other, walking down the Boulevard Montparnasse together: Dell a most distinguished gentleman, and Rappaport a sort of Quasimodo, with black untidy beard, dwarflike, clumsy and slovenly, only lacking a knife dripping with blood between his teeth to be the classical Bolshevik of Western imagination. But this uncomely exterior hid a heart of gold and an honest, witty and cultured mind. After knowing him better, no one could help loving him. He was one of the first Communists to fall into disgrace. A sincere idealist, he could not accept the new Stalin line. He made a most pathetic impression on me when I met him, after the Kirov murder. He died soon afterwards, a broken man, one of Stalin's first victims.

I have often been called by ignorant people the Hungarian Kerensky, but I must admit that there was some historical similarity in our fate. We were both defeated by the tide of Bolshevism, but while Russia stuck to Communism, Hungary succumbed to counter-revolution. Kerensky was living in Paris in those days and some friends of ours thought it would be piquant to have these two 'failures' meet. Kerensky, a small man with hair trimmed in the German fashion, did not impress me as vain and ambitious, as he has been usually depicted. Like many actors on the stage of history, he attributed his failure to some minor details or to some omission on the part of his supporters. Everything would have happened differently 'if '. . . People forget that history follows a certain pattern and that there are periods when all human endeavour is useless and the so-called 'leaders' themselves are obliged to act in accordance with history. As in Greek drama, they are puppets in the hands of the Gods. I felt this strongly during my own career — that we, whether of the Right or the Left, are subjected to historical laws as imperative as the natural laws which cause volcanoes to erupt and tides to follow the moon. That evening in the Rue du Colisée, it was argued that had Kerensky offered a separate peace to the Germans in 1917, thus satisfying the craving of the Russian people for peace, Bolshevism would have been avoided. For in those days the Bolsheviks were a negligible minority, and had Russia not suffered defeat at the front they would have had little chance of success. Kerensky disagreed; he blamed the Entente, arguing that had they given the promised assistance, Russia could have carried on the war successfully and later achieved Democracy and Socialism.

It was at this dinner that I met Prince Mirsky, an unusual and highly gifted man. A refugee from the Soviets, he nourished a deep, Dostoievskian dislike of the West, where he was obliged to dwell. He was the originator, with Goutchkov, of the Euro-Asian concept, which considers Russia a continent by itself, belonging neither to Asia nor to Europe. His appearance was by no means European. He had jet-black hair, a dead white complexion, crimson lips and an orientally shaped head and eyes. His brilliant critical faculties were greatly appreciated by the English intellectuals. In spite of his success in England, he was one of the first émigrés who returned to Russia as a convinced Communist. Soon after his return he was arrested and disappeared. His love for Russia was his undoing.

Above our flat in the Rue Stanislas, near the Boulevard Montparnasse, lived the eminent Russian lawyer and former ambassador Maklakov. There we met the aged Prince Paul Dolguroki, one of the old liberal Russians. His nostalgia for home was so irresistible that, disguised as a Russian peasant, he went back to die on his own estate. On arrival, he was shot as a spy.

Christian Rakovsky, the Soviet Ambassador in London, had now been transferred to Paris. He was a happy choice as, having lived in France before the Russian Revolution, he understood the French mentality. Commissar of Independent Ukraine after 1917, descendant of a noble Bulgaro-Rumanian family, he had opposed Stalin in defence of Ukrainian independence.

One morning I got a telephone call from him, asking me most urgently to come over to the Embassy. He was pacing up and down his study, his Alsatian dog anxiously watching his steps. I saw at once that he was facing a grave crisis. He took me into the enchanting garden of the Embassy where the lilacs were in full bloom and told me frankly — how unimaginable such a thing would be today — of the dilemma which he had to face. The Opposition, of which he was a member, was going to issue a statement condemning Stalin's China policy, the support given to Chiang Kai-shek, as well as the policy which had resulted in the breakdown of the agreement between the British Trade Unions and the Soviets, against which the Opposition had already warned Stalin. Eighty-three members of the Opposition had signed this declaration and he felt that he could not refuse to add his name to it, as he was in complete agreement, although aware that it would mean his disgrace and recall. I tried to persuade him not to jeopardize his post, as he was of such value in it, but he seemed to have made up his mind. 'One is or one is not a friend,' he repeated, 'I cannot abandon Trotsky, who counts on my support. Friendship involves duties. I must sign it.' His dog laid his wise head in Rakovsky's lap as if he understood that his master was leaving and was pleading with him to stay. Turning towards me, Rakovsky said whimsically: 'He is on your side, too, trying to make it more difficult for me.'

The night before he left I dined with him and his wife. The atmosphere was sad. No one else was there. All French Communists and fellow travellers had turned away from him. He was a lonely man, but had followed his conscience.

I related my last conversation with Rakovsky to Bogomolov, the Soviet Ambassador to Paris in 1948. He stared at me flabbergasted — not at what I had said, but at my daring to take such names as Rakovsky and Trotsky into my mouth when talking to him.

After Rakovsky's departure, the position of Soviet Ambassador to France remained vacant. It was the chargé d'affaires, Rosenberg, a man of shrewd intelligence, who carried on. This short, hunch-backed man with his air of a Jacobin fanatic, was what one called in those days *un pur*. The atmosphere of the Embassy changed, for he could not replace his engaging predecessor. Some years later he too was liquidated.

Russia was undergoing its great change at that period. The Opposition had broken down, 'democracy inside the party' was abandoned, Stalin was consolidating his power. But it was only some years later that the West became aware of this. As always, the Russian sphinx did not give up her secret.

In Paris, the foreigners' town, there was practically no intermingling with the natives. The French are reticent and suspicious and dislike the foreigner, especially when he has no money. Unlike the hospitable American or English of the upper classes, even the so-called best people in France avoided meeting strangers, for fear of having to offer them an apéritif. Of course there was no question of inviting them to luncheon or dinner. Although we met many French people, I can count on my fingers the times, during the fifteen years we spent in France, when we were invited for meals. It was a special favour to be asked for coffee. Most foreigners have had a similar experience in France. To create a neutral ground on which to meet and to save the philistines from expense, we had the idea of founding a club, an international meeting-place of the Left, where ideas could be exchanged and kindred spirits discovered. Like many bright ideas, it did not materialize. The reason was disagreement about the membership of the Communists, the eternal strife of the Left amongst themselves. I dissociated myself from the plan, and it fell through.

My closest associate and faithful friend was George Boloni, a rare man in his way, for although a member of the Hungarian gentry he had none of their prejudices and fought loyally for our common cause. The Bolonis returned to Hungary after the last war and, later, in order to keep him at a safe distance, as he was never quite trusted to toe the line, he was appointed Minister to The Hague. He stuck to his resolution never to become an émigré again, so even when I left Hungary after the Rajk Trial, he remained at his post.

The colony of foreign workers in France was very large. The official figure at the last census had amounted to about three millions. Of these the Italians were the largest group. In the mines of the Pas-de-Calais the Poles were the greatest number. In Loubaix, Lens and Biancourt a large colony of Hungarians worked in the mines. Often I visited them. Living in a close community they did not acquire the French language and kept up Hungarian national traditions. They printed their own newspapers, had their own schools, restaurants and lecture-halls, proving again how emotionally patriotic the so-called 'international' proletariat is, how deeply attached to the traditions and habits of the Motherland, eyeing with contempt and dislike those of other nations. Their sole hope was that conditions would some day enable them to return to their native soil. They thought French food uneatable, French wine abominable. And those who wanted their children to learn a foreign language would teach them Polish rather than French, 'there being so many Poles around'.

In consequence of the stabilization of the franc, unemployment increased considerably and the situation of the émigrés in the north of France became alarming.[24]

I spent much of my time playing chess in the Café de la Régence, opposite the Comédie Française. I had a passion for the game and could spend my nights at it. I played with all nationalities and all classes and it was revealing to notice that each nationality had its own approach: I had no need to ask them from which country they came, I could recognize it by their game.

Enclosed behind an iron railing the marble table is preserved on which Napoleon used to indulge in his favourite pastime. It was here, too, that Trotsky sat playing his King gambit, for which he was so well known in chess circles. For me this game was an escape; through it I could forget my cares.

It was in those days that we acquired a new member of the family. One night, when I was living in a small house in the Rue des Ursulines, I was woken up in the middle of the night by the pathetic howls of a dog. Dogs being one of my weaknesses — even during the hardest times of our life we always managed to have one — I ran out, and there, tied to the handle of the front door, sat the ugliest little mongrel of a fox terrier I had ever come across. When I tried to unfasten her — for she was a female — she bit me; for besides being ugly she seemed to have a most ungracious disposition. For several days she would not touch the food I brought. Someone who knew my love of dogs must have attached her to my door — an unwelcome present at that particular time. It took weeks for me to tame her. At last she would eat and drink, but only out of my hand. Ursuline, the name I gave her, was now adopted by the family. She completely changed her character, and became gentle, fat and complacent, smiling happily at the world whilst sitting on her hindlegs, her favourite position, in the centre of the courtyard of our apartment house, munching pieces of sugar which the inhabitants would throw down to her. When she died of old age, she was much regretted by all of us.

After Ursuline's death, Katus presented me with a chestnut-coloured dachshund puppy. His ears and paws were oversize in comparison with his small sausage-like body but his self-importance and conviction of his irresistible charm were unmitigated. As we were often on the move, and could not take him with us, we had to trust him to the care of friends, which gave him a feeling of insecurity and nourished in him a loathing for visitors, for he always feared that he would be carried off.

One day he thought of putting an end to this shameful treatment and, sensing correctly that the lady who visited us had some intentions concerning him, he leapt up in the most affectionate way and cuddled with an expression of bliss into her crêpe-de-chine lap. The lady, deeply touched, was all ready to take him away with her. Suddenly she gave a suppressed shriek and jumping up noticed that she was sitting in a pool of warm liquid. The culprit, delighted, rushed round the room in madly hilarious mood, jumping over the furniture and barking with joy. The lady refused to have anything to do with such an ill-bred dog.

Once he got publicity in the Swiss press, for he misbehaved himself in a Lausanne tea-room at the leg of a chair where a gentleman was sitting. The gentleman, who did not make any objection, turned out to be Alfonso XIII, and the article suggested that Count Karolyi's dachshund was a fanatical republican who had no sympathy with crowned heads.

In the year 1927 I published a pamphlet on land reform, addressed to the Hungarian peasantry. To get it distributed I needed the help of the underground Communist organizations. For this purpose I went to Vienna to meet Bela Kun, who lived there illegally. He was unrecognizable with his dark eye-glasses and black beard. He never left his room except after dark. He was taking great risks, for had he been detected he would have been handed over to Hungary, and this time there would have been no mercy. Conferring with Kun was most unsatisfactory, as sincerity and confidence on both sides were totally lacking. During our discussions he was continually buttoning and unbuttoning his waistcoat, a sure sign with him that he was trying to mislead me.

I was staying incognito with an Austrian worker's family, who were kept in the dark as to the identity of their guest, the man with the small goat's beard — I wore one in those days. Discreetly they did not inquire. I was called 'Herr Professor' for every German is a 'Herr Professor'.

George Lukacs, the Marxist philosopher of European standing, was living in Döblin, near Vienna. I visited him often, as I had a deep admiration for his intelligence and moral integrity. The son of wealthy Hungarian Jews, he gave up a comfortable living and chose a faith which rendered him an outcast in his circle. His parents, true to the family solidarity of the race, were trying to supply him with money, which he stubbornly refused. He lived in destitution. I often found that the so-called 'materialists' were ready to sacrifice material advantages for an ideal, whilst the main aim of the pious was worldly comfort.

Two years later I was at a meeting in the Tempelhof, Berlin. I suddenly felt two arms enlacing me in a hearty embrace and recognized my host of the Vienna days. With tears in his eyes he related to me how he had watched all through the night by my dead body in remembrance of the 'Herr Professor' and his quaint ways, how he had gone to my funeral and buried me. It turned out that he had taken me to be Landler, one of the Social Democrat leaders, who had recently died. Communists know how to keep a secret.

Until 1933 the European Left was carrying on a hopeless struggle against the spread of Fascism. It was a dire task, as the Western Democracies, not realizing the danger, welcomed any movement opposed to Communism, little caring about the methods employed.

During the first years it was mainly round Henri Barbusse and the group *La Clarté*, founded in 1919, that progressive intellectuals of all nations gathered. It was the union of those who during the war had opposed the diehards in their respective countries. It was elating to discover the many kindred spirits on 'the other' side, and justified the hope that this minority today, the persecuted of yesterday, by uniting, would become a strong influence, and would have to be reckoned with in the future.

Having joined the International Committee of *La Clarté* and of the newspaper *Le Monde*, I got in touch with many remarkable men amongst the European progressives.

Barbusse had published during the war his powerful novel *Le Feu*, which received the Goncourt Prize. It was, with Laczkos's *Men in the War*, the first violent denunciation of war and the degradation of man converted into a medium of destruction. Few works had such a stirring effect and it spread like fire through the ranks of the army. As editor of *Le Monde*, he was now fighting a relentless battle against Fascism. On the platform he cut a most distinguished figure. Tall and lean, with the sensitive features of the intellectual, he would stand, slightly bent, using freely his beautiful hands with the long fine fingers. His voice scarcely carried, and he had to make the greatest efforts to make himself heard, after which, completely exhausted, he would often succumb to a haemorrhage of the lungs. But he would not give way; with the feverish haste and mental energy of one who knew his days were numbered, he organized meetings, flew from country to country, although flying was strictly prohibited by his doctor, never failing to come to the assistance of his persecuted comrades. He even gave up writing, making the greatest sacrifice, that of his talent and finally that of his life, for he died — virtually on the platform — for the cause of the disinherited.

Romain Rolland who, partly owing to his bad health, had to live in Switzerland, sent messages, protests and encouragements from the shores of Lac Léman, where he had retired after 1914. His brochure, *Au delà de la Mêlée*, had appeared during the war, arousing many a sensitive conscience to pacifism. I visited him several times at Villeneuve, in the Villa Olga. When confronting him one immediately realized the presence of a great man. Wrapped in shawls, with his long grey cloak hanging loose around his towering but slender figure, he would take his walks in the evenings on the shores of the lake, reminding one of those nineteenth-century Romantics who before him had chosen these peaceful surroundings for work and meditation. Serene, he watched the world, free from personal ambition, suffering acutely from every act of injustice and brutality committed. He was extremely kind to anyone who needed encouragement or moral support, and Villeneuve became a sort of Mecca of Western Communists. This great pacifist accepted Communism, for he realized that it was impossible to fight Fascism with Tolstoyan or pacifist methods. One had to build; to trust and not find fault was his axiom. At that time he believed in the Soviets, in the light that was coming from the East to save Western civilization from decay.

In Hungary a bomb exploded; Beniczki, ex-Minister of the Interior and Chief of Police during the White Terror, accused Regent Horthy of having instigated in 1919 the murder of the Socialist editor Somogyi and his associate Bacso. Beniczki in his evidence disclosed the names of the criminals, who until then had never been identified. He landed in jail and was disowned by his friends. Being a legitimist, he was suspected of disclosing these facts, the truth of which no one doubted, so as to harm the Regent, who had betrayed the King. The case had much similarity with Matteoti's assassination, in which Mussolini was involved. Many years previous to Nazism, we in Europe were acquainted with its ways and practices.

Shortly after the Beniczki scandal, Hungary again got into the news. This time it promised to be more serious, for the financial interests — more important than human lives — of a big power were involved. A Hungarian ex-colonel in possession of a diplomatic passport issued by the Hungarian Foreign Office was arrested in Holland with his two colleagues as they attempted to pass forged notes. In order to dodge the Customs, the suitcases containing the forged notes bore the diplomatic stamp of the Hungarian Foreign Office. The Banque de France sent several members of the Paris Sûreté to Budapest to make an inquiry. The Hungarian Government, after having tried to hush it up, was compelled by Premier Briand to assist the French Sûreté. Prince Louis Windischgraetz was arrested and charged with being the instigator. Half official Hungary was involved: The Chief of Police, Nadassy; the Chaplain-General of the Forces, Bishop Zadravetz; the Head of the Post Office Savings Bank and a Cabinet Minister — Count Paul Teleki, close friend and relation of the Prime Minister, Bethlen. The Regent himself was supposed to have had knowledge of it. In the secret passages and dungeons of the eighteenth-century castle of Sarospatak, one of the oldest and quaintest residences of northern Hungary, which had belonged to Ferencz Rakoczy, millions of forged francs were said to be concealed. The Government's answer to the French request to have the castle searched was that it would take three months to explore it, a slight overstatement. The small fry were caught, the big fish allowed to escape. Those arrested openly admitted to the court that they needed the money to finance the Irredentist movement in Slovakia, thus proving their patriotic motives. And it was now disclosed, too, that the false sokols circulating in Czechoslovakia had the same origin.

The interest of this affair was not the fact that some individuals forged money, but that members of the highest society were involved in the scandal as well as members of the Government and that no one considered it a disreputable action; only, as it had been found out, a foolish one. All the blame was put on the Prince.[25] It certainly came at a most inappropriate time for Count Bethlen, who was trying to negotiate a loan for Hungary from the League of Nations. Eventually the Entente resumed their benevolent attitude towards Horthy's regime, which in fact had been their creation, though the terms under which it was conceived had never been fulfilled.[26] It was only the wretched émigrés who suffered, for it gave the Hungarian aliens an undesired notoriety. Many were turned out of their jobs; others, in desperate need, found it impossible to secure one. They were labelled 'Les Faux Monnayeurs'.

This forgery was a characteristic incident of the 'cold war' between Hungary and her neighbours of that period. It proved the corrupting power of chauvinism, and that the dangerous theory that 'the end justifies the means' was not a Bolshevik monopoly. It also demonstrated the frivolous attitude of the Magyar ruling class, who imagined that all things were permitted them. When a society based on the sanctity of private property sins against its own gods, when rulers break their own laws, things are going wrong. Hungary, weak and corrupt, was an easy prey to outside interference. This happened in 1941 and again in 1947. After the forgery scandal Hungary gained a new patron in the person of Lord Rothermere, the British press magnate. Hungarian propaganda was carried on in his paper the *Daily Mail*. The Hungarians hoped that through his influence the lost territories would be returned to them. They even went so far as to think seriously of offering the crown to the press lord's son, the handsome Harmsworth, thus creating a new dynasty of Rothermeres. It was humiliating to see Hungary carry on in such a foolish and undignified manner; but their hopes were soon frustrated. Lord Rothermere and the *Daily Mail* got their publicity, but Hungary did not get her lost territory. Bitter disillusionment followed, and nothing remained of this idyll except hundreds of different sorts of pipes, spices, red pepper, apricot brandy and Tokays on show in Lord Rothermere's apartment, and a monument and street name in Budapest.[27]

While the Hungarian gentry were amusing themselves in this way, the standard of living of the peasant, especially of the farm-labourer, was steadily sinking. The numbers leaving the country were increasing daily. One day I got a message to say that a party of 250 peasants from my former estate in the county of Heves were in Paris on their way to America and wished to see me. In a small bistro in the Rue Cambon, a deputation of six was waiting. It was an unforgettable, nostalgic evening, this meeting with my countrymen, my one-time semi-serfs, with their peculiar dialect and long-drawn-out broad vowels, their hanging moustaches, black suits and top boots. Holding their round felt hats on their knees, they sat in silence at the table, contemptuously sipping the French wine. Only one of them spoke. The Hungarian peasant is not talkative; he is reserved, suspicious and much too dignified to give way to any sort of emotion. 'To talk is the business of the white folk' they would say — they call women white folk. In a monotonous voice, not complaining, but just stating facts, the leader of the deputation related that their pay in Hungary for a week's work on the landlords' lands was equivalent to a few French francs; that there was no organization to defend them; that during the winter months their wives and children had to work without payment, practically as slaves, so that they might be chosen for paid work by the landlord in the time of harvest. Their earnings from spring to autumn had to keep them through the winter. They were now ready to face the strange land of America, its hard conditions and its unknown climate, and start a new life. They left their families behind to be sent for when they had secured a living. Of course their sole dream was to return to their native land with pockets filled with gold, and be free.

The worst conditions prevailed on the large estates between the two rivers, the Duna and the Tisza. The situation of the farm-labourers was appalling. The names they gave to their villages such as Sirohegy (Weeping Hill), Banomhegy (Hill of Sorrows), demonstrate the misery of their existence.[28]

Stephen Bethlen's statesmanship consisted mainly in his adroit manœuvring of the different parties, the legitimists on one side and the free electors on the other, and in preserving the ingenious myth of the kingdom without a king, of an admiral without a navy. His master-wangle was in 1921, when he brought the Social Democrats to heel, drawing up a secret pact with them. This pact, accepted by the Socialist Party under duress, made them agree to his franchise bill with its open ballot for the rural districts, and his prohibition of all farm-labourers' organizations. This meant the complete control of the peasantry, and was of major importance to the landowner Bethlen. In exchange the Socialists received permission to keep the Trade Unions and the secret franchise in towns.

The discontented gathered around Stephen Vagi and in 1925 they founded a new party of the Left to which, as the Communist Party was illegal, a great number of revolutionary youth flocked. Stephen Vagi was elected to Parliament. Judging the moment propitious, Matyas Rakosi, ex-commissar of the 1919 Commune, entered the country illegally in 1925. He was arrested with Vagi and some others and, as Hungary was under martial law, he was on the verge of being executed. Again we started to work. Through the *Ligue des Droits de l'Homme* in Paris and my Liberal and Labour friends in England, we succeeded in having the case brought before the civilian courts, thus saving their lives. Their courageous behaviour at the trial was recognized even by their opponents. Rakosi was sentenced to seventeen years' imprisonment.

In 1929, the year of the concordat between the Vatican and the Black Shirts, Henri Barbusse organized an international congress of protest in the building of the German Upper House in Berlin. I was one of the speakers. I do not remember having ever before had such oratorical success.

For the first time since 1870 the Holy See had given up the theory that it was a prisoner of the State, and had moved into the 'faithless' and 'freemason' city, thus demonstrating in favour of Mussolini's Dictatorship and Fascism and gaining for them the support of the Roman Catholic world. It seemed that my exasperation against this compromise was so roused that it made me find the right words, and the ovation I received proved that my audience was moved in the same way. In the Berlin of Weimar, liberal causes found eager response. Men like Leonard Frank, Fritz von Unruh, Carl Ussietzki, Rudolph Olden, although all Junkers by origin, supported our struggle against dictatorship. Most of them perished in Hitler's concentration camps.

Those days in Berlin were the climax of the bitter rivalry and fratricidal hatred between the two workers' parties. For fear of disturbance the Social Democratic Chief of Police had banned the traditional demonstration on May 1st. The Communists who did not conform to this order were shot at. Several days' fighting and many victims were the result. Both sides had committed great errors, but the original sin of the Social Democrats dated back to 1919, when Ebert, Noske and Scheidemann united with the counter-revolutionary detachments to crush the Spartacus movement. 'If the party needs a bloodhound,' Noske was supposed to have said, 'I will be it.' The unprincipled opportunism of German Social Democracy was responsible for keeping the Prussian military in power and for the fact that the democratic Weimar Republic existed on paper only. Thus the road was open for Hindenburg and Hitler. The frustrated workers left the ranks of the Social Democrats and it was the Communist Party that benefited. On the other hand the Moscow doctrine that one had to pass through Fascism, the last phase of Capitalism, to Communism, made the Communist Party conclude a pact with the Nazis for the elections, which resulted in the triumphant Nazi majority of 1930.

7

A SNAPSHOT OF MEXICO

IN 1928 I was invited by the Mexican Government to visit Mexico for the purpose of studying President Obregon's land reform. In spite of being often an involuntary traveller I have remained a keen one, and always seized an opportunity when offered. I shall never forget our picturesque arrival in Havana. Next to me on the deck stood a national hero from Cuba returning from exile. With tears glittering in his dark eyes, he waved his hat to the aeroplanes diving and looping over our ship to greet him, whilst a whole fleet of large and small craft escorted us into the harbour.

'Thirty-five years ago I got the same reception as today,' said Fernandoz, turning to me. I did not dare ask him why he had been exiled or what he had done, fearing to offend the hero by my ignorance. So I nodded understandingly. In one of the ships a smart bunch of nurses stood waving their handkerchiefs, for General Fernandoz was both chief physician and head of the Military Hospital. One of the boats was crowded with little girls in white, holding large bunches of flowers in their dusky arms; their white eyeballs and snowy teeth flashed in the sun.

Our entrance into Havana was spectacular. A military band in khaki played the National Anthem, occasionally drowned by the strident sirens of the ships. On the pier, to my horror, I heard a voice with a Chicago accent yelling: 'Where's the Count? *Havana News* here.' A white-clad 'Harold Lloyd' in large horn-rimmed glasses assailed me with a deluge of questions, reminding me that we were in the neighbourhood of the U.S.A. 'What do you think, Mr. Count, of our Cuban beauties?'

As the question sounded like a statement, there was not much for me to say. Taking my hesitation for shyness, and in order to spur me on, he offered me a Havana cigar. I lit it with joy and watched the blue smoke eddying in the draught of the electric fan. I answered appreciatively, 'Fine'. And my reply was instantly recorded in his zip note-book. Tomorrow Havana would read the edifying news that the foreign count thinks its beauties fine.

While we talked the ventilators unsuccessfully tried to cool the sticky atmosphere of the hotel lobby, so my tormentor suggested a swim on the Palaya Beach. We walked through the town, passing the statues of stern and dignified men murdered in revolutions. After the swim I purchased a box of Havanas for the proprietor of the Café du Dôme in Montparnasse who had specially asked me to get him one. This box of Havanas was a painful indication of human frailty. After leaving Vera Cruz, I opened it to taste one of them. Gradually there-after the contents of the box decreased so that, when I arrived in Paris, it was empty. What could I do so as not to disappoint the old chap? I went to the Rue de la Paix and bought him a box of Havanas for double the price. He was enchanted and each time I came into his café he would wink at me and say: 'Nothing like Havanas straight from Havana. Those you buy in Paris are a fake. *Je m'y connais moi. Ils n'ont pas le même arôme.'*

When I returned to the S.S. *Espagne* and entered the smoking-room there was an abrupt silence. Evidently they were discussing 'Harold Lloyd's' interview with me in the local evening paper and now, after twenty-one days' companionship on the boat, had found out what a dangerous man I was. My first chill in Havana. . . .

Whilst sitting on the terrace of the hotel in Vera Cruz, sipping an iced drink, I felt a touch on my shoulder. A young American, with a girl of Hollywood appearance, looked down on me.

'Excuse me, please, are you Prince Carol of Rumania?'

'Sorry,' I answered, 'I am neither Prince nor Rumanian.'

'The waiter told me so,' he said apologetically.

'Although I am not a Prince, will you have a drink with me? For now that you know who I am not, I will have to tell you who I am,' and I handed over to them the local paper with my photograph and the caption: 'Bolshevik Count arrives in Mexico.'

I thought my inquisitive companions would bolt at this revelation, but to my surprise they did nothing of the sort. On the contrary, after the disappointment that I was not a royal prince, they felt relieved that I was at least a count; a count one could forgive even for being a

Bolshevik. We spent a pleasant evening together and each time I noticed their interest flagging I began to tell them gruesome stories of people we had murdered. At this their eyes would light up again.

'With your own hands?'

'With my own hands,' I assured them.

They would probably have walked off had I told them that I had never murdered anyone and that I was not even a Bolshevik.

On our arrival in Mexico City the town was full of the news of President Obregon's murder, so my companions found other fish to fry and let me off.

The first thing that struck me was that the main street of the city was completely devoid of shade. The stumps of tree trunks were still to be seen in the ground where they had stood. Surprised, I asked why they had been cut down. 'Because,' was the answer, 'it is from behind those trees that Mexicans shoot their political adversaries. Trees are very dangerous.' But President Obregon was murdered in spite of the felled trees.

My stay in Mexico had a bad start. I soon contracted dysentery and had to keep to my bed for several weeks. One night I awoke to find myself at the other end of the room, although still in my bed. I tottered to the light switch, but it did not work. A shattering sound followed. In the dark, I crawled into the passage, where on all sides I heard people yelling. Then someone said: 'One cannot go down the stairs, we must use the elevator.' From every direction women and men in nightshirts and pyjamas made a rush to get in the elevator and soon we were out in the garden. It was one of those earthquakes, usual in Mexico, but disconcerting to the uninitiated. After the first they became a daily experience, but fortunately less violent.

My illness prevented me from getting round the country, and visiting the different farms as intended. Yet I concluded from what I saw and heard that, as in so many cases, the Mexican land reform was perfect on paper, but in reality did not satisfy the needs. The red-skinned farm-labourer's situation was not much improved. There were few collectives and no tractor centres; the new owners of the dwarf farms had no machinery or agricultural implements. Although I was the guest of the Government I could not praise the reform and candidly gave my opinion to the leaders — which, no doubt, they did not much appreciate. I was received by President Calles, Obregon's successor, a squat, swarthy man with a dynamic personality, who by his fanatical anti-clericalism endeavoured to divert the criticism of the Left from his militarism and unsatisfactory land reform. I was often a guest of the painter Diego Rivera, whose works I much admired. Like all great artists, he is very simple, modest and direct. Most of his works — and many of his critics objected to this — were propaganda against the exploitation of his country and the natives by foreign capital. It was from his paintings, more than from any article or leaflet, that I learnt the genuine plight of Mexico. The tired, bent backs under the wide-brimmed *carro* of the peons slaving on the vast cactus lands and haciendas of the landlords, cultivating the *pulka*, the intoxicating drink which has sapped the life-blood of Mexicans, were more expressive than any written words. In one of his famous frescoes Rockefeller is depicted swallowing gold dollars. It is the greatest proof of Diego's talent that in spite of the changing regimes his work has remained living. His critics resent his interpretation, maintaining that art should not be propaganda. But were not the medieval painters propagandists of their religion? And did not Daumier, with his killing satire, greatly contribute to the overthrow of Louis Philippe? Were not their pictures as useful as pamphlets? When I met him, Rivera was a sympathizer with Communism. When Trotsky was offered asylum in Mexico, it was Rivera who showed him hospitality. Later they disagreed — the reason was never known — and Trotksy left his house. In spite of the fact that Rivera was one of the best-paid artists, he lived in a most modest way. Once I had a lunch with him which consisted only of raw cactuses mixed with garlic. Having just recovered from dysentery I did not dare touch this peculiar concoction; when my hosts noticed my plight, they offered me an egg instead. But this was easier offered than found. A search started. Rivera clad in his *suara* and his beautiful Indian wife holding her baby in her arms, and looking like a figure out of the Bible, opened drawers and cupboards, peered behind bookshelves and canvases to find the egg. At last it was discovered underneath a large straw hat.

The effect of the ruthless Spanish colonization, although it drained the country's wealth, was, as far as culture and religion went, more apparent than profound. It is a striking fact that of the fourteen million inhabitants of Mexico today, three million do not speak Spanish. It is true they all are Roman Catholics, but only in a superficial way. One example illustrates this: I saw in a village a Calvary where to my surprise, instead of three, four crosses were erected. When I asked the meaning, I was told that the fourth was the symbol of the Indian god. When there is a drought, they visit the churches and pray with the Catholic priest that he may bring them rain; but after this service is over they light bonfires, an ancient custom of the Indians, to persuade their old Aztec god to open the clouds. Religions are mostly utilized for political purposes, but the Conquistadors minded little about spiritual penetration as long as they got their booty. In Vera Cruz I visited the palace of Cortez, where the story runs that as a Catholic he was forbidden to lie with the conquered heathen women. So he ordered a priest to stand near the bed and had the women baptized before the deed. *Après la sainte cérémonie tout est permis.* Today Mexican independence is threatened by the peaceful penetration of gum-chewing conquistadors anxious to get hold of oil wells.

Although I had only intended to remain in Mexico a month, it became five. My leave-taking was coloured by an incident which put me in a curious light.

I left Mexico City in the morning. A deputation of local Hungarians and some Mexican friends accompanied me to the station. This group, in dark cloth suits and bowler hats, made eloquent speeches to which I replied with thanks, hopes and all the rest customary on such occasions. After handshakes and bows I got on to the platform of the train. They all stood there waving their hats as the train began slowly to draw out. Then suddenly the figure of a woman, running towards me with outstretched arms, detached itself from them. It was the young Hungarian wife of a Mexican friend. I felt the blood in my veins turn to ice and recollect seeing the terrified expression of her husband and the flabbergasted look on the faces of the rest of the company. She seized the railing and I, fearing that she might hurt herself, lifted her on to the platform of the train and quickly retired into the carriage with the pretty lady gasping in my arms. She told me between her sobs that she was fed up with life in Mexico and her only desire was to go to Paris. Since she knew me to be a kind-hearted man, she felt sure I would assist her. I was stunned. Why had she never mentioned this to me before? We could have talked the matter over with her husband.

'No, no,' she sobbed. 'He would never have consented. Only after a scandal like this will he agree to divorce. All the Hungarians here and all Mexico will now be certain that we are lovers.'

This was getting embarrassing. In the first place I had very little money, barely enough to pay my ticket to New York; and then what would Katus say if I arrived home with a woman on my hands? Quick thinking was necessary, for after the first stop, in ten minutes' time, the next station was three hours away and from that she could hardly get home the same day: I was most anxious that she should spend the night with her husband. My fellow-travellers, who had witnessed this strange scene, cast reproachful glances at me, obviously considering me a vile seducer. But my efforts were crowned with success. My rash young beauty got out when the train stopped, carrying with her all my good wishes for a quick and lasting reconciliation with her worthy husband.

After many years I met her again in Europe and she told me the sequel to her adventure. She had been forgiven, but divorce followed some years later. But my reputation, I fear, suffered a blemish.

In August I sailed home on the S.S. *Cristobal Colon* via New York. It gave me forty-eight hours in the harbour of Manhattan, so I applied for permission to land. Although I had received no answer to my request, on arrival my solicitor and friend, Morris Ernst, stepped aboard and without a word took my arm and together we walked down the gangway. The authorities on the pier purposely shut their eyes. They had had enough of the Karolyi affair, it seemed.

We went straight to the aerodrome and in a two-seater plane hired by Ernst flew to Washington, where we were received by the State Department, whom Ernst succeeded in convincing that the ban on my wife and myself was unjust. It was a piece of luck that Secretary Kellogg was away in Ireland at the time. In the afternoon an outdoor meeting had been organized in Wall Street to support my plea, and I addressed some unpolitical words of thanks to the assembled crowd. I was then escorted to the boat by two members of the bomb squad; a dozen policemen guarded the pier. Whether they guarded it in case I should blow it up or to assure my safety, I do not know. My friends, Hungarians and Americans, came to see me off in order to demonstrate against the attitude of the State Department.

8

U.S.A. RE-VISITED

ON the advice of my American friends, I applied for re-admission to the States. The new administration of Secretary Stimson granted me a visa without any difficulty. Katus, as soon as the battle was won, lost interest and had no wish to accompany me.

The questions put to me at the Consulate were rather naive: 'You are not a revolutionary are you?' — 'It is useless for me to deny historical facts', I answered. 'You can look it up for yourself in the works of the period.' I noticed a pained expression on the face of the Consul, who had obviously hoped that my answer would be a categorical 'No'. So I added: 'In any case I have no intention of overthrowing the Government of the U.S.A.' This pleased him, but I could not help adding: 'But do you seriously believe that, had I such intentions, I would let you know beforehand?' He then referred to the Italian expulsion, a charge which was instantly cleared up by Count Sforza's letter, which I had received from him the day before.[29]

The campaign of the Horthy press against me was so violent that it drew attention to my meetings and they were well attended. In general it was mostly to my opponents that I owed my successes. My aim was to make the American people understand that the danger to world peace lay mainly in Fascism and Dictatorship, and that the only possible way to save Europe from a new war was to found a United States of Europe on a basis of planned economy. If this was too premature a step to take as yet, the United States of Central and Eastern Europe should be the first move towards it.

My audiences, mainly composed of Americans, were ready to listen without prejudice, even if they did not share all my opinions concerning planned and socialist economy; for the nonconformist Quaker tradition still exists among the Anglo-Saxons and at times even Wall

Street has to take it into consideration. These elements, in contrast to the newly settled emigrants, have tried to preserve the tradition of tolerance brought from the mother country. They were the founders of a new civilization, and unlike those who, having recently escaped from backward countries and being ignorant of democratic develop- ment, have to adjust themselves to an existing social order. A kind of double inferiority affects the first generation of the newcomers. Not only do they retain the serf-like servility inculcated in them at home, but the fact of being immigrants gives them a feeling of uncertainty. To counteract this, they try to become 200 per cent American. But there are others again who stick together, wedded to the habits and customs of their mother country. I met some who had lived twenty years in the States but could speak practically no English, whilst their children had already forgotten Hungarian. I was particularly impressed with this at a banquet given for me by a group of men who had formerly been tenants of mine in Hungary. They embarrassed me by kissing my hand in the feudal manner of greeting, but their sons and daughters had shaken off all traces of humility and, although dressed in elaborate Hungarian national costumes, were unmistakably the only Americans in the hall. They had that self-confident air so characteristic of Americans.

When my compatriots noticed that my lectures were well received by Americans, they boldly organized banquets, festivals and celebrations in my honour; but their pride, as I regretfully noticed, lay in being able to show me off to the Americans not as a radical, but as an ex- millionaire.

Many of them were self-conscious and apprehensive that their child- ren would look down on them. One day in a tram car I sat next to a Hungarian and his ten-year-old son. He asked me to talk English on account of the 'kid' who, he explained, was ashamed of being called a 'Hunkey'.

At a dinner offered to me during my stay in the West, I sat next to my host, one of the most distinguished members of the Hungarian colony, a wealthy and respected man. To start conversation I asked him what his business was. He looked at me with a sly, self-satisfied smile and pushing out his portly chest said: 'Vell, Mr. President, I can assure you that my business is amongst the most remunerative in the States. One can only win on it and never lose.'

Intrigued, I asked him to tell me more.

'Vell,' he continued, obviously pleased to have roused my interest and looking like a cat that has swallowed a canary, 'I fabricate a special kind of table which is in great demand. No one else knows how to do it. I have the patent.'

'How interesting! And what sort of table?'

He winked one of his small eyes and smiled with a superior air.

'Vell, it is a roulette table with a special contraption. It can be manipulated by the croupier with his leg, without any risk of being discovered. The table bends slightly, very slightly in the direction you want it to bend.' And, turning to me proudly, he waited for me to express my admiration.

I swallowed the excellent paprikas chicken offered me by my ingenious host, muttering, 'Vell, vell!'

When I arrived in Los Angeles, in the company of Hugo Gellert, a well-known Hungarian caricaturist and good friend, we were speeded at a terrific pace through the streets of the city, accompanied by half a dozen motor cycles frantically blowing their sirens.

'Is there a fire?' I asked naively.

Embarrassed, Gellert touched my foot; I had not realized that the sirens were in my honour; for a Hungarian landowner, even if his glory was past, had to be received like a maharajah.

At the Hôtel Ambassadeurs a suite of six rooms awaited us. 'But gentlemen,' I exclaimed with awe, 'I cannot possibly afford this.' After a short conference between the reception committee and the management it was fixed up. I would be the guest of the town.

Some minutes later the telephone rang and a voice said. 'Here Charlie Chaplin.' This was a pleasant surprise, for he is not only a great artist but one of the most charming men to meet. Dazzled by the Californian sun, I stepped into the cool studio where he was preparing his film, *City Lights*, expecting to see the man with the bowler hat and bamboo cane; I did not recognize him in the young man in pyjamas coming towards me with outstretched hands. The thing that struck me was his modest, rather bashful manner. His staff, awaiting his orders, were prepared to proceed with the picture, but he stopped the work and we went to a small bungalow next door, where a Chinese servant prepared tea.

'I have been working on this picture for two years and I am not satisfied with it yet. They would all like me to go in for the talkies but it would not suit what I am trying to do.'

'Haven't you thought of producing a talking picture and only yourself silent in it? Or are you opposed to the principle of it in general?'

'I could not say that,' he answered, 'but talking pictures are still technically in a primitive stage, and would therefore ruin the effect of the whole.'

We then discussed the importance of the moving picture as a means of influencing the masses, how useful as political propaganda and also how disastrous it might become. Chaplin emphasized that his art was an individual one, a personal expression of himself, without any object in view. His conversation was most lively and entertaining. He sprang from one subject to another, his shyness had vanished, he had a delightful way of making fun of his colleagues and of mimicking the 'stars' of Hollywood. This great comedian had the gift of entertaining without ever creating the impression that he was performing. He once told us how the theatre of San Francisco held a prize competition for the best imitation of Charlie Chaplin. 'Naturally, I presented myself as well,' he said. 'We were about fifty Charlies, with bowler hats and shoes like boats; but what a disappointment — I got only the seventh prize. There were six better Charlies than myself!'

I had the impression of talking to a charming, subtle and fascinating woman, although one would never call him effeminate. Most unexpectedly, his house was strangely stiff and impersonal. How could an artist live in such stereotyped, American, rather vulgar surroundings? Stairs covered with plush; sitting-room with chairs so far apart that intimate conversation is excluded. The only room which had character was his puritan bedroom, with the chaste narrow bed, books piled up at hand's reach, and next to it a dictaphone. Over it hung an accordion, and as soon as we entered he grasped this and started playing on it. He sensed that his home surprised me, and he admitted not caring for it himself, and said he would change it at the first opportunity.

Many of the famous producers and actors in Hollywood are Hungarians — Bela Zukor, Paul Lukacs, Bela Lugosi, and several others — so I had ample opportunities of visiting the studios. Alexander Korda was already in Hollywood in those days, but less known then. As I had often criticized the arbitrary way which film producers have of changing an author's original text in order to have a happy ending,

I was told by the Metro-Goldwyn-Mayer people that I should watch in their studio Remarque's film, *All Quiet on the Western Front*; this time, they assured me, I would have nothing to complain of. When it was over they asked me if I was satisfied, for all the heroes were dead. 'No,' I replied, 'you have managed to make it a happy ending anyway, for the dead are all Germans!'

It was in California that I became friends with the writer Upton Sinclair. At one of my lectures, where he took the chair, he introduced me as a living refutation of the Marxian theory, of which I was a follower, that everyone finally acts according to the economic interests of his class. My whole career, he pointed out, refuted this theory better than any argument could do.

I remember leaving Los Angeles unwillingly, as Chaplin had arranged for me to meet Greta Garbo. By the worst of luck I had to attend a meeting in San Francisco at the same time. The Committee threatened to resign if I cancelled it. While I was lying in bed, probably with the subconscious desire to be late, Upton Sinclair called on me and, seeing that I had not even started to pack, collected all my belongings, threw them into my suitcase, and put me on the train. So I never met the 'Divine Greta' as she was then called. These are the tribulations of a public man.

On my way back East I stopped in St. Louis, where there is a large Hungarian settlement. Yet it is not the Mississippi I remember, nor the tanneries and meat-packing factories. My stay in the capital of Missouri was entirely taken up by . . . but let me not anticipate. The morning after my arrival I was invited into the hall of an hotel where about twenty-five dignitaries of the city, headed by the Mayor, and half a dozen reporters for the local papers had assembled.

I was then informed that I was to be taken to see an extraordinary sight which could not and, mind you, never would be seen anywhere but in St. Louis. But what it was had to be kept as a surprise for me.

We took our places in the line of eight cars waiting for us in front of the hotel, and drove off in a procession towards an unknown destination. It was an early February morning and frightfully cold. The journey seemed interminable. After an hour's drive, the procession halted. We got out and I was guided solemnly and silently through the gates of what I realized to be the zoo of the County of Missouri. It must be some sort of seventh wonder I thought, much intrigued, a horse with the head of a man, or a woman with four breasts. We stopped in front of a large cage which seemed to me, at first glance, to be empty. My companions turned eager and expectant eyes towards me. I strained mine and then perceived something heaving on the bottom of the cage, something long and dark with yellow spots. It seemed to be all curled up. A young man stepped close to me with his pad and fountain pen ready for the offensive.

'What do you think, Mr. Count, of our snakes?'

Yes, now I had seen the snakes and also that there were two of them. I racked my brain for something to say.

'He seems to be a jolly long chap,' I said at last.

'Five yards, twelve and a half inches,' was the prompt reply.

'Wonderful,' I said, 'but why are they so motionless?'

The Mayor turned to the keeper of the serpents and repeated my question.

'They had a most strenuous night, sir,' answered the man apologetically, 'they are sleeping.'

'You mean,' said one of the notables, 'that we can look forward to a happy family event in the spring?'

'Yes, sir.'

With proud satisfaction the company took note of it.

We stood for a time, gazing in silent awe at the illustrious couple, who were breathing peacefully after the exertions of the night and taking no heed of us.

We then returned to our cars.

Wherever I went that day I was asked my opinion of the snake couple and scored my greatest success when, speaking at the Town Hall, I mentioned that not only could the inhabitants of St. Louis be proud of their acquisition, but that the snake couple could certainly hold their heads high at having been adopted by such foster-parents as the appreciative population of St. Louis.

Before leaving America, I received, to my surprise, an invitation to speak at an exclusive millionaires' club in Palm Beach. All expenses paid and a thousand dollars for telling them that their days were numbered, for in the event of war disaster would befall them and capitalism. I was the guest of Mr. and Mrs. Earl Perry Charlton, and was most kindly received, and asked to repeat my lecture in other clubs as well. The luxury of Palm Beach was dazzling. Its never-ceasing flow of champagne in spite of prohibition, its beautiful women and prosperous old men, its perfect stage setting, gave one a sensation of unreality. Those were the days of the great slump, when shares were rapidly falling and unemployment figures rising.

9

THE BIRTH OF A CONTINENT

It was a time of promise, a renewal of the world. HAZLITT

IN 1931 Lucien Vogel, Parisian editor of *Vu* as well as of various
fashion papers, asked me to join his group of writers on a visit
to Soviet Russia and prepare a special number for his magazine.
I was to write on the Agrarian Revolution, my wife on the general
aspects of Soviet life. We accepted with pleasure; it was a unique
opportunity to see the Marxist experiment for ourselves.

I had been in Russia before the war, during Tsarism, when Berchtold was our Ambassador, but I had seen only the brilliant world of
fashion of St. Petersburg.[30] The other side of the medal, the world of
the miserable *mujik*, was an unknown quantity to me. Later, during
the Galician campaign in 1915, I saw the sub-human conditions of the
natives of those regions, and this enabled me now to make comparisons
and avoid the mistakes of most Westerners, who judge Soviet conditions by their own standards.

Russia in 1931 was just moving out of its 'Sturm und Drang' period.
The Revolution seemed to have come to a standstill. The exhausting
civil wars were over; the inhuman expropriation of the *kulaks* was
slowing down; the collective co-operative farms (*kolkhozes*) were
triumphing over the State farms (*sofkhozes*);[31] the opposition was made
to toe the line and Stalin was undertaking one of his strategic moves
backwards, known as 'Real-Politik'. It was the third year of the Five
Year Plan; industrialization was advancing in great strides; the latent
power of the waterways was being used for electrification on a gigantic
scale; the Dnieprostroy, one of the wonders of the age, was being constructed with the aid of German and American engineers; the first
Soviet trial for sabotage against foreign engineers had been staged;
Bukharin, Rykov and their friends, after having been made to recant,
had received important posts; Trotsky was banished to Siberia, and

the voice of Soviet nationalism was being heard for the first time.[32]
Although Stalin was gradually building up his legend of infallibility
and extending his power daily, he was not yet the idol of later years.
It was the dead Lenin lying on his velvet cushion, with his Mona Lisa
smile, who was the worshipped god. His portrait as a child with
chubby cheeks and a wisp of hair hanging over his convex forehead,
the god-child — a conveniently silent idol — was visible in all public
places, on school walls, in nurseries and hospitals. Are dead idols less
noxious than living ones?

My attitude towards the Soviets in those days was the following: I
had always believed that to counteract the supremacy of Germany on
the Continent alliance with the Slavs was indispensable, particularly to
Hungary. Even at the time of the Tsars, however antagonistic I was
to their system, I had endeavoured to find a way to Petersburg. My
final aim, the Danubian Federation, needed the backing of its mighty
neighbour. How much more did I feel this towards the new Russia,
which had broken the old despotism and was on its way to achieve
Socialism. For the first time the exploitation of man for the creation of
individual wealth was being abolished. It was the first experiment on
the lines of those economic principles in which I believed. Although
far from having realized the paradise depicted by its enthusiasts, the
system, I was confident, bore within itself the possibility of creating a
more efficient, equitable and happy world than ours.

No signs of unemployment, the danger-mark of Western civilization, no exploitation by private capital, the surplus of production
returning to the State for re-investment; all this meant progress. Soviet
Russia was but ten years old. How could it have been expected to
achieve more in so short a time, surrounded as it was by foes? And
even if Communism, in the Marxist sense, had not been achieved, the
power of the gilded monster had been broken, as well as that of Auto-
cracy and of the retrograde, irresponsible and selfish landed gentry. A
revolution had been effected similar to the 1789 revolution in France
which gave the land to the peasants. Therefore, we, the European progressives, should approach with sympathy and understanding the
effort which was being made in 'the sixth part of the world', and do our
best to create an atmosphere which would help the country to develop
peacefully on its new lines. This would have been the only way to
check the cruel methods which were the consequence of the fear of

THE AUTHOR IN A KOLKHOZ IN RUSSIA IN 1931

MY SON ADAM KAROLYI IN SWITZERLAND

aggression. Besides, Russia meant for the working classes of Europe the materialization of their faith, which had hitherto been purely theoretical. Therefore, nothing I saw, however unfavourable, could alter my disposition towards them. In the controversy between Trotsky and Stalin about Socialism in one country, I agreed with Stalin, since I cherished no illusions about the strength of the working classes in the West. It was essential to prove that Socialism was not merely the theory of a nineteenth-century German professor which could never be carried out, but a working proposition.

As far as human suffering was concerned, was that not inevitably linked up with progress? And why did those who assailed the Soviets on grounds of inhumanity accept the cruelty of modern warfare? Why was hardship only acceptable for the sake of imperialism, but unacceptable in the cause of progress? Comparing it with previous conditions, we judged this to be progress. And even today I feel certain that many of the best men and women of those days, much of the moral and intellectual élite who opened their minds and hearts to the Soviets, did so for the right reasons. The best writers, painters, artists, scientists and philosophers fell under the spell.[33] On the other hand, capitalism was passing through one of its periodical crises, irrefutably demonstrating the defects of the system. Tons of coffee and wheat were being cast into the ocean or burnt and millions of pigs slaughtered in order to keep prices up, whilst the unemployed were starving. Every day news of banks crashing, of fortunes lost, of millionaires throwing themselves from skyscrapers, of strikes and disturbances, emphasized the disintegration of the system. The West seemed to be on the verge of foundering in economic chaos, whilst in the East planned economy, controlling unemployment and over-production, was showing its first results.

Our group consisted of Lucien Vogel with his inseparable camera strapped on his shoulder, his tartan cap on the back of his head and his tweed plus-fours; Pierre Lyautey, nephew of the eminent Marshal, a pleasant and amiable companion; Emil Schreiber, on the look-out for business opportunities, with his pretty wife; and Marc Chadourne, writer and neurasthenic, with the face of a St. Sebastian. He possessed an uncanny knack of attracting to himself, like a magnet, all possible calamities. When fountain pens, purses or cameras were stolen, they invariably belonged to him; if mail was lost, it was his; if boats broke down and trains were hours late, they were always those on which he was travelling or had booked his seat. We were accompanied by a medical expert.[34] Ex-general and ex-count Ignatiev, ex-military attaché of the ex-Tsarist regime in Paris and guardian of the funds of the ex-embassy, had after the Revolution refused to hand over these funds to the émigré colony as they requested and had returned them to the representative of the Soviet Government on the grounds that this money was Russian property whatever its regime;[35] this surprising attitude in a member of the *ancien régime* made him the most hated man in Russian refugee circles. Now he had been appointed commercial representative of the Soviets in Paris and this was his first journey home. In order to avoid the assault with which White Russians had threatened him, he boarded the train several stations beyond Paris.

It was a great moment for Katus and me when we caught sight of the large red Triumphal Arch erected at the frontier dividing the West from the East. Facing us in large letters stood: 'For the Workers of the West.' On the Eastern side of the arch: 'Communism will destroy all frontiers.'

The spick and span station was like an exhibition of the Russian Decorative Arts Pavilion in any Western capital. It was in fact the first and most impressive propaganda bureau to strike the newcomer. Special devices, gadgets, brilliantly coloured posters, gigantic inscriptions of Soviet slogans in all languages such as: 'Dumping and forced labour are lies'; 'Electricity plus planning is Socialism'; instructions on how to use soap for washing the hands before meals, how to care for the newly born, and large photos of men and women with high cheek bones and narrow, slit eyes, learning their alphabet somewhere near the Caspian Sea.

The buffet is very poor. There is no showing off to the tourist. Black, sticky bread, vodka and mushrooms (*ceps*) are the only fare. Everything functions perfectly, calm officials, elderly porters in immaculate white blouses, polite Customs officers, which make Lyautey remark that the service is more efficient than in France. I get a tape and measure the distance between the two railway lines, comparing them with our narrower ones, to the distress of Katus who fears I will be arrested as a spy, but no one takes any notice. The doctor is the only one who is made to feel uncomfortable. All his bags are opened and his collection of photographs of Parisian ladies is much appreciated. They are handed round, to the embarrassment of the blushing doctor. The emotion of General Ignatiev is touching to witness. At home in his country he assumes the duties of host and pays for our refreshments. He tells the head official that he had been a count, a general and an émigré for fourteen years, and that he is now returning home for the first time. The effect is instantaneous. The Bolshevik official falls into his arms and kisses him on both cheeks. The photographing fever takes hold of us and cameras click in all directions.

The large sleeping-car is most comfortable; everything seems more spacious, wider, larger. We have left Europe.

Katus, unable to restrain her impatience, asks the ticket-collector for his opinion on life in Russia.

'Why do you think it an improvement?'

'Because the work which was done in the past by one man is now done by two; because my daughter is attending a secondary school, which she could not have done before; and because we call each other "Tovarish" ' is the disconcerting answer.

Three weird-looking individuals are in the next carriage. The conductor whispers in our ear that they belong to the G.P.U. Are they watching us, we wonder? Ignatiev sits and drinks vodka with them, he little minds who they are, they can be the devil and his relations so long as they are his compatriots. They discuss politics and reproach the French bitterly for refusing Russia a loan. At each stop we get out and use our camera freely. At one of the stations Lyautey is surrounded by a cheering crowd, women offering him flowers and clapping their hands with joy. They point to his belt. It is a red belt. They have taken him for a Communist.

The town of Moscow, that gem of Byzantine architecture and Asiatic variety, of gilded domes and exotic shapes, is being feverishly converted into an American city. Tall concrete buildings are shooting out of the soil like mushrooms, replacing the picturesque ancient churches.

The mellow brick Tartar wall surrounding the old city and the tiny, unique, sixteenth-century chapels erected within it were, to our grief, being demolished. Lunacharsky, the writer, when Commissar for Fine Arts, tried his best to preserve these works of art, but the tram-line which brought workers rapidly to their factories had to pass there and was of greater importance than the preservation of historic relics. At night we were kept awake by the continual grinding sound of pneumatic drills and the dumping of the cobbles of the ancient pavement into the trucks.

'Do people never rest?' we asked, exasperated.

We were told then about the system of twenty-four hours' work, of day and night shifts to keep the factories running continuously and so complete the Five Year Plan before its time.

The Russians were proud of these improvements and honestly imagined that nothing like them existed in the West. Nevertheless the freedom of a woman to bear a child when she wanted, the fight against prostitution by setting up institutions for re-education — which would have gratified Gladstone as well as Lady Astor — the free schools for the psychological rehabilitation of delinquent children, all were full of promise. The charge that they existed only for the purposes of propaganda was not justified. Being model institutions there were but few of them, yet they proved that the leaders recognized certain principles, although for the time being they had not the means to instal them throughout the country. How could one expect them to guide us to the miserable quarters of Moscow, or to the concentration camps? What Government in the world would make a show of its slums, prisons or black markets?

The picture galleries and art collections — the most famous, those of Morozov and Shtchukin, with the best Picassos — were kept like sanctuaries where with wonder-filled eyes, awe-struck *mujiks* would stand gazing at the works of the masters.

It was therefore not only the economic and social aspect which seemed full of hope, but also the cultural. The artist and the man of talent enjoyed many privileges and was an appreciated member of the community. No publishers, no agents, no middlemen to exploit the writer and drain his talent.

In the Writers' Club in Moscow, the President of which was the eminent and popular writer Alexei Tolstoy, we had many discussions on the role and aim of art. The writer Lunacharsky was a man of exceptional gifts and ex-Minister for Education. He disagreed with the view of the French writers' group that art exists for art's sake only, independent of space and time, being merely the self-expression of the individual. For him, art must be the expression of its period, put at the service of humanity, to make men happier and better, and life more valuable. Picasso was the representative of *l'art de la décomposition*. Lunacharsky was frankly critical of the Soviet system of education and discussed its drawbacks freely. He did not approve of education being controlled by young people, chosen because of their political reliability but without the necessary erudition or authority; nor of teachers being subjected to Childrens' Councils, and having to seek their favour.

Anti-religious propaganda, as seen in their anti-religious museums, was mainly an effort to enlighten the backward population about primitive superstitions and the dangerous and unhygienic practices of religious sects.[36] It was a course of rudimentary hygiene.

In the market places one could still see, seated behind long tables and underneath large parasols, members of the former ruling class offering for a few kopeks the remnants of their treasures; real lace for which no one cared any longer, Fabergé snuff boxes, painted fans and ivory-handled, silver-topped canes. These unfortunate people still cherished the dream of being 'liberated' by the West.[37]

The Soviets seemed to have solved the intricate problem of minorities. The various republics incorporated in the Union had their own schools, universities, theatres, the national character of each being respected. A centralized system as far as State planning was concerned, yet decentralized culturally.

There was no sign of militarism. The unimportance and amateurishness of the Red Army was demonstrated to us at a military parade of General Budyenny, which resembled a gymkhana or a point-to-point rather than a cavalry display. Later, after the advent of Hitler, the fear of Japan and the spread of Fascism made armaments imperative and relegated social progress to the background.

The foreigners who lived in Russia in those days were an odd collection. Fascist business men, American tourists and journalists, British Socialists, French writers, German engineers. Some came driven by the urge to see the 'great experiment' at work, others in search of business opportunities, others again simply for adventure. Many of them were loyal friends to the Soviets. The reports of Walter Duranty, correspondent of the *New York Times*, helped to dispel existing prejudices. Maurice Hindus the American writer, a Pole by birth, had just brought out his great success *Red Earth*; Louis Fischer and his

Russian wife were at that time sincere supporters of the new creed. Egon Ervin Kish, the witty Czech writer, would entertain visitors of all shades of opinion in his room in the Hôtel Europe. One evening I had supper at Louis Fischer's, at which Hindus and several Russian men and women were present. In the Russian fashion, we were continually sipping tea with red wine, and the more animated the conversation grew, and the hour advanced, the more wine and the less tea was poured into the cups. The main topic, I remember, was the drastic methods used against the *kulaks*, the forced industrialization and the divergence between Stalin and Bukharin. It was not easy for outsiders, whatever expert knowledge they possessed, to disentangle the antagonisms of the different factions.

Tourist traffic was most welcome to the Soviets, for it meant foreign currency, and was widely encouraged. The squares in front of the hotels were filled with huge red and blue buses into which energetic females, members of the Intourist, working like clever sheep-dogs, guided their flocks. I remember an American woman asking the interpreter, pointing to the Red Square where Lenin's Mausoleum stands: 'Tell me, please, was Lenin a Communist? I cannot believe it.' This bunch of tourists, avid for information — meaning, as someone said, 'to see and hear everything, but to understand nothing' — had to visit the Cathedral of St. Basil, the House of the Boyar, the Trietiakovsky Gallery, the historical museum in the Kremlin. In the evening the docile flock would be taken, whether they liked it or not, to *Boris Godounov* at the Opera, and to dine at midnight to the sound of the balalaika at the Hôtel Métropole. To be *à la page* was to have visited Soviet Russia; it belonged in those days to the itinerary of the fashionable American woman when she came to the Continent. The Paris dress shows, the Gourdjeff Institute at Fontainebleau, the nudist colony in Berlin, a visit to that rising man Hitler, and last but not least an interview with a live Bolshevik in the Kremlin. On her return home, she would in all probability publish a book on Russia.

'The Bolsheviks are not sentimentalists', was the slogan of the day, and business men, no matter to which country or to what system they belonged, were the most favoured visitors. Yet none of them could compete with the Italian Fascist business men, who were the favourites. Our first encounter with them surprised us romantic Socialists of the West, who had daily witnessed the bitter struggle between Communists and Fascists, and made us wonder if Russian Communism were not following a very different path from ours and dissociating itself from the European workers' cause. In an hotel in Leningrad which had kept unaltered the atmosphere of the 'nineties, we sat at a richly decorated table, covered with flowers and evergreen plants, and surrounded by palm trees. We had had nothing to eat since the early morning and it was three o'clock, but no luncheon was served. From the hall next to us intermittent hurrahs and vivas were heard, and we suspected that the reason for the delay was to be found behind the glass door, which was covered by a curtain. Since the French have no patience where food is concerned, Marc Chadourne peeped behind the curtain and saw a table covered with the most delicious food, huge sturgeons, goblets filled with grey, shining caviare, steaming pancakes, and a mountain of ice-cream piquantly coloured, one half red, the other half green, white and red. In the top of this culinary masterpiece were stuck the Soviet and Fascist flags. The banquet was in honour of a Fascist delegation of business men. The band in the corner of the room was alternately playing 'Giovanezza' and the 'Internationale'. It was the prelude of things to come, the start of the policy of expediency so much approved by Western 'realists' but which in later years was responsible for the undermining of Communist morals. The waiter, who noticed our puzzled looks, smiled a sly oriental smile. 'This is a three-million-dollar business. This means new tractors,' and added reproachfully: 'You Francesi do not do business with us.' We conceded the privileged position of the moneylender, and waited, subdued, for our turn to be served.

There were other disquieting symptoms. One of them was the Hôtel Métropole in Moscow with its nineteenth-century atmosphere of luxury and grandeur, its humble, obsequious old waiters, who had bent their backs so long that they could not straighten them. It formed an island in the centre of Moscow, reserved almost exclusively for the entertainment of foreigners. The young women at the bar were not sent to any institution for re-education; on the contrary they were placed there specially for the pleasure of the Western diplomats. The excuse offered was that the State needed foreign currency and the ladies had to be paid in dollars or pounds. Also the diplomats had to be supplied with what they were accustomed to at home, for if restricted they would become antagonistic to the Soviets. 'We have to be realistic.' No Bolshevik would enter this place of ill-repute. He would have been discredited.

In spite of these defects, Communism was still in its heroic phase — the old Bolsheviks were still alive — and the 'pure' kept away, letting others, specially picked, do the dirty work. This was the hey-day of Communism.

It was in that summer that Bernard Shaw, Lord Lothian, and Lady Astor came to Moscow.

From an article by my wife in the *New Statesman* (1951):

The tall figure of Bernard Shaw stands on the terrace of the British Embassy in Moscow, surrounded by eager and expectant faces. Noah's Ark had not a more varied and bizarre collection of creatures. The Soviet leaders of those days, who as a rule never entered those luxurious surroundings — Communism was still in its puritan stage — have shelved their prejudices in order to meet the great playwright, and are sipping the dry Martinis and champagne cocktails presented to them on brilliantly polished silver plates. The entire foreign colony is present; what a treat after the dull, or rather non-existent social life in Moscow! Cameras click; all try hard to approach the white and bristly beard in the hope of being snapped while talking to the great man.

Shaw and the Commissar of Public Instruction, Bubnov, the man in green uniform, are having a violent discussion. The ex-general and ex-count, Ignatiev, is acting as interpreter. Shaw is talking French with a strong Anglo-Saxon accent.

'You have to create for children a life of their own. I'm sure it is a mistake, while educating a child, to think of what he will become when he is twenty. Every age has its right to existence. The fault of adults is to want children to live according to their precepts. A child is not a grown-up person, it has its own value as a child, and should not be influenced to live the life of a grown-up.'

I see Bubnov's clean-shaven skull shaking disapprovingly.

'We don't believe in isolating our children from our problems which are also theirs. We believe in bringing the child directly into real life, and not creating around it an artificial atmosphere so harmful in later life.'

I don't hear Shaw's reply; a strange profile, very pale with an Abraham Lincoln beard and the aspect of a French *Communard*, draws my attention. Leaning over the stone balustrade in a black Russian blouse, he is explaining something to a woman dressed in spotted red crêpe-de-chine. It is Radek arguing with Lady Astor about the status of the worker in the Soviet Union and in an England which he pretends to regard as ruled by titled ladies.

I turn back towards the Russian group surrounding Bernard Shaw. He is asked if he anticipates a war against the Soviet Union.

'Talking about war,' he goes on, turning to me, 'I remember an incident. After a speech of mine during the General Election of 1924, I ridiculed the slogan of the Allies, their famous "War to end War". A soldier said to me: "Why didn't you tell me that in 1914? If I had known it, I would not have gone into the trenches." My reply was: "That is precisely why I did not tell you in 1914." '

I had got my 'bon mot' and have to move on as a couple of newly arrived visitors are thrust upon Shaw.

'The reason why I talk so much,' I hear him say to them, 'is not to have to listen to what other people say.'

Lord Lothian is deep in conversation with Lunacharsky about the advantages of State planning and the possibilities of carrying it out under the capitalist system.

Suddenly, Lady Astor's red dress drops in a deep curtsy before Litvinov.

'Like a humble peasant before the almighty Tsar, I beg you to grant the demand of a person who is at present in the hands of the G.P.U.,' I hear her say as she hands him a letter.

'This has nothing to do with me. These cases are not within the jurisdiction of the Foreign Office,' answers the Soviet Minister, who seems not to enjoy the joke. It was a petition in favour of one of the 'sabotaging' engineers who had been put under arrest.

Like an advertisement in a fashion magazine, the Swedish ambassador, in his perfectly tailored brown suit, stands beside Halatov, the President of the Gosizdat (State Publishing Institution). Halatov wears a black leather coat, breeches and high boots; his olive face has a jet-black beard growing up to his eyes. Two young men are conversing in undertones, keeping apart from the rest of the company. The one with red hair looks like a film star. He is Lady Astor's son. They look around anxiously, as though wondering whether a bomb will not be hurled at them by the fanatic-looking Radek.

The American-Russian writer, Maurice Hindus, is endeavouring to approach Bernard Shaw, but in vain. The great British author is besieged. Luckily everyone can have a glimpse of him as his red face soars above the crowd.

In his slow Irish brogue he is saying: 'I told Stalin that his mistake lies in imagining that Englishmen are intelligent. I told him that Englishmen are not, and that's why they can't understand the importance of State planning. I was a Communist long before Lenin was born.'

Sir Esmond Ovey, the Ambassador, smiles at Duranty, a short man leaning on a cane:

'Of course, they don't realize that he is an Irishman, and he is growing more so every day since he has been here.'

Lady Astor, who acts as Shaw's impresario, hustles him off as he has to appear in an hour's time at the public reception given in honour of his 75th birthday.

At 8 p.m. the former Club of the Nobility, with its vast hall supported by white Empire pillars, is packed with an expectant crowd. On these shiny parquets, today's Paris taxi-drivers, the Russian émigrés, once waltzed in picturesque green and braided uniforms. It was here, too, that during the civil war Lenin and his staff had their headquarters.

After an interminable period of waiting, Bernard Shaw at last appears. He is wearing a Norfolk jacket and a shirt without a tie. He has tried his best to look Bolshevik, but he has not succeeded in losing his strikingly Anglo-Saxon air. He forms an amusing contrast to his neighbour, Halatov. It is of him that Bernard Shaw said later:

'The Bolsheviks are queer chaps. They pick out a man to accompany me who knows no language but Russian, and they sew him up in black leather; the one thing they forgot was to put in his mouth a knife dripping with bourgeois blood.'

His other neighbour is Lady Astor, who with motherly solicitude is unceasingly fanning Shaw.

Lunacharsky delivers a speech in Russian. We don't understand a word of it, but there is no doubt that he is appropriating Shaw, turning him into the precursor of the proletarian dictatorship, the 'Voltaire' of the Russian Revolution, the destroyer of individualism and the inspirer of the new collective ideology. Shaw seems rather worried about what is said about him and with one eyebrow raised, giving him a Mephisto-phelean expression, he listens attentively to the translation of the inter-preter seated behind him. But still more so are his English travelling companions who wiping the sweat off their brows, wait uneasily for what their great *enfant terrible* will say or do next.

In an impressive silence Bernard Shaw rises and addresses the audience:

'Tovarichi . . .' his voice is drowned in a storm of enthusiasm which he endeavours to diminish by adding that it is the only word he knows in Russian. He tries to assume his customary ironic tone; but somehow less successfully than at other times. One cannot help feeling that he is deeply touched by the spirit of the people, although he tries to conceal it. It is not the usual Bernard Shaw; his jokes lack their habitual flavour.

'My travelling companions are all capitalists, very rich capitalists indeed,' he continues. At this Lady Astor claps her hands in genuine pleasure, and the audience, not understanding English and imagining that it must be something revolutionary, again reacts with a new burst of applause. 'They were very worried about coming to Russia. . . .'

He goes on, but his wit dries up. And then suddenly: 'I can't talk to you as I generally do, I see in your eyes something I have never met in the audiences of other countries.'

After this he goes on in a changed voice. There is nothing left of the sardonic Shaw; an unusual earnestness has taken hold of him.

'England should be ashamed that it was not she who led the way to Communism. We let Russia, an industrially backward country, do what we should have done.'

I see Lord Astor nervously twitching his short moustache.

'It is a real comfort to me, an old man, to be able to step into my grave with the knowledge that the civilization of the world will be saved. It is here in Russia that I have actually been convinced that the new Communist system is capable of leading mankind out of its present crisis, and saving it from complete anarchy and ruin.'

How many things have changed since then! Most of the Bolsheviks who were present at this birthday party are dead now, most of them executed, and how many of those who had been ardent Stalinists have been cruelly deceived!

Bukharin, whom I visited in his office in the Commissariat of Agriculture, was theoretician number one of the party. A brilliant scholar of Marxism, he was its undisputed authority not only in Russia, but in Europe. Friend of Lenin and Trotsky, he was one of the genuine leaders of the Revolution. Head of the right wing of the Communist Party and editor of *Pravda*, he had opposed Stalin's agrarian policy of persecuting *kulaks*, advocating that they should be absorbed by the community instead of being turned into potential enemies. Youngish, with a rust-coloured goat's beard, in top boots and leather coat, with good-natured, laughing blue eyes, he had the face of a rather insignificant *mujik*. He seemed to be the same type of man as Rakovsky — sharp-minded, simple, direct, without personal vanity or ambition. He did not deny that his views differed from those of the party on the subject of agriculture; but what those views were he did not disclose to me. He had fallen into disgrace owing to his opposition, had recanted and now held an important post.

'Is it true,' I asked him, 'that the part of the Five Year Plan which concerned communal farming had to be entirely altered? I hear that the peasants who brought in land are now given a proportionate share of the profits of the *kolkhozes*? This, you will admit, is co-operative farming, but not communism.'

'You are right,' Bukharin answered in perfect German. 'You must have noticed already that we Bolsheviks don't bind ourselves in all circumstances to our theories. [This from a theoretician!] Our ideal is Communism but we are still far from realizing it. There are as yet only a few communes. Among them are the Lenin Commune founded ten years ago, the Verblud Commune and a few others. Where the peasants were less tractable we had to make concessions. Life is full of compromise. Our peasants are backward and still want to own their horses, cows, pigs and poultry; but when experience has proved to them that a communal tractor ploughs in forty-five minutes what a man and a horse plough in as many hours, they will be won over to our ideas. We started these communal farms only a year or two ago, so the peasants have not yet had time to see the results. In Pamir the tractor proved such a success that the natives brought it, as a sign of their gratitude, offerings of bread and wheat.'

'Isn't there a danger that a peasant who enters the *kolkhoz* on a property basis might after a few years of good crops acquire capital by investing his money — this being now permitted — and become the founder of a new bourgeois class?' Bukharin shook his head.

'No danger at all. The pessimists, of course, croak about peasant counter-revolution, but why should we fear the agricultural labourer becoming comfortable and prosperous? He can do nothing with his money. He cannot buy land or factories, or acquire productive capital. Money is power only when it is a means of production. People do not realize that Socialism never advocated equality. The notion that one man may not possess more than another has been attributed to us by the ignorant, unacquainted with the A.B.C. of Socialism. All the means of production — land, factories, banks and machinery — should belong to the State. When the peasant sees that the communal system gives a better yield and enables him to live in a comfortable cottage of his own, why should he want to return to a system under which he was miserable? And even should the peasant be seized by a capitalist desire to be the sole owner of the farm, he would not be able to carry it out. For the Soviet State is sovereign. The notion of a peasant counter-revolution is pure humbug. But what do you mean by class? The danger of class exists only when it can exploit the work of others. As our laws and system prevent this, we have no reason to be afraid of a new bourgeoisie. Our aim is to be a self-sufficient country. The needs of 160 million people have to be satisfied. If we export at present, it is to get machinery in exchange. We are turning bread into steel so that tomorrow steel may give us a double return of bread.' This was a peaceful version of Goering's famous 'guns for butter'.

Four years later Bukharin was executed as an enemy of the Soviets. His trial was one of the most famous in the history of political trials, and his defence and confession the most brilliant and disconcerting human document.

The former President of the U.S.S.R., Rykov, was also one of the old guard. He received us without ceremony. He still occupied the presidential apartment in the Kremlin and the door leading to it stood open. Without ringing or knocking, we entered. No servants; a long corridor and many doors. We went on opening them until at last we came to the room where Rykov and his wife were waiting for us. While taking tea, Rykov spoke freely and simply without restraint. The most characteristic difference between the old Bolshevik and the new starched, 'Gladkin' type of *Darkness at Noon* was that the former seemed uninhibited, fearless and outspoken. The new breed was suspicious, cautious, pompous and silent. One of Rykov's remarks struck me as particularly brave. He said that he had always believed in the downfall of Tsarism and that Russia would become a democratic republic, but that he had never aimed at the dictatorship of the proletariat. That had come through the war. He also told us that the collective farms were much less successful in Siberia, for the Siberian peasant, not having been a serf like the Russian, was more property-conscious. The landless *mujik* was better material for the experiment.

'We are still a continent in effervescence,' he said. 'We have not yet been able to rid ourselves of all the bad things inherited from the past, such as, for instance, the hypocrisy of family life. We have not yet succeeded in modernizing it.'

'What do you call modern family life?' Katus asked.

'A family in which the economic factor does not prevail and where women are not obliged to sell themselves for economic security.'

'But even if money is non-existent, won't power and position take its place?'

'Perhaps, but at least one decisive factor, that of wealth, will be eradicated. That is the first step.' It was the raising of women to a higher moral standard and the giving them more responsible positions which seemed to occupy Rykov. His wife, a doctor, was certainly a superior woman.

As we left, Rykov asked my wife if we had ever been in prison. Katus answered proudly: 'Yes, one night in Italy.' But that did not satisfy him. 'It is nothing,' he said, slightly contemptuous. 'You will have to be imprisoned yet . . . and you will,' he added encouragingly.

He was said to have recently given himself up to drink. Was this caused by disillusion and the apprehension of things to come? Some years later he was purged and executed.

Lenin's widow, Krupskaya, was a woman about sixty, with grey hair parted in the middle, a grave face and unusually heavy eyelids over a pair of light blue protruding eyes. She gave the impression of a very kindly schoolmistress, which she had been in her youth. Now she held a high post in the Ministry of Education, as Stalin did not yet dare to eliminate the widow of the 'Great Leader'. Rumours were spreading that she had admitted that she would never have become a Bolshevik had she not been Lenin's wife, being too sentimental and soft-hearted. Talking about her life, she told us how since her earliest childhood she had devoted herself entirely to revolutionary work; how she had given classes to workmen on her free Sunday nights at the Smolensky college; how she had met Vladimir Ilyitch during the Carnival at St. Petersburg — 'but our Carnival consisted of lectures, debates, conspiracies'. She told us of her imprisonment in the fortress of SS. Peter and Paul, of Lenin's letters to her, written between the lines with milk which had to be heated to be made visible, of their deportation to Siberia, and how they would spend their mornings in studying English and translating Sidney Webb's works into Russian; of their life in Munich, Zürich, Paris, London; the publication of clandestine literature and the periodical *Iskra* ('The Spark') which became the formative influence of Russian Socialism. The English they had acquired in Siberia was not of great help to them for, as she said, 'no one understood us, nor could we understand them'. She told us how in the British Museum, under the green lampshades, Lenin wrote his works and prepared for the struggle with the decaying Russian Empire. Half a century back, under those same lampshades, Karl Marx had written *Das Kapital*. And also how gay Lenin could be; how, in an exuberant mood, he would mount the stairs on all fours, tease and make fun of his friends with pungent, harsh humour. She spoke of their celebrated journey in the sealed carriage through Germany in 1917, playing chess all the way; and how, approaching the Russian frontier, his excitement grew and his game got worse. Although we knew much of all she told us, to hear it from one who had shared Lenin's fight and strenuous life was fascinating indeed. She spoke freely about Trotsky and admitted to liking him. 'He loved Vladimir Ilyitch very deeply; on learning of his death he fainted and did not recover for two hours. I thought then that he cared for him too much to succumb later to his "vanity". He is a domineering, difficult man.' She was living in Gorki, with Lenin's sisters, in the country place where Lenin spent the last months of his life. A large garden with unkempt lawns, beech and willow trees, and overgrown paths surrounded a white house in Empire style; striped linen covered the furniture, shuttered windows conveyed the impression of an uninhabited residence. Between the pillars at the entrance hung an oversized portrait of Lenin in a framework of faded flowers. It was here that Lenin, condemned to eternal silence, though conscious and lucid, watched the intrigues waged for his inheritance — the reins of power. Stalinists and Trotskyites fought their deadly battles round the motionless invalid of Gorki. Lenin's sister, Maria Ilyitchina, a little woman in black with a long skirt reaching to her ankles, received us. Her prominent cheek-bones and small slit eyes were those of her brother. She had joined the opposition against Stalin, but finally submitted like most of his opponents. She asked us timidly if we wanted to see the room in which her brother died. She showed us, behind a mahogany screen, the plain wooden bed, the big armchair with his cane still lying on it and the small mahogany desk at which he used to work. Three large windows looked out on the park. Katus wanted to take Maria Ilyitchina's photograph, but she refused, seeming shocked at the idea of having it taken in her brother's room. The tragedy of Gorki, the final act of the fantastic life of the creator of the New Russia, is little known. The Communists do not write about it. The man before whom millions trembled in fear, and whose name even today is a flaming spark, lay here at the summit of his power, a helpless wreck waiting for the end.

The atmosphere of the place was infinitely depressing. The garden was covered with yellow autumn leaves; the damp smell of mushrooms, thick grass and rotten tree bark filled the air. Under the columns of the façade the two silent sisters, vestals of the sanctuary, waved us farewell.

One evening we dined at the house of Hungarian friends, where we met Bela Kun. He had now settled in Moscow after leaving Vienna and seemed to have acquired more poise and frankness. He was less gushing about the merits of the Soviet Union and admitted that bitterness against the regime existed in certain strata of the population, due to the hardships of collectivization; also that social progress had lately been relegated to the background in order to achieve the Five Year Plan. Our relations were still strained. He did not like me. He was very anxious that our compatriots in Russia should not know of my presence and that my sympathy towards the Soviets should be kept dark. Since the Soviet press did not publish personal news, my arrival had not been mentioned in the Hungarian papers either. At Kun's personal wish an article I had written for *Izvestia* and which Radek, its editor, had accepted, was never published — a proof that in Hungarian matters his was the last word. The reason for this concern was

mainly his personal vanity and his fear of my influence, as he was unpopular with the Hungarian colony.[38] He never forgave me the legend
that I had handed over power to him; it detracted from his merit in
seizing it. He was an ardent Stalinist and spoke of the opposition with
contempt. He enjoyed talking about Hungary and did so with nostalgia. I was again faced by that touching patriotism of the persecuted
and despised Hungarian Jew — a curiously sentimental, masochistic
race. He would listen in for hours to gipsy music from Budapest and
recall with moist eyes the various cafés of the Hungarian capital, for
which he had an intense longing.

The most distinguished Hungarian living in Moscow was Varga,
the well-known Marxist and one of the most respected and independent
Marxist economists in the Union, although he got into controversies
with the official party line and fell into disgrace at repeated intervals.
His latest controversy came from his attitude towards American
capitalism.

The Hungarian refugees in the Union met with various fates. Many
of them were purged, of whom Kun was one; others returned to Hungary after the Russian victory in 1945. Through the Hungarians in
Moscow we gained more insight into the life of the ordinary Russian
behind the scenes than our French companions acquired through their
official investigations. The so-called Old Bolsheviks resented the
deifying of Lenin, for they used to say that it was just from such
superstitious cults that the great iconoclast had tried to liberate his
people. He would turn in his grave, they said, if he could see what
nonsense was being built up round him. Some frankly admitted to us
that, although Lenin recognized Stalin's qualities, he despised him as
a man of lesser stature.

A remarkable experiment had started in those days, which was given
up later on. This was communal housing for people belonging to the
same profession — buildings for painters, writers, sculptors, architects
and so forth. It had some similarity with Van Gogh's idea of painters
living together. To the Western mind communal life seems unbearable, but the Russian considers it the normal way of life, for he seems
not to require privacy. As a matter of fact, the word 'privacy' does
not exist in the Russian vocabulary.

The first attempt at this communal living was that of sculptors. We visited one, whose name I cannot remember, in his studio. He was a bachelor and received a yearly salary from the State of 2000 rubles, in return for which he had to deliver four works a year, whether good or bad. If he was appreciated, the State would buy more of his work and pay accordingly. He could also sell to others whatever he liked. In this way, they argued, a talented artist would be well off, and the less talented would have a chance to improve. But how many poor artists would, by delivering four works yearly, get their 2000 rubles? Who would decide whether he had talent or not? The answer was that 2000 rubles was such a minimum for existence that, if he got no more orders, he would take up another profession. So finally it was the State who decided what was good art or not. Was it competent to do so? How far the State would take advantage of this and interfere with the artist's liberty remained to be seen.

Our host was a middle-aged, hefty man, with an uncouth beard, his open shirt revealed an extraordinary growth of dark fur. He pointed out a small figurine of earthenware for which he was offered 20,000 rubles by an American and had refused.

'Why?'

'What could I do with the money?' he answered. 'I cannot rent better or bigger apartments — no one is allowed more than three rooms. I cannot get more food in the co-operative than is my share, whatever wealth I have. I have no material worries.'

'Would you not like a car?' asked someone.

'I could not use it. It would make me unpopular. The people would look askance at me and take me for a crocodile [black marketeer] and not for an honest artist. I would much rather go on foot.'

Then, looking with tenderness at the small, fine figure and caressing it with his large hairy hands — it seemed impossible that such clumsy hands could have produced so frail a thing — he went on: 'How sad it must be for the artists in the West to have to part with works they love for the sake of money!'

The irrelevance of money was perhaps the most comforting and redeeming feature of the new way of life. The harassing business of making and storing money, of competing with one's neighbour in the standard of living, so exhausting and nerve-racking for the Western man, was completely absent.

Our journey through the Russian continent was one of inter-
mittently changing impressions, varying from unpleasant annoyances
caused by trains stopping without notice in an open field for several
hours and for no apparent reason — engines and boats breaking down
and having to wait for days for communication — mails being delayed
and letters lost — water-taps dislocated — rubber-like meat floating
amongst half a dozen drowned flies in a concoction of yellow oil tasting
of turpentine ... to the imposing structure of the Dnieprostroy, storing
the waters of the Volga to supply electrical energy to the furthest
villages of Eurasia — Stalingrad growing like a mushroom out of the
earth, a modern American city with foreign engineers as instructors—
the luxurious sanatoriums and hospitals on the shores of the Black Sea
with up-to-date equipment and everywhere the joyful, laughing faces
of the young — elsewhere the wild, homeless children, victims of the
battle against the *kulaks*, sleeping in the gutter for want of a roof over
their heads, fighting for crumbs like dogs under the tables in public
restaurants — and the astounding colony of Bolshevos, a pioneer camp
for the education of these boys, the 'berprizzenii' working on the
most modern principles of child psychology. It was here that we met
Maxim Gorki who had just returned from exile. He wore a *mujik's*
brown blouse and a short beard. He had no wish to talk to the group
of Francesi, having probably had enough of Europeans in Capri.
When he was told that I was amongst them, he wanted to shake my
hand. A brief second only was sufficient to make me aware of the
indescribable tenderness of his eyes, especially when he looked into the
enthusiastic young faces in front of him. They were wet with tears. I
shall never forget his expression.

Our Russian companion, General Ignatiev, underwent a curious
metamorphosis during the journey. He changed before our eyes from
a courteous Western diplomat, the pet of the ladies, into a rough, uncouth, genuine *mujik*, who viewed us Westerners with visible disgust
and aversion. While our boat travelled through the Black Sea,
dangerously listing to one side — its helm was broken — followed by
somersaulting dolphins, Ignatiev sat at the piano playing and singing
old folk songs for the diversion of his fellow-travellers, who gathered
around him, accompanying him with guitars and song. In his white
Russian blouse, no one would have taken him for anything but a
mujik. He had completely cast off the last vestige of European manners

and grunted abusively when any of us addressed him. In his capacity of interpreter this attitude was not particularly helpful, but I never saw a happier man. He had visited his former estate, now turned into a *kolkhoz*, and was overjoyed to find on it his old valet, who had remained in the house as guardian. They fell into each other's arms. I think the predominant trait of the Russian, to whatever class he may belong, is his deep emotional patriotism, his attachment to the soil, to which he feels himself united by a sort of mystical bond. He carried with him, in a silver cigarette case, a clod of Russian earth to bring back to his mother, the old Countess in Paris.

In the stern of the ship the sailor Soviet sat in judgment on two of their men who had neglected the engines. The appointed prosecutor presented the charge. The guilty men stated their case. They did not 'confess to sabotage'. In the distance the flat roofs of the ducal palaces and those of rich industrialists, now turned into holiday resorts for labourers, shone white in the sun. It was the first time we had heard of paid holidays and free tickets for factory workers.

Georgia has a special fascination for the European. It is from those dark summits of the Caucasian range, between the Black Sea and the Caspian, that sprang the legends of the chained Prometheus, and of Jason who sailed across the waters to find the Golden Fleece.

Lying on the main thoroughfare uniting Europe and Asia, this strange country is populated by various races, peoples and religions, who have kept intact their different customs and special traditions.

For centuries they fought their battles of independence in those sombre mountains, against the invasions of Darius and Cyrus, against the Mongols of Genghis Khan and Tamburlaine, against the Tartars and Turks, against Tsarist oppression, and against the armies of Denikin, as well as against the Soviets. Djugashvili (Stalin), himself a Georgian, succeeded in subduing them and incorporating them in the Transcaucasian republics in 1922. Tiflis had been the stronghold of the Mensheviks and the scene of the ruthless repressions and purges which had caused the first dissensions between Stalin and the ailing Lenin.

The three towns we visited had nothing in common. On the eastern side, on the shores of the Caspian Sea, lies the oil-town of Baku. Approaching the town one is struck by the heavy odour of naphtha vapours. The vegetation is dried up, and the sea itself is an opaque grey, the colour of lead, with oil floating on its surface. The bleak landscape is a drab mixture of beige and chestnut colour and the oil derricks stand silhouetted against the sky like gallows.

Batum, on the shores of the Black Sea, with its abundant semi-tropical vegetation, its damp hothouse atmosphere, its luscious, over-sized gardenias, ivory-coloured magnolias and wild geraniums, its persistent and intoxicating perfume, forms a striking contrast. These two towns are connected by a 300 km. pipe-line, through which flows the oil to be shipped to all parts of the world.

Between them, at the foot of the Caucasian mountains, lies Tiflis, capital of Georgia, filled with red acacia trees and known for its excellent wines, its love-songs and the beauty of its women. Also for its legends about the lovely and cruel Queen Tamara, whose memory still lives vividly amongst the population. Near the river Kura, amongst the ragged hills, we saw the ruins of an ancient Christian monastery. Everywhere the graceful spires of minarets contrasted oddly with the giant hydro-electric station over which stood a colossal bronze statue of Lenin. Was it here that Prometheus had defied the gods by bringing to men the heavenly spark? It was an appropriate spot if so, as Lenin is considered by the Russians as the Prometheus who achieved Russia's electrification in defiance of the 'all-powerful Gods of Capitalism'.

Strange figures, wrapped up like mummies and mounted on small frisky horses, confront us on the road. As soon as they notice us they make their horses pirouette on their hind legs, and face the stone wall beside the road, waiting for us to pass. These amazons are Bashkir women, who may not face the glances of the infidel.

The military road towards Vladikavkas narrows down at Passanour and cars filled with tourists halt at a small wayside inn. In the vine-covered loggias we relished excellent wine and listened to the music of guitars. The place was filled with picturesquely clad natives, men with huge fur headgear like monumental wigs, while others wore tiny skull caps richly embroidered like a cardinal's. The men were most handsome creatures. Tall, slim, with narrow hips and broad shoulders, their small waists girt with wide, richly ornamented belts from which hung daggers and poison-containers. In days gone by the weapons, tipped with poison, would inflict a fatal wound.

An enchanting evening was spent in that remote valley, watching the white mist creeping along the foot of the mountains, while a pretty gipsy girl sang in a low and gentle voice nostalgic songs to the twang of the guitar. Hilarious with wine, our French colleagues intoned the refrain of Maurice Chevalier's latest hit, breaking the spell.

On entering the International Hotel in Tiflis we seemed to be confronted, to our surprise, with Stalin, standing behind the reception desk, in his brown Russian blouse and belt, directing the tourists to their respective rooms. The shape of the skull, the face, the dangling dark moustache, sly eyes, sensual mouth, stocky stature were all exactly like. This Georgian porter must have had the same talent for organization as his double, for the building was compelled to house ten times as many lodgers as there was space for. Beds, couches, mattresses were laid out in the lounges, halls and corridors, solving the problem regardless of comfort. Even in the daytime the place was strewn with inert bodies. After two weeks without washing I was offered a shower. Blissfully I covered the entire surface of my body with the foam of soap and turned on the tap. After some drizzling drops it dried up mercilessly, leaving me standing there like a snow man. In desperation I ran down the corridor in this peculiar attire, a towel wrapped round my loins, to complain to manager 'Stalin'.

Our Intourist guide was a curious type. Like all well-trained propagandists, she had had, at the start of our journey, an explanation for every defect we encountered. But when she discovered we were of 'good will' and had not come to prove that Socialism was a failure, she became more critical than we were. She was conservative and a typical philistine. All for preserving traditional family life, she would not consider sending *her* daughter to any communal institution, though she had shown them to us with such pride.

The trip down the Volga was most enjoyable. The boat was clean, as most of the passengers were kept below deck. Each time our boat stopped at a village we were assailed by a heaving mass of nomads, who, with all their earthly possessions on their backs, shoved their way like a horde of cattle over the gangway. It seemed to us that the entire population was perpetually on the move, crowding the railway stations, trains, boats and hotels. These broad-cheeked, Kalmuk-eyed men and women with children wrapped up in their bundles did not appear human. They were an elemental force, shoving ruthlessly forwards, over living or dead — heaving, expanding Asia on the move. They seemed irresistible, and whoever was so imprudent as to get in their way would be trampled down mercilessly beneath their rag-bound feet. In the boats they were herded on to the bottom deck, where they lay on top of each other like animals, the women spending the hours in delousing the heads of their infants or neighbours, a pastime which probably gave them the same pleasure as cross-word puzzles give to us on journeys.

We should not forget that Russia cannot be judged by European standards. What we call Russia is but a part of that hundredfold-larger body which extends from the shores of the Baltic to the Pacific Ocean, and which for several decades has been suffering the birth-pangs of a new civilization, dying and being reborn in 'sweat and blood'. Since those days other Asian countries have emerged and the West has become uncomfortably aware of their existence. Will the over-civilized and degenerate peninsula called Europe, placed at the extremity of this vast continent, be mad enough to interfere and, spurred by ignorance and greed, try to check the natural evolution of Asia? Will Europe, following the lead of those who, with the ocean as their Maginot Line, have little to fear, risk being trampled over and submerged as far as the shores of the Atlantic?

In the streets of Kharkov an old man accosted us and praised the life in the democracies of the West. He knew what Paris and London were like, it was only the silly young ones who believed everything they were told. The 'young ones' stood around and laughed. One man asked: 'Do you know anything about Trotsky? Where is he?' These incidents show that there, interest was still felt in the outside world and that had Russia not been in constant fear of invasion it would probably have developed on more normal lines. The fear of Europe relegated more and more into the background the so-called 'Europeans' inside the party, those who had more knowledge of the West, leaving Stalin and the 'Asiatics' to take the lead. A new type of Russian was gaining ascendancy — THE BUREAUCRAT. Silent, suspicious, unemotional, he sat with his long pointed pen at his vast desk, in a gloomy, empty room, slowly and elaborately copying out figures.

When meeting this specimen I thought of Beatrice Webb's statement that humanity was divided into two species: the anarchist and the bureaucrat. The period of the anarchist, of the individual, was now coming to an end in Russia. They had done their job, they had rebelled and destroyed the antiquated values of the past; now they were gradually being eliminated and superseded by the bureaucrat, the Gladkins, whose only duty was to keep the machine running.

On our return to Moscow at the end of June, we were told by Umansky, Secretary for Foreign Affairs, about the pact which Soviet Russia had renewed with Weimar Germany. Stalinism had got a successful start. News of banks crashing all over Europe came in daily. The biggest Hungarian bank, the Hitel Bank, collapsed. Strict measures were being adopted in Germany to prevent capital from escaping. Mussolini, to frighten the Democracies, predicted the proletarianization of Europe.

Leningrad was a dead city. It seemed but a monument of the 'Ten days that shook the world'. The palace of Prince Youssoupov, where Rasputin's murder had started off the revolution, the Smolny Institute, the Tauride Palace, were neglected and empty. We went to Tsarskoe Selo and saw the untouched quarters of the imperial family kept intact by the Bolshevik Government to demonstrate the philistine mediocrity of the Russian autocrats. The walls were covered with coffee-coloured flowery paper, third-rate oil paintings, cheap knick-knacks and trinkets acquired on visits to European watering-places, a glass globe with the view of Karlsbad floating in its interior, imitation flowers, and tables crammed with family photographs; the nursery of the Tsarevich held the huge, toboggan-like contraption on which the whole family used to slide — to the dismay of the Cabinet Ministers, who disapproved of the Tsar diverting himself in such an undignified way instead of attending to more serious business. All formed a painful memorial of fate's cruelty to simple, innocent humans placed in exalted positions to which they were not equal.

On the boat which carried us from Leningrad to Stettin we noticed a silent, stern man, who for most of the time sat in the bows submerged in thought. His dark face was thin and hard and completely motionless. We got to know him later as the well-known Soviet writer Constantin Fedine, who was leaving his country, never to return. He was supplied with a passport and left Russia officially. Another companion was Friedrich Wolff, the young German playwright, whose play *Ciankali* had won a great success in Berlin.

10

BEFORE HITLER

IN the year 1932 I spent some months in Berlin, writing with others on the Republic of Weimar for a special number of *Vu*.

I stayed in a gloomy flat in Kleist-strasse with a distant German relative of ours who, like most Germans in those days, was living in penury. He would saw up his heavy carved-oak furniture for firewood and his food consisted of sour herrings and lard (*schmalz*) spread on bread.

Life in Berlin preceding Hitler's seizure of power was strangely unreal. Coming home at night I would find entire families of decent-looking bourgeois with children, perambulators and dogs, sleeping under the porches and in the entrances of blocks of flats.

At the same time there were night clubs, bars and music halls galore, where champagne flowed in streams and a population gone mad danced on the brink of a volcano. In this decadent modern Byzantium, young men dressed as women would walk the streets and children of twelve would prostitute themselves. Life was carried on from day to day, as they knew that the morrow could bring only disaster. The side streets of Kurfürstendamm were gayer than Montmartre and the Berliner prided himself that there was no need to go to Paris in quest of vice; but their vice was dismal and sprang from despair.

André Germain, the French writer who had been a friend of Proust, and many other well-known people of the Paris of 1900 had made their home in Berlin, where writers, artists, actors, producers, generals, politicians of all shades and believers in the most contrasting creeds, would meet.

It was there that I made the acquaintance of Ernst Toller, author of *Massen Mensch*, who had been one of the leaders of the Revolutionary Government inaugurated by the Spartacus movement in Bavaria in 1919. He was a strikingly handsome man of engaging personality. During the war he committed suicide in America. There were also Fritz Unruh, and Erich Mühsam, the idealist and writer, who was later tortured to death by the Nazis; Piscator, innovator-producer who worked at uniting the art of the theatre with that of the cinema and had just produced *The Beggar's Opera* and *Mahogany*, the great successes of the period; Erich Remarque, whose *All Quiet on the Western Front* had, after its initial triumph, been banned on account of nationalist disturbances; Edgar Mowrer, the American correspondent, who, like most Anglo-Saxons, had come to Germany filled with sympathy for the underdog, but had soon lost it; the vivacious and attractive Mrs. Rosenheim, wealthy wife of a banker, who had been won over to the extreme Left and kept a salon of her own; the disconcerting Junker Von Salomon and Bodo Uhse the novelist, who also were bitter enemies of the Nazis.

A curious atmosphere of doom hung over pre-Hitler Berlin, as if the population had lost faith in the values of their own world. Capitalism was, it seemed, in its death agony and the republic doomed, therefore many turned to Communism whilst others adopted the new creed in the hope of saving the bourgeoisie. Bankers, wealthy business men, high-ranking officers were to be found in the ranks of the Left. Von Buller, the son of the well-known admiral, declared publicly that private property could no longer be saved and that collective economy was the only salvation, although not on the Russian model. Owing mainly to the policy of the Quai d'Orsay and to the slump, Germany was heading for bankruptcy.

In order to meet reparations they were granted long-term loans and to pay interest on these loans they had to secure short-term ones. Brüning's Government could not solve these difficulties. There were some who expected a *putsch* from the Stahlhelms (Hindenburg's party) for February 1933, when the short-term credits were to come to an end. The French, believing that German bankruptcy would prevent her rearmament, welcomed it. Hindenburg's election as President did not convince France that Germany had turned over a new leaf, although the optimistic Léon Blum wrote in the *Populaire* thanking the old Field-Marshal for having saved Germany from Nazism.

During my stay in Berlin the Junkers' Association (the German O M G E) organized the Grüne Woche. It was to demonstrate their strength and power, and intimidate the Government into refraining from interference with their lands. These Junkers, many of them fellow-travellers of Nazism, came from Silesia, Schleswig-Holstein and East Prussia. They wore short leather knickers, white woollen socks, monocles stuck in their eyes and chamois tufts in their soft green hats. I visited von Gleichen, the President of the Herren Club, the Conservative stronghold. He was supposed to be anti-Nazi, but I got the impression that the German 'Barons' still hoped to be able to use the 'Führer' for their own ends and expected him to pluck the chestnuts from the fire for them.[39]

As my work for *Vu* was about agrarian reform, I got into touch with the Green International, the organization of the revolutionary peasantry of Middle and Eastern Europe. I attended their meetings under the symbol of the 'Schwarze Fahne'. In the Reichenhall a monster gathering was held for the purpose of drawing up a unified agrarian programme on the principles of the United Front. The aim was to line up the landless agricultural labourer and dwarf-holder with the industrial worker and thus prevent this stratum of the peasantry from being used as a counter-revolutionary element, as in the past. My pamphlet to the Hungarian peasantry had by now been clandestinely distributed all over Hungary. Although the publication was limited to a thousand copies it was read by many more, being passed from hand to hand.

Europe abounded in peace-saving devices, while what was actually being allowed to happen was leading us straight to war.

In Hungary, Gombos, nicknamed Gombolini, had followed Gyula Karolyi as Prime Minister. His was a semi-Fascist regime, in close friendship with Mussolini, his mentor and model. The murderers of Erzberger found refuge on his farm, and Captain Ranczberger, who had been instrumental in the assassination of the Hungarian Socialists Somogyi and Bacso, and had disappeared for years, was now appointed bodyguard of the Regent. Aggressive propaganda against the neighbouring States was carried on more strongly than ever. While Tardieu launched the plan for Danubian economic co-operation and Briand preached European Federation, Gombos was given a loan of half a million from the French Government, to enable Hungary to order munitions from Creusot-Schneider. Against whom? Against Czechoslovakia, France's ally. (This was openly advocated in Hungary.) In consequence Creusot shares went up from 800 per cent to 1800 per cent. No wonder that the Czechs, watching the rearmament of Hungary made possible by their protector, France, did not feel too confident. Also, owing to pressure from Rome, the largest European aerodrome was built in the vicinity of Budapest, and opened by Balbo, Italian Air Minister. As Hungary could not balance her budget anyhow, and was incapable of paying for the aerodrome, a big banking house assumed the obligation.

Hungary was again showing signs of unrest. Émigrés living in Vienna were being kidnapped and dragged over the border to be beaten to death as in the 'twenties.[40] A conspiracy against the Regent was discovered and many students and workers arrested. One of them was Laszlo Rajk, who became Minister of the Interior in 1945, later Foreign Minister, and was executed in 1949 by the Rakosi Government.

II

THE HEYDAY OF FASCISM

Rien n'est perdu sauf l'honneur.

IT was in Geneva, where we had settled on account of the children's schooling, that the news of Hindenburg's handing over the reins to Hitler reached us.

Crossing the Mont Blanc bridge and passing the romantic isle of Jean-Jacques Rousseau, I remember wondering whether the 'Age of humanism', of 'Reason and Enlightenment', as we conceitedly liked to call it, had not come to an end, and we were not returning to the obscurantism and intolerance of the dark ages, to *Le Temps du Mépris*, contempt of man, as Malraux called his grim novel.

Geneva, stronghold of middle-class prosperity, seemed unperturbed. Only in the Café Bavaria, where under the caricatures of the Hungarian cartoonist Kelen, the journalists of all nations gathered for apéritifs and gossip, was there commotion.

At the start people kept repeating that Hitler in power would be milder than Hitler in opposition. *'Es wird nicht so heiss gegesssen wie gekocht'* (barking dogs seldom bite), they said, like frightened children whistling in the dark. Few realized that a storm was brewing which would soon sweep away this illustrious puppet-show. But hopes placed in the League were beginning to wane; it was becoming a dead letter, an assembly where words lost their meaning; a platform of rhetorical fireworks.

Soon the Reichstag fire put an end to optimism. The news that all over Germany Socialists, Liberals, Democrats and Communists were being arrested, murdered or taken to concentration camps came pouring in, and made us anxious for our friends. Goebbels, Goering, Streicher, the modern Machiavellis, strutted through the streets of Berlin in their brown uniforms, grinning with satisfaction. Van der

Lubbe, a half-witted boy, used by them as *agent provocateur*, was dragged, yelling his protests, to the gallows.

Although by this time I had few illusions left about politics, it was an ignoble sight to see how rapidly those who only yesterday had opposed the Nazis were now ready to assist them.

In Geneva the authorities began to watch me with suspicion. I was courteously given to understand that the Swiss Government would prefer me to move over the border with my family.

I called on Robert Dell, who was living in an enchanting eighteenth-century house, where he gave delicious meals and rare wines to his friends. He accompanied me to Arthur Henderson, whom I had known ten years before in London, with the result that I was no more molested.

As Paris now became the centre of the anti-Hitler campaign, we again took up our abode there. Its heart and soul, the organizer and wire-puller behind the screen, was Willi Münzenberg. An extraordinary man, this Willi, called the 'Red Hearst' of Germany as he was the owner of several Berlin magazines, dailies and weeklies, with mass circulations. That he was the head of the Western Section of the Comintern, I did not know. He was also the head of the 'International Workers Aid', and possessed a genius for raising money from the most unexpected quarters. He would line up duchesses and princesses with bankers and generals, who would serve as obedient pawns in his hands. All over the world Committees in Defence of the Victims of Fascism cropped up, headed by respectable Liberals and well-known fighters for progressive causes, who never suspected that they were party to a Comintern organization.

This short, squat man, with the unruly tuft of hair on top of his high forehead making him look like a spirited pony, with his glowing dark eyes, his incomprehensible Thuringian accent and his dynamic personality, was the son of a carpenter. The word impossible was unknown to him, and when he conceived one of his vast schemes it had to materialize instantaneously. This at times got him into trouble; then with the same speed he would come out with half a dozen new plans, for his stock was unlimited. If necessary, he would ally himself with the devil. *Les purs* disapproved of his cynical methods of raising money, but the party benefited greatly by his conjurings. He believed that 'money had no smell' and should be accepted from whatever quarter it came. His first lieutenant was Otto Katz (alias Simone) a man of great ability, a bureaucrat of the party machine, who, when Willi left the party, turned against him. His companion and most efficient collaborator was Babette, his wife, an attractive woman with a Prussian Junker background, who had left her wealthy husband to follow Münzenberg and share his perilous life.[41]

He came to me one day with the idea that Archduke Otto, heir to the Austro-Hungarian Monarchy, should be enlisted in our fight.

'How will you manage that?' I asked sceptically.

'I will make him see the danger of German supremacy to his dynasty and to the Roman Catholic Church.'

Some days later he reported to me his interview with Otto: 'The young man passed his exam. on Marxism and Leninism with top marks. He is intelligent and open-minded. If it depended on me, I would let him join the party at any time.'

For both, this meeting was rather compromising; yet it was a proof of their political astuteness, for to get to know the adversary's point of view is essential in a struggle. As Münzenberg had a critical mind, he often disagreed with the party line. He believed that had the Soviets not prevented the German workers from resisting Hitlerism and from declaring a general strike, Nazism could have been stopped.

Many Communists began to realize that Stalinism was ready to sacrifice international labour rather than let Russia run risks — being anxious to avoid any Left upheaval which would cause economic confusion and mean that Russia could not be supplied with the machinery and experts she needed.

The extreme Left in Europe was divided in opinion at this time. One group maintained that Russia was all-important because it was the only Workers' State; they supported Stalin's 'Socialism in one country' policy. This was the accepted party line.

The other group held that Russia on its own, without the international workers' class to support it, would be unable to survive; that it would have to compromise with capitalism, thus corrupting the Communist Party. In the event of aggression from the West, the demoralized working class would be of little help to the Soviets. These two opposing views, both of which could be justified, formed the fundamental divergence of opinion which attained its climax at the time of the Hitler-Stalin Pact. I must admit that I adhered to the

THE AUTHOR WRITING HIS MEMOIRS AT VENCE IN 1953

former opinion until the pact, though I was always in favour of freeing European Communism from Soviet leadership, a view I often expressed to my Communist friends.

The French elections had given a big majority to the *Front Populaire* and Léon Blum became Premier. Münzenberg, who had advocated this policy, was now the right person in the right place, and his activities knew no limit. Day after day new organizations were born, with different names but the same purpose. As in a marionette show, the puller of wires remained invisible.

The first activity of our committee was the publication of the 'Brown Book'. Much of the material for this was brought out of Germany by Katus, a risky performance. She had stayed in Berlin under her maiden name, searching for evidence relating to the Reichstag fire, which in those early days was still a mystery, information about concentration camps, etc. She handed the material to the French Embassy.[42] The Russian Embassy in Unter den Linden, anxious not to compromise itself by incorrect diplomatic behaviour, refused to lend a helping hand. Her situation became precarious when her cousin, the notorious Louis Windischgraetz who had played the main part in my trial and in the famous forged francs scandal and was then in Berlin, detected her presence and declared openly that he would have her arrested. But the guardian angels of children, fools and drunkards took care of her, and she escaped a fate which I prefer not to envisage. It was madness on my part to let her go, but in those days we all felt that everything had to be attempted for the common cause of preventing the Nazis from stabilizing their power. Personal considerations had to be discarded. Soon the case of Dimitrov impassioned public opinion. It became obvious that this Bulgarian Communist was innocent of the charge of setting fire to the Reichstag. The gallant fight which he put up in the Leipzig court against the vociferating Goering won many hearts, and he received invitations to recuperate in English country houses. Münzenberg organized a sham trial in London, exposing the falsity of the charge. This campaign of ours ended successfully; although sentenced to death by the Nazi court, Dimitrov was handed over to the Russians. He was saved by English and American public opinion.

On the other hand we did not succeed in publishing the facts about German rearmament in the British press. Münzenberg was receiving regular information through underground channels from munition factories, giving evidence of Germany's preparation for war. Yet, when I tried to approach editors in London in order to warn Europe of the impending danger, they turned me down with the excuse that this sort of news would only hasten the conflict, which had to be avoided by all means. We were regarded as warmongers, and told that the West was not going to risk war in order to oblige the émigrés. England was swept by a wave of pacifism. Both Right and Left were for appeasement.

In 1934 grave things were happening in Austria. Under Mussolini's pressure and with the aid of the Roman Catholic Church, the weak and short-sighted Chancellor Dollfuss crushed the Social Democrats, the sole reliable force in independent, democratic Austria. The conflict started with the refusal of the Austrian railwaymen to load smuggled arms from Italy to Hungary, a regular traffic in those days, for Mussolini was surreptitiously rearming Hungary, in contravention of the Peace Treaties. The matter was brought up by a Socialist member in the Austrian Chamber. Dollfuss could not tolerate that Austrian Labour should prevent Eastern Europe from rearming under the Duce's leadership. Labour, like Carthage, had to be destroyed. He found a willing ally in the Catholic Premier, ready to support the Rome-Berlin Axis.

After the slaughter of the workers in February and the crushing of Red Vienna, the 'Third Force' of those days, Austrian independence was at an end. Many lost their belief that progress was attainable by democratic methods, as the Socialists had imagined. All this brought me a step closer to Communism.

In the year 1934, the head of the Leningrad Soviet, Sergei Kirov, was shot dead by a *Komsomol*. Although the murder was an isolated act, Stalin made use of it to crush the opposition. It was therefore supposed by many to have been the act of an *agent provocateur*. Executions followed on a large scale. Many of the foreign Communists living in Russia, especially the Germans, disappeared for ever. Stalin effected this great change, but was anxious that the friends of the U.S.S.R. in the West should not notice it; therefore entry to Russia became more difficult for foreign Communists than for neutrals or even for those of the Right, who were mostly concerned with the general aspect of the country and not with principles. They only noticed that the Soviets had more bread, but not that they had lost their soul.

I well remember Louis Fischer, the American journalist, visiting us in Paris on his return from Moscow after the Kirov murder. He was silent and pensive. Yet, when I mentioned my doubts about Stalin's new policy, the revival of Russian nationalism, the emergence of a new ruling class, the deification of the 'Leader', he disagreed and brought up all the arguments which I would probably have used myself if confronted by the same objections. I knew later that Fischer had been as critical as myself and even more so, as he was better informed of what was happening than I was. Yet he would not contribute to my scepticism. This was the way we all felt in those days: that as long as Europe was under the menace of Hitler and Mussolini, and as long as the Russians had taken the lead against Fascism and war and for collective security, it was not for us to concern ourselves with their internal affairs. This loyalty, as we discovered too late, was grossly abused and contributed to the legend of Stalin's infallibility. Yet I remained anxious, and had many painful discussions and arguments with my Communist friends.

When the trials started in Russia and the liquidation of Lenin's friends was carried out, I wrote to Romain Rolland, whose intellectual integrity was above doubt, unfolding to him my deeply felt objections. There must be something basically wrong, I wrote, in a country where all the high officials are accused of being spies; if the accusation is just, why wash the dirty linen in public instead of hiding it from the gloating eyes of the enemy?

His answer was brief and non-committal. He also, I felt, refused to give up the last hope. Sick at heart, I realized that nothing could be done. Spain and Europe needed Russia's help. When, three years later, the German-Soviet Pact was signed, Romain Rolland turned away from the Soviets.

In 1935 the problem of the Saar became acute. It was facing the plebiscite which would decide whether it would return to Germany or remain under the control of the League of Nations. We opposed its return to Nazi Germany as the majority of the Saar population were industrial workers and because its mines and heavy industry would help Hitler's rearmament. The French middle classes were less concerned with this aspect; for them Socialism in the Saar appeared a greater menace. It was hard to make them take any interest in the campaign for its independence. The French Government, although aware of the prestige it would gain by winning the plebiscite, did not supply the necessary funds. Through my friend Pierre Comert I kept contact with the Quai d'Orsay. On several occasions I was asked to go to Strasbourg and Saarbrücken to attend meetings of the election campaign. In need of funds, I approached the rich Jews of the Saar, who I imagined would have no desire to be turned over to Hitler. I got refusals all the way. Eventually most of them died in gas-chambers. The Nazis, on their side, carried on a most violent campaign of intimidation and the plebiscite resulted in a major German victory. Aware of French impotence, even the workers voted against remaining under the League, fearing that in case of defeat the Nazis would take revenge on them.

A year later, in 1936, Hitler's armies marched triumphantly into the Rhineland. Although this flagrant violation of Locarno was a matter of life and death to France, the French Government did nothing about it. Only the blind could fail to see that we were running headlong into catastrophe.

In those days we were frequent visitors at the Faisanderie, a long, grey stone cottage built in the sixteenth century in the forest of Saint-Germain. It belonged to Lucien Vogel, with whom we had been to Russia. At weekends the Vogels kept open house for politicians, writers and journalists. They received in English fashion without ceremony, letting everyone do as they pleased. The regular habitués of the place were a bunch of White Russians, Armenians and Georgians, dark-haired women with jet-black eyes who, lying on cushion-covered low couches, would talk Russian loudly to each other, a language which neither the host nor his wife nor any of the other guests could understand.

Causette, Lucien's wife, would direct the housemaids with their delicious dishes of *lapin au vin blanc*, *artichauts fourrés*, or *civet de lièvre*, around the table, whilst everyone would be talking at the same time, as though wanting to defeat each other with words. An outsider witnessing these amiable discussions for the first time could not doubt that they would end in a free fight.

After some hours spent in the forest of St. Germain to recuperate, one would be knocked out for the rest of the week. Vogel, with his inseparable pipe, bright checked suits, tight trousers and old-fashioned choker, might have stepped out of the '90s. He was of sanguine temperament, often brilliant in his conversation, always vivid and amusing. An excellent business man, he ran his huge publishing concerns in American fashion, at the same time finding jobs for all his friends and treating them most generously. He was surrounded by Soviet Russians, journalists and officials. I remember Michel Kolzov, the correspondent of *Pravda*, a talented young man, who later was liquidated, Kantarowitz, the German Communist writer, Egon Ervin Kish, the Czech writer, several Czech politicians, smart American women, German spies and agents and adventurers from all countries. For in spite of his many-sided talents, Vogel was easily taken in, having little knowledge of people.

It was at the Faisanderie that I first met André Gide, before his journey to the U.S.S.R. I never believed that his Communism would endure and, when his novels were rejected by the U.S.S.R., and he discovered that homosexuality was not much in favour, and his name incessantly made use of by the French party, he wrote his *Retour*.

The two pretty Vogel daughters were enthusiastic Communists, under the influence of Paul Vaillant-Couturier, leader of the party. The eldest became his wife and later, when Lucien, disillusioned, turned away from the Soviets, the harmony of the family was broken up.

Madame Tabouis, who worked so hard for the Spanish Republicans and all anti-Fascist causes and whose Cassandra prophecies were often made fun of, was one of the few who saw clearly the approaching disaster. I remember meeting her after the occupation of Austria. 'Mark my words,' she said, 'Hitler's next move will be against Czecho-slovakia. And we [meaning France and England] will not stop him. We shall be forced into war at the worst possible moment for us, politically and economically.' Pierre Comert said to me optimistically: '*Nous avons touché le fond.*' How far from the *fond* France actually was, and to what depths of surrender it still could go, no one could then envisage.

We were staying at a small hotel behind the Champs Élysées, when Paris was receiving its Prime Minister on his return after his surrender at Munich. The avenue was packed with people, frantic with joy at having their skins saved at the price of betrayal. It was the most nauseating spectacle I ever witnessed. While we were reading the evening papers with the news of the German armies occupying the land of their allies, for whose defence their Government had pledged its word, the cheers and yells drowned the voice of shame. When Daladier beheld from his plane the masses waiting for him on the aerodrome and was told that it was an ovation and not, as he feared, a protest, he is reported to have said: '*Quelle canaille!*' That retribution would follow was inevitable and was felt by many.

I was taken ill with disgust and was in bed, when two women called on us. One of them, the beautiful American wife of a well-known lawyer, who became later Pétain's Ambassador, tried to cheer me: 'What is Czechoslovakia anyhow? Just a country of gipsies. Its name, Bohemia, proves it.' This was a joke, fashionable in the lobbies of the Ritz. They both deplored, as did all the *bien pensants* in Paris, Duff Cooper's folly in resigning from the Cabinet, now that at last an era of stability was assured. Duff Cooper tells in *Old Men Forget* how surprised he was when, after his resignation, he went to Paris, to find that people there were even more critical of his attitude than they had been in his own country.

After Munich we decided to leave Paris for good and all — a grievous decision to take, as it had been our home for fifteen years. We realized that France was doomed. To have come to this conclusion had taken me a long time and was truly painful, as I had started life as the most devoted and appreciative friend of the French people.

THE SECOND WORLD WAR

In war moral considerations make up three-quarters of the game; the relative balance of man-power accounts only for the remaining quarter. NAPOLEON

WE spent the first part of the year 1939 near Winchester in the mellow surroundings of a small sixteenth-century cottage.

We chose this place because our son, who was twenty years old, was completing his training nearby, at the Air Training School at Hamble. He had been brought up in England and wished to become naturalized and join the Royal Air Force. His sponsors were Lord Listowel and Sir Arthur H. Hoare, of Ovington, cousin to our friend Ruth Cavendish-Bentinck.

It was the first time that we had settled in the English countryside and got into touch with county life. It was a fresh experience, as we had until now spent most of our life in towns, my tastes being definitely urban, and our friends being politicians of the Left, journalists and artists. We had not had the opportunity to meet Conservative landed gentry.

On the Continent, especially in France, to live in the country means to retire into solitude; the only thing you have in common with your neighbours is the desire to avoid each other. Not so in England. The minute you are discovered, your neighbours call on you; if you think them pleasant, you return the call and, from then on, you are accepted. On the Continent the new people do the calling — a much less hospitable custom, I think.

I hurried to join the Winchester Chess Club, of which I later became a life-member. After my experiences in the Café de la Régence and other cafés in Paris, the fairness of the English chess-player was a treat. They did not jeer when I was losing, or try to distract my attention when I was winning. They did not find an excuse for giving up the game when they were at a disadvantage.[43]

Most of the people we met were Chamberlainites and Munichites. They would mention Churchill with apprehension as being more American than English, a disquieting figure, 'a dangerous chap, not quite what we English like'. There were some Christian Scientists among them whose faith in 'Peace in our time' was unshakable. They would whisper that Spirits of higher order had intervened at Godesberg. Proof: Mr. Chamberlain, who had been suffering from gout, had been completely relieved from his ailment during the negotiations. Also, since his return, the attacks had become rarer.

Soon the war in Spain came to its sad end and Katus went to the French camps in Argelès, to distribute clothing among the Hungarians of the International Brigade. They were kept like cattle behind wire by the French, and even the parcels sent to them by the British Relief Committees were confiscated. Treated as criminals for having fought against the totalitarian powers, and disillusioned by the Communist Party, which had fought the Trotskyites with more bitterness than Franco, they were completely demoralized. Some of them hoped to find refuge in the 'Fatherland of the Proletariat', but were turned down. The reason given was that the Soviets had had bad experience of European Communists in Russia. Only a few engineers and specialists were admitted. Several of these turned into bitter enemies of the Soviets; others, losing the faith for which they had sacrificed so much, committed suicide.

The news from Hungary was growing increasingly alarming. The country was running headlong into Hitler's arms and chaining itself to the Axis. The name Axis had been coined by the Hungarian Premier, Gyula Gombos. Laws against the Jews were passed by Parliament and Hungary was assuming politically, as well as economically, the role of Germany's satellite, supplying it with bauxite, corn and cattle.

After the occupation of Czechoslovakia, Hitler generously presented Hungary with Kassa and other parts of Slovakia. By accepting these from the hands of the Führer, Horthy lost his freedom and had to give up Hungary's neutrality, its only means of protecting itself. Horthy had even gone so far as to ask for a share of the booty, announcing with pride that his regime had been the first Fascist one. Prime Minister Bethlen declared in 1938 that, though the Hungarian Government had been free to choose, it had refused to join the Little Entente and had thus rendered an invaluable service to the Germans and made impossible the creation of a strong bloc, antagonistic to Germany.[44]

Their chauvinism prevented them from seeing that in exchange for the rectification of the frontiers they had lost the whole country.

The Hungarian elections, held in June, gave the Arrow Cross (Hungarian Nazis) 23 per cent of the votes; out of two and a half million voters, half a million had voted for the Arrow Cross,[45] an alarming symptom.

In the middle of May 1939 I took part in an international conference held in Paris to warn the Governments of the approaching danger. Twenty-eight different nations were represented.

On July 14th I watched the Grande Parade in the Champs-Élysées. It surpassed in splendour anything I had seen in previous years. Most awe-inspiring were the French and British planes that swept roaring over the Arc de Triomphe.

No one present could imagine that this magnificent army could be so completely defeated in a year's time. The confidence aroused by this display of strength was slightly shaken by the news published the very same day that the Duce had given over parts of Trieste Harbour, 'the pearl of the Adriatic', to the Germans for ten years. The *Mare Nostrum* had become a German lake. There was also another disquieting rumour going round. Two well-known journalists, correspondents of most powerful newspapers, the *Temps* and the *Figaro*, had been arrested and admitted having received three and a half million francs from the German Government. One of them, adviser to the Quai d'Orsay, was the confidant of the Minister for Foreign Affairs, M. Bonnet.

Whilst the midinettes were dancing in streets and squares in the arms of black Senegalese soldiers in their bright uniforms, and the population was elated by the sense of security which their tanks and planes were bestowing on them, the homes of 150 politicians and journalists were searched by the police — a grim forecast of coming events.

And then, out of the blue, came the shattering news of the Ribbentrop-Molotov Pact. Some days earlier Katus had been present at a party in London in the house of an Austrian refugee writer, and she told me about a heated argument between H. G. Wells and Freda Utley (expert on the Far East), who had just returned from Moscow. She had been a party member for years. Her husband, also a party member, was now a prisoner of the Soviets. They had lived for many years in Russia and she had become passionately anti-Soviet. She told my wife about the admiration which the Soviets felt for Hitlerism and said that it was most probable that the two dictators would become allies. Wells, hearing this, became exceedingly irritated and called it the rambling of the feminine mind, incapable of logic. Such a pact was impossible. A couple of days later, the news of the pact was published.

The pact had a devastating effect on Russia's friends. It again proved to us that something was happening there of which we, the European Left, were unaware. I became more and more critical of Stalinism and convinced that Western Socialism had to find a new way, emancipating itself from Russian leadership. Trotsky's warnings had seemed to me, until then, the exaggeration of a vain and bitter man. I thought that his so-called 'Thermidor' was a mighty over-statement. But now everything seemed to crumble. My Communist friends tried to reassure me, saying that Stalin's ways were inscrutable.[16] The purge-trials, and now the pact, made me realize more than ever how right I had been not to join the party, for there was a time when I had come very near doing so.

Looking at events in retrospect, there are arguments for Stalin's policy. Munich had been signed without him. It naturally made him suspect that the capitalist States would eventually unite to attack Russia, when she was not strong enough to wage war. It was better that Hitler should be the aggressor, and unite all the Russians against him. But, even admitting this, the pact was unpardonable; it was not mere neutrality, but an actual alliance with the Fascist dictators. At the same time, he urged the workers of the West to sabotage war-production, which 'would help democratic plutocracy'. Moreover, had Hitler not attacked Russia, it is most problematic whether Stalin's attitude would have changed; and in that case the outcome of the war would have been very different.

In Hungary, the Government-controlled press even stopped being anti-Russian for Hitler's sake, and acclaimed the 'two young proletarian nations' (Germans and Russians) as 'fighters against capitalism'.

The best elements in the workers' movement were bewildered and many lost their faith in Russia. It was one of those notorious Stalinist expediency measures which proved the deep contempt he felt for the European proletariat and for the Western Communist Parties in particular. It meant a great loss of prestige to the European Communists, which they have had much difficulty in recovering.

My material situation was rapidly becoming precarious. My brother Joseph, who had been presented with 40 per cent of my estate, was embarrassed by this gift. It made him appear to be profiting by the illegal and inequitable procedure of the Government towards his brother. Urged by his mother Geraldine, he declared that the entailed property assigned to him was not his, and that he would preserve it for my son Adam, whom he considered to be the legal heir. He repeated this in his will; he sent me messages that the reason for his not refusing this gift had been to keep it intact for my children; had he refused it, it would have gone to the State. Meantime, he promised to supply us with a generous allowance and urged us to start living in a *standesgemäss* fashion. He regarded as inadequate the flat Katus had bought in Paris with her inheritance. 'Buy a house in Paris, suitable to your position', and another in the country, etc... I do not doubt that this was his intention, but the way to Hell is paved with good intentions, and my brother lacked the strength of mind to carry them out. The allowance rapidly dwindled and we were lucky not to have followed his advice. We received just enough for the education of the children. After his early death, it turned out that poor Joseph had not only spent his own income, but had used up mine as well. He was incapable of handling money and his extravagant tastes, the advice he followed in his investments, and his political activities (he was President of the Legitimist Party), and sponging friends, all contributed to the ruin of the two estates. He had bought a large house in the centre of Budapest for the Headquarters of the Legitimist Party, out of my money. It was perhaps his way of making good the sins of his brother. The legitimist propaganda was thus carried on at my and my son's expense.

When he was appointed educational adviser to the Archduke Otto, the luxury in which he and his family lived in Lequetio, Spain, greatly surpassed that of the imperial household, and was not much appreciated by Empress Zita, although he extended his generosity to the Emperor's family as well.

When the war broke out, even our meagre allowance, smuggled out of the country by my sister Elisabeth in a ball of wool or in the inside of dolls, had to be stopped. Adam had now completed his training and turned out to be an exceptionally gifted pilot. In order to help us, he took a job as instructor for Civil Defence at Shanklin on the Isle of Wight. A week before the start of hostilities, owing to a defect in the plane — the joystick broke — the plane crashed. His pupil was extricated from beneath the burning plane without a bruise, whilst Adam, who had rolled into a ditch, remained unattended. He burnt to death.

The outbreak of the war found us in a semi-conscious state. On the day of its declaration, we were both in Downing Street, asking for permission to settle permanently in England. In spite of the events, Lord Vansittart had time to receive us and settled the matter. His sympathy and humanity we shall always remember.

From Hindhead, where we spent that terrible summer, we moved to Oxford in the autumn. It was in that remote environment, among the spires and colleges and green parks, that we passed the first year of the war.

After the fall of France all aliens were suspected, and the miserable German refugees were sent to the Isle of Man, in company with rabid Hitlerites. This created hysterical persecution of the already so-much-harassed Nazi victims, making them fear that they would meet the same treatment wherever they went. A tragic case was the breakdown of a friend, the German writer Rudolph Olden. He was one of the few German Junkers who had had the courage to stand up to Hitlerism. The camp commander, taking it for granted that all of them were Nazis, used to praise them for 'being loyal to their Government and good patriots'. Although his captivity on the Isle of Man was a short one, it was sufficient to shatter his faith in the democracies of the West. He decided to leave England. The boat on which they sailed ran on a mine. He refused to take a place in a lifeboat until all the women and children were saved. His wife stayed at his side. When the ship sank, they were seen in each other's arms on the sinking deck. Had he been less impatient, he would soon have lived to see the day when his exceptional gifts would have been appreciated and put to use, for nowhere were the refugees so wisely treated as in England, when the first panic was over. In France, many of them, the Socialist Ministers Breitscheid and Hilferding for instance, were handed over to the enemy or executed by the Pétainists.

A compatriot, who was also interned in the Isle of Man, told me the following characteristic incident. One night, the Hungarian internees were kept from sleeping by a terrible hullaballoo going on in the next block, where the Japanese were confined. They were cheering and yelling without stop. The next morning, the Hungarians complained to the commander and received the answer that the Japanese had been celebrating the fall of Singapore, for which they had got special permission. The champagne had made them hilarious. 'We hope this won't happen again', our flabbergasted Hungarians were told.

One day, having heard about A. J. P. Taylor, History don at Magdalen College and expert on Eastern Europe, I called upon him. When I stepped into his small study, built over the running water of a mill at Holywell Ford, he was just writing about my role in Hungarian history. Did I live up to his expectations? It is not for me to say — all I know is that we have remained friends from that day on.

When, after Pétain's Armistice, the radio announced that Churchill would speak, the foreign colony in Oxford had no doubts that he would offer peace to Hitler. They were packing their trunks for crossing the Atlantic, or preparing to take poison. I, too, could not imagine that Britain would be able to carry on by herself. My Marxist ideology had convinced me that, in the last resort, capitalist Britain would behave like capitalist France.

Churchill's great speech knocked out all preconceived theories, and gradually we began to fathom the extraordinary strength of the British people when they are in a tight corner. They were silent. It was hard to know their reactions; their faces were set, and life followed its old routine in this ancient citadel of learning and fastidious civilization. It seemed a secure haven which even the vandals of Europe could not destroy. In the Randolph Hotel, men and women, all in some sort of uniform, kept their unperturbed expression while sipping their gin-and-It. and discussing any subject except the war. The foreigners would say: 'Look at these people, they do not know that they have lost the war. They have not the imagination to realize what will happen to them when the S.S. march up High Street.'

We received a message from Caja, my wife's sister, who was in Hungary, that we were on the list of those to be liquidated when they landed. She begged us to leave for America.

The bombers were flying nightly over us to Coventry and Manchester and Merseyside. The blitz had now started in London. Through Lord Vansittart's help, Katus became a member of the Red Cross and joined the Ambulance Service.

One day, returning from London, my train was late and I arrived after curfew. Puzzled at what to do, I went up to the policeman outside the station and told him what had happened. After looking me up and down suspiciously, he told me to follow him. At the police station — for it was there that he took me — I was shown into a cell with only an iron bed in it. He wished me a comfortable night and left. This wish of his was most unlikely to be fulfilled, for the bed was short — most are too short for me — and hard, without pillows, the cell cold and the electric light from the passage shone into my eyes all night. Also, the unpleasant feeling gnawed at me that Katus must by now imagine that I had been killed in a raid.

I had no reason to worry. At two in the morning, Katus had been woken by a towering policeman:

'Are you his wife?'

'Yes . . . What has happened to him?'

'Don't you worry, lady. We've got 'im safe.'

'What has he done?' she gasped.

''E'll be all right . . . You come to see 'im in the morning and make 'im comfortable: 'e is rather cold.'

At crack of dawn, Katus, with a couple of pillows, blankets and thermos flasks under her arm, arrived at the prison as though she expected me to remain there for the rest of my life.

After an admonition from the Head of the Police not to choose trains that run late another time, we returned to our flat in Crick Road, with the resolution not to turn for advice to the police next time.

The devastating experiences of the last years had shattered faith in such established values as loyalty, courage, honesty and the capacity of self-sacrifice for a higher cause. Humanity appeared an abject mass, accepting brute force as its basic law. The League of Nations, Collective Security, the Kellogg Pact outlawing war, had proved naive dreams, scraps of paper, words without meaning. Exasperation at the hypocrisy of the democracies, at the impotence of Parliaments, conferences, resolutions and protests, was all that remained; also a deep disappointment in the masses, in the workers' movements, indignant bewilderment at the Hitler-Stalin Pact. But now something unexpected was happening. Churchill's dramatic speech, the epic of Dunkirk, the Battle of Britain, the fortitude of people in the blitz, had the effect of a camphor injection. The Continental exiles, chased from one country to the other, defeatist and hopeless — many committed suicide — found a new stimulus to life. Defeat was being converted into victory, not through material superiority, but through those spiritual values which they had mocked at and imagined dead. Those who had believed that it was sheer madness on the part of Britain to resist began to wonder if victory was not more a 'moral or psychological issue than a physical one'. Life and its inscrutable laws were defeating logic. Mathematically, Britain had lost, but mathematics seemed not the last word. There were other things that counted as well.

Thus, the vulnerable island, Churchill's fortress island, became the haven of the shipwrecked, where, although life was physically unsafe, uprooted humanity acquired a more substantial safety. They became aware of belonging to a community which, having accepted them, would protect them. For it is not the fear of death that matters most, it is the fear of being an outcast, of belonging nowhere.

The arrogance of the German émigré, whether Aryan or Jew, who prided himself on German efficiency — they were nicknamed *bei uns* for exalting the German way of life over the British — faded away and their advice on how to win the war was less heard. England's unobtrusive spiritual climate affected these heavily tried people, though often subconsciously. The attitude of the Government was a constant source of surprise to the foreign colony. However bad the news was, it was not kept back from the public, as was usual in countries on the continent. The press was not an organ to mislead, to fabricate lies, to raise unreasonable hopes. Neither did it excite to hatred of the enemy. Its frankness at times even appalled us. The public were handled as adults — the only way to render them so. Mass hysteria was completely absent, in time of defeat as in that of victory. In fact it was Dunkirk, the defeat turned into victory, that the British seemed to be the most proud of. They are not flag-conscious. Even after their greatest victories the streets were not decorated, there were no demonstrations, no marches, no military bands; proving more than anything to what a height their civilization had reached. What a contrast to the noisy celebration of *Sedans Tag*, carried on all over the world where a German happened to be, and the statues erected, even before the victory, to General Hindenburg: *Der Sieger!*

Only on Victory Day was London decorated.

In the winter of 1941 Katus managed, after many difficulties, to have herself transferred as an ambulance-driver from Oxford to London. Although I did not see the necessity of her driving in the blackouts and fighting fire-bombs, we had to give up our comfortable flat in Crick Road and settle in Hampstead, for *homme propose et femme dispose.* We found a ground-floor flat in a large modern block on Haverstock Hill, comparatively safe, so that during the raids the neighbours would crowd into it, whilst Katus would satisfy her unwholesome passion for firewatching on the roof of the flats with the other members of the team, selected from the block's inhabitants.

I remember a specially bad night. All round the horizon flames were devouring the city. The anti-aircraft guns on nearby Primrose Hill were shaking the concrete building. We had just got the belated news that Caja, who had been on her way to join us, had been killed by a bomb in Yugoslavia. She had been working for the Allies and now that the Germans were to march through Hungary she had to escape. She was a rare person, courageous, talented and beautiful. At the time of the Spanish war she had worked for the Republicans in Spain and, although for some years an ardent legitimist, she had become a Socialist in the 'thirties and a passionate anti-Nazi.[47]

It was a tragic night. It seemed as if the dark forces had all united to destroy the civilized world; but the next morning was a perfect spring day, the sun was shining with special intensity over the mutilated and still burning city, as if to offer consolation to its sorely tried inhabitants.

We took the Underground to the East End and walked through streets covered with wreckage; we climbed over the smouldering debris out of which St. Paul's stood in a landscape of devastation, alone, as if liberated. It had acquired a fresh importance, showing façades until now concealed. The air had that special quality only experienced on islands, radiant and with the taste of sea. It was strangely exhilarating, like champagne. Lorries drove by, filled with firemen and volunteers. In their fierce faces, blackened with soot and shining with sweat, their teeth shone white. Bruised top-hats — they must have picked them up from under the debris — were tilted with a flourish on the back of their heads, and they sang and cracked jokes with the passers-by, in voices hoarse with fatigue ; but the expression in their eyes was that of grim defiance.

Shopkeepers were sweeping up the glass in front of their shattered premises, humming popular tunes. It was an impressive sight to see these people amongst the ruins of their property, accepting it all without lament and with a smile. I remember an old woman who was looking for something amongst the debris. Turning towards us, she said: 'It's the third time 'e's bombed me. My girls says I must leave. Not me.' She shook her head. 'I'll not give 'im that pleasure. That's what 'e wants; make everyone uncomfortable.'

On the door of a partly destroyed public house, I read the following notice: 'This establishment stays open during air-raids; in case of a direct hit, we close at once.'

This walk through devastated London on that bright May day was a great experience. It proved that property is, after all, unimportant, and that to be alive in the radiant air was the only thing that mattered. Since then, London and England have grown close to our hearts — an affection which will never wane.

Hungary had for long been regarded, not only by the German and Italian dictatorships but also by the Western democracies, as a bulwark against Bolshevism. It was therefore not surprising that the semi-Fascist regime installed in Hungary should become Hitler's ally.

The pact of 'eternal friendship' signed with Yugoslavia by the Hungarian Government on December 12th, 1940, was carried out under German pressure, Berlin hoping in this way to chain the Yugoslavs more solidly to the Axis.

On April 2nd, 1941, at Horthy's order, Hungary declared war on her 'eternal friend' and invaded Yugoslavia. Count Paul Teleki's

Government was mainly responsible for this pro-German policy, as he had introduced the anti-Jewish laws and had given his consent to Hitler's armies marching into Rumania, thus giving up neutrality. In exchange, they had received some parts of Transylvania. The Regent himself had hurried to kow-tow to Hitler, so as to secure something of the Rumanian spoils, reminding him again that Hungary had been the first Fascist State before the Führer or even the Duce had founded theirs — which, by the way, was perfectly true.

Teleki realized his mistake too late. His personal atonement — he committed suicide — proved that he was aware of the gravity of his acts, but it did not help his country.[48]

The pro-Nazi Bardossy assumed the Premiership. To rouse the passion of the population the Luftwaffe arranged an attack on Kassa, telling the Hungarians that the bombing had been done by Soviet planes.

I was now being assailed from all sides to start a free Hungarian movement, uniting all those outside the country who opposed Horthy's pro-German policy. I hesitated, as many of my countrymen were non-political and had just been caught up by events, which had prevented them from returning home. I feared spies. Moreover, I did not approve of the official British propaganda towards Hungary. I did not believe that the B.B.C.'s kid-glove way of handling my country would obtain the desired results. The broadcasts were addressed only to the higher civil servants, and took no heed of the lower middle-class, intellectuals, workers and peasants who, although they had little influence now, were the only ones who could be relied on if a change came. It was odd to hear the wireless saying that the Hungarian members of the Cabinet, who had adhered to the Tripartite Pact,[49] were the ideal leaders of Hungary. These tactics, obviously used in order to win over the ruling classes, had the contrary effect. They encouraged wishful thinking and made them confident that, in spite of their support of the Nazis, they would not be held responsible, as the Allies had understood clearly that they were unable to do otherwise. It strengthened their traditional sitting-on-the-fence and the belief that they were the pets of the British, with the label 'handle with care' attached to them. They were convinced that Hungarian feudalism was greatly appreciated by the English Lords who, they thought, were the masters and who, in the event of German defeat, would stop the Russians from bombing or occupying their country. Had they not got their pipe-smoking Admiral who could talk English and resembled Earl Beatty? It made them feel safe and smug and that it was pointless for them to get into trouble with the Germans.

In the second half of the war, the B.B.C. adopted a different line and appealed to other strata of the population as well, but it was already too late. Hungary was chained hand and foot to the Germans. Mr. Hohler, third secretary to the Budapest Legation, told us on his return that the entire ruling class had turned pro-German and they could count on their five fingers the few who dared to be seen with the British.

After endless discussions, I started the New Democratic Hungary Movement, to which the majority of our countrymen all over the world adhered.[50]

In Chicago a mass meeting was organized on the basis of my pro-gramme and that of the Danubian Federation. The Communists, being cut off from Moscow and without instructions, were like lost babes in the wood. They were muddling along, attacking my policy as being too friendly towards the Czechs, as the majority of their London Club was composed of chauvinist Hungarians and Slovaks.

Thus the paradoxical situation arose that the ex-Horthyites and Communists joined hands on 'patriotic' grounds against my movement. I had always been incapable of following the principle of 'my country, or my class, right or wrong'. I felt that the fact of belonging to a country or a party made it incumbent to discern its faults and help it to improve. At times I hurt the feelings of my compatriots, who preferred flattery to criticism.

The Foreign Office was only willing to recognize my movement if all the different Hungarian associations joined it. I refused to col-laborate with the dissident diplomats in London as long as they were in touch with Tibor Eckhardt, who had started a movement of Free Hungarians in New York.[51]

After much hesitation, the leader of the London group, Zsilinski, who had been First Secretary at the Legation, agreed to my wish, and unity would have been achieved had he not, on the day after signing his break with Eckhardt, committed suicide. His motives were personal. The other members of his association were of no political importance, and collaboration was therefore dropped.

When Hitler attacked Russia we were at a party in Hampstead. Those present were mostly of the Left, an M.P., writers and journalists. We betted as to how long it would take for the Germans to beat the Red Army. There was no question of the Soviets being able to resist them. The most optimistic said six months. I betted four, while the majority thought four weeks.

During that summer of 1941 everyone was watching, their eyes riveted anxiously to the map of Russia. At the same time we were enjoying sudden calm and quiet nights, bombing having completely stopped. The exhausted population could breath again, sleep again. The popularity of the Soviets increased daily. Stalin's scorched-earth cry and the heroism of Stalingrad were the second epic of the war. The new and unexpected Soviet patriotism and the efficiency of the Red Army were a revelation.

Although my faith in Stalinism had dwindled and I became more and more critical of his methods, I now had to admit that the industrialization of Russia was the key to its resistance, and that industrialization of such a vast continent in such a short time could only have been accomplished through blood and sweat. No one could doubt that after the decisive victory of Stalingrad Russia would play the foremost role in Eastern Europe. Therefore, our grudge against Stalin's methods, which did not accomplish Socialism in our fashion, had to be stored up for later on.

After the defeat of Voronezh, where the Second Hungarian Army was routed, Prime Minister Kallay tried to put out feelers to the West through the Horthyite diplomats who were living there. The Hungarian ruling class had begun to realize that the war was lost and their only concern was to save the regime. All nationalist bodies were united in a single National Defence Association under Major Magashazy, Horthy's former aide-de-camp, which had an uneasy resemblance to Hitler's S.S.

Our New Democratic Hungary Movement, or rather my wife, set up a club in Connaught Square, where our members could meet, discuss and listen to distinguished British personalities who came to lecture. Our aim was to offer opportunity to Hungarians to know more of Great Britain, its institutions, customs and literature, so that on their return home they might turn the knowledge to profit. The

President of the Club was Lord Wedgwood, who was well acquainted with Hungarian affairs, as he had been at the head of the Parliamentary Commission at the time of the White Terror. Many well-known people gave their names as patrons.[52]

One day, Jan Masaryk, Czechoslovak Foreign Minister, came to speak and emphasized what he had often told me in private — that Czechoslovak-Hungarian friendship would be possible only with a Hungary which would honestly accept the Karolyi programme. I could not help remembering Franchet d'Esperey in Belgrade seventeen years before: 'Ralliez-vous autour de Karolyi. Il est votre seul espoir.'

The Hungarian colony was much impressed and they joined my movement with increasing trust. I myself was confident that the Czechs' policy was turning over a new leaf and that they at last realized that Federation was as much to their advantage as to ours.

These gatherings in the very heart of bombed London during a bitter war were comforting. They proved that there are values common to all civilized people, which cannot be destroyed and which unite, beyond all prejudices, those who believe in them.

Hitler's easy conquest of Europe was a flagrant proof that in our mechanized age small nations cannot exist on their own. London, the centre of the Resistance, where refugees from all parts of Europe assembled, was the propitious place to work out the principles of a United Europe on a federal basis. If this could at last become reality after the war, the suffering and destruction would have been worth while.

The idea of a federal Europe was based on an alliance of several regional federations, in which our Danubian Federation would have formed a part. It was our particular concern, and war-time London offered the right time and place to launch it.

We therefore set up a Danubian Committee in which all Eastern European countries except the U.S.S.R. were represented by delegates. It was important to get to know those with whom later one could collaborate.[53]

Inside the various national groups political differences were acute, each arguing that it was they alone who represented the real opinion of their country. It was odd to watch these bitter foes, who loathed each other more than they did their neighbours, trying to adopt the

British way of conducting political controversies. From time to time one would see murderous glances exchanged in silence. But the 'glittering eye' of Captain Robinson, our circus tamer, kept control.

The President of the committee, the Yugoslav Minister Gavrilovich, had been Ambassador in Moscow and was a follower of General Mihailovich. He was an astute politician and a charming man. There were English members as well, experts on South-Eastern Europe.[54]

The Poles, when the news of the Russian victories came pouring in, became more and more dejected and finally resigned from the committee.

The greatest difficulty was the handling of the Russian problem. Russia being our most valuable ally, no one dared oppose her outspokenly. But each controversy inside the different groups was determined by their pro- or contra-Soviet attitude. The anti-Soviet members wanted to include the Greeks and the Turks as well. Another divergence was caused by the social problem and that of the distribution of the land. My group was for planned economy and radical land reform, with Customs union within the States. Each State had to give up part of its national sovereignty. Others desired a purely political alliance, each State retaining its sovereignty and economic independence — a sort of enlarged Little Entente.[55]

In the Royal Institute of International Affairs at Chatham House, a study group was formed under the chairmanship of Sir Frederick Whyte, to work out, with the help of the various peasant leaders of Central and Southern Europe, a common agricultural programme. Daniel Arnold, an expert scholar, and myself were invited to represent Hungary.[56]

During these war years I got into close touch with Jan Masaryk, Foreign Minister of the Czechoslovak Government in exile. When I met him first, in 1930, my impression had not been a favourable one. He struck me as a mixture of a smart and frivolous Austro-Hungarian officer — he had served in the imperial army — and a superficial Yankee — his mother was American. I thought him a shallow sybarite, *un bon viveur*, to whom nothing really mattered. It took me some time, as I am not a good judge of human nature, to detect that this attitude was just a mask to conceal a very valuable, deeply human and sensitive person. Although his father's genius must have weighed on his youth, he was the worthy son of his great parent. He was imbued with his father's philosophy, his high moral standards, his idealism and nobility, and he tried to remain true to them all his life. Attached with every fibre of his being to his own country, he was free from the particular form of chauvinism so characteristic of most East European statesmen. He was not afraid to admit that his country was not entitled to certain parts of northern Hungary. He was wise enough to understand that to retain unnatural frontiers was the greatest danger and that the future could only be solved through federalization, giving frontiers much less importance.

He did not agree with Benes's minority policy, or with his plan of exchange of population. In spite of his American mannerisms, he was primarily a European. He had much understanding of social problems and of the necessity of evolutionary change. After Munich he felt that he could not rely on the West. He was deeply and unrelentingly bitter. He despised the French for their treachery, for having, as allies, delivered his country to the Germans.

A man of great charm, Jan was a delightful companion, witty and humorous, easy-going, informal, without any sort of affectation or pomposity.

I remember one evening when he dined with us at our small Queen Anne house in Church Row. There were only the three of us and Katus had cooked the meal. He seemed to be happiest when in informal company. He was what the Viennese would call *gemütlich*. His favourite position was to sit with his legs pulled up underneath him, and joke at himself and at some of his pompous colleagues.

Jan was a man without ambition, devoid of vanity. That evening he told us that he would be the happiest man on earth, could he live for the rest of his life in Czechoslovakia on a modest pension, with time to play the piano — as a young man in the States, during his father's exile, he had earned money by playing in public places — reading and seeing a few of his friends. He liked good food and drink and the company of women. 'Who knows what will happen after the war when we return?' he would say sceptically. 'Will they want us? Won't they kick us in the pants? There will be others, new men who worked underground, more suited for the job. I would not mind that. They should only let me live for the rest of my days in my own country. I have had enough of being an exile.' He greatly admired the British and said that, if he could not live at home, he would choose England. In the worst moments he would try to keep cheerful, although underneath he could be, at times, frightfully dejected and would even mention suicide.

I saw him a week before his death, and will say more about this later.

Masaryk was not what one would call a strong man. In the last resort, he would give in. He gave in to Ripka, to Benes, to Clementis, to Fierlinger. Broad-minded, civilized, sophisticated, he was detached, giving perhaps at times too little importance to matters which to others seemed essential.

Benes was in every way the opposite of Masaryk. One could hardly carry on a conversation or argument with him. He would start by asking you to put forward what you had to say; he would listen attentively and, when you had finished, ask: 'Have you anything to add?' Then a long speech would follow, clear, precise, going into every detail, diplomatic, shrewd, completely lacking spontaneity. When Hitler took Czechoslovakia, he never doubted for a second that war would be the consequence.

Like Masaryk, he could not forgive the Western democracies for the Munich Pact, and could never be made to trust them again. This was the reason why he turned towards the East, towards the Soviets.

Benes, who had often assured me that he was in favour of Federation, changed his mind at the end of the war. He did not admit this openly to me, but avoided discussing it, on the excuse that it was too early to go into details, as we could not know what the general conditions after the war would be. He said that a homogeneous Slav State must be formed, and favoured the expulsion of the non-Slav population, Germans and Hungarians. I deduced from his changed attitude that he had reached an understanding with Moscow.

The uprooting of a population of 3 million Germans and 700,000 Hungarians was not only inhuman, but completely unnecessary if there had been Federation. I came to realize, with a heavy heart, that the Danubian concept had been dropped by him. His Slav chauvinism, encouraged by Moscow, had gained the upper hand.

Clementis was, without doubt, the strongest personality among the Czech politicians. A silent, shrewd, stubborn man, with a deep scar over his eye, he was a fierce opponent. An independent thinker, although a Communist, he disapproved of the Stalin-Hitler Pact and left the party at that time. Later, when Stalin needed every able brain in Eastern Europe, they forgave his 'sins' and he rejoined the party.

In spite of his Marxism, he was a short-sighted chauvinist and I never managed to get to any sort of agreement with him. He believed that the only way of extracting the poison of Magyar chauvinism out of Slovakia was to chase the Hungarians from the country, and would not concede that this action would only spread hatred and render future understanding more difficult.

In 1943, through the Soviet Ambassador Maisky, I got in touch with Matyas Rakosi, in Moscow. He was now the head of the Hungarian section of the Communist movement in Russia.

Maisky was very different from the usual Stalinist diplomat. The ten years which he had spent in London had had a noticeable effect on him. He would not start a conversation, as so many of the Communists did, with a lecture on Marxism, or bring in Marx on all occasions to stop argument. He was easy to talk to, would discuss all subjects freely. He and his wife were among the most popular diplomats in London.

Rakosi had been urging me to make a common front with the ex-Horthyite émigrés and to demand, through the Kossuth radio (Russian controlled) or other available means of propaganda, the recall of the Hungarian regiments from Russian territory and from Yugoslavia to their own frontiers. I refused the first request and was sceptical as to the second, knowing that even Horthy would have liked to do this, but could not, as it would have entailed breaking with the Germans. Moreover, the location of the recalled troops was a delicate question, as Hungary did not wish to give up her recently acquired territories. It was obvious that these demands were put up by the Russians and were transmitted to me by Rakosi. Mine to him were of a different nature. I proposed to go to Moscow and form, under its own colours, a Hungarian brigade recruited from the sixty to seventy thousand Hungarian prisoners in the U.S.S.R. who, at the time of liberation, would march into Budapest, as the French General de Gaulle entered Paris before the Allied armies. Maisky approved of the idea. Rakosi never answered. I realized later that it was not in line with Russian thought to win over the people of the defeated countries. They desired military victory in the old-fashioned way.

On March 17th, 1944, the Germans took complete control over Hungary. Neither the army, the police nor the Government put up any resistance. Horthy appointed Sztojay, Hungarian Minister in Berlin, his Premier. The Headquarters of the Social Democrats were seized and their leaders, as well as those of the Peace Party (the illegal Communist Party) and the Smallholders, went into hiding. The Hungarian Resistance acquired its first martyrs.[57]

Their programme, which was surreptitiously circulated, was in its broad lines that of the October Revolution of 1918. Democracy, distribution of the land, nationalization of the key industries. I could only agree with it; and a united front on those lines, with members of both of the hitherto antagonistic Hungarian movements in Britain, was hatched.

Now that the defeat of the Germans was certain, my popularity increased daily. I was reluctant to form a Hungarian Council with the elements of the Right, doubting their sincere change of heart; but Chichaev, representative of the U.S.S.R. to the Czechoslovak Government in London, urged me most energetically to do so. He was clever and had a sense of humour, so rare in the modern Russian. It was through his mediation that our council, of which I was elected President, sent a memorandum to the temporary Hungarian Government in Debrecen, formed by the parties of the March Front. General Miklos was elected its Premier. Debrecen and the east of Hungary had been captured by the Russian General Voroshilov. Chichaev's attitude and the information I gathered from him gave me confidence in Soviet policy in Hungary. He desired my return at the earliest date and assured me that his Government would see with satisfaction my election as President of the Hungarian Republic. I answered, undiplomatically, that they must not imagine I would play the role of a Quisling to Russia. He smiled as usual, but my presidency was no more mentioned. I would not be surprised if Zoltan Tildy's candidacy[58] was due to my bluntness. If so, I was for once well served by it.

The London National Council was an unwholesome concoction. The Right and the Left of the emigration, after having contrived to convince the British authorities that I had not a single follower at home, now started to boost me. They needed my name for Hungary. At the same time they tried to carry out their respective policies under my auspices. The ex-Horthyites, realizing that Hungary, after the

Allied victory, would have to undergo a great change, were anxious not to miss the bus. For this they were dependent on the good will of the Communists. On the other hand the Communists who, by now, had got their instructions to win over the chauvinist element, outdid them in patriotism. The Hungarian Communist Party went so far as to expel from its ranks a member who declared that St. Stephen was a feudal king. The Communists, as well as the ex-Horthyites, considered Left Socialism as the greatest danger. When Oscar Pollak, leader of the Austrian Socialists, asked the Hungarian Council to take part in the rally of May 1st, with the Labour Party and Aneurin Bevan, the Hungarian Communists opposed it.

It was pitiful to watch the leaders of the London Hungarian Club wretchedly following, like robots, the orders of Moscow which, naturally, could not judge a situation which it did not understand. Their blind obedience was of little help to them, for after their return most of them were liquidated. To have spent the war years in England seemed to be sufficient to rouse distrust in those Stalinist days. Theirs was a tragic fate.[59]

Now that I had united the different factions in the Hungarian Council, the B.B.C. was ready to broadcast my messages to Hungary. I sent an S.O.S. in which I appealed to my countrymen to join Tito and Benes against the Germans. Its effect was atomic. The German papers raged and the Hungarian ruling classes were seized with panic, for they knew now that they had lost the game.

I had made up my mind *not* to leave England unless I received a unanimous invitation from the Hungarian Government and from all parties of the National Front. For twenty-five years a generation had been reared on the calumnies of the official Horthy propaganda against me; to slip in at the call of a minority would have been, I felt, a mistake, especially in a time of such injured national feelings.

If a freely elected Parliament should abolish the law of 1923 which had declared me guilty of high treason, I would be ready to return, and only then.

Katus had a relapse of her illness and was being treated in the Midhurst Sanatorium, whilst I myself was laid up in London, with an occasional charwoman to look after me. This gave me a good excuse not to follow the call. It was a harassing summer, spent in suspense.

In November I called on the Foreign Minister, Ernest Bevin, to tell him that I was probably returning home in the spring and to thank him for England's hospitality. He was very friendly, and his straightforward simplicity made an excellent impression on me. He mentioned how difficult the Russians were, and wished me good luck in my dealings with them. I suggested that a loan to Hungary would be a wise move and asked him who was the person in the Foreign Office whom I could contact concerning Hungarian affairs. He supplied me with the name, and the next day I got an appointment with the gentleman. He was not friendly. He made it clear to me that he saw no necessity to discuss Hungarian affairs with me, as all the information he needed came to him from the British envoy in Budapest, Mr. Gascoigne. I should see Mr. Gascoigne; Mr. Gascoigne was on holiday in the country. He could not see me.

The B.B.C. also stopped mentioning me to Hungary and refused my wife's broadcasts. Although disappointed, I did not give up hope that in time I could be of use in promoting good relations between the country which had become my second home and my native land, although it now belonged to the Slav bloc. I considered this to be my special mission, as I was *persona grata* to the Soviets. All through the years, I had never attacked the Soviet Union, in spite of the continual prompting of my followers to do so. But if the advice of some minor and prejudiced official in the Foreign Office was to be followed, there was not much hope left for this.[60]

In December 1945, an official letter from the President of the House of Deputies, Ferencz Nagy, reached me, informing me that I had been elected as non-party member for the City of Budapest, and was requested to take up my duties. Of the Hungarians living outside Hungary, only four were elected, including Bela Bartok, the famous composer, Professor Rusztem Vamberi, George Boloni, who had headed the Hungarian Resistance in France and myself. There also came a letter from the Social Democrat Party, asking me to return.

In January 1946, Mr. Bede, who was appointed Hungarian representative in London, brought me letters from Arpad Szakasirs, President of the Social Democrats and from Matyas Rakosi, both repeating their request for me to return. Also wires and messages from William Böhm that my election as President of the Republic was absolutely certain if I returned immediately. From the Communist side, too, came a message that Rakosi was backing my nomination. My friends were becoming restless and were starting to reproach me for expecting too much. Still nothing official came from the Government. I was pleased for, had it come, I could hardly have postponed my return; but my health and that of my wife were still a valid excuse.

In February the Protestant clergyman Zoltan Tildy became President. I received the news with a sigh of relief. He had been little known before and had acquired popularity when he joined the March Front.

In March the Assembly declared null the law which had seized my property, thus returning to me my entire estate and confirming the services I had rendered my country in the past. I also received from the Government an official invitation to return. My rehabilitation was complete.

The press announced the news that I was returning on May 1st.

Much had changed in Hungary during the last year in favour of the Right wing. The new leaders were less particular than we had been in 1918, but shrewder, and elections had been held inside the Trianon borders. The Smallholders Party gained 57 per cent of the votes, for right-wing elements, who had no other party to join, voted for it. It was filled with urban bourgeois elements, who had no connection whatsoever with peasants. It was a vote against Socialism and the Soviets. Ferencz Nagy became Premier.

On the other side, members of the Arrow Cross, in order to save themselves, joined the Communist Party, who accepted them, as they needed members from wherever they came. The Russians did not interfere. Old animosities and feuds flared up again and the Communists, to regain their popularity of the days of the Resistance, became more nationalistic than their nationalist opponents, and even sent out shock troops into the villages to build up destroyed churches. But this was of little help to them, for few were taken in by so obvious a gesture.

PART FIVE

THE END OF THE JOURNEY

In my end is my beginning. T. S. ELIOT

I RETURN HOME

And where I did begin there shall I end—
My life is run his compass.   SHAKESPEARE

IT was May 8th, 1946. Seated in a car and followed by an escort of others, we drove out of Vienna, eastwards, towards home. Twenty-six years of banishment now belonged to the past.

How often had I visualized this moment in all its detail. How often did it haunt my dreams, although my inveterate pessimism did not allow me to believe it would ever happen.

When the four towers of the fortress of Pozsony appeared on the horizon, it seemed to me that the metaphor 'My heart leaps up' was literal truth.

At the frontier a group of unknown people, a delegation, is waiting for us. President Tildy's representative, a corpulent, bald man, makes a flowery speech. I answer in a few words. My throat feels very dry . . . It is strange, I had never before been sentimental about frontiers . . . How irrational these emotions are, and what surprises our nature keeps in store for us.

We get into the President's car of an American make, and a smartly groomed colonel, Tildy's personal guard, takes his seat at the back.

Now we are on Hungarian soil. My wife presses my hand. The broad highway along which the Germans had retreated is in parts destroyed; right and left of us large stretches of uncultivated land . . . rattling horse-carts on the stony, dusty road, low huts, brown, yellow earth, burning sun and the wide horizons of the plain . . . this is my Hungary. 'Asia begins on the Landstrasse. The road out of Vienna is the East' said Metternich.

On both sides of us squat the old villages, spread out in the sunshine, with their little white houses and red-tiled roofs. They have not changed since we saw them last. They are gay with the national colours and lined up all along the road are schoolchildren behind their teachers, waving little flags. Women throw bunches of wild flowers at the passing cars, and grave-looking men in dark clothes stare at us. Cheers.

Is all this an official show ordered by the Government? What have these villagers heard about me during these twenty-six years? Was not my name taboo all over the country? Change of sentiment does not occur in so short a time. Only one outcry struck me as spontaneous, and it came from a young woman who, running up close to our car with a bunch of spring flowers, exclaimed: 'Oh! how old he is!' Had she expected to see a young man? I do not know but, anyhow, I was sorry to have disappointed her.

The welcome of Gyor was a very different matter. The factory workers were all out on the street, surrounding the car, cheering. Excited faces, genuine cordiality. Through rows of cheering people we are conducted to the Town Hall for the Mayor's banquet. Anxious to reach Budapest before dark, I cut the speeches short and we hurry on. I do not feel the fatigue of the journey, although when I left London I had been ill. This first contact with an enthusiastic crowd in my own country has a healing effect. I feel like an old hunter who hears the blast of the horn. The bitterness of the past has faded away; only pity, affection and tenderness are left.

After Komarom, the Danube. The grand old river had remained unaltered through all changing times . . . and Hungary . . . perhaps Hungary, too, had not changed; for nations and peoples are not altered by events. The road now turns upwards and from the hills of Pillis, I recognize Mount Gellert, with its white Citadel . . . O-Buda, the boundary of the capital. Here the official reception is held. The Mayor of Budapest heads the deputation. A band plays the national anthem; speeches, flowers, banners. I am received with the ceremony due to a Head of the State, for the Coalition Government, headed by Ferencz Nagy, leaders of the Smallholders' Party, is keen to demonstrate the legality of the October Republic, of which I had been the President.

We now drive through the ancient part of Buda, past the tomb of Gulbaba, dating from Turkish times. In the long main street the houses seem naked, their surface is ripped off as though they had been skinned. From the damaged windows national banners are dangling. I cannot recognize my Budapest; as in dreams when, although one is aware of a person's identity, he yet seems completely different. A sad encounter.

I had not wished it this way, nor at this price. My gratification is complete, but at what a cost! Catastrophe, destruction, bloodshed and much suffering. As in 1918, after the crime was committed, those responsible are gone, fled or in hiding. Our third Mohacs. Shall I be able to help?

We drive towards the quay. The pillars of the bridges stand out of the Danube, the rest is submerged, a desperate sight. We cross the heaving pontoon bridge and turn into the Egyetem utca, towards the Karolyi house. Someone is talking to me, but I do not hear what he says. I see the puckered façade of the old house, like a face marked with smallpox. The traces of bullets, the smashed windows. The street is packed with the waiting crowd. We slowly turn through the gateway and stop under the columned porch. A woman in tears rushes towards us and falls into my arms. It is my wife's sister, whom we had not seen for many years. Now we are in the glass-covered hall, ascending as in a dream the shallow steps of the wide staircase. I do not recognize the faces, my vision gets blurred. Is it really I that am standing here? The Minister of Justice, the Social Democrat Ries, hands me a massive key and speaks: The stolen property returns to its rightful owner ... The wrongs done to you ... I cannot follow ... I am struggling to control my nerves. Memories are crowding one upon another ... faces ... ghosts ... Uncle Alexander, my grandmother, my father ... Bakos, my loyal valet, who put an end to his life by throwing himself out of the attic window after I left ... It was here that my son Adam was born; he who could not be near me today. Yet this house is more than my home. Hungary's history is woven around it. It had been the heart of the revolutions. It was here that in 1849 Lajos Batthyanyi had met his end. It was here that Haynau, the hyena of Brescia as the Italians called him, signed his infamous death warrants. And it was here too that, in October 1918, we had first formed the National Council. Tivadar Batthyanyi, Martin Lovászy, John Hock and others ... these are no longer here, my colleagues, comrades-in-arms, friends all dead — my enemies as well — I would have liked them to be present today. And I, too, so different from what I was.

What we had tried to do and failed, could it be achieved now? Now that we were in a more favourable situation, now that Hungary had a Great Power to back her? The present leaders would have to be wiser than we had been, they would have to learn from our errors, keep their faith intact, but a faith without illusion.

Ries has now finished speaking. I had not heard a word of what he said. Now I have to answer. The microphone is turned towards me. I say some words about the house having to become the property of the town. My voice falters, it is agony to go on.

I see the rigid face, as though carved in stone, of an officer in front of me; his cheeks are wet with tears.

The fantastic tale of my life has come to an end. The wheel has come full circle. I am back from where I came, never, I think, to leave again.

The old house, bought at the time by the city, had been used for years as a picture gallery. Now they offered us one of its wings, converted for the purpose. But Katus, with feminine instinct, preferred to postpone acceptance. It was she now who was the pessimist. We walked into the library, which I hardly recognized. The shelves were empty, the books had all been sold by auction twenty years ago.

Stepping on to the balcony, we looked into the park, now turned into a public garden. In the middle I noticed a large statue. It had not been there in my time. 'Who is it?' I asked my neighbour. An embarrassed silence followed. My bad eyesight prevented me from recognizing it. 'Who is it?' I insisted.

My secretary, the enthusiastic Havas, whispered in my ear: 'Bishop Prohaszka.'

Anti-climax. Bishop Prohaszka was the Patron of the White Terror and one of the most ardent opponents of the Socialists. He had started as a liberal, broad-minded churchman and, for this reason, I had asked him to marry us during the First World War.

'This, I am afraid, will have to go, if you want me to live here,' I said, turning my back on the Bishop.

It seemed strange that all through the last year the Government had not removed this Gessler's hat, put there to insult the October Revolution. I heard afterwards that the Social Democrats had demanded its removal, but the Communists, playing the clerical card, had insisted it should remain.[1]

After the ceremony in the old house, the second item of the programme followed: my visit to the President of the Republic, Zoltan Tildy.

In front of a modest villa in the Andrassy Avenue, now Stalin Avenue, I took the salute from the Republican Guard, ordered there for the occasion.

Tildy, a man of small stature, the typical Hungarian country clergyman, had in no way an impressive personality. After we had exchanged the usual formalities, the cameramen flashed their magnesium lights on the 'two Presidents shaking hands'. As the crowd that had gathered outside the windows was clamouring for me, I spoke some words to them from the balcony, emphasizing that they should give their support to the President in whom we all had entire confidence. I pushed him to the parapet where, being short, he was scarcely visible. But it seemed that I had done the wrong thing. Icy silence followed. We retired in haste, as this part had not been in the programme. Tildy's face wore a sour expression. This he put on whenever we met, and only lost when he became convinced that I had neither the intention nor the desire to take his place, which was not an enviable one.

Exhausted after this day of emotion, we were at last permitted to retire to the apartment reserved for us by the Government at the Hôtel Gellert. This hotel, on the embankment of the Danube, is a huge, super-ornate building in Oriental style, and had been erected after we left Hungary. Its swimming-pool with waves, and its thermal waters, had an international reputation.

We were the guests of the Government, which had provided for our journey as well, until my material situation should be settled.

The first week a personal guard of honour was assigned to me, and a decorative, heel-clicking colonel followed me wherever I went. I discovered later that he had been Horthy's personal aide-de-camp.

When I laid my tired head on the pillow that night, being in Hungary seemed as unreal as a dream. Of one thing I felt certain: whatever happened, I would never become an émigré again.

The next day a grand reception was arranged in Parliament. To the sound of the National Anthem, with Katus at my side, I ascended the broad stairs leading to the Hall of the Assembly.

The members of the Government received me on the landing. The Premier, Ferencz Nagy, with the oratorical talent native to the Hungarian, made a clever speech. His astuteness and poise impressed me, for I was told that he had been a hairdresser's apprentice in his early years, and had had no political training.

Then I was escorted by two members of the Cabinet into the Hall of the Assembly where, under the high glass dome, in the centre facing the Speaker, a high-backed armchair was placed. There, floodlit by powerful flashlights, I had to take my place. Totally blinded, I sat, feeling very uncomfortable, with darkness surrounding me like a black veil. It flashed through my mind: Am I on trial? It was the clapping that reassured me. Now, one after the other, the party leaders proceeded to the Speaker's chair and greeted me in turn. Listening to them I kept wondering, was it really I to whom these eulogies were directed? How many hours and days I had spent here in the past! I remembered the exciting time of my struggle with Tisza; his stern, owl-like face with the black-rimmed spectacles, seemed to glare at me through the dark. I saw Andrassy's slim figure, curled up in his seat; Apponyi's imposing beard and hooked nose with its wide nostrils; and Batthyanyi's congested face, with its shrewd smile.

Were they witnessing what was happening in 'their Parliament', in 'their Hungary'? What did they think of the homage given to that 'madman' Michael?

I was roused from my reverie by some words which had a special sound. They were simple, direct, without clichés and seemed to come straight from the heart. Although this was the shortest speech of all, I was deeply moved by it. It brought into the darkness a breath of air from the Hungarian plains. I was told that the young man who uttered it was Laszlo Rajk, Secretary of the Communist Party, who had organized the Resistance against the Germans.

Now came my turn to speak. For more than an hour I spoke into the dark world surrounding me, and only the cheers made me realize that I had an audience. When I mentioned my wife's name and said that without her help, her love and her courage, I would not be here today, the whole house stood up and, turning towards the gallery where she was seated, gave her an enthusiastic ovation. How happy I was to have been able to offer her this tribute.

Then, from the terrace of the Parliament where twenty-three years previously the Republic had been declared, I addressed the assembled crowd. There was not a voice to disturb the harmony of the day. It seemed as though I had won the race with History.

At the Gellert hotel I was visited by politicians of all shades of opinion, from the old as well as the new regime. Delegations of students, peasants, bourgeois, nobles, thronged our apartment, mostly to vent their grievances and to ask for assistance. These people imagined that I had a magic wand which could cure all their ills. We opened an office for the investigation of complaints and, if they were justified, we pestered the authorities until something was done about them. The authorities were filled with goodwill and in most cases we were successful.

Old servants, ex-employees, managers, people whose existence I had completely forgotten, appeared like ghosts out of the past. Many had suffered on account of their association with me; others, to save themselves, had most probably howled with the wolves. Few are those who keep their integrity in time of upheaval! But we had not come to retaliate or pass judgment.

The aged Swabian peasant farmers who, fifty years before, had saved me from under my wrecked car, were now on the list of those who had to quit their farms owing to the exchange of population policy. Believing themselves to have a special claim on me, they appealed for my aid. I tried my best on their behalf, not only for sentimental reasons, but because I strongly disapproved of the policy. Yet my intervention was unsuccessful. I avoided my own class as much as possible and few ventured near me. Some of them had a strange mentality. They told Katus that they had been praying for our early return, but had been disappointed.

'Why?' she asked surprised.

'Because we trusted that, being one of us, you would come to our rescue.'

'Did you help us when we were in trouble?' she answered. 'Did you not join in the campaign of calumny against Michael?'

But in the morning, when I plunged into the swimming-pool of the hotel, I was at the mercy of everyone. I remember someone whom I refused to see doing the 'crawl' in a circle round me, recalling old days and reminding me that we were relatives. Could I put in a word in his favour to General Voroshilov, as he had always been a friend of the Russians. I decided to bathe at six in the morning, so as to avoid the swimmers with the tide.

My cousin George Karolyi did not belong to these. A legitimist and a 100 per cent reactionary, he had the courage of his opinions and consequently got himself into trouble with the different regimes. He had been for years the black sheep of the family, having committed a misalliance by marrying a Jewess without money. I had sided with him against the family, and for this reason he had harboured a soft spot in his heart for me and did not attack me like the others. But he could not forgive me for criticizing our class openly to the 'plebs' and now that I was 'up' again, he refused to approach me with any requests, although he knew that I would willingly have helped him. I had respect for his pride.[2]

The Government had arranged everything so as to make our visit as pleasant as possible.

Every morning the manager of the hotel appeared, inquiring as to our wishes. After living on rations for so many years we enjoyed with special relish, but with an uneasy conscience, the tasty Hungarian specialities — spring chicken with cream, cucumber salad, fried veal, cutlets overhanging the plate, goose-liver, crayfish in their shells. We suspected that these luxuries were unattainable by the 'ordinary mortal'. Coming from austere England, where the black market was scarcely known, into a country hardly recovered from the devastation of the siege and the burden of two occupying armies, we were surprised to see that the first-class hotels and restaurants had everything you wished for, whilst schools had to close for want of food, and patients in hospitals were under-nourished.

My criticism of the inequitable distribution was not appreciated by those responsible, who argued that, even if food control were stricter, the difference would not cover the need. Economically they may have been right, but they ignored the psychological and moral aspect which, at times, is of even greater importance.

After a week's indulgence I told the *maître d'hôtel* that my favourite dish was dry beans and that we would eat veal no more, for veal must become beef and feed a greater number. He looked at me shocked and, I suppose, believed that the great heat — the day was very hot — had sent me mad. Dry beans had been the sole food during the siege. By the way, many who had suffered from chronic stomach disorder owing to rich food had been cured by this diet. I was not being ascetic, for dry beans are one of my favourite dishes.

The black market was flourishing, prices soaring high and the pengo losing its value. The peasants, as in 1919, distrusted paper money and refused to sell their produce. The only way for the citizen to get food was to go and fetch it himself in the countryside. The pontoon bridge was thronged with well-dressed, middle-class women and men, with huge bags tied to their backs, filled with potatoes, vegetables, pork etc. In exchange for these, they had given clothes, shoes, cameras and so on. This bartering, *battyuzas*, was strictly prohibited, as it encouraged the black market; but, as so often happens, the small fry were caught and locked up while the big fish, with their cars and bribes, got away with it. Eventually it was stopped.

The prisons were filled with young boys who had committed the 'crime' of filling their hungry stomachs with food not belonging to them. They would loot bakeries and sweet-shops. These children were herded together in filthy adult prisons, awaiting trial; there were too few judges and the reformatories had been destroyed in the siege. Katus, who refused to join any organization of a political nature, took up the cause of these 'delinquent' boys, and founded a home for them near Budapest.[3]

About this time inflation started and prices were changing from hour to hour. I had seen this happen after the last war, but nothing comparable to what was happening now. One of its causes was the seizure of the coal mines by the Russians; another, the high cost of reparations payable to them. In 1946, 65 per cent of Hungary's total production went to them.[4]

To the amazement of the economic experts, after the dollar had attained 29,667,000,000,000 pengo, the currency was stabilized.

On August 1st, the new florin was issued. This bold and arbitrary measure, carried out by the Communists, proved a success and raised their prestige in the eyes of the country. The new salaries were calculated on a very low scale. The Russians made some concessions over reparations and the Americans restored to Hungary the 32 million dollars which they had seized in time of war.

All impartial observers admitted that the Soviets treated Hungary in a more liberal fashion than the neighbouring States. They respected the Yalta Agreement and things seemed to develop in a normal way. The competence of the Hungarian Communists enabled the Russians to keep to their policy of non-interference, and the ability of the ruling classes to adapt themselves to those in power was most useful. The Hungarians are realists and, having learnt from the Germans to respect the strong hand, were willing to co-operate.

The Smallholders' Party, an amorphous mass, was composed of all sorts of different elements, at loggerheads with each other. The Prime Minister, Ferencz Nagy, a weak man, could not impose his will on them. Although a bitter opponent of the Communists, he gave way to their demands to purge his party of the reactionary elements which had infiltrated into it. He thus antagonized those who had put their hopes in him, without winning the goodwill of the Communists, who were well aware that he was not their friend and who used him for their own ends.

He expelled from his party his most able associate, Desiderius Sulyok, who then founded a party of his own. The Smallholders were thus gradually being ground between those who had given Nagy their support, in the hope that he would protect them from the Communists, and those who, recognizing the inevitable ascendancy of the Communists, wished to gain merit by disorganizing the forces of the Right. These crypto-Communists, who rendered the greatest service to the Communist Party, received high posts. Nagy himself was carrying on his difficult and double-edged game. So the coalition which, at my arrival, seemed to be a masterpiece of political balance and astuteness, was falling apart.

Some urged me to form a party, a request I categorically refused. I had made up my mind to keep a free hand and not touch party politics.

Although the Russians made themselves inconspicuous and few Red soldiers were to be seen in the streets, the population could not forget the days when the Soviet general had let the army run amok. Those who had put their trust in the Red Army had been cruelly disillusioned. The Communists admitted amongst themselves how much their prestige and popularity had suffered by it. It was alarming to meet this hatred in all quarters, and any time I mentioned the 'Liberating Red Army' in public, a hostile silence followed.

The memorial erected to the glory of the Russian soldier on the summit of Mount Gellert, dominating the town, was considered as a deliberate insult[5] especially by the women, whose memory of the

Red soldier was not a pleasant one. Even the land reform carried out by the army, did not mitigate the anger against them. It was the deportation of civilians to Russia that most incensed the population. I continued to harass General Voroshilov and the Minister Pushkin about these, and received promises, but no results.

I only once had a spectacular success, when I intervened concerning my nephew, Ilona Cziraky's son, who had disappeared after the fighting had ceased. A Russian soldier brought him home to his mother, all the way from the Urals, where he had been interned. It was a gesture to demonstrate their goodwill towards me. Unfortunately, I could do nothing about another nephew, George Pallavicini[6] who, although a most courageous member of the Hungarian Resistance and interned in Dachau, had been arrested by the Russians. Even the Hungarian Communist Party intervened on his behalf. He disappeared without trace.

The Deputy Minister, Matyas Rakosi, was considered the ablest member of the Cabinet. Many years of solitary confinement had made a strong impact on him. A man in prison, if weak, gets his spirit broken and adopts the attitude of a slave. If strong enough to resist submission, he turns into a rebel. In some cases he becomes both. In Rakosi the rebel was strengthened, but having been for sixteen years a slave-victim of a primitive, inefficient and brutal system, that of Horthy's Hungary, he became conditioned to be a slave-dictator of another system, as brutal, but more reasonable — an edifice built on a logical concept.

Rakosi is shrewd, amiable and diplomatic, and reminded me at times of the old Serbian Minister Pasich, who would go on speaking for hours so as to avoid embarrassing questions. Although he has no Pasich beard in which to hide his sly smiles, he also has the trick of wrapping up in a long-winded speech one single point of importance. He expects you to disentangle this from all its unnecessary wrappings. He also appears not to listen, although you can be sure that he has not missed a word or an intonation. He moves with great difficulty, owing to the treatment received at the hands of the Horthy police. When he was arrested the soles of his feet were beaten to shreds, so that for years he could hardly stand on them.

He speaks several languages fluently, which he learnt during his prison years. He is self-educated and his astounding memory serves him well. When he wants to impress his visitors, he brings out a flow of names, dates, statistics, figures, facts and witty anecdotes, but conversation with him is hardly a two-sided affair. He would derive great pleasure from making a foreigner understand that he, Rakosi, knew more about his country than he did himself.

His jovial and paternal ways made him popular in those days, among the bourgeoisie and even among the diplomats of the West. He seems always ready to oblige and has a sense of humour. He plays his part well but, as Cardinal Mindszenty said to a foreign visitor: 'His bite is worse than his bark.' Although I recognized his merits, I never fell under his 'notorious charm'. I mistrusted his smooth and amiable ways. He would put people into pigeon-holes according to his preconceived ideas and treat them accordingly, in consequence underrating his opponents — always a fatal mistake. But circumstances were in his favour, and until now he has managed to keep his ship afloat with great astuteness.

With Erno Gero, Minister of Public Works and Reconstruction, I got on much better. One knew where one stood with him. In a brief, matter-of-fact way he would deal with the essential problems, and in a short time, without unnecessary talk, would accomplish more than any of his colleagues. He is a good listener and does not get involved in theoretical discussions about dialectical materialism with those who know the lesson as well as he. He was the hardest worker at his office, always the first in the morning and the last at night. But, exacting as well, he would demand 100 per cent efficiency from his staff. They feared but respected him for his exceptional gift for organization and his austerity. Although his position in the Government seemed a secondary one, I suspected that in the Cominform it was higher than Rakosi's.

Zoltan Vas, head of the Financial Department, was also a remarkable man. The way he managed to restore the country's finances bordered on genius. But he was far from having Gero's or Rakosi's personal integrity. He was a *bon viveur*, cynical, a lover of women; many discreditable stories circulated about him. Rakosi, Gero and Vas had spent most of their lives in Russia, had become Soviet citizens — Rakosi even married a Kalmuk-Russian — and had been trained in the Stalinist methods. From the Soviet point of view they were entirely reliable. Keen Russian patriots, they had all the prejudices and limitations which patriotism involves.

The Muscovites had, over the others, not only the advantage of their exceptional training but also the support of the Red Army, which was not negligible. It was their job to keep the Hungarian Communists in check, for Stalin feared no one more than those who tried to achieve Communism in a manner different from his own.

To the Hungarian team of Communists who had worked underground in the Resistance belonged Laszlo Rajk, Gyula Kallai, Erik Molnar and others. In the first months of the so-called 'liberation' it was they who played first fiddle, as it was Soviet policy to back the nationalists, a policy followed wherever the Red Army entered.

Laszlo Rajk became Secretary of the Communist Party and later Minister of the Interior, the most responsible office of the time. It was he who reorganized the police force. Not having received a Soviet training, he approached Communism in a different, more romantic, idealistic fashion, believing that its moral and human aspect was of major importance. He believed in the people and loved them, but if he thought the cause required it he could be hard and uncompromising, and would carry out the orders of his superiors unflinchingly, taking the responsibility on himself if necessary. He was tall, with a high forehead, a bold and honest look and a straightforward handshake. His good looks made him the show-piece of the party. The love and devotion of his subordinates, who were ready to follow him through hell, made him a leader of men. But, without ambition or vanity, he wished to be a soldier and not a general. He was a man of action, loyal to the path he had chosen; not an intellectual, not a vivisector of ideas. He was an easy prey. That his comrades could act as they did, he certainly could never have imagined.[7]

While the conquest of Hungary was still going on, orders for agrarian reform were given out by the Red Army. The reason for this urgency was to induce the peasants, who were still fighting on the side of the Germans, to desert. At the Congress in Debrecen, where the Russians launched the reform, the leaders of the Hungarian parties had been invited, but obtained no hearing. The reform was codified on March 15th, 1945, and carried out by the peasants themselves. The dwarf-holders and the agricultural labourers put up in the villages their own committees of claimants, controlled by a commission from the Ministry of Agriculture. Peter Veres, leader of the National Peasant Party, headed the commission.[8]

The brilliant Soviet economist E. Varga pointed out that this hastily carried out land reform was prejudicial to agriculture. The breaking-up of the big estates into smallholdings brought many new problems. One of the greatest was the necessity of finding about 400,000 homes for the new proprietors. Another was the lack of agricultural implements. Huts were erected without even the most primitive sanitary installations. The Troglodytes, about whose misery so many books had been written in the past, although they were now landowners, remained in their caves. The agricultural labourer of the past, however much exploited by the big landowners, had at least a pigsty to sleep in, and found work on the landlord's estate, even if on starvation level. Now some of the new proprietors had no roof above their heads and no landlord to provide them with work or food. This period of transition engendered discontent, which was exploited by the Church and its Primate, Cardinal Mindszenty. Our land reform of 1919 seemed, in comparison, a mild affair.

It was tragi-comic to be told by the former landlords how much they regretted that they had not backed my reform in 1919, for, had they accepted in time, they would not have been completely destitute today. The Communists, fearing the resistance of the peasants, did not dare to introduce collective farming, though collectivization, if carried out in the right way, is, I believe, the only solution, and was the final aim of the Communists.

My visit to Parad and Kalkapolna, the estates which I had, in part, distributed amongst my tenants twenty-seven years before, will always remain in my memory.

We arrived in Kalkapolna at the very spot where, in March 1919, the actual division of the land had begun. It was a mound, on the top of which was a stone memorial, erected in commemoration of one of our victories against Austria in 1848. From there, Katus and I both spoke to the peasants assembled below. They had come from all parts of the county. Although their weather-beaten and furrowed faces, with the drooping dark moustaches, appeared the same, they were different. Their eyes had not the wonder-gazing look of that rainy March day in

1919, but seemed harder, more demanding, more alive. Through what years of misery and pain we had all passed since! They had been robbed of what I had given them; cruelly punished for having dared to hope for a better life. There were years of misery, and then the war and the Russian occupation. In the heat of the blazing sun and the scorched yellow earth, they remembered the March distribution. They had never quite believed in it at the time, for their intuition was deeper than mine; they knew that their lords were invincible, even if their own crazy Count stood up on their behalf. Only the might of the Red Army had been able to defeat their lords.

This time it was real, but mixed with horror and grief, as reality so often is. They were critical and discontented, as peasants usually are; they grumbled on principle, for, if they did not, their masters would think them satisfied. Grumbling for them is a sort of self-protection, a warding-off of envy, for to be envied is dangerous.

The injustice of the distribution was, of course, their main topic, for some had got more, some less than their share. Some Fascists, who had joined the Communists, had managed to get land allotted to them. These good Heves peasants fancied that, now I had returned, all injustices would be remedied.

They were also incensed that the Red Army had carried off their sons and daughters to work as slaves in the Ukraine, on the ground that, as it had been devastated by the German and Hungarian armies, this was a kind of rough justice.

We listened to their complaints and Katus was taken into a hut, where she received men and women who followed each other in procession with their requests and grievances.

After the meeting we changed into horse-carriages and drove on to Parad. The officials and journalists returned to Budapest and we were now on our own at last, accompanied only by our closest friends. The Government had not manifested much zeal in the affair: the papers scarcely mentioned it and the cameramen had been kept from following us. It was a genuine home-coming, spontaneous and therefore more dear to me. Yet it was less the return of the revolutionary leader after years of banishment than of the lord of the manor. Every village we passed had put its own mounted escort (*banderium*) with horses carefully selected for the occasion. With flying banners they galloped on both sides of us, clad in their national attire: immaculate white-pleated and starched linen drawers like skirts, embroidered flowery waistcoats and round black felt hats decorated with feathergrass, a profusion of red, white and green ribbons gaily floating in their wake, like coloured serpents.

At the entrance of each village a new escort took over, the previous one returning to its base. In one of them we noticed a young girl rider of about fourteen. This was a revolutionary innovation, unimaginable in my day. The splendid horses were well-fed and glossy and I was surprised at seeing so many. I was told that they had been concealed from the Russians and had been brought out for my sake, at the risk of requisition. This was a touching proof of the genuineness of their welcome.

Our carriage pulled up in the village squares, where cakes, bread and wine were offered us. We climbed on to the tables and answered the greetings of the inhabitants. In one place, a peasant recounted how he had heard me speak fifteen years before in Chicago, and how I had said: 'In fifteen years' time, no one will envy a Hungarian landlord.'

They told us how the spokesmen of the Horthy Government had tried their best to turn them against me, and added: 'But we did not believe them. The worse things they said about you, the more we trusted you, for we knew you were on our side.'

Towards the end of the day, intoxicated by wine and talk, they started dancing and singing. The more wine drunk, the light and sparkling wine of the Matra, the more out of tune the singing became. There was endless rejoicing into the far evening and Katus had to dance the *csardas* until she was exhausted. I shall always remember the sparkling eyes and shining face of my loyal secretary and friend, the poet Andrew Havas, singing hoarsely, the others all joining in, the refrain of the song composed by the peasants during my exile: 'We are wet and cold and hungry. Let us bring back Michael Karolyi.'

We spent the night of this memorable day in the cottage of a superintendent of the estate, next to my second country house Sasvar (Eagle's fortress). There was nothing of a fortress about it and still less of an eagle. It had been used as billets, first by the German and then by the Russian Army, and was dilapidated and partly destroyed. Very soon it would become a ruin, mellowed by age. It had already acquired a dignity which it never had possessed in its heyday.

And now, on to Parad. In 1923, after its confiscation, it had been turned into a fashionable spa, because of the healing qualities of its waters. The main building, the house in which we had spent the early years of our married life, had been reserved for the members of the Horthy Government at a preferential tariff.

It was haunted with ghosts and the memory of the first night after our wedding, when we had crossed the mountains on foot in the rain; the strange beginning of an adventurous life.

From the narrow balcony of our large bedroom with the four-poster bed, we looked down over the valley to the other side of the hills where, in my youth, I had planted beech trees. They had grown high now and covered the slopes. How often did I think of them during the years of my exile, wondering how much they had grown or if they had been cut down, and should I ever see them again?

We went into the billiard-room with the low ceiling where, after our shooting parties, my friends used to collect, to boast over their Tokay of their sporting exploits — a conversation that had always bored me. I remembered small Boli, the unfortunate Premier of later years (Count Paul Teleki), who for years was my regular guest. Did he, I wondered, ever remember those days, when he stayed there during my absence?

Here, too, in most of the rooms soldiers had been quartered. Men in uniform become like beasts. Although Parad is surrounded with forests, they had used the furniture as fuel and the parquet floor had been torn up for tables. The paper had been torn from the walls, laying bare newspapers printed twenty years before, which had been used as padding. The speeches and articles of the men of the Horthy regime stared at us from all sides, a catastrophe for those who were now protesting that they had always been to the Left.

My encounter with Parad reminded me of those painful meetings, after many years, of people who were once in love. The object of one's desire has grown fat and heavy, her skin has turned dull and she has had many lovers! It was Parad, but at the same time it was not Parad. We fell silent and kept away from our companions. We tried to discover something of the older days, but only the air and the weather were the same.

Although it was supposed to be mine now, we knew that we could never live there again. We hurried back to Budapest.

I was gradually discovering Budapest again, its long-forgotten streets and alleys, the grandeur and aloofness of the Danube, its quays where, even in those days, smart-looking women were chattering in the sunshine, and men in cream-coloured linen suits were lounging in deck chairs.

Whatever happened these people would never give up their easy-going habits, their hedonistic approach to life. I was struck by the oriental character of Hungary. Men and women could be found at any time of the day at the public swimming-pools, lolling on the sunny slopes of Mount Gellert, strolling leisurely along the *corso*, or sitting gossiping in the cafés sipping chocolate or coffee, submerged by a tower of whipped-cream. The women looked elegant in their home-made dresses, made out of mattress or curtain materials.

I was happy to walk the streets, the Vaczi utca (Budapest's Bond Street) the Kossuth Lajos utca, and the Vorosmarty Ter, and to linger in front of the shop-windows, still filled with attractive goods, or dine in the garden-restaurants, under vine loggias, and be welcomed by beaming waiters. The gipsy band would play its familiar melodies; their repertoire had remained unchanged for half a century and is as imperishable as the old river itself. I had always been exasperated by the sentimental monotony of the gipsy music, but now I was more lenient, even towards that. Or was it that my hearing had become worse?

One day, we had been invited to a gala performance of *Richard III* at the Nemzeti Szinhaz (National Theatre). The management of the theatre had reserved the presidential box for us, as Tildy was not to be present. As soon as we entered the entire audience jumped to their feet and gave me a most hearty and spontaneous ovation. It was a surprise to me, the audience being purely bourgeois, from whom I would never have expected such an enthusiastic reception.[9]

Budapest, the town of my youth and early loves, of carefree years and sentimental worries, of idealistic dreams and bitter disappointments, this hated and much loved city, lost for so long, was now, at the close of my life, found again.

2

OUR LIFE IN THE PEOPLE'S DEMOCRACY

I speak of Peace while covert enmity Under the smile of safety, wounds the world. Henry IV

I HAD been asked by Premier Nagy to be the Government's unofficial representative and councillor at the Peace Treaty in Paris in 1946.

The Minister of Foreign Affairs, Gyongyosi, headed the Hungarian delegation. He had been Minister of Education in the Debrecen Government[10] and later became Foreign Minister. A cautious, timid man, white-haired and handsome, his performance at the Palais Bourbon was not a brilliant one. He spoke no French and the speech he read was scarcely comprehensible. This would have mattered less, had he been able to convey to the world that Hungary had genuinely changed, or was on the way to change.

Far from doing this, he claimed the territories returned to Hungary, as a reward, by the Führer. This was to pour oil on fire. It gave us a bad press. Gyongyosi's speech was addressed to the Hungarian nationalists. It made it easy for Masaryk to reply that the speech could just as well have been delivered by Count Bethlen.

That Russia dropped the Hungarian claim against Rumania for part of Transylvania was a bitter disappointment. Prime Minister Nagy had received the impression in Moscow, where he had gone on the eve of the Peace Conference, that Stalin would back Hungary. Stalin backed Rumania.

Dejected at the way things were turning, I often visited Jan Masaryk in the rue Matignon. I appealed to him to use his influence on behalf of the 500,000 Hungarians outlawed by the Slovaks. Masaryk, sitting on his crossed legs as was his habit, shared my indignation. 'How can you imagine that I approve such inhuman proceedings,' he said. 'Don't forget that I am Thomas Masaryk's son. But it is not me you should try to persuade, but Clementis.'

333

He, for his part, reproached me for Gyongyosi's speech. 'It is you who should have represented Hungary; that would have convinced us that Hungary is genuinely turning over a new leaf. After such a speech, Gyongyosi must go.'

In the autumn of 1946 we bade farewell to the West, with special tenderness towards our little house in Church Row, where we had spent the exciting war years, and returned for the second time to Budapest.

The anniversary of the October Revolution was to be celebrated in a grand fashion by the Social Democratic Party and the Trade Unions. I was to have been the principal speaker. Owing to bad weather my plane had to land at Munich and I could not attend the meeting. Katus who had returned earlier, took my place and spoke to the large crowd on Parliament Square.

The situation had much improved since we left. The Communists had been admirable in their efforts to repair the destruction caused by the Red Army and the Germans. The currency was stabilized, bridges rebuilt, wreckage cleared, factories reopened. Their dynamism dragged the apathetic population in its wake, and even those who were hostile or neutral had to recognize their merits. Their competence, energy and, at times, a wise sense of diplomacy and even tolerance when the interest of the party required it, were recognized by everyone. Although feared, they were admired. The bourgeois parties were of little consequence, having no definite programme, and no leading personalities.

As Hungary had been systematically demoralized by dictatorial regimes for so many years, its recuperation in so short a time could not have been expected. When corruption has penetrated the viscera of a nation, it is hard to eradicate.

Each regime had laid hands on the property of the supporters of the previous one, or rather of those who did not change rapidly enough.

During the last years of Horthyism the property of the Jews was offered to the loyal Fascists; now the property of the Fascists went to the Jews. Thus, 'the sanctity of property' had lost its prestige, and capacity for indignation was at its lowest ebb. Lawlessness having been experienced for so many years, there was no reaction against it. If people lose the capacity for indignation at injustice, orderly society is doomed.[11]

We had now found a modern villa on the Rözsadomb (Hill of Roses) overlooking the town, and the curves of the silver Danube on the horizon. The house belonged to the brother of Rassai, from whom we rented it. I lived there in a private capacity; members of the Cabinet and leading personalities visited me in my retirement and kept me in touch with events.[12]

The Economic Council was working out a scheme for the restoration of my property. This was an impossible undertaking, for as soon as Parliament had declared invalid the law that had confiscated my estate, not only the estate itself, but its twenty-three years' revenue, should legally have been restored. But Hungary's entire budget would not have been sufficient for this, and naturally I did not dream of demanding it. The regime in those days was still a bourgeois one and, although my arable land came under the land reform, there remained forests, apartment houses, Parad Spa, the house in the Egyetem utca, as well as the 300 acres due to active anti-Fascists.

As I am not good at dealing with business matters, I appointed someone to take this up with the Economic Council on my behalf. The result was that 2 per cent of what the State owed me was to be restored to me, invested in Government bonds and State enterprises, on which I would only have the interest. The house in the Egyetem utca, which had been returned to me with such ceremony, remained the property of the city, but some rooms in it were to be used by us as a *pied-à-terre*.

One day I drove to Foth, the home of my childhood, where my aunt, née Fanny Apponyi, the wife of my mother's brother Laszlo Karolyi still lived.

There stood the large cream-coloured house, with its columned façade, forlorn and abandoned, in the big, unkempt park. The spacious lawns and gravel paths had become meadows strewn with wild flowers. The rooms were empty, the furniture had been stacked in heaps reaching the ceilings. One part of it was used as a home for children, and dark-eyed youngsters were playing on the terraces. They were, I was told, Greek orphans from the civil war, in the care of the People's Republic.

Fanny had two rooms allocated to her, for she had been a model *châtelaine* and the villagers had not forgotten what she had done for them in the past. She had the gift of organization, and had put up hospitals, dispensaries, nurseries and also a model village, called Zebegeny, one of the show-pieces of Hungary. This Potemkin village misled the foreign visitor into believing that the idyllic existence of the white-washed, thatched-roofed cottages, decorated with gay geraniums, was normal peasant life. Pretty society girls, barefooted and in picturesque peasant costumes, with the names of flowers as 'alias', would receive the tourists, surprising them with their knowledge of English. Her niece Geraldine Apponyi who later became Queen of Albania, had been one of these receptionist-girls.

Now Fanny lived in one of the bathrooms of her château, which was cluttered up with furniture and a multitude of knicknacks, old prints and fifteenth-century miniatures. The bath was full of manuscripts and books. She had chosen it because it had an easily heated iron stove in it. There she sat with her typewriter, working on the life-story of Stephen Karolyi our great-grandfather, surnamed the 'Builder of Churches'. Completely submerged in her work, she did not mind about anything else, as long as she could remain in her bathroom. She did not complain or feel bitter, and even the noise of the Greek children did not seem to worry her.

I knew that she had associated with my bitterest enemies, that the Regent Horthy and his family had been her closest friends, but now all this receded into the past.

In her youth, she had lived in Paris, in their house on the Quai d'Orsay, where she was known for her beauty and elegance. Little of these remained now, with the exception of her hair, which had still kept its golden hue and of which she was still proud.

Laszlo, her husband, had been much older than herself, and their marriage had not been a happy one. I had, in those days, taken the firm resolution not to marry a woman so much younger than myself. Luckily for me, I did not keep it.

We sat on the terrace, which faces the wide avenue from where the city is seen in the distance. The ancient lime tree in the centre was perhaps the only thing that had not altered. It was one of those hot summer evenings, typical of Hungary before twilight, when it seems as if the world had ceased to breathe. A white haze lay motionless on the earth. The grasshoppers ceased their chatter. Then, slowly, one by one, the frogs began their hoarse and monotonous conversation. I missed the despondent barking of the village dogs, belonging to these hot summer nights. There were no dogs in Hungary then. The Russian soldiers had shot them all. To possess dogs seemed to them a bourgeois indulgence.

Nostalgia for the past turns that past into a luminous garden of Eden, without shadows, with half-remembrances, a hazy world, looked at through pink gauze.

'O me, what I was for years, now dead. . . .

O to disengage myself from those corpses of me, which turn and look at where I cast them. . . .

To pass on . . . and leave the corpses behind.' *Walt Whitman*

It was in the summer of 1947 that I visited Marshal Tito in the country near Zagreb. He was then the most popular statesman of Eastern Europe and Yugoslavia, and held up as a model to the rest of the Peoples' Democracies. It was for this reason that Belgrade was chosen for the Cominform's Headquarters.

Yugoslavia's position was a unique one, for they had not been liberated by the Red Army, but had gained freedom by their own heroic struggle. They had built up their organizations through underground village cells, which were kept going after the liberation, and their system developed from these. Its roots grew therefore out of the people themselves, and it was not forced on them from above.

Tito had visited Budapest during the autumn and had been given a glorious reception.[13]

The Marshal made an even greater impression on me than I had expected. Somewhat diffident, it was only after a time that he warmed up. He spoke little and listened with attention. He did not use the Marxian jargon or the habitual clichés. He surprised me by his objectivity when talking about his opponents, Mihailovich and others, and seemed to me very well informed. There was no bitterness or recrimination towards Hungary, nor did he show any signs of chauvinism.

I was convinced that collaboration between our countries was not only possible, but of absolute necessity. His specifically Yugoslav Communism was not blindly following the Russian pattern. As he proved later, he saw that every country has different problems to solve and each must tackle them in its own particular way. I noticed that he scarcely mentioned the Red Army or the Russians, as did countries such as Hungary, which had been the allies of Hitler and so had to overdo their loyalty to the Soviets.

When bidding him farewell I thought how lucky Yugoslavia was to have such a leader.

Although the right moment for instituting the Federation of the East European States had come at last, Slovak chauvinism hampered the project. Hungarian disloyalty to the Czechoslovak State was used as an excuse for chasing 500,000 Hungarians out of Slovakia. The Czechs seemed to have forgotten that in 1939 the majority of the Slovaks had received with joy their emancipation from Prague. The Slovak Communists backed this policy and rejected the protests of the Hungarian Communists. It seemed that Moscow was unfavourable to Federation and was kindling dissension. Like the Habsburgs, Russia appeared to be following the policy of 'Divide and Rule'.

Hungary, for her part, was doing the same to the Germans. It was pathetic to see the trains puffing slowly towards the West, filled with Swabian farmers' families, children and infants at the breast, crammed into cattle-trucks, singing nostalgic songs of farewell.

The rich farms were turned over to the primitive peasants of northern Slovakia who, having been landless, were ignorant of how to run them. True, most of these Swabians had sided with the Germans, but so, too, had the Hungarians. Only those who had been active Nazis should have been expelled.

When Rakosi and Gero launched Federation at the Communist Congress in Budapest, I still had hopes that something might be done.

The relations with the Social Democrats were still normal, the unity of the working class seemed solid, the attacks were concentrated on the right wing of the Smallholders' Party, which was made up of those who, though antagonistic to the new regime, had taken shelter in it.

One day, from the windows of the Hôtel Gellert, I watched the arrival of Cardinal Mindszenty to read mass in the Rock Chapel, built in a cave on Mount Gellert. It had little in common with a religious ceremony. Thousands of people were gathered on the hillside. Everywhere loudspeakers were amplifying his words, which were interrupted by cheering and applause. It was a political demonstration, much resembling an electioneering meeting. All those who were against the new regime had united in this demonstration, the only safe outlet for their pent-up antagonism.

The Government had been surprisingly patient. They dared not molest the Cardinal, although his attacks on the Government through his pastoral letters, instructing the priests to preach against the land reform, were very harmful. He felt safe, for the stand he had taken against the Germans made him popular, and he was convinced that the country would rise in revolt if a hair on his head were touched.

Early in the year I had been asked to be President of the Hungarian group of the inter-Parliamentary Commission, which was going to hold its conference at Cairo. I accepted, on condition that all parliamentary parties would be represented in our group. I had an unpleasant controversy with Rakosi, who objected to Dezso Sulyok, leader of the Party of Freedom. I was as well aware as Rakosi that Sulyok was not a supporter of the regime,[14] but I believed him to be an asset to our delegation. I won, but Sulyok withdrew his nomination.

The conference was of importance, as this was the first time since the war that Hungary had been in contact with the democratic parliaments of other countries. The outstanding member of the conference was its President, Lord Stansgate, whose remarkable tact, knowledge of international affairs and European culture were admired by all. He spoke half a dozen languages without any accent; in his company one could never pass a dull moment.

Other members were Count Carton de Wiart, ex-Belgian Prime Minister, a man of great distinction, with a remarkable wife; Monsieur Boissier, a Genevan patrician, with the special quality of fastidious culture and perfect taste characteristic of some of the Swiss patrician families.

The first encounter between West and East went smoothly, in perfect harmony. Both Lord Stansgate and I hoped to bring about the adherence of the U.S.S.R. to this organization; this would have greatly enhanced its importance. The next conference was held at Rome when I had the occasion to visit Nitti, my old friend of emigration days, who had returned, as he had always predicted in his optimistic way, after Mussolini's fall. That he had predicted it ten years' earlier was of no importance. He was now living all alone in a modest flat in an apartment house, looked after by one of his grandchildren. He had lost his devoted wife, his two sons and his beloved daughter. Although much aged, he still had his former wit and preserved a large store of venomous irony. Inexorable as in his Paris days, he realized that Fascism had not yet been completely eradicated from Italy, but he had no sympathy with Nenni and the Left. He seemed a lonely man. He died in 1952.

When the trouble started in Greece the U.S.S.R. felt unsafe in Eastern Europe, and their apprehension grew when the Marshall Plan offered American aid. Although the U.S.S.R. could not supply this aid, and was in dire need of it itself, it opposed the plan, fearing that the penetration of American capital would mean that in the event of a conflict these border-states would be used against the Soviets.

The more the antagonism between East and West grew, the more acute became the controversy inside the Hungarian coalition. Czechoslovakia and Poland, tempted by Marshall Aid, were hesitant to follow Russia in their refusal. It was then that Stalin told Masaryk bluntly that the Marshall Plan's intention was to isolate the U.S.S.R. True to the old Bolshevik conception, Stalin was convinced that the West would finally attack Russia and that the Marshall Plan was its first strategic move. Turning the screw on their neighbours and subjecting them to Soviet control were natural outcomes of this fear.

The more that was heard of Western Union, the Atlantic Pact, and plans for German rearmament, the more rapidly did Stalin proceed with the Russianization of Eastern Europe and the more solid and impenetrable did the Iron Curtain become.

The Czechs, reluctantly, had to give way — Munich was still fresh in their memory. Masaryk on his return told Ripka: 'We are nothing but Russia's vassals.' It was inconceivable for either of our countries to risk a break with the Soviets, the only safeguard against future German revival.

I therefore completely agreed with the Communists that Hungary should remain independent of American capital and the economic tutelage of the U.S.A.

The only alternative was a federal bloc, independent both of the West and the East. The Bulgarian leader, Dimitrov, declared himself as late as January 1948 in favour of it, extending it to Poland and Czechoslovakia as well.[15] But such a bloc could only come into existence with Russia's help, so the suspicion that it was an anti-Soviet move had first of all to be eliminated.

The predominance of the Smallholders' Party and the flirtation with the West would surely make Russia suspicious and anxious to tighten her grip. So when the elections of 1947 gave only 14 per cent of the votes to the Smallholders' Party, I supported the Government, hoping that the new balance of power between the parties would promote the Federation. Even today I believe that a courageous attitude on the part of our leaders — Tito's way in Yugoslavia — would have compelled Stalin to consent to it, for he would have been confronted not with one country alone, as in the case of Yugoslavia, but with a united front. But our bad luck was to have no such leader. Rakosi's playing with the idea of Federation misled me. I hoped that the Soviets would recognize that in the long run it was to their interest to have the united European States as a protection. But Stalin, made uneasy by Western policy as applied in Greece and by the Marshall Plan, thought force more effective and would not take the risk involved in independence. The right to criticize had gradually been completely wiped out of the Cominform.

The Smallholders' Party had to come to heel and this was done by arresting its secretary, Bela Kovacs, who was said to be involved in a plot. I never doubted that plans for seizing more power had been hatched by the Smallholders' Party, but the dimensions of the plot discovered then were probably much exaggerated. More serious was the military conspiracy of some generals belonging to the old regime. That the two had any connection with each other was not proved.

While Ferencz Nagy was on holiday in Switzerland he received a message from his own Government advising him to remain where he was and resign, for if he returned he would be made responsible for the choice of his colleagues involved in the plot. The Government even sent his American Super-Ford to him, as well as his small son. Everything was done to induce him to remain away. This manner of getting rid of political adversaries was novel and used effectively in other cases as well.

The Government, knowing my views and wanting to keep me as their friend, continued to kindle hopes in me that the possibility of a Federation still existed. They suggested that I should be appointed Minister in Prague, a minor post which they thought I would turn down. They were surprised when I accepted with pleasure. I went to

Prague to see Benes and Masaryk, who were pleased at my nomination; but the Government, at the last moment, changed its mind and begged me to accept Paris instead. I was disappointed at first, but after some consideration I accepted. The reason was that, as the Prague post was out of the question, the only way of fostering my aims was through Paris.

Moreover, the cold war had already started and Moscow did not believe in the importance of diplomatic representation in the West; one reason the more for accurate and unprejudiced information.

The great danger for dictatorships is that their diplomats are afraid to report the true situation. Their reports must fit into the theory of Marxian dialectics, of Historical Materialism. The Government expects from its envoys the justification of its official policy. Many calamities in the past were due to this sort of information leading to erroneous deductions.

I felt I might be of real use in the West especially as, having lived in France for so many years, I had knowledge of their politics and psychology. I made up my mind to tell the truth and nothing but the truth, whether they liked it or not. I was perhaps the only one who could indulge in this luxury, as I was independent, and the Government would have to accept it from me.

Finally, I wanted to keep out of internal politics and doubtless the authorities themselves thought it wise to have me out of the country when the Russianization started.

3

MINISTER IN PARIS, 1947-1949

They spared no human hecatomb to build the pedestal for their truth...
The counterpart to their absolute faith in a metaphysical idea was their absolute
distrust of living people.   TROTSKY about Robespierre

AFTER Premier Nagy resigned my predecessor, Paul Auer,
was recalled from Paris but, like so many others, he felt it more
prudent to disobey the summons.

To the general surprise and to the embarrassment of M. Gauquier,
French Minister in Budapest, a most gifted man with an exceptional
knowledge of Eastern countries and of Soviet Russia in particular,
with whom it was a pleasure to work, my appointment was not
confirmed by the French for three months. I heard later that it was
due to Léon Blum, who felt bitterly about the Hungarian Government's treatment of the Social Democrats. I had not expected
this opposition from Blum, whom I had considered as a friend,
although I did not always agree with his politics. (I remember how
affectionately he embraced me when we met in London in 1944, after
his liberation from the Nazi camps. But those were still the 'happy days
of the war'.)

Before I left for Paris, Gyongyosi, Minister of Foreign Affairs,
Rakosi and Gero accepted my proposal to launch a periodical in Zürich
which would sponsor the idea of the Federation in the West. I had
therefore every right to believe that Moscow was not antagonistic to
the idea, and this gave hopes for my mission in Paris.

During the first two years, 1947 and 1948, although the cold war
had already started, the diplomats of the two hostile camps still visited
each other, and life was pleasant and civilized.

The greatest diplomatic event of the first year was the farewell party
given by the British Ambassador, Viscount Norwich, and Lady
Norwich at the sumptuous British Embassy. Winston Churchill, who
was passing through Paris, was there too.

I also paid a private visit to the Ambassador — a most pleasant one, due probably to both of us sharing the opinion that the German danger was still acute. As he was on the eve of leaving the Embassy, he was candid about his disagreement with the official British stand in the German matter.

My conversation with the American Ambassador was of a different kind. It had little of the usual diplomatic subtleties and Mr. Caffery surprised me with the blunt statement that in a very short time the U.S.A. would be ready for war 'and will wage it, if Russia won't listen to reason'. Of course I knew that he was keeping to the fashionable 'treat them rough' maxim, so I did not feel impressed. In general, the diplomats of the U.S.A. made no effort to maintain the traditions of diplomatic etiquette and never returned courtesies received from countries on the other side of the curtain. Lacking the century-old training of diplomatic intercourse, they did not waste time on such cumbersome relics of past ages.

I had often heard from colleagues that to be a successful diplomat in France was a costly business. One's safe has to be well filled with what are called private funds, the use of which is strictly confidential. It was embarrassing at first to find that everything had its price and that neither the politics nor the artistic achievements of your country are mentioned in the press, except for a consideration. Sometimes a case of Tokay, liqueur, Barack, or *foie gras* would do the trick. One soon had to give up the illusion that the cause itself would be sufficient to arouse interest.

One day we excited the suspicion of the British Council. This happened in the following way: Katus had asked Louis MacNeice to give a performance at the Legation. It consisted of reading his poems, accompanied by his attractive wife, who played the guitar and sang. Although my staff did not see the necessity for cultivating English poetry at the Hungarian Legation, the evening proved such a success that they had to admit that art is the best medium for international understanding, and that it could even lift for some brief hours the weight of an iron curtain. But the British Council, I was told, suspected that this had some political significance. The real reason, that Katus loves poetry, they did not suspect, for it would have been too simple.

The U.S.S.R. receptions in the rue de Grenelle differed from the others through their strange custom of dividing their guests into two categories: first class and second class. This meant that on arrival, the secretary at the top of the stairs would, after inspecting your card, direct you to the first- or second-class reception halls. The first class had the privilege of being served with caviare, champagne, strawberries, pineapples, salmon and sturgeon; the unfortunates of the second class had to content themselves with sandwiches, chips, apples and vodka. To the first class belonged the ambassadors and ministers, members of the French Cabinet and the leaders of the parties; to the second the ordinary M.P.s, journalists and members of the Communist Party, friends of Russia, and other mortals of lesser importance.

I could not help recollecting with nostalgia Stephen Rakovsky's receptions in 1926, and how one felt a fresh breeze from a new world when one entered the Soviet Embassy of those days.

To promote the East European Federation, I suggested that once a week the representatives of the interested countries should meet socially with their wives and daughters, to exchange ideas and get to know one another. The proposal met with sympathy from the Russian Ambassador Bogomolov, and so we inaugurated our 'Thursdays', held in turn in the different Embassies.

The Polish Ambassador, the young and handsome Putrement, was a thorough Marxist and a clear-headed, able man. He had been a writer and journalist and an expert football player. Matches between our staffs were arranged, though when the Ambassador entered the field, thrusting everyone aside who was bold enough to approach him, our team had no chance. My help, I am afraid, would not have been of much use. Putrement was most of the time in serious difficulties with the French authorities. He told me how on one occasion his courier, a woman, was arrested and kept in prison because she refused to hand over the contents of the Polish diplomatic bag. Expecting any moment a raid on his Embassy, he had armed his staff to the hilt — an unusual procedure in the centre of peace-time Paris. Even his pretty wife, who looked like a lady of the court of Marie Antoinette, had probably learnt to handle a gun.

The Yugoslav Ambassador, Marko Ristic, a surrealist poet who knew France and its literary circles well from pre-war days, a gentle, charming intellectual and an idealistic Communist, was most endearing. His receptions near the Trocadero had that special quality of simplicity, directness and warmhearted spontaneity characteristic of the Yugoslavs. Together with his clever and attractive wife, the Ambassador-artist had actually created within the walls of his sumptuous Embassy a ground where the most antagonistic elements met and felt immediately at home. Marshal Tito could not have had a better champion of his cause than this young and fascinating couple.

After the Czech crisis, when the Ambassador resigned and joined the camp of the dissidents, he was replaced by Hoffmeister, also a writer of distinction. The Peoples' Republics excelled in intellectual diplomats.

I was now asked to take over the posts in Belgium, Holland and Luxembourg, which I visited in turn to present my credentials. Our republic was restricted in diplomats and therefore accumulated several posts in one.

In February 1948 I visited Benes, Masaryk and Ripka in Prague, to try to come to an agreement about the minorities in Slovakia. Benes had been affected by his recent stroke and was not in a fit condition to negotiate. I had placed all my hopes in Masaryk. It was about two weeks before his death. He wore his arm in a sling and was visibly in pain. He had a wound in the palm of his hand, and had been twice operated on for it. The doctors had assured him that it was not cancer. 'The worst of it is,' he said wistfully, 'that I cannot play the piano and probably never shall again.'

During our talk, Clementis, without being asked, repeatedly interrupted us. Masaryk seemed nervous in his presence, and I had the impression that he feared him. He watched him anxiously when he entered and spoke to him with formal politeness, which was not Masaryk's usual way. I knew that Clementis was intractable and that my seeing him would be of no avail. My trust in a settlement rested on Masaryk's personal prestige. 'That man controls me,' he said when Clementis left the room.

At the entrance of the Czernin Palace a group of men and women were waiting. An old woman with a shawl on her head came up to Masaryk, who had accompanied me, and offered him a small bunch of spring flowers. She was followed by a peasant with a large watermelon. Masaryk tucked the gifts under his arm. 'What do they want?' I asked him. 'Nothing, it is like this every day,' and his eyes suddenly filled with tears. 'They do not ask for anything, they just want to see

me, and show their affection. I really believe they care for me, oh how
I love them.'

When I heard the news of his death I did not believe the official
version of suicide. That the doctor was prevented from examining the
body spoke against suicide, but on the other hand Masaryk's position
was insoluble. He was torn between different loyalties. Whether he
was actually killed or killed himself is, I think, of minor importance; if
it was suicide, it was not a voluntary act. A humanist and democrat,
having passed his life in the struggle for liberty — how could he have
accepted the servitude of his people and totalitarian dictatorship? I
was deeply affected by his death.

The last of our 'Thursdays' was a memorable one. It was held at
the Soviet Embassy and was, I think, about the middle of May.

At the beginning these meetings were easy-going and informal, and
fulfilled their purpose: the exchange of ideas. In time they turned more
and more into lectures delivered by Bogomolov. The shrewd diplomats of the satellite States, although they knew European politics as
well as the Russian Ambassador, sat in silence and nodded approval.
On that special afternoon the atmosphere was strangely tense; the
reason for this only one of us knew.

Madame Bogomolov, a frail and very young woman, who suffered
from heart trouble and was overworked as she had the position of
councillor in the Embassy, was not there, being ill. The Ambassador
received us alone, in front of a ready-laid tea-table. There were no
servants to wait on us, and Bogomolov seemed strangely absent-
minded, so that he even forgot to offer us tea or strawberries and
cream — an unpleasant omission as the day was hot and we were
thirsty. Marko Ristic, who had usually been a keen contributor to
our discussions, was noticeably silent and Bogomolov did not seem
to be aware of his presence. I, as the veteran and not belonging
to the Communist Party, had a unique position, and could indulge
in the role of *enfant terrible*. Putrement seemed to be the favourite
today. Hoffmeister and I got some friendly glances, but Ristic sat
at the end of the table like a naughty boy in disgrace. As our thirst
became unbearable, our eyes were riveted on the unoffered tea and
the cold drinks in front of us. At last Katus, unable to resist temptation, helped herself to the strawberries. That broke the tension and the

Ambassador started pouring out the drinks. Had it been mere neglect owing to his obvious preoccupation, or was it a gentle hint that Russia had a lot of good things to offer, but could, if it pleased her, deny them to the unruly boys?

Later I heard from my friend Ristic that the controversy between Tito and Stalin, which had already been going on for some time, had now entered an acute phase. Some weeks afterwards the Cominform's letter to Tito was published. Stalin had now committed his most fatal error.

For some time I imagined that Hungary could take on herself the role of appeaser, and that a way would be found to patch up the breach. I mentioned this on several occasions to Rajk, who had now succeeded Erik Molnar as Minister for Foreign Affairs, but he was adamant against it.

The controversy with Tito had greatly weakened the International Workers' Movement and the fusion of the Communist Party with the Social Democrats therefore became of vital importance to the U.S.S.R. This was concluded in Hungary on April 17th, before the actual break with Tito took place. Instrumental in the Hungarian fusion were the leader of the Social Democrats, Arpad Szakasirs, and Stephen Ries, Minister of Justice. Their party had been undermined by the Communists, and those who opposed fusion had been pushed aside, so now there was no one to resist it. They had lost their standing with the workers. Antal Ban, who had belonged to the left wing of the Social Democrats and had opposed the union, was accused of corruption and had to leave. He fled to Switzerland. Anna Kethly resigned from the leading position which she held in the party, but stayed in the country. As is often the case, women gave evidence of greater pluck than men.[16]

What was happening made me feel that I could no longer be of use in Paris. The Federation, my main reason for accepting the post, was now completely dropped. I was approaching my 75th birthday; it would be a good opportunity to tender my resignation. But I was prevented from doing so for the following reason: Cardinal Mindszenty had been arrested on the ground that his actions were endangering the State. His pastoral letters addressed to the clergy — the village priest is the most powerful propagandist — were direct attacks on the Government's agrarian policy. The Government had shown excessive patience and the measures they at last had to take were in self-defence. Had they let him carry on his activities, a revolt of the peasants would probably have resulted, the bloody suppression of which would have been worse than the Cardinal's imprisonment. Moreover his unauthorized negotiations with the Americans and Cardinal Spellman about the Crown of St. Stephen were a serious breach of confidence.[17] If priests become political and act accordingly, they should not be surprised if they are treated as politicians by a dictatorship. His actions had exceeded his competence as Primate, and his guilt would have been easily proved had he received a fair trial.

My resignation at that precise moment would have been interpreted as a demonstration in favour of the Cardinal. At that time I assumed that the trial would be properly conducted — I was not prepared for the methods which were used.

Colonel Hodgson, Australian Minister, called on me several times for a visa, as he wanted to see the Cardinal in jail. In spite of the right of all Governments to refuse visits to their prisoners — what would Franco or Mussolini have answered to such a request? — I thought it wise, in this unusual case, to allow the Australian Minister and the French Abbé Gau, who had voiced the same desire, to see for themselves that the Cardinal was not ill-treated and that the rumour concerning his having been murdered was false.

I did not mince my words in writing to Rakosi and Gero, letting them know what disastrous effects the trial was having on public opinion in the West. I kept to my resolution of telling them the truth, although I agreed with Oscar Wilde that 'to give advice is always dangerous, but to give good advice is positively fatal'.

At the beginning my reports had been circulated in all Hungarian Legations as models of how reports should be constructed, but those about Mindszenty did not get the same reception. I thought it important for me to stay at my post for this very reason, as my successor, I feared, would be less outspoken. At last the Government agreed to the visas, but not that Mindszenty should be visited in his cell. I did everything I could to persuade them to have the Cardinal's sentence changed into exile in Rome. It would have been the only way to remedy the trial which had been so shamefully conducted.

When none of my advice was followed I announced my wish to return to Budapest and tender my resignation.

I received several letters from Rajk begging me to reconsider my decision. He pleaded that I should not abandon them now, when they were having such a difficult time, and when my support was so much needed. He agreed that I should return to Budapest for a while to talk matters over.

John Eros, who had been the first Chancellor of the Legation, became on my recommendation Minister in London. But when recalled to Budapest, suspecting that he would be purged, he resigned and disappeared in the London wilderness.

Peter Mod, the Councillor of the Legation, and Andrew Havas, were expected to make me change my mind. Theirs was a hopeless task. Peter Mod was a personal friend of Rajk and had worked with him in the underground. He was a slim, austere-looking man, silent, punctual, efficient and with a sound judgment. He tried, poor fellow, to persuade me to stay. He seemed to know all the arguments which Katus and I were having in the dead of night about my resignation. How he managed this has always intrigued me.

Andrew Havas, who had been my secretary in London during the war, and whom I considered my most loyal friend, tried to persuade me as well. His faithful eyes, shining with tears, watched me wherever I went, hoping against hope that I would alter my decision. He had attached himself to me at a time when it was the fashion amongst the émigrés in London, to say: 'Whatever happens in Hungary, one thing is certain, that Karolyi will never return.' My 'friends' called him the 'crazy poet' who follows lost causes. He had been tortured in the Horthy prisons as a youth, and had left the Communist Party at the time of the Hitler-Stalin Pact. When the Hungarian Party was in need of every able man, he joined it again, and the lost sheep was re-admitted again to the fold. Trusting in everyone, believing the best of most people, he would find an excuse even for those who had played him the vilest tricks. He had attempted the impossible — to serve the party and remain loyal to me. This was incompatible and became his personal tragedy. He used to say: 'If I am purged it is I who will be in the wrong. I will die with the cry of the Jacobins on my lips: "*Vive la République!*" and add my own "*Vive le Communisme!*" '

In July I returned to Budapest for a short visit to hand in my resignation, but with the intention of carrying on until the appointment of my successor. I still hoped to convince Rakosi that the Cardinal should be exiled to Rome.

As soon as I arrived I called on Rajk. In the waiting-room of the Foreign Office I met the French Minister, Gauquier, who was also waiting to be received. When Rajk appeared in the doorway, he asked us both to enter. To discuss our matters in front of the French Minister was certainly unorthodox and made it clear to me that Rajk was not interested in what I had to say, and that his post as well as mine had become irrelevant. I remained silent, and Gauquier complained about some visas which had been refused to his compatriots. Rajk was extremely absent-minded, although his attitude was, as usual, composed and calm. Before I left, he said that he would let me know when he could see me the next day. Since his resignation from the Ministry of the Interior after his visit to Moscow, Rajk had been a mere figurehead at the Foreign Office.[18] He had no power. Actually the Foreign Ministry was divided into Eastern and Western sections. The Eastern was undoubtedly of greater importance and was conducted by Andrew Berei, a party man, who was, though not in name, the real head of the Foreign Office, controlling Rajk himself.

The next morning Katus rang me from Paris, with the news that Peter Mod had suddenly been recalled to Budapest, that he had taken the plane and was bringing me a letter from her. She also said that the Russian Ambassador and Foreign Minister Vyshinsky, who should have come for luncheon, had postponed the appointment, so I had no need to hurry back.

It was most surprising for Mod to leave when I was away without even letting me know. Also that Rajk, who must have known about it, had not mentioned it to me.

I received no word from Rajk the next day, nor did Mod appear. After a couple of days I rang the Minister's office and got the answer that Rajk was too busy and could not see me. The town was full of rumours that he had been arrested and taken to Moscow. Everything in Budapest can be controlled — economics, politics, parties, people — but one thing is invincible, and that is the tongue of the people. No guillotine, gallows or firing squads have the power of shutting mouths.

At last Katus's letter reached me, but it was not Mod who brought it; Mod had disappeared. Where was he? No answer. Had the plane arrived? No answer. To my surprise, Rajk's private secretary, a woman, was assigned to me, as well as his car and chauffeur, for the duration of my stay in Budapest.

Getting more and more anxious and puzzled, I called on Berei to discover the truth concerning the rumours of arrests. He denied them point-blank and added that in any case it had nothing to do with the Foreign Office.

'It is inadmissible,' I retorted, 'that a member of the Cabinet should not be informed of such important events.'

The same evening a member of the Communist Party, whose name for obvious reasons I cannot disclose, told me that Rajk had been arrested on the very day when I had visited him; he gave me the list of highly placed officials and journalists who had been arrested with him. They were eight in number. Peter Mod did not figure on the list. In spite of Berei's refusal to see me under the pretence of urgent work, I forced his door at ten at night and laid the list in front of him.

He turned livid. Staring at the paper he muttered: 'From whom did you get it?'

'That is my business,' I answered. 'I return distrust for distrust. Now we are quits.'

I immediately got on to Rakosi and Gero, but they wrapped themselves in a mysterious silence, assuring me that as soon as they knew more they would communicate with me. The charges had probably not been worked out yet. They hinted that Mod had been in the service of the Deuxième Bureau.

'If so,' I retorted, for of course I did not believe this absurd charge, 'it is I, the head of the Legation, who am responsible for not having detected this earlier. You must proceed against me as well.'

'You are not responsible. Spies can infiltrate anywhere,' was the answer.

I left in despair for Paris, to wind up the matters pending at the Legation.

On arrival I was informed by the Quai d'Orsay that the First Councillor and the Second Secretary, Mod and Havas, would not be granted their return visas to France. What I had suspected now became clear to me — that much had been happening of which I was totally ignorant. I then realized that if the Minister of a totalitarian State is not a party member his role is restricted to representation only; that, however devoted his staff may be to him, they cannot play fair.

Those last months in Paris were a nightmare. For weeks news of Rajk's arrest was not published. I shall never forget Mod's pathetic little wife, whose ghastly pale face with its bewildered and frightened expression, haunted the Legation. She appeared dutifully at all functions, regularly followed the courses in Marxism inaugurated by her husband — the only sabotage I could discover in Mod's activities, as nothing renders Marxism so unpopular as to be compelled to attend lectures on it — even participating in the discussions. Every day her cheeks grew hollower and her face, with its perpetual forced smile, seemed to be turning into a skull. She applied for a visa to return, hoping that she could be of use to her husband. Katus and I both tried to dissuade her from returning, but in vain. Her worst torment must have been that she could not express her fears, even to herself, for that would be disloyalty to the party. She would not admit the evident truth that her husband had fallen into disgrace. The party could not be wrong: Peter could not be wrong. How could she reconcile the irreconcilable? We feared for her mental balance and, although I was the only person with whom she would talk, I could not give her the comforting words she was expecting. At last she got her visa. A member of the Legation who accompanied her to the station saw on the paper-stand the announcement of Rajk's arrest. Hoping that now at last she would understand and turn back, her companion handed her the paper through the window of the compartment. Mrs. Mod gazed at her, her face turned a shade paler still, but she did not make a move to get out. The train pulled out slowly. That terrified look of a tortured child was the last we ever saw of her. On arrival she disappeared. I bombarded Berei with wires asking for news of her. No answer came. I was told much later that she had committed suicide.

Now that the news of the arrests had come out, the Hungarian papers published daily an avalanche of wires from workers and peasants demanding that this 'human vermin', these 'poisonous vipers', should be ruthlessly wiped out. One after another, my staff was being ordered home. The same was happening at other Legations. Velics, our Minister in Rome, the only professional diplomat and a Catholic, remained loyal to the 'hand that fed him'.

He had a hard time when the Mindszenty trial was on, and was about to obtain a favourable compromise with the Vatican, when he was ordered home.

One never knew if the man who the day before was still the messenger of the Government would not on his return be arrested as the agent of a foreign power.

Our press attaché in Paris, Ferencz Fejto, was recalled as well.[19] He asked my advice. I could not take on myself the responsibility of urging him to return.

Paul Ignotus, cultural attaché in London, although aware of the risk he was taking, returned home, believing that having served the regime he must remain consistent. He told me, and this has worried me since, that he was following my example.

My Legation was crumbling to pieces. The position of my wretched successor was not enviable, now that the cold war was acquiring new vehemence.

Soon afterwards Zoltan Szanto arrived to replace me. He knew as little as I did about the Rajk affair and made the following unguarded remark: 'One thing is certain, that whatever he has done was not out of ambition or vanity, for everyone knows that he is devoid of both.'

My much-tried nerves needed a rest and I went to Châtel-Guyon for a fortnight.

About July 15th a special diplomatic messenger arrived from home to give me at last 'all the information I was asking for'.

To listen to the absurd explanations of the wretched messenger was perhaps the hardest ordeal I ever had to go through. It sounded like a second-rate detective story, unconvincing, illogical, contradictory, heedless of the most elementary human psychology.

The story they wanted me to believe was that Rajk had been a Horthy informer since 1933, an American agent since the liberation, and a Tito spy for the last two years.

I had made up my mind to listen to everything he had to say without arguing, as argument was futile. He knew that I knew that what he said had nothing to do with the truth, but that he had to deliver the message.

But at last I could not restrain myself and burst out: 'If Rajk was an agent of the West, why did he disclose the famous conspiracy of the

Smallholders at the time when he was Minister of the Interior? Had not Rakosi expressed his deepest thanks to Rajk for his revolutionary vigilance? He would have rendered the most valuable service to the U.S.A. had he helped the plotters to accomplish their aim and draw Hungary over to the Western side, as was officially stated at the time. This agent of Washington seems not to have been a very useful one to his masters.'

There was no answer to this, except that the acts of such black souls are incomprehensible to ordinary mortals.

He then produced a document signed by Rajk's own brother, stating that in the year 1933 it was he who had liberated Ladislas from prison, on condition that he would join Horthy's secret service.

Rajk's brother had been a notorious Fascist and had served a term of imprisonment, after which he had managed to leave the country.

'How is it possible that he is back in Hungary?' I asked.

'Why not? Are we not a free country in which anyone may live if he pleases?'

'The word of a Fascist is not a sufficient proof,' I said.

And then he brought out his trump card: in 1938 Rajk was excluded from the party owing to his Trotskyist activities.

'How could you trust an ex-Trotskyist with the most important post, that of the Ministry of the Interior, at such a dangerous moment, when the Smallholders' Party had the majority? And how could he belong to the Politburo until the very last?'

The embarrassment of my visitor now became obvious. He began to stutter. He muttered that Russia had not informed them of Rajk's expulsion.

'But later, at the time of the liberation, when you entrusted Rajk with the most vital post of Minister of the Interior, why did they not let you know? And what about his courageous behaviour in the Spanish Civil War?'

'His wounds were accidental,' he replied.

I was no longer listening. I was thinking how easy it would have been for Rajk, as Foreign Minister, to escape had his conscience troubled him.

'Had Rajk any connection with Tito? Did he disagree with the attitude of the Cominform towards Yugoslavia?' I asked, trying to detect the real reason behind the story.

'Not at all,' was the prompt and categorical answer. 'I am afraid I have not convinced you,' he went on, 'but Rakosi asked me specially to tell you that all the relevant documents will be at your disposal when you return. He hopes you will do this as soon as possible.'

The same night I wrote to Rakosi that in the event of Rajk's conviction, he must not count on my support.

I received a stiff answer: he regretted that I was showing such lack of confidence in the Government and in him.

At the end of August I took the train for Budapest hoping against hope to be able to help the arrested men. At the station an official delegation was waiting for me. Also a bunch of students, probably ordered there by the Government, gave me a 'spontaneous' ovation.

My first visit was to Rakosi. In spite of our unpleasant exchange of letters, he received me cordially. He showed me triumphantly Rajk's signed confession and asked me to stay for the trial, which was starting on September 17th, so as to hear and see for myself. He emphasized how much they appreciated my loyalty in contrast to the other diplomats.

The version of Rajk's 'crimes' was now a new one. It was built up on a Titoist conspiracy, which at the time of his arrest had been positively denied. The brother's letter was no longer mentioned.

The necessity for the trial became more and more evident. Rajk had to be eliminated because he proved to be a potential danger to the Stalinist policy in the Balkans. He was courageous, he was popular, he refused to be Moscow's slave, he dared to raise his voice in the Politburo, of which he was a member, until the very last. He had to be used against Tito, against the independence of Yugoslavia, which had dared to inaugurate a Communism different from Stalin's. Two birds had to be killed with the one stone.

Soon the other Peoples' Democracies staged trials of the same pattern, against Gomulka, Kostov, etc. The Hungarian Government had no choice, and I feel certain that they were not happy at having to stage this trial. Gero, when I challenged him, was more astute. I said: 'No one will believe the rubbish about Rajk even if he confesses. Nothing will harm your regime more. You will lose many friends. Why not prosecute him for what he has done, and let him defend himself?'

Gero remained silent. Then he said: 'Rajk and his followers have committed unpardonable offences. His Titoism is a danger. We know that he conspired with Tito, but we have no proof of it. He must be liquidated. But to tell the entire truth to the public would be madness. They would not understand. They are not politically ripe enough. Whether he was actually a spy or not is irrelevant, for in its essence it comes to the same thing: committing treachery or being a spy. The crudeness of the charge is only the mechanical side of it, and of no importance.'

'But if you cannot reveal his treachery, as you call it, to the people, why not reveal the conspiracy to me and to those who have been your supporters?'

He shook his head. 'You have to trust us.'

My apartment in the Egyetem utca was now ready. The rooms where I had lived as a student, had been arranged in exactly the same way as in those days. I thought it would be my last abode. But the curse of Baroness Orczy was apparently coming true.[20]

No one seemed interested in the coming trial, and nobody dared mention Rajk's name. The public seemed completely apathetic, they obviously did not believe in the charges but considered Rajk and the other accused as dead men. Those who were antagonistic to the regime were pleased that the revolution was devouring its own children, the Communists were apprehensive that one day Rajk's fate might be theirs. The amorphous mass of non-politicals were uninterested.

Havas, who had been recalled and had received some minor appointment, had been convinced of Rajk's guilt. He had in the past been one of his friends and admirers. It was horrifying to hear him say that Rajk had betrayed us all and that Mod, too, had been a traitor. This change in Havas was perhaps the most uncanny and grievous of all. He seemed not to be himself. He died in prison some years later.

One day I had a luncheon appointment with Paul Ignotus, the press attaché of the London Legation, who had returned at the call of the Government and had been given a remunerative position as translator at international conferences. His father, a well-known writer, had died recently. I had been seeing quite a lot of him. He was a most careful, diplomatic man, with much humour and a rare capacity for seeing the different facets of problems. Politically he was a Liberal, but in recent years he had joined the Socialist Party. His sister was the owner of a first-class small restaurant in the centre of the town. It was there that we should have met. I waited for ten minutes, a quarter of an hour, half an hour.

Then suddenly, his sister, who had been sitting silently at the counter, came up to me; her face was distraught, her eyes filled with tears. She whispered in my ear: 'Pali has been arrested,' and she returned to her place, as silently as she had come.

I went straight to Gero and guaranteed Ignotus's loyalty. 'It's madness, what you are doing. How can you expect that anyone will return after this, when this is what happens to them?' Gero showed surprise and assured me that he would look into the matter. I got the impression he was not deceiving me, for the secret police had authority to act on their own.

One of the worst features of totalitarian States is that people in the highest positions are not always informed of what is happening; decisions are taken behind their backs by the secret police. Ignotus was not released, but tried *in camera* and sentenced to ten years' imprisonment. What he had done was never revealed.

Before returning to Hungary I had still cherished the illusion that I could, with the remaining shreds of my personal prestige, be of some help to the arrested men; but I soon discovered that during my absence the situation had much changed. My friends feared to be seen with me and came no more to the Egyetem utca. Those few who risked it were watched. The weight of an alien power became more and more evident and one had the feeling that the leaders themselves were no longer in control. The Government were obeying orders, but what else could they do? If they refused, it would have been their turn to be 'vaporized' and another shift, more servile still, would take over. They had gone too far. Courage such as Rajk's was not usual.

The plan for East European Federation had now been entirely dropped: Dimitrov, its champion, had been taken to Moscow where, incidentally, he died; the campaign of calumny against Tito and Yugoslavia was carried on with bitter intensity.

In spite of all this I was still determined to remain in my country and end my days in the old house. To become an émigré again was unimaginable. It would have meant siding with the enemy, especially as the situation looked very much like war in those days. I did not believe it possible to hang in the void like Mohammed's coffin, and I had always used the argument that one had to choose which side of the barricade one was on. I did not believe in a third way. There were no masses behind a Third Force. The English way of life is not suited to the Continent. The threat from German Nazism and international Fascism has not yet passed.

To live in a capitalist world from where the atom bomb would be used on the East seemed an impossible decision for me. I belonged to the East and my place was there amongst my people, whatever errors they were committing. How well I understood Masaryk's dilemma! But to remain in Hungary during the trial, to attend it, as the Government had asked me to do, would have given the impression that I approved. Most probably statements would appear in the press in my name and my denial would not.

I had, therefore, only one alternative. To return to Paris and get help from Left international channels, the only ones which could wield influence, making the instigators of the trial realize that they were losing their most loyal friends and risking a split in the party.

With the firm intention of returning one day, I left Budapest. Yet the Gods willed differently.

Katus was prepared for the worst; she did not believe that I would get out, and was ready to return and join me. But, to the surprise of all, my visa was granted without the slightest difficulty. It was a generous act, as they knew how strongly I dissented.

When I crossed the frontier at Buchs, I sent a wire to Katus: '*Les canards ont bien passé.*' It was a phrase we used when we had overcome a difficulty. It had its origin in the caption on an engraving which had hung in my nursery in Foth. It depicted a row of ducks crossing the river.

4

OPERATION HEARTBREAK NUMBER TWO

Se taire, c'est laisser croire qu'on ne juge et ne désire rien. CAMUS

I ARRIVED in Paris on September 17th, 1949, the day the Rajk trial started.

I do not wish to show in detail the absurdity of the charges, for that would be banging at open doors. Since then everyone, even the thinking Communist, has understood that the trial was staged to discredit Titoism and eliminate Rajk and his companions, whom Stalinism considered as obstacles to the Russianization of Hungary.

I will only mention some facts, to prove how little trouble was taken to make the trial convincing.

The arrest had been effected first; the accusation concocted afterwards. No plot was discovered; not a single piece of evidence was produced by the State Prosecutor. The accused had to prove their guilt themselves, by confessing it. The witnesses for the prosecution were all police agents, or Nazi spies dragged out of prison. The defence had no witnesses. The advocates of the accused did not attempt to defend them. The judge was chief prosecutor. The procedure of the trial followed the pattern of the Moscow trials.

But why did the accused confess? That our scientific age has its own methods of making a man confess to no matter what crime, and even of making him believe that he committed that crime, is now common knowledge. After Stalin's death the Russians themselves admitted in an official statement that improper measures were used to induce the doctors (in the famous trial of 1951) to confess that they had murdered Zhdanov.

That Rajk wished for death, that he refused to appeal for clemency, that he took all responsibility on himself for what he had done — what this was did not, of course, come out in the trial — and exonerated the others, was not surprising from such a man. Whatever the methods used to break his resistance, the inner core of a human being remains unchanged.

Rajk could not imagine life except in the service of the party. What else remained to him but to die? When the death sentence was announced, I wired Rakosi, asking for a reprieve. There was no answer.

In those days of anguish I was searching for a way to refute the confessions of Rajk, on a point on which I had personal knowledge.

Reading the report, I noticed that Rajk confessed to having supplied Sulyok with a visa, in order that this 'enemy of the Peoples' Republics' should work against Hungary in the West. I knew this to be untrue. In the presence of Dinnyes (ex-Prime-Minister), Rakosi had told me that he was going to give a visa to Sulyok to leave, as he considered him a danger inside the country, and that he was even ready to give him financial aid if necessary.

Here was my chance to testify on a point about which I had personal knowledge, and because of which I could demand a new trial. To take this decision was not easy. It meant burning my boats, for I had no illusion that Rajk could be saved. It meant that I could no more return to Hungary, that my name would be erased from Hungarian history, that the peasants would be made to believe that I had joined the camp of 'the Landlords'. This threat had been insinuated to me previously.

After many sleepless nights, I decided to take the decisive step. On October 13th I sent a wire to the President of the Hungarian Republic, offering to testify, in front of the courts if necessary, that Rajk's confession as regards Sulyok was contrary to facts known to me, thus throwing doubt on the rest of his confessions. I referred to what Rakosi had told me in the presence of Dinnyes, and requested him, in view of this evidence, to postpone the sentence, and order a new trial. If I had no answer within twenty-four hours, I said I would publish my wire.

Again no answer. The international press published my wire in full and *L'Humanité*, French organ of the Communist Party, printed the answer of the Hungarian Government: that I had joined the capitalist-imperialist camp, for I was too old and ill to resist their influence.[21]

Rajk and his seven colleagues were hanged.

I became, for the second time, an émigré. All my belongings were seized as they had been twenty-eight years before. This time there was no hope of return.

THE LAST WORD

FAITH WITHOUT ILLUSION

I have loved justice and hated iniquity: therefore I die in exile. GREGORY VII

MY critics could call me inconsequent. And so I was — inconsequent to my theoretical beliefs, to reason; but not to myself. Was it not the same indignation which had turned me into a rebel twenty-eight years earlier and made me join the progressive Left? Indignation against the injustices and hypocrisy of a clique, exercising unlimited power.

In both cases, now as then, personal interest was against my decision, and in both cases I was attached by emotional bonds to those from whom I dissociated myself.

One's acts are mostly determined by one's temperament and not by reason; this accounts for the fact that the same sort of experience repeats itself during the course of one's life, predestining the person to a particular fate. Mine was to be homeless.

It would have been impossible for me to live in my country without protesting against the violation of those moral principles which I believe to be the basis of Socialism. For Socialism is not only an economic, but an ethical, issue. The liquidation of capitalist society will be of little use unless a higher, more equitable and freer order takes its place.

I have always followed thought to its conclusion, hating half-measures, and refusing to pour water into wine. This uncompromising attitude is perhaps due to that secluded, anachronistic upbringing which protected me from direct contact with life.

At the beginning it was difficult to find a harmony between my life and these fascinating theories, and only an entire break with the past could accomplish it. The distribution of my land supplied the break. With that action I burnt my boats. Now I became free to follow the road to Socialism and lead the life I had longed for, but for which I was neither suited nor prepared. Gradually all vestiges of the past had to

365

go overboard. Yet somehow I never managed to get closer to the people with whom and for whom I worked. I felt unhomogeneous in their company, an eternal outsider; their ways and their customs were alien to me. From this came my loneliness. I lost my own milieu, but did not gain another. These saw in me the aristocrat who for some incomprehensible and mysterious reason had joined them. To some it seemed fishy, to others naive.

Yet there were moments, at large public meetings, when I felt understanding and love, emanating from the crowd, overwhelm me like a tidal wave, as if, for a brief moment, barriers had been swept aside and I was one with this trusting mass of humanity.

My faith in Socialism compensated me for much that I had lost, for in spite of my inveterate pessimism I never doubted that one day it would materialize, and that our struggle was indispensable to progress. Socialism meant and means for me today — for I have remained an unrepentant Socialist in spite of the conversions fashionable in our time — the only cure for the ills of our society.

I have never been convinced by the argument that no good can ever result from bad actions. The results of our actions are mysterious, not in our power to solve. The span of our lives is short, history can be judged in many ways, and good and evil are relative. Did not the betrayal of Judas make redemption possible to the believer?

We have no other standards than those of our individual consciences. In historical perspective, the crimes of Henry VIII, of Peter the Great, of the French Revolution fade away and only the achievements remain. The horrors of war have not kept Governments from waging them, and have those the right to preach political morality and condemn 'expediency' who remained silent at the time of Hiroshima and are ready to use the H-bomb to extend their power and protect their wealth? I do not believe that any of us who live in this harsh age, and who have all been to some extent responsible for its misery, have the right to preach morality. Neither should the ex-Communist, the 'renegade' believe himself justified in serving as the torch-bearer of a new anti-Communist crusade on moral grounds, because his own hopes have been frustrated. Although not a member of the Communist Party, I had been a sympathizer; and when I write this I think of myself first. It is not a reason for those who have erroneously taken Stalinism for Communism to commit the even greater error of believing that under the leadership of the U.S.A. as it exists today (after turning away from the great Rooseveltian conception), propagating hatred and reinforcing reactionary elements in Germany and all over the world, anything worth while and lasting can be achieved. Under the disguise of fighting Bolshevism, America is now hoisting back into the saddle the Nazis and Fascists of yesterday, herself using the same methods against which she is launching her crusade, and trying to make the world forget the six million victims destroyed in gas chambers. I refuse to believe that the only alternative to this is the slave camps of Russia or a third world war.

Although aware that Stalinism was not Socialism, I believed that it was the first step towards it, as it had done away with the exploitation of man by man, the State having taken over the means of production. In the Europe of Mussolini, Hitler, Franco and Horthy, Russia was, before the war, the only power capable of defeating those aggressive creeds. One had to choose. There was no other way. During a battle, the man who walks between the lines is inevitably shot down. I had no wish to investigate the errors of the U.S.S.R. as it was not the Russian system that we wanted to follow blindly, and 'objectivity' would but have weakened the impetus of the fight. A soldier during the battle is not expected to be objective. Greater dangers are at closer range. The issue was not Socialist democracy versus Communist terror; it was to prevent Nazi terror from expanding and establishing itself in Europe. This was the main duty of every progressive European, and what was happening in Russia was of secondary importance. The time would come later to do things in a more civilized way than that adopted in Russia. For we believed then, as even today some naive Communists believe, that once in power, Russian tutelage would cease and the new creed, fashioned to European standards, would be realized in a way more suited to each particular country. All Communist parties are fundamentally Titoist. That it meant complete Russianization and the installation of the Stalinist system, they only discovered when the Red Army marched into Eastern Europe. It has been one of the lessons of the aftermath of war that the attraction of Communism was greater in the parts where the Allied armies had control, and the Western ways of life were more appreciated where the Red Army was supreme. Every regime is more alluring from afar.

Stalinism rejected the Leninist and Trotskyist conception of the

'State withering away', of 'Democracy inside the Party'; for the leaders of the Russian Revolution in 1917 anticipated democracy as soon as a majority was gained for Communism. Without the majority's active support and its free co-operation, the regime could not survive in its primary conception. It was here that the engine slid off the rails; for terror once accepted has its own momentum, its own laws, and cannot be stopped when we deem it necessary. In all systems based on force, contempt for the masses predominates. The principle of '*Tout pour le peuple, mais rien avec lui*' was that of Stalinism, just as it was that of the feudal aristocracy in the past. That centralized power in a totalitarian State has all means to annihilate resistance, and that scientific interference with the individual can kill all critical capacity and produce such mental conformity that authority becomes invincible, are indisputable facts. Marx could not reckon with this, or with many other factors unknown in his time. The infallibility of the deified leader made Socialist development impossible and led to the corruption of the whole.

After my break with the Hungarian Government in 1949, international reaction rejoiced, expecting me to adopt the Kravchenko attitude and reveal inside information. They were soon disappointed. For the same reason, I fear, this book will not live up to their expectations. Unable to protest at home against what was happening, I refused to play the enemy's game. So I fell willingly and consciously between two stools, the only place I could honourably take.

What about Hungary's future? As with all small nations today, it cannot be solved separately, but is closely linked to the future of Europe. Twice it has missed the democratic bus — first, in 1918, the Entente prevented it; then, in 1947, the Russians. As long as the re-armament of Europe continues, producing poverty and the proletarianization of its citizens, as long as it becomes more and more enslaved economically to the U.S.A., so long will Russian mistrust and apprehension continue to grow and her grip on her satellites become fiercer.

The more a man has to lose, the more he dreads war. Therefore it is in the interest of the West to give the Soviets time to raise their standard of living. To avoid the catastrophe which today seems inevitable, the recognition by the United States of the new China, which is rapidly becoming a Great Power, a policy of 'Hands off Asia' and a Europe, self-sufficient, independent and neutral, collaborating closely with a Socialist Britain, freed from American pressure, are essential. In an atmosphere of *détente*, the peoples of Eastern Europe could at last unite on the Yugoslav pattern and, on a Federal basis, regain their liberty from the U.S.S.R. and form a link between the two antagonistic ideologies. Not being directed against the Soviets, this union would ease the tension. For it is only by postponement that the final conflict c. 1 be avoided. An East European Socialist Federation would be the first step to a larger European unity and a powerful factor in the destiny of the world, strong enough to escape becoming the battlefield of rival imperialisms.

Socialism will come to Europe and the world in a different way from that imagined by the nineteenth-century revolutionaries, but it will come all the same, in the shape of Welfare States, making capitalism in its ancient form and *laisser-faire* a savage vestige of the past.

Is this a dream? 'But are not the dreams of one generation, the realities of the next?'

Now that all passions are spent in me, I know that what finally prevails is not what one was aiming at — the absolute — but something akin to it. But for the young, passions, struggle and illusion are a vital necessity. It is only by errors, by disappointments, by lost battles, that men learn, and start afresh. I believe that a new synthesis will emerge out of the present conflict of ideas and opposing social forces, IF THERE IS TIME.

I often wonder whether, if I had to start again, I would act in the same way, cherish the same hopes, follow the same urge for bettering the world. I believe I would. For we all have our particular destiny to fulfil, our part to play, and it is for history to judge how far we succeed in contributing something of value.

I owe much to my enemies, perhaps even more than to my friends, for the never-subsiding hatred and wrath with which they honoured me for half a century contributed greatly to what I became, and helped me to find myself. They stimulated my work, they spurred me on, like a vitamin injection. They hardened me and stung me out of the apathy and laziness inherent in my nature, defeating the pessimism which at times of depression tempted me to give up. No one, I believe, served me as well as my zealous adversaries. I am grateful to them and offer them my sincerest thanks.

Now, at the age of seventy-nine, in a small village among the undulating Mediterranean Alps, with few friends left — but they the more dear to me — with my truest one at my side, I am ready to face that greater and everlasting solitude from which there is no return. I should not be sincere if I added that it is without regret.

Vence,
September 1954

NOTES

NOTES

PART ONE [pages 15-56]

[1] Leopold Berchtold, Austro-Hungarian Ambassador in St. Petersburg, later Foreign Minister of the Monarchy and author of the notorious ultimatum to the Serbs in 1914.

[2] André Tardieu, then editor of the foreign affairs section of *Le Temps*, and later French Prime Minister.

[3] The Karolyi family received with the title of count the right to have eleven points instead of the nine usual for the coronets of counts: the only Hungarian family with this privilege.

[4] The leaders of the Party of Independence were Count Albert Apponyi and Francis Kossuth.

[5] The idea of a Federated Austria had already arisen in 1871, in the time of Prime Minister Hohenwart, who believed in it for the purpose of strengthening the Monarchy against the Magyars and the Germans. He succeeded in persuading Francis Joseph to have himself crowned in Prague as King of Bohemia. This plan was torpedoed by Julius Andrassy senior, who feared that a settlement with Bohemia would weaken Magyar supremacy in the Empire, as well as endanger Hungary herself. The Czechs would then be able to back up the Slavs in Hungary, while the German element in Austria, hostile to Federation, would try its best to ruin the Monarchy and thus seek to chain Hungary more closely to Berlin.

[6] Fiume, on the coast of the Adriatic, belonged politically to Hungary and was its only seaport. Its population was Italian, but it never ceased to be a South Slav aspiration, as it belonged geographically to them. The Fiume Resolution of 1905 was aimed against Vienna and offered political co-operation with the Magyar Independence Party. It was a complete *volte-face* of the Jellachich policy of the past. But soon afterwards Francis Kossuth, leader of the party which had won the elections, introduced an Anti-Croat Bill by which the Hungarians were given complete control over the Croat railways, administration and staff.

[7] The Jews, who were easily assimilated in the West, in Hungary did the assimilating: the Hungarians adopted many a characteristic of the Jews. This psychological penetration made those who wished to preserve unaltered the characteristics of the Magyars uneasy: the instinct of self-preservation was the basis of the Jewish persecutions which broke out periodically, in spite of the Jews being most loyal and patriotic towards their adopted country. After 1918 the Rumanians, too, were able to assimilate with astounding rapidity the conquered Hungarian population in the islets of Transylvania.

PART TWO [pages 59-119]

[1] A new law had exempted the owners of big entailed estates (the *Majorats Herrn*) from military service on the ground that they were indispensable on the land. The more is the credit due to the exceptions, such as my brother-in-law Esterhazy, who, demonstrating against this law, volunteered for the Galician front, and was killed in action.

[2] Delegations: A body composed of members of the Hungarian and Austrian Parliaments, meeting once a year. They were independent of each other, not bound by instructions, and not responsible to the two Parliaments which nominated them. In case of disagreement they were to sit together and reach a decision by a single majority vote.

[3] Our memorandum ended with these words: 'As it is of paramount interest to the Dynasty, to Hungary and the Dual Monarchy, that Rumania should not attack us, the above-named deputies [who signed the memorandum] regard it as their patriotic duty to the dynasty to communicate the foregoing, for absolutely confidential use. They do so in order also not to incur the responsibility of failing to make a communication of such vital interest.'

[4] Karolyi Party, Social Democrats and Radicals. Neither the Social Democrats nor the Radicals were represented in Parliament. The Radicals represented the intellectual middle class, mostly Jews. Their leader was Professor Oskar Jaszi.

[5] Erzberger, leader of the Centre, demanded Parliamentary rule in Germany and the declaration of the war aims.

[6] Under this agreement only those who could read and write and were over twenty-four were to be enfranchised — Hungary had 33 per cent illiteracy — with the exception of the holders of

the Charles Cross, who were to be eligible without any age or educational qualification. The ballot was to be secret only in the towns; open voting to be continued in the country districts.

[7] The reply was: 'The terms upon which the United States would consider peace have been repeatedly and with entire candour stated, and it can entertain no proposal for a conference upon a matter concerning which it has made its position and purpose so plain.'

[8] Later, when he became Premier, he said in Parliament: 'In this State, where private property is sacred, to ask for land reform is like asking for my pants.'

[9] Julius Maniu, leader of the Peasant Party, played an important role in Rumanian politics after the last war. He was imprisoned by the new regime.

[10] F. Milan Hodza in Bohemia, Pribicevich in Serbia and several others.

[11] The text was: 'In accordance with the will of her people, Austria will become a Federal State, in which each race, within its natural domain, shall form its own National State. The union of the Polish territories of Austria with an independent Polish State will thereby in no way be prejudiced. The town of Trieste, inclusive of its territories, receives, in accordance with the wishes of its population, a special position.'

[12] Lansing's Note was as follows: 'The President deems it his duty to say to the Austro-Hungarian Government that he cannot entertain the present suggestion of that Government because of certain events of the utmost importance which, occurring since the delivery of his address of January 8th last, have necessarily altered the attitude and responsibility of the Government of the United States. Among the fourteen terms of peace which the President formulated at that time occurred the following: "The peoples of Austria-Hungary whose place among the nations we wish to see safeguarded and assured, should be accorded the freest opportunity of autonomous development." Since that sentence was written and uttered to the Congress of the United States, the Government of the United States has recognized that a state of belligerency exists between the Czecho-Slovak and the German and Austro-Hungarian Empires, and that the Czecho-Slovak National Council is a de facto belligerent Government, clothed with proper authority to direct the military and political affairs of the Czecho-Slovaks.

'It has also recognized in the fullest manner the justice of the nationalistic aspirations of the Jugo-Slavs for freedom. The President is therefore *no longer at liberty* to accept a mere autonomy of these peoples as a basis of peace, but is obliged to insist that they, and not he, shall be the judges of what action on the part of the Austro-Hungarian Government will satisfy their aspirations and their conception of their rights and destiny as members of the family of nations.'

[13] Later on, the Reaction, in order to undermine our regime, spread the false rumour that Andrassy had received a wire from Ambassador Dutasta from Berne, informing him that Clemenceau and Foch were ready to sign a separate peace with the Monarchy without demanding great territorial sacrifices. As later works on the history of that period have proved, there was not a word of truth in this story.

PART THREE [*pages* 123-164]

[1] Andrassy, who could no more consider himself Foreign Minister of the joint Monarchy, telephoned me from Vienna requesting me to accept his services, as he had hopes of obtaining some concessions from the Entente. I communicated this request to my Ministers, pointing out that it would be more advantageous for us if those who had been responsible for the disaster were to take the blame for it instead of us. This was also the point of view of Victor Adler, the leader of the Austrian Social Democrats in Vienna. I was unanimously out-voted.

[2] In the afternoon of October 31st, my wife received a message from a cousin of hers that Tisza was in danger; suspicious-looking individuals were lurking around his house. Katus telephoned me immediately and I gave the necessary instructions. Katus later telephoned her cousin to ask if everything was all right. Our enemies whispered that she, informed of the conspiracy against Tisza's life, had inquired by telephone 'if the deed had been done'. That was one of the legends circulated against us. The person I suspected of being the instigator of the murder became later one of the leaders of the White Terror.

[3] The Workers' Council, formed in June 1918, sent their representative, Desiderius Bokanyi, to take part, and General Staff Officer Stelly was appointed as military expert. The deputation was representative of the forces of the Revolution: Baron Hatvany, newspaper owner and Liberal, was also asked to join. Jaszi and myself were the political delegates, and there were also economic experts on fuel and food. At the last moment the Soldiers' Council nominated Captain Csernyak as its representative, arguing that it was the army that had secured victory for the Revolution. We were therefore bound to include Csernyak in the delegation, for it would have been unsafe to snub this powerful organization, which could have caused serious trouble at home during our

absence. No doubt he brought a touch of the times with him, in his fantastic self-designed uniform.

⁴ After the demobilization we were permitted six divisions of infantry and two cavalry divisions under arms, for the maintenance of order.

⁵ This line ran from the rivers Szamos, Besztercze, the town of Marosvasarhely, the river Maros as far as its entry into the Tisza, the towns of Szabadka, Baja and Pecs, through the river Brau to the Croatian frontier.

We also had to hand over some of our railway engines and coaches, the exact number not being specified. The German regiments inside Hungary were to be demobilized within a period of ten days and were to leave the country.

⁶ We said in our telegram that we accepted, in principle, the terms of the Belgrade Armistice, as they were similar to those of the Italian Armistice at Padua. But our Government would sign only on condition that the Entente respected, until the signing of the Peace Treaty, the present frontiers of Hungary (with the exception of Croatia and Slavonia) and would protect her against attacks from the Germans, Rumanians, Czechs or South Slavs. Until the signing of the Peace Treaty, we would retain the administration of the whole of the Hungarian territory.

⁷ The daily journal *Vilag* interviewed Franchet D'Esperey in 1925 at the time of my trial, and he again emphasized most categorically that Foch on the Western front, Diaz in Italy, Allenby in Syria, and he in the East, possessed equal powers. The Armistice with Hungary therefore belonged to his sphere. He repeated again that, had we not signed, he would have ordered the Serbs to march into Budapest. Besides, the Belgrade Armistice was more favourable than that of Padua, since it guaranteed that the occupied territories would remain under Hungarian administration. The mistake was not in the terms of the Armistice itself, but in the fact that they were not respected.

⁸ The Parliament voted unanimously for the Republic.

⁹ The Pragmatic Sanction, the legal charter of the Habsburg Monarchy, settled the succession on the female line, and recognized the separate existence of Hungary.

¹⁰ To illustrate how little knowledge our peasants had of what a republic was, the story was told that, in one of the villages, they complained that the Republic lasted only one day. 'The gendarmes came and took it away.' The 'Republic' for them was the spoils they had collected from their neighbours, in the first days of the Revolution. When order was re-established, they thought the Republic had ceased to be.

¹¹ The extent to which any ordinary welfare measure could irritate and alarm our ruling classes might have been comic if the situation had not been so tragic. To quote an example: One of our greatest needs was clothing for the soldiers who returned from the front in rags. The Red Cross, of which my wife was President, was entrusted with collecting suits from well-to-do members of the community. Those possessing more than ten suits had to give one. This emergency measure was regarded as Communistic and from then on my wife was labelled 'Red Catherine'. The same anti-social attitude was shown when living quarters were requisitioned from those who had unused premises in large houses.

¹² Clause 17 of the Armistice: 'In case of recurring disturbances, the neighbours could intervene to restore order and defend their safety.'

¹³ Colonel Vix not only conspired with the friends of Germany behind our backs, but he was also unscrupulous in his private financial dealings. One of his officers was found to be involved in unlawful monetary operations, and his protection was even extended to the Hungarian black marketeers. (*In the Fire of two Revolutions*, by W. Böhm, p. 103.)

Things reached such a pitch that Böhm, the Minister of War, handed in his resignation. Thereupon Cunningham, the head of the British Mission, intervened and asked him to withdraw his resignation, since the actions taken by the Entente were not directed against the Karolyi Government (as our opponents put it), but against the Austro-Hungarian Empire, which they had defeated in war. He mentioned the sympathy of the British people towards our new democratic Hungary, provided it would not turn Bolshevist. He also stopped Vix carrying out one of the punitive measures which he had threatened on account of the resistance of the local Hungarian population in the border towns.

The unpardonable mistake of the French Government was to give such unlimited power to a complete blockhead who had never held responsible position and knew nothing of the country or the people with whom he had to deal. A man of his calibre should never have been appointed as an all-powerful dictator in control of Hungary. His political outlook was that of an army sergeant swept off his feet by the flattery of Hungarian princes and counts, who used him for their own purposes, sending reports against our regime through him to Paris, to make the situation untenable. As such things occur after wars, and often cause dangerous misunderstanding, I think it useful to mention this.

[14] My wife, who was distressed by the ill-treatment of political prisoners, arranged for them to have blankets, pillows and books. As a result, the Communists considered her one of their sympathizers and turned to her in several cases when they needed help. Soon a painful incident occurred. Under the disguise of the International Red Cross, a young woman called Rappaport was suspected of working for the Bolshevists. My brother-in-law, Festetich, Minister of War, had her arrested. My wife, as President of the Red Cross, whose members are immune, protested against her arrest, as there was no proof of guilt and, on her own authority, gave instructions (of which she informed me later), that the girl should immediately be released, conducted to the Austrian frontier and expelled. It was typical of the prevailing situation that the police, anxious to gain favour, seemed only too happy to accept her orders and open the prison gates. The girl was taken by night to the Austrian border. When my brother-in-law discovered that the bird had flown, he protested to the Council of Ministers, but no one could tell him who had issued the order for her release. My wife then told him the truth, adding that she had not informed me of what had happened. He was deeply outraged and I cannot blame him.

[15] Later the legend grew up that I had had hundreds of innocent people executed when I was President of the Republic. In fact no one received a death sentence during my period of office except one common criminal. As I am against capital punishment, I commuted his sentence to one of imprisonment.

[16] Impatient at the slowness of the reform, the landless peasants seized the land by force in several places, chasing away the landlords. On my father-in-law's estate they plundered the castle of Tisza Dob (my wife's birthplace) and, breaking up the furniture, used it for their fires and the tapestries for skirts for their wives.

[17] My wife's family had left for Switzerland. In those anxious days, Katus appealed to her stepfather Julius Andrassy to lend a helping hand in uniting the country, for we were heading for catastrophe. She received the answer that no co-operation was possible and that his only wish was that the situation should become worse.

[18] They had even taken part in the new nominations which their colleagues had put forward, knowing that it was all unnecessary. They had but one request and that was the liberation of the Communist leader, Bela Kun, and his followers.

[19] Garami and Peidle were the only ones who refused to unite with the Communists and resigned.

[20] Two weeks earlier, William Böhm had requested me to authorize him to wipe out the Communists in the country, whom he estimated at about 1000. 'I will never consent to it,' I answered.

[21] The election was carried out on the basis of the party list and I read with surprise that an individual called Michael Karolyi was heading one of the lists. The people were therefore convinced that I was actively supporting the regime, a method of falsification which, in later years, became quite a usual element in the struggle.

[22] Harold Nicolson in *Peace Making* gives a vivid account of his visit with Smuts to Hungary — a most crushing description of the Hungarians.

[23] Commissar Hamburger was trying to make Bela Kun appoint me as adviser for the distribution of the land.

[24] Esterhazy was so anxious to remain on good terms with his 'friends', that he even told them of his intention to shave off his beard. In a letter to President Garbai he proposed to have his name altered. I imagine the reason for his shattered nerves was the cruel joke which some hooligans played on him. One morning he was arrested by armed men, who stood him up against a wall while measurements were taken for his coffin. After this they released him.

He was also greatly concerned lest he should be put on the Black List with us, after the return of the Reaction. He was not, for dictatorships are ready to forgive cowardice, but never conviction. For weeks he carefully prepared his escape, training himself by extensive walks, gradually increasing in length; discovering ways to avoid villages; remaining without food and drink for hours; getting expert knowledge of the countryside. Anxious also about our fate, he provided us with the key to one of his gamekeepers' lodges, where we could safely hide.

[25] When our turn came to need help and my sister Pappenheim asked one of the Apponyis to send news to us concerning our children, who were with her, he refused on the grounds that it would compromise him to be in communication with us. This is only one instance of how many of our relations and friends returned 'evil for good'. Human nature is laid painfully bare in times of upheaval.

[26] When the demobilized soldiers' delegation, a couple of days after his seizure of power, demanded from him the 5400 kronen subsidy which, incited by the Communists, they had been asking from us, Kun replied: 'If you start pestering me with your claim for 5400 kronen, you will get 5400 bullets under your skins.' He had well learnt his lesson in Russia.

[27] When Gyula Karolyi and Paul Teleki in Szeged and Stephen Bethlen in Vienna begged

Franchet d'Esperey to attack Hungary, he answered: 'Do you imagine that I will consent to French blood flowing for Hungary's internal affairs?' But as long as they did not have to take any risks, these predecessors of the Vichyites did not mind collaborating with the enemies of France, the Germanophiles.

[28] Berend, the well-known children's doctor, was killed on this occasion.

PART FOUR [*pages* 167-311]

[1] On the liner to New York, I tried to explain to Bakos the change in time: that when it was 12 o'clock in Paris it would be only about 10 in mid-ocean. He would not believe me. One morning he came into my cabin beaming with satisfaction. 'I caught the rogues,' he whispered. 'I actually saw them turning back the hands of the clock.' He had waited, concealed behind a curtain, until midnight and caught them doing the trick. After this I let him have the satisfaction of telling his friends on his return to Hungary how he had outwitted the foreign rascals, adding no doubt that 'masters are so easily fooled'.

[2] *Documents on British Foreign Policy*, p. 196 — Report of Mr. Balfour on July 26th, 1919.

[3] It became in later years a cause of many bitter feuds and blackmail. Count Theodore Batthyanyi, having had the temerity to ask Pallavicini for an acount of the missing millions, was expelled from the Hungarian National Casino on the pretext that he had been a member of my cabinet — though he and Pallavicini had been hand in glove when organizing the attack on the Legation.

[4] The following incident is typical of those times. Some soldiers had taken hold of an officer who was specially hated for his cruelty towards his men and decided to execute him. A young Communist who was present was trying his best to prevent the murder and convert the officer to the 'New Idea', as it was called in those days. The officer threw himself on his knees in front of this 'Saviour', assuring him that he now understood the crimes he had committed in the past and would atone for them in the future. They fell into each other's arms, and the would-be executioners parted filled with the uplifting feeling that they had by their merciful attitude gained a new recruit for the struggle to achieve Paradise on earth. When, some weeks later, 'The White Terror' swept over Hungary, this 'converted' captain headed a detachment of terrorists, to avenge himself for his humiliation. These experiences, which were numerous, later effected a change in these romantic Communists.

Many considered Communism as the Christian ideal carried to its furthest consequence. They had a decidedly Christian approach to it. One often heard biblical sayings such as: 'It is harder for a rich man to get to heaven than for a camel to pass through the eye of a needle.' Or: 'If you have two pennies you have to give one away', etc. brought up by Communists.

[5] During the last days of July a mysterious incident occurred which was never properly cleared up. Two Ukrainian officers, supposed to be emissaries of Rakovsky, Governor of the Ukraine, arrived in Budapest for the purpose of recruiting for the Soviet Red Army amongst the Russian ex-prisoners of war. They were officially provided with a special train and all facilities to visit the country. It was soon discovered that they had come to make contact with the discontented elements of the ultra-Left whose revolutionary units had lately been dissolved, and to propagate the idea that Hungary was not a Proletarian Dictatorship but a Dictatorship of the Bourgeoisie. They incited them to get rid of the Social Democrats first and then exterminate the bourgeoisie. A plan of action was set for July 21st when Kun was to be forced to resign, the Social Democrat leaders arrested, the bourgeoisie massacred and Samuelly made the new Dictator. Twenty-four hours earlier Kun was informed of the plan. He gave orders to Samuelly to execute the two Ukrainian officers. This was carried out instantaneously. At his trial Kun was charged by the Horthy courts with this double murder, but of course no mention was made that in this way he had avoided a large-scale massacre.

[6] Workers and peasants were hurled alive into burning furnaces, a proceeding jokingly called 'using them as fuel'. Innocent Jews were dragged out of a train and hung on trees in the forest of Orgovany. Wives of Communists were raped by officers and then turned over to the ranks. The editor of the Socialist Paper, Somogyi, and his associate, Bacso, were one day found murdered in the waters of the Danube. Although well known, the murderers were not arrested. It was supposed to have happened with the consent of the Regent.

[7] The British High Commissioner, P. B. Hohler, the leader of the Inter-Allied Military Mission, Brig.-Gen. R. N. Gorton and Admiral Sir E. Troubridge, stated in their reports of February and March 1920: 'There is nothing in the nature of a terror in Hungary' and that life is secure, here as in England. Although Troubridge remarked, in parenthesis: 'B. Somogyi the Editor of the Social-democratic paper, was murdered yesterday.' He described Admiral Horthy as a strong

character and a man of Liberal tendencies, and the Government as a Christian Government in a Christian country.

[8] One of the stories circulating about us was that the young woman with me was not my wife. Catherine Andrassy, as a good Catholic, was supposed to have left the revolutionary Karolyi and returned to her parents. It was a Hungarian woman who spread this story in Florentine society, adding that she had been present at our wedding, having been Catherine's best friend.

[9] Imperiali was a frequent visitor at our pension, as he was the friend of an American woman writer who published a novel about those days of turmoil, in which we all played a part. Its title was *The House of Hate.*

[10] The battle of Menton when Mussolini marched his army into unresisting Menton in 1941.

[11] When the Hungarian Government was recognized by the Supreme Council in 1919, November 26th, the following conditions were made: 'The Hungarian Government shall secure to every Hungarian Citizen full civil rights, including freedom of Press, freedom of Assembly, the free expression of political opinion and universal suffrage resting on an impartial, secret and democratic basis.' These conditions were never fulfilled. The dominant view in Liberal and Left circles in England in 1924 was that the loan should be considered in its economic aspect only and assistance should be given unconditionally, for the help of the League was intended for the people and it was not supposed to worry about the form of Government in the country concerned. If the Government is reactionary or even if it has warlike aims, they argued, the League should not interfere but give the loan.

[12] Count Sigray had been my envoy in Switzerland during the Karolyi regime.

[13] The intrigues against my wife started with the customary vehemence. Mrs. Despard, a charming old lady of Victorian type, had invited her to her flat in New York. As soon as this became known, the wife of one of the greatest landowners of Slovakia, who in consequence of the Czech land reform had lost most of his property, called on Mrs. Despard and informed her that her guest had had her own parents executed in Budapest during the Red Terror. Mrs. Despard was on the point of cancelling her invitation when the unsuspecting Katus arrived and all was cleared up, her hostess deciding she never wanted to see the landowner's wife again.

[14] The Prince was married to a cousin of my wife.

[15] Louis Hollo and Desidéré P. Abraham.

[16] Owing to my reputation as a pacifist, there was no likelihood that the Central Powers would initiate me into any of their military plans. Windischgraetz had the stupidity to accuse me of having given away to the French — in the autumn of 1917 — the plans of the German offensive on the Chemin des Dames. First, the offensive was by that time already a thing of the past; secondly, it was a French and not a German offensive, and ended in German victory. This proves that my 'betrayal' was not very efficacious. No one, save in a terrorist court, could have given credit to such an absurd tale.

Chemin des Dames

News of General Nivelle's plans leaked through to the enemy, and the whole detailed plan, with every unit and objective named, fell into the enemy's hands on April 6th, 1917. Nivelle knew of this but did not inform his Government or make any important change in the order of battle.

The attack, fixed for the 12th, had to be postponed from day to day because of disastrous weather: cold rain fell in torrents and every morning the barometer was at 'Stormy'. The French attacked on the 16th. Black troops, employed as 'attack fodder', were so numbed that they could not fix their bayonets. They groped along miserably and soon fled in disorder.

Nivelle extended the battle and renewed every few days partial attacks between Soissons and Rheims. By the end of April 1917 more than 20,000 prisoners and 150 guns had been taken at a cost of 118,000 casualties. (These figures have been disputed.) Nivelle was *limogé*, and Pétain was made C.-in-C.

[17] Declaration of Renaudel: 'The Prince is not only ignorant but he is lying. He is ignorant because he says that Moutet and I belong to the extreme Socialists, whereas everybody knows our opposition to the extremist standpoint. I give my word of honour that I have never met Mr. Desidéré Abraham either in Switzerland or anywhere else and have had neither written nor spoken communication with him.'

[18] Léon Blum wrote as follows: 'Although this story is founded on information furnished by the espionage service of the German General Staff in Budapest and claims to be supported by Emperor Wilhelm II, I declare that the whole story is a tissue of lies and I wish to denounce it with the greatest vigour. I do not know either Michael Karolyi or Desidéré Abraham. Never in my life have I seen them nor have I ever had any kind of direct or indirect intercourse with either of them. During the war I was not in Switzerland. If the other statements of Prince Windischgraetz are as well founded as these above, then again I deliver the same judgment on

them. I felt myself bound to make this statement not for the sake of Karolyi, whom I do not know, but for the sake of truth.'

[19] According to Hungarian law, accusations are only accepted as true if confirmed by witnesses.

[20] Clemencau's letter: Le soussigné certifie n'avoir jamais eu aucun rapport d'activité politique avec M. le Comte KAROLYI, n'avoir entretenu avec lui aucune relation d'aucune sorte au cours de la grande-guerre. J'engage formellement à ce sujet ma parole d'honneur et suis prêt à répondre à toute question qui me serait posée à cet égard.

Paris, le 28 novembre 1927.
Signé: G. CLEMENCEAU.

[21] Before we left the States, the resumption of my wife's interrupted lecture tour had been arranged for the following autumn; but when she applied for her American visa at the Consulate in Paris she was refused. The reason was obviously that the campaign in our favour had created much embarrassment to the State Department and they were not keen to hear of us again. Mr. Kellogg had been nicknamed 'Frightened Nelly'. Many public figures sponsored my wife, and Senator Wheeler demanded that the reasons for the ban should be given. Kellogg refused to disclose the source, everyone suspecting that it came from the Szechenyis. Some years later, under Stimson's administration, we were granted visas and received entire satisfaction.

[22] Before leaving England, as we were approaching the tenth year of our exile, we applied for Hungarian passports in order not to lose our nationality. We had been using Yugoslav ones presented to us as a matter of courtesy. Some English friends accompanied the children to the Hungarian Consulate. Their passports were refused on the ground that they had voluntarily accompanied their parents into exile. (The eldest was three years old when we left.) Later, a well-known English politician approached the Hungarian representative in Geneva on their behalf, but was refused as well. So we remained stateless.

[23] Victor Basch was one of our first friends in France. A small, aggressive man of Hungarian-Jewish origin, with encyclopaedic mind and erudition, he was a brilliant combination of German and Latin cultures. During the German occupation his French compatriots and 'patriots' picked him out of a convoy taking him and his wife to a concentration camp (they were both eighty years of age) and murdered them on the roadside. He had been the *bête noire* of the French Right for his courageous stand in the Dreyfus case.

[24] My wife conceived a scheme for starting a colony in Saskatchewan or Alberta to settle Hungarian workers on free land in close community. The idea was to establish it on the Dukhoubor or Mennonite system, in which land, stock and equipment are owned in common. We planned to settle with them and organize the colony ourselves. The Dolhin district near Winnipeg and the House district in the Rocky Mountains seemed the most suitable for the purpose. Katus travelled to Calgary, examining the land and conferring with the local authorities. The homestead being completely uncultivated, it would have taken years to make it arable. For the better land, a price had to be paid. The Government was ready to give a loan, so the difficulties could have been overcome; but the press got hold of the scheme, and notices appeared that political refugees, Liberals and Socialists, were to be settled in Canada. As our people had no passports, only French identity cards, the Canadian Government went back on its promise and the scheme had to be given up. It was a great disapointment for our wretched miners, who by now had lost their jobs and had put their last hopes in this prospect. This failure turned out later to be a blessing in disguise, as the year 1928 brought the disastrous drought and many foreign settlers, as well as Canadian farmers, died miserable deaths.

[25] Windischgraetz's wife, Maria Szechenyi, indignant that 'Pirincz' as they called him, was made the scapegoat, gave her husband's diary with all the compromising facts and names to Imre Karolyi and George Pallavicini, who then made an attack on the Prime Minister Bethlen. Bethlen challenged Imre Karolyi to a duel, trusting to settle the painful affair in this convenient and traditionally Hungarian manner.

[26] The Clark Agreement of 1919.

[27] The Hungarians were very puzzled that Lord Rothermere's son was not named like his father, but was called Harmsworth. They concluded that the English language was somewhat peculiar: the name was spelt Rothermere, but had to be pronounced Harmsworth.

[28] In 1930 when the census was taken, 67 per cent of the population was entirely landless and had less than the minimum for existence. Thirty-six big landowners owned more than 12,000,000 dwarf-holders. In the last forty years mortality had increased by 50 per cent. Farm-labourers' wages corresponded to twopence a day for 12-20 hours' work. Many worked in winter without pay to ensure their harvest work. When there was a special crop of grapes, they were paid only with rotten grapes which the landlords could not sell.

[29] Sforza's letter: 'It is true that Karolyi was expelled from Italy while I was still in power. I showed Giolitti the report on my investigations, a report that was absolutely in favour of Karolyi.

But Giolitti informed me that some White Russians were plotting against the former head of the Government, whom they did not want in Florence, and that it would be very embarrassing for us to have, in the person of Karolyi, a centre of and a pretext for agitations and disorders. I made no objections. But I think it is my duty in view of so many silly legends to state that the prohibition of his stay in Italy had no other reason.' In his book he repeated this statement.

[30] My cousin Nadine Karolyi, Leopold Berchtold's wife, was known for her complete disregard of the ways of the world, not too useful for an Ambassador's wife. She was not vain and minded little about dress. At one of the glamorous court festivals she arrived in a raincoat covering her evening dress. She had forgotten to get an evening wrap.

[31] The *sofkhoz* was state land on which the agricultural labourer worked as wage-earner, employed by the State. He did not share in the produce of the farm, as in the *kolkhoz*.

[32] 'In February 1931 Stalin openly appealed to Russian nationalism.' (Deutscher, *Stalin*, p. 323.)

[33] Barbusse, Romain Rolland, André Gide, Auden, Isherwood, Day Lewis, Stephen Spender, Dreiser, Dos Passos, Arthur Koestler, Richard Wright, Upton Sinclair, Seghers, Brecht, Steinbeck and many others.

[34] He was one of the French doctors who signed the shameful document in 1952, demanding the severest treatment for the Russian doctors who were on trial before Stalin's death. These same doctors were rehabilitated later on and declared to be heroes of the nation.

[35] A play had been written on the subject, and produced in Paris.

[36] A certain sect of which the Grand Duke Dimitri was said to be the patron exercised castration and cut out the breasts of women.

[37] The popes, merchants, *kulaks*, gendarmes, bourgeois and their progeny belonged to the class of the *lishenetz*, who were deprived of their citizenship for three years.

[38] Inside the Hungarian Communist Party, there was a bitter controversy amongst the Kunists and the anti-Kunists. The anti-Kunists were for Jeno Landler, who had been President of the Commune in 1919. The difference was in the handling of the peasant problem. Landler and his friends wanted me to assume a leading role in the agrarian reform, as Kun when in power had committed grave mistakes. Kun opposed this.

[39] In those days in Berlin, I saw much of the writers Sinclair Lewis and Dorothy Thompson, who had just become engaged. They had also attended the Congress. Miss Thompson, whom I had met years before in Yugoslavia, had set up a most competent office where day and night, young and old, males and females, were working for her devotedly. When the news of the Vienna disturbances came in, she decided that Sinclair Lewis would have to write the story. Admitting no impediment, she dragged him mercilessly from his bed, where he had been resting and hoisted him into a plane specially hired for the occasion. They arrived in time to give a thrilling account of the civil war in Vienna.

[40] For instance Roboz, a Hungarian journalist.

[41] Greta Neumann sister of Babette-Neumann published her reminiscences under the title: *Under Two Dictators*. Wife of a German Communist, she had been interned in Russia and delivered at the time of the Stalin-Hitler Pact to Germany.

[42] The Embassy official with whom Katus was in contact was not too discreet, and gave away my wife's activities to a German woman friend of his. The French are not good at keeping secrets.

[43] I remember the Russian world champion of chess, Alekhine, who used to come there as well. One day the proprietor of the Café Régence had challenged him to a game. With a patronizing smile he had accepted, but to the amazement of the onlookers he could not manage to beat his challenger. The champion, livid in the face, refused to finish the game, using as excuse the noise of the café, and walked out.

[44] *Darkest Hungary* by Paloczy Horvath, p. 115.

[45] Members of the Arrow Cross were Archduke Albert of Habsburg, my brother-in-law Alexander Festetich, and members of the Palffy and Andrassy families.

[46] Anatole France writes in *La Reine Pédauque* about the Catholics: 'If they offend your reason, it is because they are superior to it and because they accord with the true ends of man and not with the ends which are apparent to them.' This could as well be said about the Stalinists.

[47] Caja, Princess Odescalchi, my wife's sister, had been organizing, with Countess Elisabeth Szapary, the Polish Relief for the refugees pouring in from Poland. After Caja's death the British officer with whom she escaped found on her letters of recommendation to the British authorities from O'Malley, British Minister in Budapest, referring to her dangerous work in favour of the Allies, organizing sabotage in Poland.

[48] The disruption of Yugoslavia was an aim common to Italy and Hungary, and the training on Hungarian soil of Pavlevic and the other Croat terrorists who were to murder King Alexan-

der in 1934 was the first step in a process from which Germany reaped the ultimate benefit in 1941.

[49] The Tripartite Pact, signed by Germany, Italy and Japan on September 27th, 1940, to which Hungary, Rumania and Slovakia adhered later.

[50] Branches of my movement were formed in New York by Professor Rustem Vambery, son of the famous explorer, Moholyi Nagy the artist, Laszlo Fenyes, the ex-Hungarian M.P. who was much respected for his courage and integrity; in Hollywood by the well-known actor Bela Lugosi; in Mexico, Canada, Bolivia, Argentine, Chili, Brazil, Algiers, Palestine and Switzerland as well, for the purpose of promoting the war effort in all directions.

[51] Tibor Eckhardt was a well-known political figure. His past record could not inspire confidence. He had been President of the 'Wakening Magyars', the first terrorist organization to hunt down Communists, Jews, Socialists and Liberals. He had voted for the anti-semitic laws. He had represented Hungary in 1934 at the League of Nations, when Hungary was accused of the assassination in Marseilles of King Alexander of Yugoslavia and the French Minister, Louis Barthou. During the war the Hungarian Government had supplied him with a visa to New York, as Britain had refused his entry.

[52] H. N. Brailsford, Julian S. Huxley, Augustus John, Stephen Spender, A. J. P. Taylor, Vernon Bartlett.

[53] Michael Padev for Bulgaria, Dr. Kunosi for Czechoslovakia, Dr. Decebal Mateescu for Rumania and Rudolf Bicanic for Yugoslavia.

[54] John Parker, M.P., Doreen Warriner, author of several works on Eastern Europe: *Economics of Peasant Farming, Eastern Europe after Hitler* and others.

[55] In a brief outline, the main principles were: a Federal Europe; formed by the alliance of several smaller regional Federations: Common Customs frontiers, Uniform currency, Common foreign policy, Common army, Centralized treatment of Social problems, Unification of penal codes, etc. The Regional Federations would work out plans for their own planned economy, co-ordinated in the Central Federal Authority. The Danubian Federation, in spite of its predominantly agricultural character, should have an industrial as well as an agricultural plan, industries being encouraged to utilize local raw materials.

Not only economically but politically, too, the maintenance by each participant nation of its own language, culture, racial customs and religion should be upheld. The Federal Parliament could be organized on the 'Migratory system', and would hold sessions in each of the capitals of the participant States. The experience of the last twenty years has shown that it is not enough simply to transfer the ownership of land from large to small owners; it is necessary to have much stronger forms of collaboration in production, and to convert the old ways of farming. In Czechoslovakia the division of large estates raised the standard of living through intensive farming, and even the corn yield rose because more livestock meant more manure. In Rumania where there was no intensification, the standard was reduced by the land reform, and the old estate system kept going.

[56] Its members for Czechoslovakia were—Ladislas Fierabend (Minister in the Czech cabinet) Jan Lichter; for Greece: C. Capernaros; for Poland: Mikolajczyk and W. Kulerski; for Rumania: Pavel; for Yugoslavia: Milan Gurilovics, Fran Gabrovsek, Rudolf Bičanič (member of the Croatian peasant party. He had been imprisoned in 1932-35. He was Director of the Economic and Social Research Institute and the Peasant Co-operative). Subject of discussion between these peasant leaders of Central and South-Eastern Europe was the solution of the agrarian reform after the war. Sir John Russell's plan consisted of raising the standard of living by producing more milk, meat, eggs, and other products of higher money value than that of wheat, with the help of Western Europe (especially that of Britain and America). The objection to this plan was that Western Europe had not the capital needed to industrialize a population of 100 million people. I suggested the creation of large co-operatives on the big estates, which by the use of modern machinery, freeing man-power, would enable wheat and other cereals to be produced in large quantities. Intensive farming would produce more valuable foodstuffs and so would not need Western capital.

[57] They were Bajcsi-Zsilinszky, who with some others attempted a military revolt and was executed. Also a workman called Nadas who was trying to organize sabotage. Prince Odescalchi was hanged by the Germans when he wanted to desert to the Allies; before the execution he had taken off all his clothes so that, as he said, the Germans should not profit by them. He walked stark naked to the scaffold. The leader of the Social Democrats was Szakasics, Imre Kovacs was leader of the National Peasants' Party, and Laszlo Rajk of the Communists.

[58] Zoltan Tildy had been a legitimist in the past. He was the leader of the Smallholders, joined the Resistance and went into hiding.

[59] The President of the London Hungarian Club was Zoltan Rado, a journalist. On his return

he was executed as a Western spy. He confessed to all charges in the usual way. The two other leading members disappeared. Once, towards the end of the war, I was descending the Hampstead tube lift with one of the most intransigent Communists. 'I wonder,' he said wistfully, 'if one day, we will not think with regret of the time spent in London?' Two years later, when he had been purged, I remembered his strange presentiment.

[60] It is odd that the 'well-informed' British authorities have at times let themselves be misled by Hungarian ex-Nazis. These opponents of ours bragged openly that they would find ways of preventing my wife from going to England, because they knew her attachment for the country.

PART FIVE [*pages* 315-361]

[1] Two years later, Katus was woken up in the middle of the night by the ring of the telephone. A voice said: 'We have just knocked the Bishop down, it should have been done long ago.'
The next day, the papers were full of the outrage. Some Social Democrat students had done it. The Communists vociferated against it and threatened to punish the guilty. The clerical youth, having found the head untouched, placed it back on the socket, and surrounded it with flowers, giving it a tragic aspect.

[2] George Karolyi was one of the best known figures in town. Every child would recognize the very tall, ghastly pale, man with the black beard, which gave him an uncanny look, and his three Pekinese dogs, which he led on a long leash. When he had tired of his Jewish-actress wife, he took a mistress, an Englishwoman, with whom he would travel all over Europe, at times accompanied by his wife and their daughter, who would have to go second-class while he and his mistress travelled first.

[3] The funds for this Boy's Home had been collected in England by Katus on her return to London. Through personal friends and an advertisement in *The Times*, she managed to get a thousand pounds and, with the help of U N R R A, got the entire equipment from surplus army stocks. The home, based on up-to-date principles of psychology, became a model institution. Katus spent all her time in running it, and even lived on the premises. In 1950, the Government socialized it.

[4] Two British economists, Tom Balogh and Miklos Kaldor, both of Hungarian origin, drew up a report on the financial situation, which seemed at the time disastrous. When we left, after a stay of four weeks, it did not seem possible that Hungary could avoid a complete economic and financial collapse.

[5] One of the best-known Hungarian sculptors had erected the statue, an archangel beneath whose wings stood the conquering Russian soldier. In Vienna the statue was called 'The unknown father'.

[6] George Pallavicini junior was the eldest son of my brother-in-law, who had been my enemy. I had never met the son, but had heard of his exploits in the Resistance.

[7] Rajk was said to have opposed the way the Mindszenty trial was conducted. He was supposed to have argued, in the Central Committee of the party, that if expediency made it necessary to eliminate the Cardinal he should be shot, but not made to suffer the comedy and hypocrisy of a trial.

[8] The land reform law of 1945 expropriated all holdings over 140 acres. The large estates of the magnates, over 1400 acres, were expropriated entirely, leaving no remainder, in order to prevent the large landowner from retaining even a fraction of his former holding, which might serve as a foothold to regain his power. The total land expropriated amounted to about 8 million acres or 35 per cent of the land. Of this total, 4.7 million acres were divided amongst 650,000 families of landless labourers or 'dwarf' peasants, in the form of independent farms, averaging 12 acres in size (Doreen Warriner, *Revolution in Eastern Europe*). The landlords who had been active in the Resistance could keep 100 acres, the peasants, 200. Out of the 750,000 claimants, 600,000 were satisfied. By the end of the first year, 5,700,000 acres had been distributed. This meant that many got only 3 acres, thus multiplying the number of dwarf-holders, and increasing the difficulty of planned economy. The peasants called this hurriedly distributed land the 'Davaj-land' for the Russian soldiers would urge the population to work with 'Davaj' meaning: 'Hurry on – move on.'

[9] When I returned to London I was surprised to hear that a man, entirely unknown to me, had written in a London paper of which he was the editor, that on my arrival in Hungary I had spent my time in attacking Britain, biting the hand that had fed me, and that, not daring to move freely, I was escorted everywhere by a Communist guard.
As every word in this statement was untrue – in my first speech in Parliament I had paid special homage to England, and my wife was the President of the Anglo-Hungarian Society, with Zoltan Kodaly, the well-known composer, to foster good relations between the two countries,

etc. — I thought of taking a libel action against him. But it happened at the time when Harold Laski had lost his case and my English friends advised me against it, as I could not prove that this article, which appeared in a scarcely known magazine, could do me any harm.

[10] The story circulating in Budapest concerning Gyongyosi's appointment as Foreign Minister was that when the Red Army conquered Debrecen they were much impressed by the quantity of books in Gyongyosi's shop, for he was a bookseller. This convinced them that he must be a very clever, learned man, and they chose him as Hungarian Minister for Foreign Affairs.

[11] The property of pro-Germans or Fascists who had fled to the West was seized and declared 'deserted property'. Those who had gained merit in the Resistance or émigrés who returned could pick out a house or some furniture they fancied, which would then be requisitioned by the Government on their behalf. The Smallholders' Party was supposed to have been less discriminating in these matters, having little interest in the good reputation of the régime, as their influence was daily dwindling. The execution of the President's son-in-law for having smuggled valuables out of the country was a demonstration to discourage abuses.

[12] A rather curious incident occurred in those days. We were both invited to a party for December 13th 'Lucza Day'. It is the custom to summon spirits and have prophecies told. Unmarried girls put a pair of men's pants underneath their pillow and the man of whom they dream will become their husband. There was a strange woman in the company who spoke no Hungarian, and was of Rumanian origin and a clairvoyant. Our identity had not been revealed to her. She told Katus that we would not stay in Hungary nor end our days there, but would soon leave for a foreign country. This unexpected prediction cast a gloom on the company and caused embarrassment to our host. It was the last thing we had expected to hear in those days.

[13] Marshal Tito had demanded that his own police should, for reasons of safety, be entrusted with the reception. Rajk, who was then Minister of the Interior, incensed by the slighting of the Hungarian police, wanted to resign, but was ordered by his party to remain and to comply with Tito's wishes. In the trial against Rajk, after Yugoslavia became the black sheep, Rajk was charged with having given way to Tito, his 'friend', against Rakosi's special orders.

[14] Sulyok later dissolved his party, in order to demonstrate that a true opposition was not possible.

[15] Tito's and Dimitrov's meeting and their visible understanding were a good sign towards the possibility of Federation; also that *Pravda* published in its entirety Dimitrov's declaration concerning Federation. But some days later there appeared in the same paper a notice that the editors had not adopted the same position towards the Federation or towards a Customs Union between the mentioned countries. On the contrary, they did not believe in the necessity of any sort of Federation, Confederation or Customs Union, these being problematic and artificial, but were for the consolidation and the defence of the independence and sovereignty of the countries concerned. This created the impression that it was not the wish of the Soviets to have on their borders a second Federation which could and probably would adopt a line independent of Moscow. Dimitrov hastened to recant, as did the Belgrade Press. A month later Stalin disowned *Pravda*, or rather himself, and categorically demanded, in front of several press representatives, that a Federation should be formed as soon as possible between Yugoslavia and Bulgaria, without Albania. Ferencz Fejto, in his book *Démocratie Populaire*, reports that Tito explained the change in Stalin by saying that at that time relations with Russia were already strained and Stalin feared that Yugoslavia would fall out of his sphere. A Federation with Bulgaria would have meant that the Yugoslav Communist Party would have been forced into a minority and would have had to toe the line. Tito noticed the double-edged demand, and opposed it.

[16] Another exceptionally courageous woman was Margit Schlachta, who was the only one to cast a vote against the declaration of the Republic in the Parliament of 1946. She had been active in saving Jews at the time of their persecution by Hitlerism but, being a fervent Catholic and a Conservative, she turned frankly against the new Hungarian regime after the liberation. She had been imprisoned by the Arrow Cross. For this reason she had been elected to the new Parliament. On one occasion during a session in Parliament, wanting to demonstrate my respect for her courage, I sat down next to her, although I knew that in the past she had always been one of my fiercest opponents. She was surprised and visibly pleased, for she was very unpopular in the new Hungary for her outspoken attitude and her situation was becoming daily more precarious.

[17] Cardinal Mindszenty requested Cardinal Spellman to prevent the Crown of St. Stephen from being returned to Hungary, and to have it deposited in Rome instead.

[18] When Rajk had been ordered to Moscow, before his resignation as Head of the Ministry for Home Affairs, the news was spread that he had been shot at the frontier whilst attempting to escape, as he was on the eve of arrest.

[19] Ferencz Fejto, journalist and writer, author of *Les Démocraties Populaires*, *Joseph II*, and other works.

[20] One of my uncles had built a house for his mistress. After his death she was turned out by the family. She then put a curse on all Karolyis that they should never settle anywhere. This became true, not only in my case.

[21] The French fellow-travellers and Communists outdid even the Hungarian papers in the abjection and servility of their articles, although they could not have doubted the falsity of the charge. At the very last a group of intellectuals, Martin Chauffier, Vercors, Claude Bourdet and others signed a petition, but it was too late to have any effect.

INDEX

INDEX

387

INDEX

INDEX

INDEX

INDEX